THE DEVELOPMENT
OF AN AMERICAN
CULTURE

THE DEVELOPMENT OF AN AMERICAN CULTURE

SECOND EDITION

EDITED WITH AN INTRODUCTION BY

Stanley Coben
University of California, Los Angeles

&
Lorman Ratner
University of Wisconsin, Parkside

St. Martin's Press   New York

E
169.1
D47
1983

36,096

For information, write St. Martin's Press, Inc.,
175 Fifth Avenue, New York, N.Y. 10010

cover design: Nancy Kirsh
book design: Nancy Kirsh and Judith Woracek

cloth ISBN: 0–312–19665–2
paper ISBN: 0–312–19666–0

CONTENTS

PREFACE

The first edition of *The Development of an American Culture* offered a wide-ranging, yet coherent collection of essays in American culture written by leading historians. We invited a group of outstanding scholars to present their best thinking on what they considered especially important periods and topics in their fields of interest. The resulting collection spanned the course of American history, focusing on periods and social groups that have been most influential in shaping American culture.

The critical acclaim accorded the first edition and the success reported by the many college teachers who used the book in the classroom and kindly shared their experiences with us have encouraged us to revise and add to the volume. Since publication of the first edition, Americans have experienced dramatic and, for many, disconcerting changes in their national life. To bring these changes into historical perspective, we have invited three distinguished authors—Peter Clecak, John Buenker, and Tamara Hareven—to write essays for this new edition. In addition, our original authors have revised their essays. As a result, more than half the book is new.

As with the first edition, teachers of college courses in American social, intellectual, or cultural history should find that this volume helps to provide a framework for organizing their courses. Although the essays deal with particular periods and are arranged chronologically—the last two addressing contemporary matters but reaching back to the nineteenth century for perspective—all the authors look forward and backward to other periods. Thus, while reading essays treating fairly brief time periods, students will gain an understanding of the overall development, over a much longer time, of an American culture—

its subcultures, ethnic and racial groups, economic structure, and popular attitudes toward the nation.

This volume had its beginning in our search for materials for our own courses in American social, intellectual, and cultural history. It may also be useful as either primary or background reading in a variety of other courses. In whatever ways teachers may choose to use it, we trust that the book will enrich its readers' understanding of where Americans have been, where they are now, and where they might be going from here.

Stanley Coben
Lorman Ratner

THE DEVELOPMENT
OF AN AMERICAN
CULTURE

INTRODUCTION
CULTURE, SOCIETY, ETHNICITY, CLASS, NATIONALITY, AND HISTORY

Stanley Coben / UNIVERSITY OF CALIFORNIA, LOS ANGELES

Lorman Ratner / UNIVERSITY OF WISCONSIN, PARKSIDE

The concept of culture stands as one of the central ideas in modern social science. In the early twentieth century, it was developed largely by anthropologists—including Franz Boas, Bronislaw Malinowski, Edward Sapir, Margaret Mead, Ruth Benedict, Leslie White, Alfred Kroeber, and Claude Levi-Strauss[1]—from

[1] Of these pioneer twentieth-century cultural anthropologists, Franz Boas contributed to the development of the concept of culture largely by stimulating the interest of others—anthropologists, sociologists, psychologists, and political scientists—including his own students, among them Kroeber, Sapir, Benedict, and Mead, to mention only those cited in this introductory paragraph. However, Boas's *The Mind of Primitive Man* (New York, 1911); and his *Race, Language, and Culture* (New York, 1940) lent the prestige of the foremost American anthropologist in the early twentieth century to the legitimacy of the concept of culture. Boas's influence is ably explored in George W. Stocking, Jr., "The Scientific Reaction Against Cultural Anthropology," in Stocking, *Race, Culture, and Evolution: Essays in the History of Anthropology* (New York, 1968), 270–307.

Nevertheless, the books and articles by the anthropologists listed below provided the basic foundation for early- and mid-twentieth-century theoretical under-

1

nineteenth-century German and, to a lesser extent, British and French origins. This concept has become the basis for what a few theorists have argued already is a science of culture.[2] Certainly a distinct body of thought dealing with the meaning of culture seems to be developing, fostered both by an abundance of theoretical speculation and by the collection and comparison of data from thousands of cultures and subcultures. Scholars in every social science and in some of the humanities have contributed to this development. Archaeologists; art historians; social, intellectual, and political historians; sociologists; literary critics; and philosophers have taken part, although anthropologists continue to play the leading role.

Many economists, sociologists, and political scientists with practical rather than theoretical objectives have become part-time culturologists. Their interest stems in part from their observations of the inadequacy of some economic or political explanations of social change—that massive injections of capital, technology, or

---

standing of the meaning and influence of culture. For important samples of their work, see: Bronislaw Malinowski, "Culture," *Encyclopedia of the Social Sciences* IV, 621–46 (New York, 1931); *A Scientific Theory of Culture* (Chapel Hill, 1944); Edward Sapir, "Culture, Genuine and Spurious," *American Journal of Sociology* XXIX (1924), 401–29, reprinted in Sapir, *Selected Writings of Edward Sapir...* (Berkeley, 1949), 308–31, and several other essays reprinted in *Selected Writings;* Margaret Mead, *Coming of Age in Samoa* (New York, 1928); *Growing Up in New Guinea* (New York, 1930); *Sex and Temperament in Three Primitive Societies* (New York, 1935); Ruth Benedict, *Patterns of Culture* (Boston, 1944); Alfred L. Kroeber, *The Nature of Culture* (Chicago, 1952); Leslie A. White, *The Science of Culture* (New York, 1949); Claude Levi-Strauss, *Les Structures Elementaires de la Parenté* (Paris, 1949); "Language and the Analysis of Social Laws," *American Anthropologist* LIII (1951), 155–63; *Totemism* (Boston, 1963); *The Savage Mind* (Chicago, 1966). Levi-Strauss's place among twentieth-century contributors to the meaning of culture (Levi-Strauss prefers the phrase "structural anthropology") is growing more secure in the United States as his books and essays are translated into English. There is insufficient space in this essay for a discussion of the increasingly overlapping concerns of American cultural, French structural, and British social anthropology, or for an analysis of the differences in social structure and orientation that continue to keep these concerns from becoming identical.

[2]For example, A. L. Kroeber and Clyde Kluckhohn, *Culture: A Critical Review of Concepts and Definitions* (New York, 1952); White, *The Science of Culture;* and Kroeber, "The Concept of Culture," *American Anthropologist,* LXI (1959), 227–315; Ralph Linton, *The Cultural Background of Personality* (New York, 1945); Stuart Chase, *The Proper Study of Mankind* (New York, 1948); Julian Stewart, *Theory of Culture Change* (Urbana, 1955); and several essays in Raymond Firth, ed., *Man and Culture* (New York, 1958).

military force have failed to bring about desired changes in preindustrial or prenational societies; that establishment of nationhood in the "third world" does not make ethnic and class loyalties within a nation's boundaries less potent. In "first world"
countries—socialist as well as capitalist—conflict based on cultural differences, in the name of ethnic, racial, religious, subnational, and even sexual differences, seems to have grown in intensity and frequency during recent years. Austria, Belgium, Canada,
Denmark, France, Rumania, the Soviet Union, Spain, the United
Kingdom, the United States, and Yugoslavia all have experienced
serious and sometimes violent conflict of this sort.[3]

Historians increasingly find the concept of culture useful as
they widen their field of inquiry and attempt to understand the
lives of ordinary people. They recognize the need to consider the
influence of the family, ethnicity, or local and national subcultures and institutions in history, although they remain perplexed
about the relative weight to be assigned to these factors and
about the precise relationships between "society" and "culture"
in history. A leading Soviet social scientist indicated a similar
reexamination of historical concerns when he acknowledged in
1980 that "certain important characteristics of ethnic communities, *culture in particular* [emphasis added], do not easily lend
themselves to [Marxist socioeconomic] historical periodization."[4]
The editors and authors of this book would carry the point further and argue that no other historical variables can be understood without considerable knowledge of the culture or cultures
that affected and formed them.

The first task in studies of cultural history is a definition of
culture itself. For over a century, the various meanings given to
the term *culture* by social scientists have contended with a human-

---

[3]Nathan Glazer and Daniel P. Moynihan, eds., *Ethnicity: Theory and Experience* (Cambridge, Mass., 1975); M. Hechter, "Ethnicity and Industrialization," *Ethnicity* III (1976), 214–24; Wilton S. Dillon, ed., *The Cultural Drama: Modern Identities and Social Ferment* (Washington, D.C., 1974); Walker Connor, "A Nation Is a Nation, Is a State, Is an Ethnic Group, Is a . . . ," *Ethnic and Racial Studies* I (October 1978), 377–400; "Nation-Building or Nation-Destroying," *World Politics* XXIV (April 1972), 319–55; "The Politics of Ethnonationalism," *Journal of International Affairs* XXVII (1973), 1–21; "The Political Significance of Ethnonationalism within West- ern Europe," in Abdul Said and Luiz Simmons, eds., *Ethnicity in an International Context* (Edison, N.J., 1976), 110–33; Werner Feld, "Subnational Regionalism and the European Community," *Orbis* XVIII (1975), 1176–92.

[4]Victor I. Kozlov, "The Classification of Ethnic Communities: The Present Posi- tion in the Soviet Debate," *Ethnic and Racial Studies* III (1980), 123–39.

istic usage connoting an ideal standard of intellectual, artistic, and moral cultivation. The English poet and essayist Matthew Arnold popularized the latter definition with his famous statement in 1869 that culture consisted of "a pursuit of total perfection by means of getting to know, on all matters which most concern us, the best which has been thought and said in the world. . . . Sweetness and light are the main characteristics [of culture]."[5] Although Arnold's usage persists today, and traces of it have even found their way into this volume, the broader anthropological meaning seems one of the most fertile ideas available to historians, and this book is organized around it.

Social scientists who have attempted recently to define culture seem to agree that its essence consists of a set of distinctive patterns of behavior based largely on systems of concepts and values prevalent among a group of human beings. This meaning differs more than generally is realized from what is usually considered the original anthropological definition, given by British anthropologist Edward B. Tylor in 1871: "that complex whole which includes knowledge, belief, art, law, morals, custom, and any other capabilities and habits acquired by man as a member of society." To Tylor, culture was a relatively concrete concept and an aggregate of components of nearly equal importance.[6] Specialists a century later, however, increasingly regard culture as an abstraction defying exact definition, a largely unverbalized and implicit system or pattern used by individuals who must synchronize their behavior despite their disparate points of view. Furthermore, some aspects of culture are now considered far more significant than others.

To modern theorists, culture is a system that makes possible a high degree of both uniformity and diversity among individuals in a society. The shared knowledge of behavior patterns by members of a culture imposes a high degree of similarity in action and style. However, the same knowledge also enables individuals with a variety of motives to meet in thousands of standardized relationships involving detailed mutual expectations, ranging from the most intimate marital relationships to formal business deal-

[5]Matthew Arnold, *Culture and Anarchy* (reprinted: Cambridge, England, 1960), 48–9.

[6]Edward B. Tylor, *Primitive Culture* (London, 1871) 2 vols., I, 1; George W. Stocking, "Arnold, Tylor, and the Uses of Invention," in Stocking, *Race, Culture, and Evolution*, 69–109.

ings. Anthony F. C. Wallace, an anthropologist who specializes in the connection between culture and individual personality, declares that "society is . . . built upon a set of continually changing social contracts made possible by human cognitive equipment. Culture can be conceived as a set of standardized models of such contractual relationships."[7]

In studying culture—or anything else—selected factors are, as anthropologist Edward Sapir wrote, "intrinsically more valuable, more characteristic, more significant" than the rest.[8] The most important cultural phenomena, those most inclusive and crucial to cultural integration, are related to style. Like culture itself, *style* is a difficult word to define precisely. However, few scholars—including historians—doubt that cultures (such as Hopi Indian, Harlem, Scarsdale, South Boston, East Los Angeles, and Las Vegas) do differ in style, and that if these differences are identifiable, we should be able to describe them.

Our view in this book is that the primary elements in cultural style are ideas and values (including ideas concerning the meaning of symbols). The task of deciding which ideas and values are "intrinsically more valuable, more characteristic, more significant" in a culture or at a given time in a culture's history may elude exact measurement. Nevertheless, scholars learn to sample and weigh evidence within the limits of their cultural bias and personal interests. Despite the availability of some hard data, such as demographic and voting statistics, this sampling and weighing process remains an art; accuracy is made possible only by developing a high level of sensitivity, critical judgment, and experience.

Members of a society share the prevailing cultural tendencies in different degrees. These differences can be traced to factors such as age, gender, ethnicity, nationality, and social class. In studying the United States our authors found unusually wide variations ascribable to racial differences, especially to the forced two-hundred-year immigration of Africans, who then were held as slaves. During certain periods, cultural variations in the United States can also be traced to distinctions between urban and rural life and between geographical areas, most dramatically between North and South in the decades preceding the Civil War.

The difficult task for our authors of discussing the existence in

[7]Anthony F. C. Wallace, *Culture and Personality* (New York, 1961), 1–2.

[8]Sapir, "Culture, Genuine and Spurious," 401–2.

the United States of many diverse subcultures has been settled by the decision of most to devote primary attention to the dominant ideas and values that exercised decisive influence over the development of American institutions and public policies. These ideas and values also penetrated almost every subculture and ethnic, class, and subnational group, permeating most of them for generations. Undeniably, American historians have paid insufficient attention to counter-influences, of the subgroups upon dominant ideas and values, as well as to the effects of the subgroups upon each other. However, most of our authors decided that only certain of these relationships could be explored carefully in this volume. Problems concerning ethnicity, gender roles, family, and even generational dissidence generally have been discussed in separate essays.

The difficulty of dealing not only with a variety of complex subcultures but also with a great range of personality types within these groups currently leaves most social scientists and historians who consider the task in despair. Possibly this difficulty will remain until we can describe subcultures and personality types and their interactions more precisely with the aid of more sophisticated quantitative techniques or, more likely, further theoretical advances.

Meanwhile, the concept of culture provides historians with an extremely valuable intellectual tool in dealing with certain types of questions and material. Consider two of historians' most perplexing issues: to what extent do individuals affect history, and to what extent do individuals act as agents of the culture? In one of the classic works in cultural history, *Jackson: Symbol of an Age*, John William Ward demonstrated that impressions of President Andrew Jackson held by large segments of the American electorate were closer to certain popular ideas peculiar to the time and crucial to American culture in the period than they were to Jackson's actual career and character. Ward argues that although Jackson was admirably suited to act as a symbol of his age, the condition of American life in 1828 dictated that someone quite similar would have been created under a different name if he had not existed.[9] Ward carries his analysis further in an essay in this volume. Although some individuals, such as Napoleon Bonaparte and Adolf Hitler, undoubtedly have influenced major historical events and tendencies, in the history of a culture influential

[9]John William Ward, *Jackson, Symbol of an Age* (New York, 1955).

people are as likely to be intellectual or religious leaders as political figures.

A related problem is the question of whether, in general, history can be understood best in terms of long-term cultural processes. Philip Bagby, one of the most thoughtful and persuasive of the historians who have taken the extreme cultural view, declared in 1958: "History is most likely to become intelligible if individual historical events are seen as instances of cultural regularities and our inquiries are pursued on the level of culture." However, the vagaries of history occasionally exert a drastic effect upon a culture. Certainly American culture was altered by variation in geographical habitat, such as that which occurred when the early settlers from Europe reached the North American wilderness, and also by contact with members of other cultures, such as the Indians, the slaves from Africa, and the millions of immigrants from semifeudal European and Mexican peasant societies.

The overarching problem in the writing and study of cultural history—incorporating those issues already mentioned—lies in the nature of the fundamental relationship between a culture and its history. In this interrelationship the two seem always to be working upon each other—a culture giving broad historical movements their form, history reinforcing and occasionally even transforming a culture. Cultural history provides a perspective in which both culture and history are illuminated. It also brings the two together, an act of considerable importance that still takes place too infrequently. Alfred L. Kroeber, an anthropologist whose contributions to the theory of culture are monumental, declared, "When we now proceed to consider systematically the sciences of man as a whole or of human behavior as they are sometimes called, there would appear to be two considerations that cannot be omitted; first, the historical approach, and second, the concept of culture."[10]

From time to time some of the most fertile historians have expressed an appreciation similar to Kroeber's of the reciprocal importance of history and culture. The annual meeting of the American Historical Association in 1939 was devoted principally to papers emphasizing "the study of history from the standpoint of the total culture." The meeting discussed three main topics:

[10]Alfred L. Kroeber, "An Anthropologist Looks at History," *Pacific Historical Review*, XXVI (1957), 281–87.

"the technique of cultural analysis and synthesis, the cultural role of ideas, and cultural conflict and nationality groups." Unfortunately, the program was arranged so haphazardly and the choice of scholars from other disciplines was so consistently inappropriate that the meeting and the book of essays that issued from it probably set back the progress of cultural history.[11] Subsequently, historians have made sporadic appeals for more sophisticated cultural history, and an increasing number of brilliant studies provides conclusive evidence that the approach has a bright future. Students of American history who wish to test this assertion for themselves might read the accounts of the development of American black culture by John Blassingame, Lawrence Levine, Carl Degler, Herbert Gutman, and Eugene Genovese; the efforts to delineate a nineteenth-century American female culture by Barbara Welter, Nancy F. Cott, and Carroll Smith-Rosenberg; and the essays on American Victorian culture by contributors to a special issue of the *American Quarterly.*[12] The essays written for this book supply evidence to bespeak promising developments in cultural history.

In the essays that follow, all planned and written for this book, the authors have not attempted to provide a comprehensive survey of the national culture or cultures in all periods. Rather, they have explored periods during which important aspects of American culture became significant—or at least obvious—concentrating usually on the groups most involved in these changes. Although the essays are too complicated to summarize here, a few of the threads that run through them should be noted.

In the opening selection, Alden Vaughan describes the scat-

[11]Caroline F. Ware, ed., *The Cultural Approach to History* (New York, 1940).

[12]John W. Blassingame, *The Slave Community* (New York, 1972, 1979); Lawrence W. Levine, *Black Culture and Black Consciousness* (New York, 1977); Carl N. Degler, *Neither Black Nor White: Slavery and Race Relations in Brazil and the United States* (New York, 1971); Herbert G. Gutman, *The Black Family in Slavery and Freedom 1750–1925* (New York, 1979); Eugene D. Genovese, *Roll Jordan Roll: The World the Slaves Made* (New York, 1974); Barbara A. Welter, "The Cult of True Womanhood, 1820–1860," *American Quarterly* XVIII (1966), 151–74; Carroll Smith-Rosenberg, "The Female World of Love and Ritual: Relations Between Women in Nineteenth Century America," *Signs* I (1975); "Victorian America," *American Quarterly* (December 1975), reprinted as Daniel W. Howe, ed., *Victorian America* (Philadelphia, 1976).

tered European outposts of the mid-seventeenth century, separated not only by distance and a terrible communications system, but also by loyalties to different segments of European society, especially different religious groups. In the seventeenth century, Vaughan concludes, centrifugal forces seemed stronger than centripetal, a variety of cultures appeared to be developing, and the English North American colonies appeared headed for balkanization. This process was checked, Vaughan implies, largely by the similarity of the experiences and aspirations of the New World colonists. Internal migration, non-English immigration, a religious pluralism enforced from London, and a tightening of the British imperial system swung the balance decisively toward cohesion and, ironically, toward a nationalistic movement for independence.

Robert Middlekauff is concerned with the meaning of the symbols that aroused popular enthusiasm during that independence movement. In important respects, he finds, the Revolution resembled a Protestant revival, a struggle for true Christian liberty, with America serving as the instrument of Providence. Tom Paine mobilized popular support for the rebels in what seemed like an ambiguous situation to some colonists by identifying monarchy with popery. As a consequence of symbols connected with the American Revolution, "the culture was explicitly pledged to a political process that took its power and its limits from the people." The Revolution itself became the primary symbol of a promise and a prophecy that "pervaded every attempt of the revolutionary generation to understand what they had done."

The crucial egalitarian and pluralistic elements in American culture were nourished despite a powerful counterattack after the Revolution from conservative Protestant clerical and political leaders. These people still hoped, early in the nineteenth century, for "a stable commonwealth evolving in an orderly manner under the restraining hands of a paternalistic government in open alliance with established religious institutions." W. David Lewis describes the reforms instituted during this period by men basically conservative, if not reactionary, who made the most concerted attempt in American history to impose from above a single value system for American culture. Responding to the rapid political changes and social upheaval associated with the Revolution, motivated largely by doubts and fears and by a yearning to preserve the certainties of the past, they attempted to provide psychological substitutes for the aristocratic and religious barriers to change that existed in older cultures. Recognizing the futility of trying to arrest the growth of egalitarian democracy in every sector in the society, the conservatives made an effort instead to inculcate within Americans respect for order and propriety. Many reform movements originated as part of this effort; "civilization" was promoted on the western frontier, and religious revival movements were launched.

Although vestiges of the counter-revolution survived—in the form of rigid Sabbath observance and hostility to such activities as card playing, dancing, horse racing, and the drinking of alcohol—the crusade itself failed miserably. Even the revivals became infected with unorthodox ideas. On some issues, evangelical Protestant sects joined Catholics and non-English immigrants in defeating the conservative reformers. Despite deflections here and there, the culture continued to evolve on its egalitarian, pluralistic course.

The fervent popular beliefs that doomed the conservative reaction are abstracted by John Ward from the political speeches and essays of the period from 1820 through 1850. Few contemporary authors speculated about the philosophical bases of America's unique form of government. One person who addressed this issue, George Sidney Camp, explained that most of the "chief speculators" of the day concerned themselves not with political theory but with "merchandise and real estate." Ward explores the political rhetoric of the era in search of the democratic assumptions of the time—"what uncommon hopes motivated the politics of the age of the common man." For that period, at least, when the level of political consciousness in most men was high, Ward asserts that politics was an excellent guide to cultural values.

At the heart of these implicit beliefs, Ward finds a widespread contempt for all human authority and established organizations that bordered on anarchy. Fundamental law for most Americans existed not in the Constitution, but in nature. Its true interpretation could be found not in the decisions of judges, but in the will of the popular majority. The form of United States government, so in accord with divine will, determined the citizens' character and their culture. It was widely believed that because of this ideal political form and the intrinsic moral equality of all white men it was unnecessary for Americans to plan for the good society. Divine favor and political subservience to the will of the infallible majority would guarantee success in the long run.

Carl Degler examines the subcultures most responsible for the swift disruption of these pleasant myths. Millions of Negro slaves in the South did not share basic elements of the dominant culture. Largely because of the presence of these blacks, a regional culture developed in the South different in important respects from the cultures of the North and West, which came increasingly to resemble each other.

The Southern ideal life style—essentially that of the country gentleman freed by slaves from any form of manual labor— seemed so unlike the Northern style, at least to Southerners, that planters who pushed their slaves hard in an effort to increase profits were referred to contemptuously as Southern Yankees. Even the burgeoning romantic nationalism of the mid-nineteenth century could not overcome these cultural disparities, and in the face of worldwide hostility to their "peculiar situation," the Southern states seceded and attempted to form a society that could ward off the threats to their unique culture.

During the Reconstruction era the revolutionary ideal of the fundamental equality of all men finally was applied to blacks. Degler traces the partially successful attempts to assimilate the former slaves through the Reconstruction period and into the present. "In cultural terms," he concludes, "the ending of Radical Reconstruction meant that the United States was not to be a unified, homogeneous nation but a federation of regions still, in which each section would be free to pursue its own social patterns."

The belief that Christianity and democracy were related formed the vital core of the progressive effort to revitalize American society early in the twentieth century. This same belief had sustained the faith of the Jacksonians almost a century earlier. Many of the peculiarities of the progressive movement, Clyde Griffen finds, can be attributed to the predominantly white, middle-class, Protestant, native-born leadership whose value system included important vestiges from an earlier society. The reformers described by Griffen were not the only group involved in the progressive movement, as he observes, but they supplied most of the leaders and gave the crusade its dynamic spirit.

Even more remarkable than the progressives' tendency to confuse, or at least to blend, Christian and democratic ethics, says Griffen, was their certainty that complicated economic and social problems could be reduced to simple moral questions for which Christianity had clear answers. This touching optimism, this faith in the efficacy of Protestant middle-class paternalism, was hardly the stuff from which a radical reform movement could be made.

Nevertheless, the progressive spirit did unify a wide spectrum of reformers with different interests in support of specific measures. Griffen suggests that the Communist revolutions in Europe and the "Red Scare" of 1919 in the United States frightened the Christian reformers, perhaps with a sudden vision of what a too literal reading of the social gospel might lead to. During the 1920s, moreover, the intensity of religious commitment decreased among the urban middle class. The progressive spirit then largely dissolved, and the reform movement lost its essential cohesion.

Historians have noted that the generation that came of age just before, during, and just after World War I—in the cities of Europe even more than in the United States—seemed in important respects to be a different breed than their elders. Loren Baritz, reviewing the intellectual crisis of the 1920s, presents an interpretation of what may have been either an advanced stage of cultural disintegration or the beginning of a cultural resynthesis.

The inherent pluralism of American society, hidden temporarily by the progressive crusade, reappeared in full force after World War I. Baritz observes that the intellectual and artistic elite were not the only critics of the direction in which the United States was moving. Their opponents were no less adamant. A provincial newspaper editor, complaining of the huge number of unassimilated immigrants in the country, declared that this undigested urban lump was forcing its own immoral standards—including drunkenness and Sabbath breaking—upon the rest of the United States: "They govern our great cities . . . , the great cities govern the nation; and foreign control or conquest could gain little more, though secured by foreign armies and fleets." The Imperial Wizard and Emperor of the Ku Klux Klan announced in the mid-1920s that his organization would battle Jews, Catholics, Negroes, and intellectuals in order to return power in the country to the "not overly intellectualized, but entirely unspoiled and not de-Americanized average citizen of the old stock."

According to Baritz, the Klan, Prohibition, and immigration restrictions all were evidence of the temporary victory of Americans with rural and small-town origins. The village, he asserts, "was in virtual control of America's public life during the twenties, and the dismay of the writers and artists cannot be fully understood in any other context." The intellectual, and other urbanites, struggling with problems of modern life of which provincial Americans seemed altogether unaware, found the situation grotesque. It was this attitude that led F. Scott

Fitzgerald to write from Paris, "Can you name a single American artist except James and Whistler (who lived in England) who didn't die of drink?"

Although the Great Depression and then World War II gave all Americans concrete objectives and tasks, Baritz asserts that these events "did not solve but at least temporarily obscured the peculiarly modern anguish." He concludes: "With peace and returning affluence, with skirts rising again and traditional morality declining again, those now old questions reasserted themselves."

Just when there seemed a possibility that American culture might fly apart from the violence of its various internal conflicts and contradictions, the terrible depression that began in 1930 promoted a deceptive return of cultural community and cooperation. Warren Susman describes the eruption of literary sentimentalizing about "the people," the gigantic effort to document the national life and values in art, reporting, social science, and history. New communication forms—pictorial magazines, the radio, and motion pictures—also played a part in creating an impression of coherence. Above all, the popularization of the concept of culture itself reinforced a social order that had been deteriorating rapidly and helped create a desire to participate somehow in the community among those who might otherwise have encouraged revolt. Perhaps, Susman suggests, because of this desire for commitment and the pervasive idea of culture, the dominant mood of the period, even among intellectuals, was not rebellion but acquiescence in established social and economic structures.

The last three essays in this volume bring changes in American life since the 1930's into historical perspective. In examining what he and many others have termed the Movement—as well as the reaction to it—Peter Clecak discusses in a highly innovative and persuasive fashion the impact of social culture and political dissent in the 1960s on American politics and culture. While Clecak perceives the Movement as a complex, multifaceted phenomenon, he argues that it served primarily as a vehicle for individuals seeking a fuller sense of personal identity. Clecak concludes that the cultural history of America from the late 1950s to the late 1970s should be viewed as one period with two parts—a period of dramatic changes followed by a time of consolidation and consideration of those changes. How deeply these have affected American society and what we have termed an American culture cannot yet be determined accurately, though Clecak clearly considers these shifts important.

John Buenker urges us to recognize that recent immigrant groups and black Americans have related to their adopted society in three ways—political, economic, and personal—and that the extent to which members of these ethnic groups have been assimilated into that society differs for each of those areas of their lives. In politics, he finds that ethnic ties remain a powerful factor in determining voter behavior and political involvement. In economic life, Buenker claims that ethnic identity, more than economic class, has barred upward mobility for most American ethnic groups over several generations. And, Buenker concludes, "By far the least assimilation and acculturation has taken place at the primary level of society and culture." He goes on to assert that "most immigrants and many of their descendants have preferred to live much of their personal lives among 'their own kind.' " Consequently these ethnic groups have lived in a state of tension with the dominant culture, and to varying degrees they continue to do so.

Cultural change in the face of the pressures caused by economic development (often referred to vaguely as "modernization") has led many Americans to bemoan what they perceive to be the weakening of family life. Tamara Hareven makes a strong case against such an assessment of the history of the family in America. She argues that "what we are witnessing is not a fragmentation of traditional family patterns but rather the emergence of a pluralism in family ways." She insists that concern over family breakdown has characterized all periods of American history despite the belief in a mythical golden age of family life in preindustrial America. Hareven contends that family life now is more stable than in nineteenth-century America because of the greater opportunity for generational continuities afforded by earlier marriage and longer life expectancy. Hareven's findings provide a classic example of how careful historical scholarship can correct a popular contemporary perspective.

Furthermore, Hareven's essay contains evidence important for the study and understanding of women's history. Throughout almost all of American history, the overwhelming majority of females have lived their lives very largely within families. To the extent that a distinctly female subculture has existed and continues to exist in America—at least within the middle class, where research on the topic has been concentrated so far—our understanding of its nature and of its importance would be affected strongly by the aspects of family history Hareven has uncovered.

The pluralism in family types described by Hareven introduces new and significant elements into the American culture that began to develop in the American colonies. That culture flourished in the mid and late nineteenth century and in somewhat altered form remains an important part of twentieth-century American society. The distinct black subculture introduced in Carl Degler's essay also has exercised a strong effect, even on middle-class American culture. The ethnic subcultures, and twentieth-century black culture, described by John Buenker, provided new variables for anyone seeking to understand American culture. The changes in the dominant culture wrought by the cultural reform movements treated by Peter Clecak, and the continued existence of the subcultures that emerged from those movements, served to modify American culture. It is to be hoped that the complexities that these authors—and indeed every contributor to this book—have added to the already complex concept of an American culture will only encourage the thought with which we began this project. Our thought was that our volume should encourage readers to engage themselves in the process of understanding what America has been like for those who helped create and develop the nation, how America's cultural heritage affects all its inhabitants now, and what American history suggests about the most probable paths into the future.

SEVENTEENTH-CENTURY ORIGINS OF AMERICAN CULTURE

Alden T. Vaughan / COLUMBIA UNIVERSITY

In the early seventeenth century the prospect seemed remote that America would eventually hold people from scores of disparate heritages living in general, if tenuous, harmony. To Europeans, and also undoubtedly to the American Indians—soon to be overwhelmed by history's largest migration—the emergence of a coherent American civilization seemed improbable. Instead, the pattern of future settlement appeared to be separate and varied clusters of transplanted or indigenous people. Until late in the century the dominant characteristic of American culture was its fragmentation—not only geographical but political, ethnic, and religious as well.

The reasons are clear enough. There were, in the first place, differences among the North American mainland colonies that derived from the variety of national origins. Unlike the colonization of Central and South America, which from the beginning was almost exclusively Spanish, European settlement north of Mexico was international. At various times during the seventeenth century, five colonizing powers owned settlements along the Atlantic coast: the Dutch at New Netherland from 1609 to 1664 and again briefly in the 1670s; the Swedes in the Delaware Valley from 1638 to 1655; the French in Canada and the Mississippi Valley after 1608 and at various times in Florida, Maine, and northern New York; the Spanish in Florida as early as 1521; and, most significantly, the English after 1607 in a semicontiguous chain of outposts stretching from Maine to the Carolinas. Moreover, the Indian population between the Atlantic coast and the Mississippi River was divided into scores of nations or tribes exhibiting a wide variety of languages and customs and profound differences in political and territorial objectives. The area east of the Appalachians thus held a checkerboard of national spheres of settlement representing overlapping claims and rival interests. There was good reason to fear, as J. H. Plumb has observed, that North America would succumb to balkanization.[1]

Such a possibility stemmed only in part from the variety of nationalities; equally important was the disunity within the British sphere. Instead of a single colony in the New World, England had several settlements, and unlike their European neighbors, the English colonists rarely joined hands in common cause. More often they bitterly debated their rights, religions, and boundaries. At the same time, each English colony looked to the mother country for protection, supply, and guidance, thus reducing the needs and opportunities for intercolonial cooperation. And as England's national unity temporarily succumbed to religious-political segmentation in the seventeenth century, parallel factions emerged in America; each colony in British America thereafter gave allegiance to a different segment of the homeland. The mother country did possess a few men like John Smith and Richard Hakluyt who were interested in English colonization per se, harboring no preference for any colony so long as it was English. But most promoters, adventurers, and settlers had far narrower vision: their loyalties were restricted to a single strand of English society for which they sought an exclusive outpost in the New World. Each party hoped its own brand of religion or political theory would someday gain supremacy throughout the British dominions; in the meantime each asked to be left alone in its New World haven. And in order to be free to chart its own course—as well as to get necessary supplies and additional immigrants—a colony needed powerful friends back home. To such friends and to sympathetic elements in the general population, each colony appealed. Thus the Catholics of Maryland looked for help from English Catholics; New England tracts were directed primarily at England's Puritan community; Quaker merchants sought commercial ties with their religious brethren in the mother country.

[1] J. H. Plumb, introduction to John R. Alden, *Pioneer America* (New York, 1966), xxiv.

During most of the century, the Anglicans of Virginia had the easier task of appealing for spiritual and material help from the dominant religious and political power in England, although even the Virginians found themselves allied to a minority faction during the 1640s and 1650s. As the conflicts at home became increasingly bitter during England's century of turmoil, the English outposts in America likewise drew still further apart. The centrifugal forces seemed stronger than the centripetal.

Yet partly because of changes taking place in Europe and partly because of the realities of life in the New World, the disunity of the American colonies would last less than one hundred years. While American society was sharply segmented in the seventeenth century, it was also developing the characteristics that would one day reverse the trend of mutual exclusiveness; parochialism would in the end give way to more insistent tendencies toward social and political integration and to the emergence of commonly held values and aspirations that heralded the emergence of a truly American culture.

I

Until the dawn of the eighteenth century, the dynamics of fragmentation plagued British America. Much of the blame—or credit—must be assigned to the Crown, for from the outset of English colonization it encouraged the creation of essentially private settlements that could limit admissions as they saw fit. To Englishmen of the seventeenth century this seemed only natural, for it was in keeping with their understanding of the prerogatives of privately sponsored communities. Nor did it seem odd that in the second Virginia charter the Crown itself mandated a fundamental restriction on settlement: "wee would be lothe that anie person should be permitted [in Virginia] . . . that wee suspected to affect the superstitions of the Churche of Rome."[2] Virginia was to be an English colony, but not a colony for all Englishmen.

Still, for almost two decades Britain's first colony remained a truly national enterprise. Private investors cooperated with the Crown in the administration of the colony, Puritans worked side by side—though not always peacefully—with Anglicans, and

[2]Samuel M. Bemis, ed., *The Three Charters of the Virginia Company of London* (Williamsburg, Va., 1957), 54.

noblemen as well as gentlemen, yeomen, and laborers helped carve an English outpost in the wilderness. Despite rampant dissension within the Jamestown settlement and its offshoots, British America began as an attempt to transplant English culture—which under James I was relatively stable and homogeneous—to the New World. The architects of empire even hoped to incorporate neighboring Indians into the new society, provided that they first succumbed to English notions of "civilitie" and Christianity and acknowledged English authority.[3]

Until 1620 it was conceivable that the Virginia Company of London would expand its holdings and impose on all British settlements a homogeneous political pattern—much as took place in the French and Spanish possessions—yet one that, unlike New France and New Spain, would find room for the whole spectrum of British life. The almost defunct Virginia Company of Plymouth, which held title to the northern half of England's New World claim, had failed to plant a permanent colony despite temporary success in 1607 at the Sagadahoc River in Maine; absorption of the Plymouth company's title by the London company would have consolidated England's territories under a single corporation. But the intensification of religious and political strife in England, the settlement of New England by Puritan factions, and the dissolution of the Virginia Company itself soon ended such a prospect. With the revocation of Virginia's third charter in 1624 and its replacement by royal control, the die was cast for British colonization in the seventeenth century. Henceforth colonies were established piecemeal, some by private corporations, some by one or more proprietors; and the authority extended to companies and proprietors varied widely. So did the size and viability of their territorial assignments, for the boundaries were often contradictory and frequently overlapped each other and the territories held by other nations. The home government, however, rarely seemed to care, for throughout most of the seventeenth century the Crown, and briefly the Commonwealth, stepped into colonial affairs only to issue or revoke a charter or to impose an occasional imperial policy. Otherwise each colony was on its own.

The new tone in British settlement was rapidly reflected in Virginia. With the shift in leadership that accompanied the repeal

[3]Early Virginia is discussed thoroughly and perceptively in Edmund S. Morgan, *American Slavery—American Freedom: The Ordeal of Colonial Virginia* (New York, 1975).

of its charter, Virginia became almost exclusively Anglican in
theology and royalist in imperial politics. At the same time, the
colony continued to strengthen tendencies it had had under corporate leadership: representative government based on county
units, an economy dependent on tobacco, a social elite that increasingly emulated the English gentry, and, most portentous for
the future of American culture, a labor system centered on indentured servitude and Negro slavery.

Any free man, regardless of national origin, was welcome to
join this New World outpost so long as he abided by the colony's social and political premises and took an oath of allegiance to the English sovereign; servants and slaves were
admitted with the understanding that their masters were responsible for their outward conformity. Everyone else was de-
cidedly unwelcome. Hence Englishmen who still held to the
Church of Rome continued to avoid Virginia, and a sporadic
effort to purge neighboring Maryland of its Catholic influence
remained a pet project of many Virginians throughout the century. No more welcome were Puritans—whether from New England or old England made no difference—for to Anglican royalists their countrymen of the Puritan persuasion represented a
threat to the foundations of society. If the Virginia colony had
no Bishop Laud to harry the Puritans out of the land, it did
have a governor "and some other malignant spirits" in full
sympathy with such a policy. The few Puritans who put Virginia's exclusiveness to the test soon wearied of harassment
and moved on to New England or to Maryland, their departure
hastened by an act of the legislature requiring the governor to
oust all religious nonconformists.[4]

During the Commonwealth period, Virginians had cause to be
concerned about their future position. Persistent rumors told of a
Cromwellian plan to force the royalist colony into palpable loyalty
to the Commonwealth, but it never came to pass—nor is there any
evidence that the Lord Protector considered it seriously. On the
other hand, the English Civil War encouraged thousands of Anglican royalists (including the forebears of George Washington) to
migrate to Virginia; thus at the Stuart Restoration the colony's

[4][Edward Johnson], *Johnson's Wonder-Working Providence, 1628–1651* (New
York, 1910), 265. For Virginia's treatment of Catholics, see Andrew White, "A
Relation of the Colony of . . . Maryland . . .", in Peter Force, comp., *Tracts and
Other Papers Relating Principally to . . . the Colonies in North America* (4 vols., repr.
Gloucester, Mass., 1963), IV, no. XII, esp. 17, 43–44.

European population was ethnically and religiously as homogeneous as ever, a condition conducive to continued separateness. By the end of the century, Virginia was, as it had been since the 1620s, overwhelmingly English in national composition, Anglican in theology, royalist in sympathy, and economically dependent on the export of tobacco, with the corollary phenomena of ruralism and inheritable bondage. This is not to say that Virginians got along with each other in the 1660s and 1670s any better than they had in the colony's first decade. Social strife—especially local uprisings by a "giddy multitude" of "Poore Endebted Discontented and Armed" men—culminated in the virtual civil war of 1676. But a striking characteristic of Virginia's turmoil was its isolation from the other colonies. Only neighboring Maryland felt any impact, and most of Maryland's chronic troubles stemmed from its own internal dynamics.[5]

Throughout the seventeenth century, Maryland, no less than Virginia, wished to go its separate way, though for somewhat different purposes. The object of George Calvert and his son Cecilius was essentially defensive: to create a colony where Catholics could worship without fear of molestation. In a militantly Protestant empire, Catholics could hope for no more. Exclusion of Protestants from Maryland, had it been considered at all, would have invited attack; it was much wiser and more in keeping with the liberal taste of the proprietor to maintain equality in worship, government, and landholding.[6]

From its founding in 1634, the Catholic colony was open to Protestants. Although the Calverts' charter made them "absolute lords" of Maryland, their coreligionists formed a numerical minority (though not a minority of the leaders) in the first expedition to the new colony. Accordingly, the proprietor prohibited religious controversy, and not surprisingly when such controversy eventually developed the Protestants, not the Catholics, were to blame. When the Protestant majority meted out harsh punishment to Catholics during the turbulent 1640s, the second Lord Baltimore countered with that curious milestone on the

[5]Virginia's internal strife is analyzed in Morgan, *American Slavery—American Freedom*, especially the middle chapters, and in T. H. Breen, "A Changing Labor Force and Race Relations in Virginia 1660–1710," *Journal of Social History*, VI (1973), 3–25.

[6]Charles M. Andrews, *The Colonial Period of American History*, II (New Haven, 1936), 276–281; David B. Quinn, *The English Discovery of America, 1481–1620* (New York, 1974), ch. 14.

road to religious liberty, the Act of Toleration. Proposed by the Catholic proprietor, passed by the Protestant legislature, and enforced sporadically by the mixed population, the act had equal parts of modern toleration and medieval bigotry. The complete freedom of worship it extended to all Trinitarians was offset by the mandatory death penalty for all blasphemers and outspoken non-Trinitarians.[7] Fortunately, the full penalty of the law was never applied. In any event, before the century ended, the proprietor renounced the Church of Rome and endorsed proscriptions against the Catholics. Maryland had failed to become the Catholic haven its founders had intended. It remained, however, a society quite distinct from its colonial neighbors. Although it emulated the plantation society of adjacent Virginia, it remained a far more open, though equally turbulent, community. Its religious diversity was responsible in part for its uniqueness, but important too were the growth of coastal ports, a greater variety of crops, and proximity to the Quaker colonies of the Delaware Bay. Moreover, Maryland and Virginia were almost constantly at odds. For much of the century they wrangled over title to Kent Island in Chesapeake Bay, and during the times of extreme crisis, such as Virginia witnessed in 1675 and Maryland in 1689, neither colony proved a comfort to its neighbor. To the casual observer the Chesapeake colonies might well have belonged to rival empires.

Significantly different in purpose and character from Virginia and Maryland were the Carolinas. Although officially one colony throughout the seventeenth century, the ink was barely dry on the charter of 1663 before settlement below Virginia centered on two widely separate areas. In the southern portion, Charles Town (later Charleston) had by the 1690s emerged as the nucleus of a cosmopolitan community based on slave labor, large plantations, an active trade with the Indians for deer skins, and—despite its apparent incompatibility with peaceful interracial commerce—a lucrative export of Indian slaves to the West Indies. Settlers poured into the region from England and the Indies (many bringing their African slaves) and most conspicuously from France after Louis XIV resumed persecution of the Huguenots in 1685. In 1700 Charles Town boasted two thousand inhabitants and there were another three thousand in the vicinity. By that date blacks

[7]H. Shelton Smith, Robert T. Handy, and Lefferts A. Loetscher, *American Christianity: An Historical Interpretation with Representative Documents*, I (New York, 1960), 35–39.

had become a substantial portion of the region's population, and within a decade they were a majority. Thus by the turn of the century the long-range economic and social configurations of South Carolina were clearly visible. So too was its lack of identification with the Albemarle Sound area to the north. There settlers from Virginia had spilled across the border into the rugged pine country and turned to the production of naval stores, hemp, and tobacco. North Carolina, as it would soon become known, showed few similarities to the Charles Town area: no large towns emerged, few plantations were established, slavery languished, and the population remained predominantly English and Anglican.[8]

Neither section of the Carolinas quite fulfilled the proprietors' hopes for abundant revenue, nor did either abide long by the Fundamental Constitutions of Anthony Ashley Cooper and his philosopher-physician, John Locke. Their attempt to impose a rigid social hierarchy on Carolina came to nought in the "free air of a New World."[9] Locke's quasi-feudal Grand Model called for a permanent landed nobility dominating the numerous but politically powerless freeholders and an even larger and less influential tenant class. The plan was never fully implemented, largely because of widespread resistance from an antiproprietary faction that would not willingly relinquish its control over the region to the proprietors in England or to their handpicked grandees in America; nor would the Albemarle settlers yield to the proprietors' agents in Charles Town, which after 1670 became the titular center of Carolina. What emerged instead was a bipolar colony in which the two centers had little contact with each other and where the attitudes and experiences they did share could not overcome the influence of their distinct environments and disparate populations. In many respects Carolina epitomized the centrifugal temper of the seventeenth century. Long before 1700 it was clear to all that its two regions were entirely separate, a fact acknowledged early in the next century by the creation of the royal colonies of North and South Carolina.

By the end of the seventeenth century, then, four English out-

---

[8]M. Eugene Sirmans, *Colonial South Carolina: A Political History, 1663–1763* (Chapel Hill, N.C., 1966), pt. I; Converse D. Clowse, *Economic Beginnings in Colonial South Carolina* (Columbia, S.C., 1971); and Hugh T. Lefler and William S. Powell, *Colonial North Carolina: A History* (New York, 1973).

[9]The phrase was originally applied to New England but fits as well the whole Western Hemisphere.

posts had been planted in the southern latitudes. They resembled each other very little, and probably no visitor suspected that in another century and a half they would join an attempt to form a separate southern nation. For as Carl Bridenbaugh has pointed out, there was no South in the colonial period; the English settlements below the 40th parallel had many latent similarities, but they neither acknowledged nor sought any intercolonial ties or regional identity.[10]

While the South was clearly not a section in the seventeenth century, New England was. The qualities that mark a section—strong similarities in institutions, aspirations, attitudes, and ethnic background—were abundant in New England. Throughout the century it was common to speak of "Boston in New England" and to designate a resident of any of the Puritan colonies as a "New Englander." Whether or not that term encompassed Rhode Island was always debatable. In point of fact the people who settled in the smallest colony differed from those in Massachusetts, Plymouth, Connecticut, and New Haven in theology only, and not always fundamentally even there. However, that in itself was a reflection of the seventeenth century's penchant for fragmentation: even in highly homogeneous New England there took root a colony of anti-Puritans—"Rogue's Island" as the Puritans were fond of calling it. When in 1643 the four Congregational colonies formed the Confederation of New England for purposes of defense and mutual aid, Rhode Island was not invited to join.

To most New Englanders of the seventeenth century, religion was the central feature of their society. At least that was the contention of the lay and clerical founders of each of the Puritan colonies and of the principal spokesmen in succeeding generations. Shortly before his departure for Massachusetts in 1630, John Winthrop contended that "planting a Colony in New England [is] for . . . the glory of God and the service of his Church." In 1697 John Higginson, son of one of the first Massachusetts ministers, reiterated the point: New England "was indeed planted, not on account of any *Worldly Interest*, but on a Design of Enjoying and Advancing the true *Reformed Religion*."[11]

[10]Carl Bridenbaugh, *Myths and Realities: Societies of the Colonial South* (Baton Rouge, La., 1952).

[11]Massachusetts Historical Society, *Winthrop Papers* (5 vols., Boston, 1929–1947), II, 163; Higginson, introduction to Cotton Mather, *Magnalia Christi Americana* (London, 1702; repr. New York, 1972), [A3].

Higginson overstated the case. Economic, political, and social motives were present, too, and for some colonists these must have been paramount. But many, probably most, of the early immigrants to New England came primarily because of dissatisfaction with the orthodoxy of England, and they had no intention of traveling three thousand miles in vain. The result was a society infused with religious intensity both in form and ethos. In Plymouth and Connecticut no less than in Massachusetts Bay and New Haven Colony, church and state formed a close partnership. Like any partnership, this one involved occasional overlaps of effort and interest, and the proper function of each partner is almost impossible to describe with accuracy. Yet the broad outlines of the "New England Way" are clear enough: the Puritan colonies would be Bible-centered communities in which, insofar as human frailty permitted, all actions had to accord with God's rules for civil and religious society. Winthrop thought of New England as "a Citty upon a Hill" to which the eyes of European heretics and Indian heathens alike would turn—at first, perhaps, with skepticism but in the end with admiration.[12]

The Puritans assumed that in order to carry out their religious and social experiment it had to rest in the hands of those who had conceived it and, later on, of heirs equally committed to its success. This required the exclusion of anyone who threatened the basic character of the community. Hence a Massachusetts law of 1637 forbade strangers to remain in any town for more than three weeks without explicit approval from the magistrates. In defending the regulation, Winthrop argued that "if the place of our cohabitation be our owne, then no man hath right to come into us etc. without our consent. . . . We may lawfully refuse to receive such whose dispositions suite not with ours and whose society [we know] will be hurtful to us." A few years later Nathaniel Ward, self-styled "Herald of New England," put the same sentiment more bluntly when he observed that dissenters from the New England Way had "free Liberty to keepe away from us, and such as will come to be gone as fast as they can, the sooner the

---

[12]*Winthrop Papers*, II, 295. The best brief introduction to the founding of Massachusetts is Edmund S. Morgan, *Puritan Dilemma: The Story of John Winthrop* (Boston, 1957). On the nature of early Puritan society, see especially Stephen Foster, *Their Solitary Way: The Puritan Social Ethic in the First Century of Settlement in New England* (New Haven, 1971).

better."[13] Those who tarried or, worse still, insisted on preaching their own brand of religious or political philosophy were to be forcibly expelled. So Roger Williams discovered in 1636, the Antinomians in 1638, and the Quakers in the 1650s and 1660s. The lesson was also impressed upon such lesser-known non-Puritans as Thomas Morton in 1628 and again in 1630, John and Samuel Browne in 1629, and Philip Ratcliffe in 1631. These people were deemed dangerous, for reasons theological, social, or political, to the survival of the experiment and therefore were sent away, though not necessarily with bitterness. (The classic example of amity in the face of expulsion is the role of John Winthrop in aiding Williams to escape to another part of New England rather than be shipped back to England. Winthrop and Williams remained friends, despite their theological differences, and after the death of the Massachusetts governor in 1649, Winthrop's eldest son continued to be a frequent correspondent of Rhode Island's founder.) Similarly, a Massachusetts ordinance of 1647 denied entrance to Jesuits unless shipwrecked or on diplomatic or business errands. Visiting clerics such as Father Gabriel Druilletes, who in 1650 was entertained by John Eliot and other Puritan spokesmen, were welcome as long as they made no attempt to settle or to proselytize among the New Englanders.[14]

While New England, then, shared with the other colonies a desire to remain aloof from the rest of British America, it applied this preference more consciously and more extensively than did the other American settlements, directing its resentment of interference against the government of the mother country as well as against individuals from Europe or from sister colonies. In the mid-1630s and again in the 1670s and early 1680s, Massachusetts successfully resisted efforts to revoke her charter, even to the extent of building a fort in Boston Harbor to repel a possible British expedition against the colony. Later, after the crown finally succeeded in nullifying the Massachusetts charter of 1629, it failed to seize Connecticut's because obstinate colonists hid their document in an oak tree—though the charter was canceled none-

[13]*Winthrop Papers*, III, 423; Nathaniel Ward, *The Simple Cobler of Aggawam in America* (London, 1647; repr. ed. by P. M. Zall, Lincoln, Neb., 1969), 6; Nathaniel B. Shurtleff, ed., *Records of the Governor and Company of the Massachusetts Bay in New England* (5 vols., Boston, 1853–1854), I, 51–54, 74–75, 88, 196.

[14]Shurtleff, *Records of Massachusetts Bay*, II, 193; Reuben Gold Thwaites, ed., *The Jesuit Relations and Allied Documents* (73 vols., Cleveland, 1896–1901), XXXVI, 87–95.

theless. And during England's brief experiment in imperial consolidation that merged the colonies from New Hampshire to New
Jersey into the Dominion of New England, the Puritan colonies
brought Governor Edmund Andros persistent anguish and imprisoned him as soon as news of the Glorious Revolution reached
America.[15] New England acted in self-righteous independence on
other matters, too. In 1659 Massachusetts decided that it was
better to hang Quakers who defied banishment than to ship them
back to England. In the execution of three men and one woman
between 1659 and 1663, the Puritan commonwealth carried to its
logical but frightening extreme the theory that each colony was
accountable only to itself—a theory to which all colonies tacitly
subscribed. By hanging the Quakers for persistently disrupting
the colony's social and religious stability, the Puritans gave notice that they would go to any length to preserve their definition
of orderly society and proper behavior. Fortunately for dissenters
in all of the colonies, Massachusetts had so overreached its legitimate powers that henceforth the Crown and Parliament kept a
closer rein on colonial autonomy.

During the first two-thirds of the seventeenth century, New
England was isolated from the rest of British America not only by
choice and by the distinctiveness of its culture, but also by the
geopolitical realities of New World colonization. Until the British
conquest of New Netherland in 1664, the Dutch enclave posed a
formidable physical and cultural barrier between England's
northern and southern colonies. Even after the arrival of English
administrators and the promulgation of English laws brought *de
jure* English control, New York's predominantly Dutch culture
continued to separate the northern and southern spheres of British influence. Eventually the colony of New York would become
almost as anglicized as its neighbors, but in the seventeenth century, Dutch flavor remained strong in language, law, architec-
ture, local polity, and religion.

Having been conquered rather than created, the British colony
of New York did not owe its early development to English fac-
tionalism. It did, however, have a heritage almost as inimical to

---

[15]The best discussions of New England in the 1670s and 1680s are Viola Flo-
rence Barnes, *The Dominion of New England: A Study in British Colonial Policy*
(New York, 1923); Michael Garibaldi Hall, *Edward Randolph and the American
Colonies, 1676–1703* (Chapel Hill, N.C., 1960); and David S. Lovejoy, *The Glorious
Revolution in America* (New York, 1973).

colonial unity. Although from the start the Dutch had welcomed immigrants of diverse ethnic groups, spokesmen for the Dutch Reformed Church tried hard to preserve a semblance of religious purity. Backed by Governor Peter Stuyvesant and the burgomasters of New Amsterdam, Reverends Johannes Megapolensis and Samuel Drisius urged the directors of the Dutch West Indian Company to prohibit migration into the colony by Jews and Christian clergymen of non-Reformed persuasions. Letters to the Classis in Amsterdam warned of attempts by several religious sects to hold public services; the Classis in turn voiced dismay at the idea of a Jewish synagogue "for the exercise of their blasphemous religion." Nor were the civil and ecclesiastical rulers of New Netherland sympathetic to the early Quaker settlers, whom they imprisoned, fined, and banished. Under the Duke's Laws of 1665 freedom of worship was granted to all Christians, but in practice it was a limited freedom that did little to encourage immigration by religious minorities. Despite New York's broad ethnic diversity (which included clusters of French, Swiss, and Sephardic Jews in addition to Dutch and English groups), its religious diversity proved almost as limited as Boston's: in 1687 only four faiths practiced openly in New York City—Dutch Reformed, Lutheran, French Calvinist, and Anglican—and the Anglicans had to share quarters with the Dutch church until late in 1697.[16] Furthermore, the earlier Dutch pattern of manorial estates along the Hudson and the presence of a powerful Indian confederacy in the Mohawk Valley kept Englishmen from flocking to the newly acquired colony. Of course there were exceptions. Robert Livingston, for example, had qualities and aspirations ideally suited to the time and place; he gladly settled in northern New York after a brief sojourn in New England.[17] Others would follow but in such sparse numbers that New York retained its Dutch character well into the eighteenth century.

During the latter half of the colonial period, Pennsylvania rivaled New York as the most cosmopolitan colony. However, Penn-

[16]J. Franklin Jameson, ed., *Narratives of New Netherland, 1609–1664* (New York, 1909), 391–402; Smith, Handy, and Loetscher, *American Christianity*, 59–78; Wayne Andrews, ed., "A Glance at New York in 1697: The Travel Diary of Dr. Benjamin Bullivant," *New York Historical Society Quarterly*, XL (1956), 62. On intolerance, see *A Narrative of a New and Unusual American Imprisonment . . .* [1707], in Force, *Tracts and Other Papers*, IV, no. IV.

[17]Lawrence H. Leder, *Robert Livingston, 1654–1728, and the Politics of Colonial New York* (Chapel Hill, N.C., 1961), ch. I.

sylvania's claim to religious, ethnic, and economic variety rests primarily on its performance in the eighteenth century, not the seventeenth. From its founding in 1681 until the turn of the century, Penn's proprietorship contained only a few thousand Quaker farmers surrounding a small but expanding Quaker village.[18] Pennsylvania's eventual rapid growth was partly a result of the Quakers' sincere toleration of newcomers, but even where toleration and ethnic variety were championed, seventeenth-century colonies clung to the notion that each had a special purpose and distinct character that set it apart from the rest of British America. Despite his cordiality toward all faiths and nationalities, William Penn intended his colony to be a "Holy Experiment," which to Penn meant much the same as Winthrop's "Citty upon a Hill." Penn wanted his colony to be a Quaker refuge and to retain a Quaker character; it therefore needed a Quaker proprietor and Quaker political control, and for several decades it enjoyed both. Still, in many ways the last of England's seventeenth-century outposts reflected significant trends in British America. Pennsylvania's relative heterogeneity, its tolerance, and its commercial bustle heralded a new century in which the colonies would begin to exhibit characteristics that outsiders, as well as the colonists themselves, would recognize as distinctively American.

II

Members of a culture often are unaware of the forces that bind that culture together. Such certainly was the case in the seventeenth century when few British colonists knew or cared about the characteristics they held in common with any but their immediate neighbors. But to the historian looking backward, one of the most striking features of early America is the similarity of its immigrants and of their experiences in the New World.

Sheer physical hardships provided one kind of shared experience, for the American environment could be as treacherous as it was bountiful. Thousands died on the ships that safely navigated the Atlantic, while some vessels foundered without survivors. Second- and third-generation Americans of course escaped the danger of the trip, but they knew of it from relatives and friends or from

[18]The best study of early Pennsylvania is Gary B. Nash, *Quakers and Politics: Pennsylvania, 1681–1726* (Princeton, N.J., 1968).

awaiting the arrival of still other immigrants. And the ocean crossing was merely the first step. Partly from the natural hazards of the land and partly from physical weakness aggravated by the voyage, the mortality rate in the early colonies was frightening. Well chronicled are the losses of the first winter at Jamestown when 63 of 105 perished, and the first winter at Plymouth that claimed 52 of 101, while in Massachusetts scurvy took scores of "the poorer sort of people" in the months following the arrival of the Winthrop fleet. Nor was the American environment any respecter of persons: William Bradford's wife drowned within a week of the *Mayflower*'s arrival; Governor Carver of Plymouth Colony succumbed to disease during the winter of 1620/21; and less than a month after his landing in Massachusetts Bay, Governor Winthrop recorded in his journal that "my son Henry Winthrop was drowned at Salem." Before the year was out Winthrop had also recorded the deaths, probably from typhus, of Lady Arbella Johnson and her husband Isaac, of the Reverend Francis Higginson, and of Edward Rossiter, one of the colony's magistrates.[19] Almost every seventeenth-century plantation suffered comparable losses, and in many cases the high mortality rate lasted long beyond the first years. So discouraging were the hardships and so dim the prospects that some colonies witnessed periods of heavy emigration, especially Virginia, where a combination of departures and death by disease and Indian massacre left a population of only 1,275 in 1624, despite the arrival of more than four thousand people since 1618.[20] Gradually the dangers of travel and adjustment to the new environment eased as some of the hazards were prevented by improved timing of arrivals and by remedies for certain diseases. Nevertheless, throughout the seventeenth century mortality rates remained depressingly high, especially in the Chesapeake colonies.[21]

For most Europeans who survived the rigors of migration, and

[19]James Kendall Hosmer, ed., *Winthrop's Journal: "History of New England,"* *1630–1649* (2 vols., New York, 1908), I, 51–53; John Winthrop to John Winthrop, Jr., 9 Sept. 1630, in *Winthrop Papers*, II, 314.

[20]Wesley Frank Craven, *The Southern Colonies in the Seventeenth Century* (Baton Rouge, La., 1949), 138, 146–147.

[21]Recent investigations of southern demography include Lorena S. Walsh and Russell R. Menard, "Death in the Chesapeake: Two Life Tables for Men in Early Colonial Maryland," *Maryland Historical Magazine*, LXIX (1974), 211–227; and Darrett B. Rutman and Anita H. Rutman, "Of Agues and Fevers: Malaria in the Early Chesapeake," *William and Mary Quarterly*, 3d ser. XXXIII (1976), 31–60.

for those who were born and raised in America, daily life offered an abundance of hardship and toil. That most immigrants survived and many prospered may reflect the natural selectivity of the emigration experience. The first generations of British Americans were not a cross section of Europeans but rather a special breed: the hardy variety that pulled up stakes—out of hope or desperation—and risked the dangers of an ocean voyage to plant new homes in the wilderness. The qualities that Oscar Handlin found among the "uprooted" of the nineteenth century apply in large measure to the men and women of the seventeenth-century American colonies.[22] But at least one difference is central; the special challenge that the first immigrants faced was more physical than cultural. If the adjustment was not intrinsically more difficult than that of later centuries, it demanded, at any rate, a particular kind of men and women: young, adventurous, energetic, optimistic. They had to have the initiative and grit to embark on a three-thousand-mile voyage fraught with danger to reach a land where hardships might outweigh opportunities. Those very hardships, however, created an unconscious bond between the first European Americans, English and non-English alike. Seventeenth-century Americans knew intuitively that they were not quite like their cousins who stayed in Europe.

Equally unrecognized at the time but equally important in forming a basic tie among American colonists was their similarity of outlook on a number of fundamental aspects of their society. Most European Americans, for example, had brought in their cultural baggage a preference for life as they had known it in small English villages. Because there was usually a choice of precedents to follow, the patterns that emerged in America were not exact reproductions of old England: adaptation, experiment, blending, and discarding occurred in the social laboratory of the New World.[23] Still, almost everything that did emerge was fundamen-

[22]Oscar Handlin, *The Uprooted: The Epic Story of the Great Migrations that Made the American People* (Boston, 1951).

[23]Sumner Chilton Powell, *Puritan Village: The Formation of a New England Town* (Middletown, Conn., 1963); Darrett B. Rutman, *Winthrop's Boston: Portrait of a Puritan Town, 1630–1649* (Chapel Hill, 1965); John J. Waters, Jr., "Hingham, Massachusetts, 1631–1661: An East Anglian Oligarchy in the New World," *Journal of Social History*, I (1967–1968); Kenneth A. Lockridge, *A New England Town: The First Hundred Years* (New York, 1970); David Allen Grayson, "A Tale of Two Towns: Persistent English Localism in Seventeenth-Century Massachusetts," in H. C. Allen and Roger Thompson, eds., *Contrast and Connection: Bicentennial Essays*

tally English: the forms of land ownership and cultivation, the system of government and the basic format of laws and legal procedures, the choices of entertainment and leisure-time pursuits, and innumerable other aspects of colonial life. At heart this was an English land. In 1700 probably 70 percent of the European settlers in British North America were English, 20 percent Scotch, Irish, or Welsh, and the rest divided among several other nationalities.[24] While there were a few pockets of non-British settlement—Dutch in New York, Swedish in the Delaware Valley, French in Charleston, and German in Pennsylvania—they were conspicuous exceptions to the dominant pattern.

So were the substantial numbers of Africans imported into British America in the closing years of the century. By 1700 they comprised about 5 percent of the total non-Indian population and were a majority in some areas of the South. They also formed an appreciable minority in several northern cities. Meanwhile the Indians, despite rapidly dwindling numbers, still constituted a sizable portion of the total population in the territory claimed by the British government. Most of the Indians, however, were outside the areas of effective English control—in northern New York and western Carolina, for example—and thus in a sense were part of a separate and shrinking Indian America. They nonetheless exerted a profound influence on the British settlements and ultimately on the formation of British-American culture.[25]

The Indians also played a tragic role—as a formidable and persistent foe who generated a bond of shared enmity among the European settlers—in the formation of American identity. Perhaps this role was inevitable given the nature of European expan-

---

in Anglo-American History (Athens, Ohio, 1976); and T. H. Breen, "Transfer of Culture: Chance and Design in Shaping Massachusetts Bay, 1630–1660," *New England Historical and Genealogical Register*, CXXXII (1978), 3–17, are among the many recent works that give attention to the transfer of English ideas and practices.

[24] There is no accurate way to measure ethnic distribution, but as late as the federal census of 1790, approximately 80 percent of the white population was estimated to be of British stock. See *The Statistical History of the United States, from Colonial Times to the Present* (Stamford, Conn., n.d.), 756.

[25] The range and depth of Indian influence has only recently come under serious investigation. An older study is A. Irving Hallowell, "The Impact of the American Indian on American Culture," *American Anthropologist*, LIX (1957), 201–217. Some important suggestions can be found in James Axtell, "The Scholastic Philosophy of the Wilderness," *William and Mary Quarterly*, 3d ser. XXIX (1972), 335–366.

sion and European ethnocentrism. The circumstances of colonization almost assured conflict. English imperial spokesmen and virtually all European colonists assumed that Christian nations had
a right to take the heathens' land (often but not always with
compensation), to proselytize among them, and to exercise political jurisdiction over them, although where tribes were militarily
strong that jurisdiction was temporarily waived. The Indians, of
course, saw the situation much differently. Although some individuals and tribes welcomed English settlement because of immediate strategic or economic needs, most Indians resented and
eventually resisted European encroachment. It came to that in
Virginia almost from the outset, in New Netherland by 1643, and
in New England by 1675. Despite many instances of friendly relations between colonists and Indians, conflicting interests and irreconcilable attitudes caused the European population to view
the Indians with suspicion, scorn, and fear, and often to advocate
their removal or destruction. Such an attitude was not necessarily held by colonial leaders who feared Indian retaliation, and it
was often resisted by colonial clergymen who hoped for massive
conversions, but increasingly it characterized the bulk of British
America's colonists. That was especially true on the frontiers,
where irresponsible elements of both races often clashed far from
the reach of Indian or English authorities.[26]

From the earliest days of exploration and settlement, Indian
arrows and tomahawks claimed scattered victims among the
newcomers. In 1622 the massacre of more than three hundred
Virginia settlers on a single day made clear that even long-estab-
lished communities were susceptible to attack. But the lesson
bore repeating, as the Virginians themselves discovered in 1644,
the Dutch in 1641 and 1663, the Carolinians in 1671, and the New
Englanders four years later. By 1700 perhaps five thousand colonists had been slain by Indians, while vastly more of the natives
had fallen to colonial arms. And even the colonists who never
fired a musket or confronted a hostile Indian could not escape the
vicarious experience, especially after 1682 when narratives by
former captives emerged as a uniquely American literary genre.

[26]Among the rapidly growing literature on Indian-European relations in early
America, the following focus on the seventeenth century: Allen W. Trelease, *Indian
Affairs in Colonial New York: The Seventeenth Century* (Ithaca, N.Y., 1960); Alden T.
Vaughan, *New England Frontier: Puritans and Indians, 1620–1675* (Boston, 1965);
and Francis Jennings, *The Invasion of America: Indians, Colonialism, and the Cant
of Conquest* (Chapel Hill, N.C., 1975).

Stirred by stories of wilderness marches, scalpings, and torture, the colonial mind soon lumped all natives together as implacable enemies.[27]

Indians were not the British colonists' only foes. Several European powers also provided an important impetus to the creation of cultural bonds. England's seventeenth-century New World outposts may often have been unfriendly to each other, but at least they saw the need to resist encroachment by Spain, France, or the Dutch Republic. In the 1600s, there were abundant opportunities for rallying against a national foe: against the French in the 1620s, against the Dutch in the 1650s, 1660s, and 1670s, and against the French again in the 1680s and 1690s. Always there was fear of attack from the Spanish lands to the south, although not until the last quarter of the century did the English colonies show much inclination to cooperate in their own defense. While it is impossible to measure precisely the impact of international rivalry on the colonial mind, it undoubtedly helped to create a sense of British-American unity and self-consciousness. It also helped to insure a continuing dependence on the mother country, a condition that has too often caused historians to overlook the parallel trend toward intercolonial cohesion.[28]

Perhaps the best example of seventeenth-century America's fundamental unity in the face of ostensible fragmentation was in the realm of religion. British Americans could argue heatedly and interminably over the relative merits of "grace" and "works" as criteria for salvation or over the requirements for baptism, yet we can now see—as they could not then—that their entire debate took place within a remarkably solid consensus. Most early immigrants were Protestants. In 1700 probably 95 percent of the Europeans in British North America claimed affiliation with Protestant denominations; Roman Catholics numbered only a few thousand, Jews

[27]Aspects in the formation of Anglo-American hostility toward the Indians are analyzed in Richard Slotkin, *Regeneration through Violence: The Mythology of the American Frontier, 1600–1800* (Middletown, Conn., 1973); Karen Ordahl Kupperman, "English Perceptions of Treachery, 1583–1640: The Case of the American 'Savages,' " *The Historical Journal*, XX (1977); and Alden T. Vaughan, " 'Expulsion of the Salvages': English Policy and the Virginia Massacre of 1622," *William and Mary Quarterly*, 3d ser. XXXV (1978), 57–84.

[28]A comprehensive account of international conflict in early America is Douglas Edward Leach, *Arms for Empire: A Military History of the British Colonies in North America, 1607–1763* (New York, 1973).

even less. A majority of the Protestants belonged to the Church of England or its offshoots.[29] In fact, much of the century's religious conflict occurred because Englishmen on neither side of the Atlantic could agree on the exact doctrine of the church, and various sects emerged on the basis of their minute differences, in defiance of their substantial accord. For underlying these differences was a broad common heritage. Drawing largely on Lutheran or Calvinist precepts, most British Americans viewed the fundamentals of Christianity in much the same light: almost all were Trinitarians and most adhered, at least nominally, to a belief in predestination and in salvation only through the grace of God. At the same time, the Protestant majority enjoyed a binding tie in its opposition to the Church of Rome's version of Christianity.[30]

A similar bond of agreement underlay denominational differences over church polity. Prominent in the debates of seventeenth-century Anglo-Americans were organizational concepts: hierarchy, synod, presbyter, episcopacy, congregation. Yet throughout the century most Americans practiced an effectual congregationalism or something approaching it. In Anglican Virginia, local vestries selected clergymen and determined parish policy without the aid of bishops or archbishops, because the Church of England sent none to its American outposts. Likewise Roman Catholics in Maryland and elsewhere managed their ecclesiastical affairs without a resident hierarchy. Although the Dutch Reformed Church, the majority faith in much of New York and New Jersey, was theoretically under the Amsterdam Classis (it had no counterpart in America), the individual congregations were largely on their own. The Quakers, who in a sense had no formal church structure, nonetheless had silent assemblies of "Friends in the Truth." These took guidance from monthly meetings, which bore many similarities to New England congregations, and from quarterly and yearly meetings, which represented larger areas and decided major issues. And if the Quakers had no "hireling clergy," they did have religious spokesmen who increasingly served many of the ministerial

[29]In the absence of reliable statistics, estimates of religious distribution are at best educated guesses based on contemporary materials that suggest the religious composition of each colony. The best general guide to religious demography is Edwin Scott Gaustad, *Historical Atlas of Religion in America* (New York, 1962).

[30]The best modern history of American religious development is Sydney A. Ahlstrom, *A Religious History of the American People* (New Haven, 1972).

functions of more traditional churches. The Presbyterians and Congregationalists had almost identical polities: the former had separate congregations under loose supervision from representative synods; the latter had theoretically independent congregations, which in fact were scrutinized rather closely by advisory synods, clerical associations, and each other. In sum, from Massachusetts to South Carolina ecclesiastical organization among all faiths was predominantly local and quasi-democratic.

If most Anglo-Americans remained unaware of their basic similarity in theological thought and organization, they were probably also unaware that they had come from the same class of English society. Seventeenth-century Americans brought with them from Europe a deep consciousness of class distinctions, rife with implications for social and political inequality, and many settlers would have been aghast at the idea that they were essentially of the same social stratum. Yet they had to know that there were very few nobles among them, and they must also have realized how few paupers there were—a situation that would change in the next century. And although each New World colony did contain an array of class distinctions in which the gentry cherished their social superiority, the yeomen jealously guarded their independence, and the "meaner sort" paid grudging honor to their betters, in America it was difficult to keep people in their stations. Otherwise there would have been no need for such sumptuary laws as the Bay Colony passed in 1658, admonishing "men or women of mean condition [who] take upon them the garb of Gentlemen by wearing gold or silver lace, or buttons, or points at their knees, or . . . walk in great boots or scarfs."[31] Such regulations invariably failed. Because the immigrants to America boasted no prominent church officials, very few peers, and only scattered representatives of the more prosperous gentry, colonial social structure was relatively free from the massive weight of tradition, overwhelming political privilege, and vast ranges of wealth—though pockets of gross inequity had surfaced in Virginia by the third quarter of the century and elsewhere soon after. In the eighteenth century the narrowness of social and economic range would disappear almost everywhere: in the Chesapeake colonies and South Carolina where a burgeoning slave population vastly outnumbered the planter-owners, in New York where a few

---

[31]*The Colonial Laws of Massachusetts, reprinted from the Edition of 1660, with the Supplements to 1672* (Boston, 1889), 123.

landed gentry and merchants contrasted sharply with the lot of tenant farmers, and in New England where a handful of merchant families achieved handsome fortunes and social influence. But throughout the first century of colonization the narrowness of socioeconomic distinctions helped to give the American colonists a latent sense of common identity.

Paucity of class distinctions reflected not only the relatively narrow social spread among the immigrants but also the economic opportunities awaiting them. Some colonists were already aware of America's unparalleled possibilities and perhaps sensed the implications that such opportunity held for most white American males, although the full impact was probably not evident until the following century, when Franklin and Crèvecoeur elevated upward mobility into an American creed. Most seventeenth-century colonists saw only that in their own immediate locality there existed a world of economic choice not known in the mother country. Men grew rich who had before been only comfortable, and poor men often became landowners. These people also acquired many of the prerogatives that accompanied property ownership, such as the right to vote and to hold office. The exercise of political privileges, in turn, often helped to lower class barriers.

Economic opportunity was available not only to Europeans who arrived as free men, but to some extent also to the tens of thousands who arrived as indentured servants. Their service rarely lasted longer than four or five years; thereafter the more fortunate males eventually became landowners, while the rest of the men and most unmarried women probably acquired jobs at wages considerably higher than they could have commanded in Europe. This is not to deny frequent instances of hard usage and occasional cases of dire poverty. Nor is it to overlook the growing number of black and Indian slaves who shared none of the economic benefits. British America was by definition a land of opportunity for Europeans and of exploitation for all others.[32] In

---

[32]The opportunities and the plight of white bound labor in early America must be gleaned from a long list of older and more recent works. Among the most important are Richard B. Morris, *Government and Labor in Early America* (New York, 1946); Abbot E. Smith, *Colonists in Bondage: White Servitude and Convict Labor in America, 1607–1776* (Chapel Hill, N.C., 1947); and Russell R. Menard, "From Servant to Freeholder: Status Mobility and Property Accumulation in Seventeenth-Century Maryland," *William and Mary Quarterly*, 3d ser. XXX (1973), 37–64. The interconnections between exploitation and opportunity in the oldest mainland colony is the principal theme of Morgan, *American Slavery—American Freedom*.

fact, a fundamental assumption that stimulated a sense of being American among transplanted Europeans was that Africans and Indians were outsiders—non-Americans—by whom British America defined its racial and cultural perimeters.[33]

At the same time, the early colonists were gradually beginning to lose their own national identities. In America the English immigrants became exposed to the non-English elements that entered British America in growing numbers in the last quarter of the century—willingly (in most cases) from various European nations and unwillingly (in all cases) from various African states. This ethnic blending resulted in a slow dilution of cultural Englishness and the gradual emergence of an eclectic Americanism. That trend was not universal throughout the colonies nor did it occur without a counter trend in some areas toward heightened Anglicization, but what Crèvecoeur later saw as "this new man, the American" had begun to take shape by the end of the seventeenth century.[34]

Coeval with a lessening of British America's ethnic homogeneity were conflicts of interest between some of the colonists and the imperial government that in the long run made many of them less grateful to the mother country. Ostensibly every seventeenth-century Englishman who moved to America retained his attachment to king and country. And no doubt the majority continued to do so. Yet quite obviously most of the Englishmen who migrated to the New World were unhappy with conditions at home, which in turn predisposed them to favor colonial over imperial interests. The contest over the Massachusetts charter and later over the Andros regime, the squabbles over the tobacco tax in Virginia, and the series of Acts of Trade and Navigation that were enacted in the second half of the seventeenth century are cases in point. None of these episodes tore the imperial fabric. To many colonists they were simply family quarrels, and most colonists

[33]The standard work on Anglo-American attitudes toward blacks is Winthrop D. Jordan, *White over Black: American Attitudes toward the Negro, 1585–1812* (Chapel Hill, N.C., 1968). An indication of how thoroughly blacks and Indians were segregated from British-American society, even in the north, can be seen in Boston's early eighteenth-century legislation for the regulation of blacks, Indians, and mulattoes, in *A Report of the Record Commissioners of Boston, Containing the Boston Records from 1700 to 1728* (Boston, 1883), 173–177.

[34]J. Hector St. John de Crèvecoeur, *Letters from an American Farmer* (New York, 1957), 35–64.

perhaps gave them no thought at all. But each episode revealed to
a growing number of Americans that the home government was a
rival as well as a friend and protecting power. Except for the few
who held positions within the imperial bureaucracy, the colonists
were increasingly ready to question the wisdom and righteousness of the imperial administration. The widespread resistance to
the Dominion of New England and the vigorous support in Maryland, New York, and New England of the Glorious Revolution
reflect the political awareness of colonial America. It also prefigured an American stance that would eventually prove inimical
to a trans-Atlantic empire.

III

Out of the similarity of experiences, outlooks, and aspirations of
the first European Americans came a culture that had enough
internal homogeneity to overcome concomitant tendencies
toward separation into unconnected national or denominational
entities. This development of a sense of American community
became stronger as internal migration and the increase in non-
English arrivals broke down old patterns of isolation and aided in
the diffusion of a common culture, a culture at once distinctively
American and increasingly intercolonial.

In large part the integration of British America stemmed from
a new attitude toward religious exclusiveness and its corollary,
religious intolerance. During the second half of the seventeenth
century, there grew rapidly in England, and somewhat less rapidly in America, the belief that the only solution to the constant
mayhem of religious controversy was a form of toleration that
allowed dissenters from the majority faith to practice their beliefs
openly, provided they did not try to undermine the state. One by
one the colonies relaxed their legal and social strictures against .
the immigration of dissenters, while some colonies, most notably
South Carolina and Pennsylvania, actively recruited newcomers
whose religion did not coincide with the majority's. Thus there
slowly emerged a new kind of religious pluralism in which groups
of differing faiths were separated not by colonial boundaries but
by town or neighborhood lines, or by no geopolitical lines at all.
By the end of the seventeenth century, the denominational maps
of Pennsylvania, New York, and Maryland resembled patchwork

quilts, and no colony was without sizable minority enclaves. Despite pockets of bitter religious and ethnic prejudice, the rigid exclusiveness of the early decades had been shattered.

The most remarkable change in religious demography took place in New England. Under the quasi-liberal policies of Charles II and James II, and the more truly liberal by-products of the Glorious Revolution, the Puritan colonists could no longer oust with impunity those who agitated for Baptist procedures or Anglican worship. Continuing pressure from non-Puritans in England and New England brought almost complete disintegration of the Massachusetts Bible Commonwealth during the last quarter of the seventeenth century. By 1680 the Baptists were numerous enough to have their own church buildings, and Governor Andros insisted on Anglican services in South Meetinghouse from 1685 until King's Chapel opened in 1688. By early in the next century Boston also had houses of worship for Quakers, Presbyterians, and French Calvinists.[35]

The breakdown of religious exclusiveness also had important political implications. In Massachusetts non–church members had been allowed local political privileges in 1649; in 1664 they became eligible for the colony-wide franchise as well, largely because of pressure from the mother country. Under the new charter of 1691 all religious restrictions were prohibited. Elsewhere religious limitations on political participation diminished in practice if not in law, although the trend was not without exceptions. In Maryland, for example, Roman Catholics actually lost ground: early in the eighteenth century Maryland's legislature and proprietor, now an Anglican, disenfranchised Catholics on the assumption that "if Papists should continue to be allowed their vote . . . it would tend to the discouragement and disturbance of his Lordships Protestant government."[36]

In other respects the empire had also grown more cohesive during the seventeenth century. The first step had come as early as 1624 with the revocation of the Virginia charter, but the trend

[35]Dates of church buildings are given on the map of Boston by John Bonner in 1722 and subsequent revisions. The 1722 map is reprinted in Walter Muir Whithill, *Boston, A Topographical History* (Cambridge, 1959), 23. Although there were no Roman Catholic churches before the nineteenth century, some practicing Catholics may have lived there as early as 1687. See *Report of a French Protestant Refugee* (Brooklyn, 1868), 30.

[36]*Abridgment and Collection of the Acts of the Assembly of the Province of Maryland* (Philadelphia, 1759), 197.

is more clearly reflected in the progressive decline of powers granted in proprietary charters. The Calverts in 1632 received almost limitless authority over Maryland; less was allowed to the New Jersey and Carolina groups in the 1660s and 1670s. By William Penn's day the proprietorship was curbed by restrictions that made clear that Crown and Parliament considered Pennsylvania a British dependency, open to all loyal subjects and an integral part of the imperial scheme. In 1692 the Crown suspended Penn's jurisdiction over the colony; when he regained it in 1694 he had still less autonomy than before. And two years later Parliament tightened its system of trade and navigation acts and authorized the creation of vice-admiralty courts in America. Although the great consolidation experiment of the Dominion of New England had failed and a similar plan to fuse the southern colonies into a single jurisdiction never materialized, by the end of the century it was apparent that the purpose and character of colonization had changed. The apartness enjoyed for varying periods by the early colonies was no longer possible, regardless of the intent of colonial leaders. It was in large measure England, rather than America, that curtailed exclusiveness and inaugurated a trend toward colonial intercourse that would one day become a stepping stone to nationhood.

IV

As the century of colonization gave way to the century of revolution, it was still too early to speak of American nationalism, too early to call the American a "new man." It was not too soon, however, to see a new culture slowly emerging in the British mainland colonies, a culture at once pervasively English in character and yet not wholly English, at once overwhelmingly European in population and yet not exclusively so. By the end of the seventeenth century the predominant culture of colonial America, despite significant local and regional variations, had a solid core of shared characteristics—in language, literature, law, theology, political ideas and institutions, and economic opportunity, to name but a few. The next century would intensify some of those characteristics, especially the ascendancy of English ways, the increase in religious pluralism, the acceleration of ethnic heterogeneity, and, most tragically, the growing polarity in wealth and status between a small colonial elite and a large slave caste. The eighteenth century would also make contributions of its own to American unity and identity: the Enlightenment with its profound influence on political and intellectual life, the international wars with their exacerbation of Anglo-American tensions, the Great Awakening with its powerful but ambiguous impact on secular and religious thought, and the rise of provincial cities as foci for commerce and communication and of colonial colleges as centers for American learning and cultural exchange.

But the seventeenth century had laid the essential groundwork. By its end the bulk of European Americans could identify with each other on the basis of common attitudes rooted in the similarity of their backgrounds and experiences. The several colonies differed sharply on a number of matters of great importance to them, but what we can see now better than they could then is that their differences were, from the start, more of form than of substance and that as the eighteenth century approached, the grounds for their differences gradually diminished. By 1700 a consensus of sorts had been reached on most matters that had separated the colonies throughout the previous century—a consensus that proved a necessary precursor to revolutionary America.

THE RITUALIZATION OF THE AMERICAN REVOLUTION

Robert Middlekauff / UNIVERSITY OF CALIFORNIA, BERKELEY

Shortly after the United States Senate convened for the first time in April 1789, it engaged in one of those farces that have enlivened its proceedings ever since. The Senate held in its hands the inaugural address of the President, and it believed that it had to reply. Framing the response proved less troublesome than sending it with proper address to the President. What was he to be called anyway? Vice-President Adams, presiding energetically over the Senate, plumped for "His Highness the President of the United States and Protector of their Liberties." Over in the House of Representatives, James Madison averted his gaze from this pseudomonarchism and quietly addressed the House reply "to George Washington, President of the United States." The Senate eventually agreed that republican simplicity was the only appropriate guide and adopted the practice of the House, but not until it had listened to the Vice-President's pleas for giving the President high-sounding titles and not until it had coaxed the House into sending representatives to a conference committee, which thrashed about and decided nothing. The only title that emerged from this episode was tagged to John Adams, thereafter celebrated as His Rotundity.[1]

[1] For a good, brief account of this affair see Irving Brant, *James Madison: Father of the Constitution, 1787–1800* (Indianapolis and New York, 1950), pp. 255–57.

John Adams appears ridiculous in this episode: his insensitivity to the American revulsion against anything smacking of monarchy was monumental. But in his concern for form, his feeling that even a simple republic required conventions and symbols, he was sound. Americans had felt this need for a very long time, and acutely, ever since they began resisting Parliamentary attempts to tax them in 1764.

Almost all people have experienced at various times the need to express their values and intentions in some sort of forms—especially in symbol and ritual. The need seems to be an essential part of human nature, related to aesthetic and even religious concerns. Ritual and symbol permit expression of the highest values, and they satisfy impulses for order in relationships among human beings and their ideals.

The formalism of social movements may have several uses, of course. In primitive social movements—that is, in premodern and preindustrial movements—form assumes a far more important role than content, at least in providing the essential unity holding participants together. The failure of a medieval king to be crowned and anointed with the correct ritual might have seriously compromised his claims to the allegiance of his subjects. Today in many religious groups baptism, marriage, or any other sacramental observance that is not celebrated according to prescribed form lacks authority. Baptism is of course an initiatory rite in many Christian groups—by it people are admitted to the church or, as one group of Congregationalists used to insist, by it their memberships were confirmed. Besides bringing people together, a joint act of worship or any ritualistic act performed in a group may impart a sense of community, a kind of emotion common to the group, and may discipline it and give it a sense of purpose. Symbols may contribute similar kinds of emotion, summing up in themselves the leading desires and impulses of a group. For more than a century in the American colonies, the church building, from the New England meeting house to southern Gothic churches, must have performed this function, evoking the most important values and aspirations of its members.[2]

Apart from religion, colonial life was not especially rich in symbol and ritual. Politics began in factions and remained factional until the Revolution was well advanced. If they opposed

[2]The paragraph owes much to E. J. Hobsbawn, *Primitive Rebels* (New York, 1963), pp. 150–74.

the representatives of the Crown, colonial factions had to tread a narrow line between legitimacy and disloyalty, a situation that discouraged the invention of formalistic observance. Membership in the empire supplied all the forms British subjects could ask for anyway—a king still carrying a faint whiff of divine origin, a structure of administrative officials all conscious of their place in the apparatus of empire, and the conventions regulating the relationship of Crown and commons. If the factions organized themselves along other lines, as in Rhode Island, where Wards opposed Hopkinses and where force, knavery, and nastiness probably repelled any attempts at ritualization, the transitory character of the groups never permitted symbolic forms to develop.[3]

Where organization intruded into other areas of colonial affairs, ritualization of function appeared only casually. Merchants joined one another in colonial cities but interest overruled everything else; guild and artisan organizations developed late in the colonial period and assumed a few of the forms marking comparable nineteenth-century organizations. The absence of guilds seems startling; as pale as they are, modern unions in the United States have succeeded in perpetuating a more colorful ritualistic life. The difference in style lies partly in the difference in class. Eighteenth-century artisans in cities were usually aspiring merchants and often engaged in mercantile activity. Though this activity was usually only a sideline that contributed to their main efforts, it blurred their economic interests, and they experienced difficulty in locating themselves socially. Their lack of a clear sense of identity inhibited the ritualistic expression so characteristic of guilds in the next century, which usually were composed of members beset with no such doubts.[4]

Not even the violence that filled colonial life supplied much ritual. There were rebellions before the Revolution in all the colonies, but none aimed at independence or at separation from Britain, and none lasted long enough to develop its own forms. Rather, almost all clung to the fiction that they represented legitimacy and its forms. Rebels uniformly professed loyalty to

[3]For the Ward-Hopkins contest, see David S. Lovejoy, *Rhode Island Politics and the American Revolution, 1760–1776* (Providence, R.I., 1958); and Mack Thompson, "The Ward-Hopkins Controversy and the American Revolution in Rhode Island: An Interpretation," *William and Mary Quarterly*, 3d Ser., 16 (1959), 363–75.

[4]For information about artisans see Carl Bridenbaugh, *The Colonial Craftsman* (New York, 1950) and *Cities in Revolt: Urban Life in America, 1743–1776* (New York, 1955).

Britain—and believed it. A profession of loyalty imposed the use of a ritual already long established, as in Nathaniel Bacon's "Manifesto," which proclaimed that the Rebellion of 1676 in Virginia aimed "at his Majesties Honour and the Publick good."[5]

I

Of all the crude social movements in the colonies preceding the Revolution, only the revivals—and in particular the Great Awakening—created their own ritualism. Revivals of religion depend upon meetings, and even the simplest of these meetings usually offered a ritualized performance, which created relationships between revivalist and listeners, among the participants themselves, and, it is hoped, between the initiates and some higher being. The first such gatherings began in New England as a communal exercise in renewing the church covenant. After a brief sermon by the minister explaining what was required of the church, the members were asked to rise silently as a token of their devotion. This simple ceremony held possibilities for extension that did not escape the ministers, who soon enlisted first the congregations and then nonmembers as participants; sermons grew more hortatory and the purpose of the ritual assumed larger proportions. By the time of the explosions of the 1740s, a highly structured ritual had developed, the climax of which saw the mass undergo conversion, an initiation that sealed them to God and to one another. The progress of awakening enthusiasm from community to community also followed a ritualistic path, with a minister making his way from one community to the next, holding meetings, confronting the Devil and his agents, and bringing the populace to the faith.

The revolutionary movement that began in the 1760s and that carried through to independence displayed many of the characteristics of a revival. It was larger and more complex, of course, and it was defined primarily by its substantive issues. (The revolutionary movement was value-oriented, to use the jargon of sociologists, in a way the Great Awakening was not.) Before 1776 the movement gained its cohesion at the top, in particular from groups that took a name rich with symbolic meaning, the Sons of Liberty. The Sons had a variety of tactical objectives throughout this period: at times

[5]Robert Middlekauff, ed., *Bacon's Rebellion* (Chicago, 1964), p. 20.

they simply wished to force the resignation of crown officials—the Stamp Distributors in 1765, for example. As they grew in sophistication, they managed boycotts and joined merchants and artisan groups in enforcing nonimportation agreements. They also collected arms, drilled their followers in military tactics, and prepared for war. All these activities contributed to resistance against parliamentary measures of imperial reform and to the development of a revolutionary tradition.[6]

The Sons chose to develop resistance and to create a revolutionary tradition in still other ways, most importantly by ritualizing the movement against Britain and giving it symbolic expression. Here their activities approached in technique those of the revivalists. Like the revivalists, the Sons of Liberty depended upon the public meeting. Although these meetings occurred in various places, the favorite spot up and down the Eastern Seaboard came to be the vicinity of a "liberty tree" or, in many cases, a "liberty pole." The first liberty tree seems to have been a stately elm near the Boston Common, designated the representative of liberty on August 14, 1765. The occasion was an attempt to bring Andrew Oliver to resign his Stamp Distributorship. Oliver gave up his office, and the tree gained the fame that was to make it an emblem of liberty—and the model for dozens of others in all the colonies.[7]

There is no need to pause too long over the meaning of the liberty trees or the liberty poles as symbols. By themselves they symbolized freedom and evoked the strong emotions of resistance to attempts to subvert freedom. The historical origin of the poles doubtless was the maypole of English country life (perhaps the first to appear in America was at Merrymount in Plymouth Colony). The maypole had served originally as the emblem of the lower classes' disaffection from their social betters, and it soon took on the obvious sexual connotations seen in it by a later age, which has gone to the school of Freud. (The sexual significance of the liberty tree was suggested long before Freud, of course; Joel Barlow in the eighteenth century traced the liberty tree to phallic symbols common to ancient mythologies.) As a symbol the liberty tree expressed a subtle meaning dependent upon the context in

[6]For the Sons of Liberty and their activities, see Edmund S. and Helen M. Morgan, *The Stamp Act Crisis: Prologue To Revolution* (Chapel Hill, N.C., 1953).

[7]Arthur M. Schlesinger, "Liberty Tree: A Genealogy," *New England Quarterly*, 25 (1952), 435–58.

which it was used. In part what was attached to it was even more important for meanings, one suspects, than the Americans were aware of. The Liberty Tree in Boston, for example, was usually adorned with effigies of the Devil and his local representatives, the assorted officials of the Crown.[8] The confrontation intended may have been good against evil, the tree of course in this case representing the forces of good. At the grand celebration of the repeal of the Stamp Act in the spring of 1766, the symbolism was even more explicit. A large obelisk of oiled paper was to decorate the tree (it burned up before it could be placed). It was to be illuminated by several hundred lamps, and on its side were pictures of the tree, with an angel hovering over it, and an eagle in the branches.[9]

Any Protestant would have recognized the meaning of this tableau: the struggle between imperial and colonial powers was the age-old conflict of the forces of dark and light. Good was arrayed against evil in the American resistance to illegal taxation. The theme was honestly felt in a culture that still retained its Protestant cast and that instinctively thought of politics, like everything else, in moral terms. Something of the same meaning surely was implicit in the series of ceremonial burials of liberty poles that occurred in the 1760s and the 1770s. The religious significance of this ceremony is plain; the ritualized manner of the performance, with truth, liberty, and evil taking allegorical forms, could not escape anyone.

Numerology was employed in much the same way, for example in the episode of the Massachusetts circular letter. Sent by the Massachusetts Assembly in 1768, the circular letter called the attention of the other colonial assemblies to the Townshend Acts. Its phrasing and tone were moderate, but the Grafton ministry thought it seditious and saw in it an opportunity to smash the colonial opposition. The ministry ordered the Massachusetts Assembly to rescind the letter and the Governor to dissolve the body if it refused. The members refused, of course. The vote was ninety-two to seventeen, and the Sons of Liberty under Sam Adams's tutelage began to celebrate the glorious ninety-two and to execrate the cowardly seventeen. At this time John Wilkes in England was trying to stay in the House of Commons; his slogan was "45," the number of the issue of his newspaper that the

[8]*Ibid.*, passim; Esther Forbes, *Paul Revere and the World He Lived In* (Cambridge, Mass.), pp. 101–2.

[9]Forbes, *Revere*, pp. 115–17.

English government had suppressed. The Sons of Liberty in Boston sent him two turtles, one weighing forty-five pounds, the other forty-seven pounds, for a total of ninety-two pounds—the number synonymous with patriotism in Massachusetts. The number ninety-two was celebrated in other ways, too: Paul Revere fashioned a silver punch bowl, dedicated to the "Immortal 92" and engraved with slogans and symbols, among them "Wilkes & Liberty" and "No. 45." Here the technique—which may seem strained today—may have derived from the Protestant fascination with eschatological numerology, which sometimes expressed the opposition of good and evil in numbers.[10]

Even the simple act of wearing homespun as a part of the boycott of British goods, which seems devoid of any motive except economic coercion, was freighted with Protestant concern. The use of homespun was one part of the general repudiation of English corruption, and the resolve to wear it was testimony in favor of purity in thought and action. The Association, the large-scale boycott and nonimportation agreement adopted by the First Continental Congress in 1774, pledged Americans to a wholesale reform: "we will, in our several stations encourage frugality, economy, and industry, and promote agriculture, arts and the manufactures of this country, especially that of wool; and will discountenance and discourage every species of extravagance and dissipation, especially of horse-racing, and all kinds of gaming, cockfighting, exhibitions of shews, plays, and other expensive diversions and entertainments."[11] In this context homespun became emblematic of Protestant values.

[10]See Arthur M. Schlesinger, *Prelude to Independence: The Newspaper War on Britain 1764–1776* (New York, 1958), pp. 36–37, and the newspapers cited there. The Sons of Liberty in Petersham trimmed the town's Liberty Tree so that ninety-two branches remained. In South Carolina, the number twenty-six was celebrated because twenty-six members of the Assembly defied the Governor and passed resolves supporting the circular letter. For an example of Protestant numerology, see Elisha Rich, *The Number of the Beast Found Out by Spiritual Arithmetic* (Chelmsford, Mass., 1775). Rich says of the Antichrist: "Observe, that although it [Antichrist] numbers so many: yet the number seven, or sevens is never once brought into the reckoning, but it lacks one of that number by which GOD would have the true CHURCH distinguished from the false. For the BEAST comes to six hundred and sixty six, but not seven or sevens, and so the Beast lacks one in each number" (p. 23).

[11]Samuel E. Morison, *Sources and Documents Illustrating the American Revolutions, 1764–1788* (2nd ed. Oxford, Eng., 1953), p. 124. Edmund S. Morgan, "The Puritan Ethic and the American Revolution," *William and Mary Quarterly*, 3d Ser., 24 (1967), 3–43, provides an excellent discussion of the relationship between Protestant values and the revolutionary movement.

The Congress also called upon Americans to repent and reform before invoking divine aid against the British government. It suggested that Parliament's oppression was punishment for the Americans' sins and could be lifted only by an act of national self-purification. This theme was also featured in countless sermons of the 1760s and 1770s. Such preaching employed a device much older than the colonies; used in the revolutionary situation, it explained current griefs and offered a way out of them.[12] In a peculiar way this sort of ritualization, playing on old, conventional themes in a familiar tone, probably offered some reassurance. The problems, it implied, only seemed new—in reality they were the old ones of good against evil; their form was new but the old remedies were sure. All in all, this was a masterful, if instinctive, formulation of revolutionary affairs.

If the revivalistic impulse contributed so much to the revolutionary movement and if Protestant values inescapably found expression there, so also did Protestant expectations about the future of America. Although the American sense of order curbed "enthusiasm," there were unspoken millennial hints in American revolutionary thinking. Any revolution rests on the assumption that things can be made better—this one seemed to Americans to forecast the New Jerusalem, the new heavens and the new earth of the thousand years. Despite their concern for property and taxes, the Americans were not what their fathers called "carnal chiliasts," seekers only of earthly abundance. Their utopianism was in some measure a response to the evils they perceived in English life, bribery in politics, decadence in manners, and infidelity in religion, and hence they were committed to a general reformation of morals and institutions.

Politics, more than anything else, demanded reform, which began with the resistance to Parliamentary measures and royal officials in the 1760s. Americans hesitated for years to attack the monarchy openly, but that reluctance vanished early in 1776 with Thomas Paine's *Common Sense*. With his delicate ability to read public sentiment, Paine sensed that the monarchy was a kind of image, or idol, for Americans, and his role was that of the iconoclast. He played the part with great skill, treating the monarchy as a remnant of heathenish and Jewish superstition, which had

---

[12]Perry Miller, "From the Covenant to the Revival," in *Religion in American Life: American Religion,* James Ward Smith and A. Leland Jamison, eds. (4 vols., Princeton, N.J., 1961), I, 326–34.

been transformed into modern despotism. His conclusion must have seemed obvious in this context: monarchy was the enemy of freedom in religion as well as in politics, "for monarchy in every instance is the Popery of government."[13]

The revolutionaries' concern for reform had yet another source: evangelical Protestantism, which had been preoccupied with social reformation as a fulfillment of history—thus the calls for Americans to attain a purified society, with simple and sinless institutions. In this millennial state, bliss would be enjoyed as long as purity and simplicity lasted. Even the "life, liberty, and pursuit of happiness" of the Declaration of Independence gained resonance in this context of millennial expectation.

During the period before independence, millennialism proved to have great allegorical utility, which could be elaborated and extended as the conflict with the English government developed. At the beginning of the revolutionary movement the Americans applied the symbols of millennialism to specific men and measures. By the end in 1776, when American purposes had expanded from resistance to independence, they gave these millennial symbols broader, even typological meanings. Such development can be seen by comparing sermons preached in 1766 with those of 1776. For example, on February 14, 1766, a sermon was preached around the Liberty Tree in Boston in which the doctrine was inspired by the thirteenth chapter of Revelation, "where the wolves of our day are so plainly pointed out."[14] This chapter describes two terrible beasts: the first, with seven heads and ten horns, the preacher asserted "sets before our eyes the wicked Earl of Bute." The seven heads represented the offices he held; the crowns on them indicated that he was royally appointed; the horns he soon fixed on the heads of "honester men." This beast continued in power for forty-two months, and by the calculation of the minister preaching this sermon, so did Bute. The second beast had two horns, like a lamb, and spoke like a dragon; this

[13]Thomas Paine, *Common Sense and the Crisis* (Garden City, N.Y., 1965), p. 22. Americans in New York City carried out another kind of iconoclasm when they pulled down an equestrain statue of George III in Bowling Green in 1776. Had there been more such statues, there surely would have been more such iconoclasm. For similar episodes in the French Revolution, see the account by Stanley J. Idzerda, "Iconoclasm During the French Revolution," *American Historical Review*, 60 (Oct., 1954), 13–26.

[14]*A Discourse, Addressed To The Sons of Liberty, At A Solemn Assembly, Near Liberty-Tree in Boston, February 14, 1766* (Providence, R.I., 1766), p. 3.

monster was George Grenville, whose mark was the Stamp Act. Thus the crisis of the Stamp Act was treated as an old prophetic scheme: the beast, or the Antichrist, and its creation, the Stamp Act, opposed Christ and his own, the Americans in the wilderness. This design appeared clear to all a month before the Stamp Act was repealed. The end of the prophecy could not be doubted; just as the beast was slain so also would the Stamp Act be killed.[15]

How this symbolic representation could be extended to give larger meaning may be seen in a sermon preached in New York almost exactly ten years later in January 1776. By now the American struggle with Britain was completely absorbed into Biblical prophecy. The sermon pictured the church in the American wilderness and emphasized God's commitment to America, where the church and Christian liberty would survive. It was an optimistic statement identifying the American cause with "the Protestant cause in general." The "American quarter of the globe," it announced, is reserved by Providence for the church, free of tyranny and free to enjoy "right of rule and government, so as not to be controll'd and oppressed by the tyrannical powers . . . represented by the Great Red Dragon." The war of Britain upon America was described as a war on God, and God's support of America was not doubted: "we have incontestible evidence, that God Almighty, with all the powers of heaven, are on our side. Great numbers of Angels no doubt, are encamped round our coast, for our defense and protection. Michael stands ready, with all the artillery of heaven, to encounter the dragon, and vanquish this black host." As in 1766, victory awaited the powers of good, that is, the good in the New World where liberty "has been planted. . . . These commotions and convulsions in the British empire, may be leading to the fulfillment of such prophecies as relate to his [the Devil's] downfall and overthrow, and to the future glory and prosperity of Christ's church."[16] In this formulation the purpose of the American struggle had been broadened so as to coincide, in defense of Christian liberty, with the final epic conflict with sin.

This exalted expression of the meaning of the war with Britain spoke to the deepest impulses in Americans. It defined liberty and union in Christian terms; it reconciled the defense of property

[15]The quotations are from the *Discourse*, pp. 4–5.

[16]Samuel Sherwood, *The Church's Flight Into The Wilderness: An Address on the Times Containing Some Very Interesting and Important Observations on Scripture Prophecies* (New York, 1776). The quotations are from pp. 18, 24, 46, 49.

with the defense of good (they were inseparable, it suggested). It posed the struggle in the terms most congenial to Americans—in moral terms, with America serving as the instrument of Providence. In the next eight bloody years, it invested sacrifice with Christian meaning and thereby released those energies of Americans that would sustain them to the end of the war.

II

Independence did not bring Americans to a repudiation of these old Protestant values, but it did begin a fresh tendency toward a secular culture. Historians of religion in America have taught us that secularization in America began in the seventeenth century, perhaps almost simultaneously with its founding. Secularization, they maintain, expressed itself institutionally: in a church organization that saw the laity progressively assume authority in discipline, management of church affairs, and even the definition of doctrine; and in the altering of church-state relationships in favor of the voluntary principle. Secularization also expressed itself in values: in the decline of traditional piety or its conversion into ethical and humanitarian impulses; and in the indifference that found people taking their definitions of life's purposes and concerns from authorities other than religion—reason and science, business and politics.

The Revolution contributed to this process by redirecting American energies and by wrenching American thought and feeling into some new forms. The ritualization of the Revolution helped to create, but more importantly to express, new values whose sources lay, to a large extent, outside the forms themselves.

With independence, the Revolution itself became a symbol, evocative of a complex tradition of liberty and sacrifice. Perhaps in the incantations to American sacrifices during the war lies the strongest link to the Protestant past with its emphasis on sin and affliction. As a symbol, the Revolution was celebrated through other symbols and an intricate ritualization drawing on the familiar devices of meetings, holidays (the Fourth of July was preeminent), medals, paintings, statues, and hero worship. A part of this process was plainly deliberate and self-conscious. Thus in ordering medals struck in France, Congress declared their purposes to be "grateful to the illustrious personages for whom they are designed, worthy the dignity of the sovereign power by whom they are presented, and calculated to perpetuate the remembrance of those great events which they are intended to consecrate to immortality. "[17] During the Confederation period fifteen medals were authorized by Congress commemorating such events as the evacuation of Boston by the British; the surrender of Burgoyne at Saratoga; the engagements at Stony Point, Cowpens, and Eutaw Springs; the capture of Major André; and the victory of the *Bonhomme Richard* over the *Serapis*.

Although medals and meetings espoused a simple patriotism calculated to strengthen national feeling, they also presented the Revolution as an event having transcendent meaning. No doubt the connection between this conception of the Revolution and the remnants of the eschatological vision lie here. The connection may be seen in a proclamation of 1776 commemorating the Battle of Lexington, which stated, "From this day will be dated the liberty of the world." In the same year a Massachusetts minister compared the robust liberty in revolutionary America to that in other benighted parts of the world where it was "gasping for life." America's Revolution was described in 1780 as being in the service of such less happy areas: "Our contest is not merely for our own families, friends, and posterity, but for the rights of humanity, for the civil and religious privileges of mankind." And David Ramsey, the historian of the Revolution, who watched its course, agreed with foreign opinion that the Revolution marked a new age in history.[18]

The Revolution as a symbol of promise and prophecy pervaded every attempt of the revolutionary generation to understand what they had done. This tendency is especially apparent in the symbolic meanings attached to the Union. Although after 1776 the Union remained "elusive in its form and function," it commanded emotional and intellectual attachment as the means for the American experiment.[19] There was resistance to this concept, of course, and opposition to what it meant when it was translated into power relationships in government. Those who

[17]Julian Boyd ed., *The Papers of Thomas Jefferson* (17 vols. to date, Princeton, N.J., 1950–), XVI, 53.

[18]The quotations and the citation from Ramsey are from Wesley Frank Craven, *The Legend of the Founding Fathers* (New York, 1956), pp. 59–60.

[19]Paul C. Nagel, *One Nation Indivisible: The Union in American Thought, 1776–1861* (New York, 1961), p. 15.

persisted in seeing the Union as America's hope wished to strengthen it, and those who valued the states or other local authority opposed attempts to add to its power. Advocates of state sovereignty proved as fully aware of the connections of form and function as any devotee of the Union. In 1783 the freeholders of Fairfax County, Virginia, expressed their fears about the encroaching Union thus: "We like not the language of the late address from Congress to the different States [urging that Congress be given powers to tax].... The very style is alarming.... Forms generally imply substance."[20] This last point—"Forms generally imply substance"—probably put the matter too strongly for the exponents of the Union. Their conception, the prevailing one, was of the Union as a means by which revolutionary ends might be achieved, not as an end in itself. In the most frequently used language, the Union was the "foundation," the "tie," the "bounds," the "remedy" for political diseases—it was not an end, nor an absolute. As a means, the Union would ensure happiness and peace. It would, in Hamilton's phrase, serve as a barrier to faction and insurrection; Madison in the Tenth Federalist conceived of it as an agency by which the worst effects of political faction might be controlled. Useful in domestic politics, it would serve American interests abroad by focusing power, which had been tending to fragment among the new states, against European enemies.[21]

For some Americans the Union evoked the Revolution's dedication to the principle of democratic consent as the basis of government. After all, the early resistance to Britain rested on the right of people to be taxed only by political bodies in which their representatives sat, and the Constitution, in the procedure by which it was drafted and ratified and in its substantive commitment to popular interest and the general welfare, institutionalized a broad-based government. Other Americans resisted these propositions and urged that the states alone could be relied upon both for the protection of rights and as the mechanisms through which popular consent should be registered. But in either case the culture was explicitly pledged to a political process that took its power and its limits from the people.

[20]Quoted in Alpheus Thomas Mason, *The States Rights Debate* (Englewood Cliffs, N.J., 1964), p. 22.

[21]For language describing the Union I have relied on *The Federalist;* see in particular essays 2–10, 39, 84.

Form did not control substance in 1789 when the new government commenced its operations and would not begin to until the great romantic outpouring of the nineteenth century, when a secular cult would grow up around the Union. In the eighteenth century, as a symbol, the Union was unavailable to those who would have made it the basis for a secular ideology because it was still imprecise in meaning. Yet even though it was an inexact symbol, and seemingly invited only experimentalism, the Union contributed to secularization, as indeed it expressed it. For its very character as a means opened the way to new centers of thought and purpose. It permitted, for example, the development of a national politics. In time such new purposes would find ritualized expression.

Yet a Protestant culture survived the Revolution intact, committed to traditional purposes and means but also subtly liberated from them and prepared for further revolutionary change. With disestablishment accomplished in several colonies and threatened in all, the church as an institution seemed less self-contained and more dependent upon popular desires in order to perpetuate itself. By itself, this new condition of financial precariousness did not impose a greater sensitivity to secular purposes. But considered with the strengthened authority of laymen and the increased authority of the national state, disestablishment inevitably resulted in renewed secularization. Revivals would break out again at the end of the century, but despite their familiar incantations to original sin and human depravity, Protestantism would have to accommodate itself increasingly to nonreligious values.

The proclivity to see things in moral terms persisted; it is one of the enduring American characteristics. Many of the old symbols survived, too, with undiminished evocative capacity, though they were susceptible to fresh interpretations. The liberty tree, for example, took on meanings defined more by politics than by morals. The problems of the society offered further promise of secularization—especially the need to ease sectional tensions. And the questions surrounding the national government's role in economic life, which would receive a neomercantilist resolution under Hamilton's careful tutelage, carried the state far away from any religious issues.

The ritualization of the Revolution in the eighteenth century remained faithful then to revolutionary values, clarifying and expressing them. Revolutionary experience itself was so evocative of the colonial past, and still so promising of the future, that in some measure it acted to check for a time the extravagant ritualization of the intense sense of American destiny and the absolutist conceptions of America that would appear in the nineteenth century. Yet by the end of the Revolution, ritualistic and symbolic expression had taken on an ambiguous character, still indebted to the past, but holding promise of development.

JACKSONIAN DEMOCRATIC THOUGHT: "A NATURAL CHARTER OF PRIVILEGE"

John William Ward / AMHERST COLLEGE

When, in 1834, George Bancroft remarked on the need for a book that described the nature of American democracy, a correspondent replied that "no dependence can be placed upon any treatise that has yet appeared which professes to discuss [the business of government.] You must draw upon your own resources, you must think—and think alone."[1] Similarly, Orestes Brownson thought no American had produced a "work on politics of the slightest scientific value."[2] And when Harper and Brothers brought out George Sidney Camp's *Democracy* in 1841, the publisher drew attention to the curious fact that it was the first book "the express design of which is to elucidate the democratic *theory*."[3] Camp, in his own introduction, dwelt at length on the anomaly that "in a democratic country, where self-government has been successfully exercised by the people for nearly three-quarters of a century"

[1]W. S. Wait to Bancroft, October 15, 1834, cited in Arthur Schlesinger, Jr., *The Age of Jackson* (Boston, 1948), p. 309.

[2]*The United States Magazine and Democratic Review*, XIII (1843), 129.

[3]George Sidney Camp, *Democracy* (New York, 1841), p. iii.

there was no literature on democracy to which one might refer "the young democratic disciple."[4] There was no *"connected and philosophical exposition of the peculiar theory of democratic government,"* insisted Camp, and the result, he pointed out, was that Americans "journey on, living in the rich experience and practical enjoyment of democratic freedom, but in the entire and reckless indifference to its abstract principles."[5]

Camp tried to account for the dearth of theoretical interest in America's triumphantly successful practice by observing, with mild wit, that the "chief speculators" of the day were "in merchandise and real estate." Camp thought that "political opinions seem to have retrograded since the Revolution"; the majority of "educated" people in the United States did not, he believed, understand the nature of freedom or "the maxim of the natural equality of mankind." Having won independence, with a continent to conquer and a nation to make, Americans were content "with the practical results" of their political system, hardly inclined to the "patient study of its abstract nature." We have been "all action," said Camp. "There has been no room for the thinker; he has been jostled to one side."[6]

Yet Camp's own book suggests it was not simply the activism of a practical people that discouraged intellectual speculation in the business of politics. At one point Camp observed, "Government, like religion, is essential to our happiness, and was designed by the Author of our being for universal use; it is a proof of the justice and propriety of a scheme of government, as it is of the genuineness of a religious system, that it may be easily and universally comprehended."[7] "Nothing," he wrote, "can be more simple than the theory of republican government. It may be readily comprehended by the plainest minds; it appeals to the first maxims of common-sense observation, and the universal principles of morals."[8] If, as Camp had it, the chief merit of the American system of politics was that it needed no philosopher, it is hardly surprising that it did not get one. The limits of plain minds and the first maxims of common sense do not define re-

[4]Camp, *Democracy*, p. 10.

[5]Camp, *Democracy*, pp. 12–13.

[6]Camp, *Democracy*, pp. 14–15.

[7]Camp, *Democracy*, p. 89.

[8]Camp, *Democracy*, p. 88.

sources that promise to sustain intense speculation. Yet the curious result has been to make speculation on Jacksonian political thought a risky enterprise. There is an implicit logic, an unstated argument, that defines the assumptions of American democratic political thought of the early nineteenth century, assumptions that contemporaries took to be nothing more than the common sense of the matter. One must make that hidden logic explicit in order to catch a glimpse of what uncommon hopes motivated the politics of the age of the common man.

Further, the similarity Camp saw between religion and democracy suggests a way of looking at the political thought of Jacksonian America. Politics is many things, but before it can be any of the particular activities one normally associates with it, politics necessarily involves an expression of the cultural values that make politics possible at all. Camp thought that Christianity and democratic liberty "flourish best on the same soil" because of "strong points of similarity between them." Not only were both universally true and easily understood by all people everywhere, but because both rested on self-evident principles, both were hostile to "precedent or authority." Both "inculcated the same contempt for human authority, the same regard for the poorer and humbler classes, the same disregard of merely adventitious and accidental circumstances, the same paramount authority of principle." And, although both had "for their basis the law of benevolence," both, Camp pointed out, "have borne the reproach of being disorganizing and anarchical."[9]

For Camp, the similarities between Christianity and democracy proved that both were true. For us, the similarities suggest also the pervasiveness in his time of a common way of apprehending the relation of the individual to society. The question of that relation, the relation between the one and the many, is inevitably a matter of politics, but the answer to the question involves more than politics. It involves the values of the general culture of which politics is but one expression.[10] Michael Chevalier, the

[9]Camp, *Democracy*, pp. 180–81.

[10]Sidney Verba has used the term "political culture" to denote the "psychological orientation to politics." See his essay, "Comparative Political Culture," in *Political Culture and Political Development*, eds., Lucian Pye and Sidney Verba (Princeton, N.J., 1965). I refer rather more simply to the expression of the general values of the culture in the idiom of politics. See Talcott Parsons, *The Social System* (Glencoe, Ill., 1951), pp. 126–27, and especially the introduction to Parsons, et al., *Theories of Society* (New York, 1961).

French Saint-Simonian who had visited and written about the United States before Camp published his book, had this in mind when he said of the United States, "Under the influence of Protestantism and republicanism, social progress has been achieved by pushing the process of division to its extreme, that is, individualism; for Protestantism, republicanism, and individualism are all one." Chevalier, along with his fellow countryman Tocqueville, had observed the centrifugal impulse in American society, the extremity of division in which "individuals have cut themselves off from each other," but his observation did not stop with what Camp termed "the reproach" of seeing nothing but disorganization or anarchy.[11] Chevalier recognized that in the United States, Protestantism, republicanism, and individualism were simply different aspects of a comprehensive system of values. Despite "the process of division," each derived its sanction from the good of society. Or, to put it another way, the discovery of assumptions that underlie Jacksonian democratic thought may lead to a better understanding of the political thought of the time but it may also lead to a problem that lies beyond politics and finds its answer only in the values of the general culture.

I

In 1824 Andrew Jackson received a plurality of the popular and electoral vote in a four-cornered race for the Presidency, followed by John Quincy Adams, William Crawford, and Henry Clay. Since no candidate had a majority, selection devolved on the House of Representatives, where choice, according to the provision of the Constitution, lay among the three leading candidates. Clay, now excluded as a candidate, threw his political influence behind Adams, and after Adams became President he named Clay his Secretary of State, placing him in the office that at that time was the conventional stepping stone to the Presidency. Immediately, Jacksonian partisans raised the cry of a corrupt bargain between Adams and Clay and began the campaign that was to bring Andrew Jackson to the White House in 1828.

Against this background Jackson decided, in his first message

[11]Michael Chevalier, *Society, Manners and Politics in the United States*, trans., ed., and with an introduction by John William Ward (New York, 1961), p. 356; the first American edition of Chevalier's book was in Boston in 1839.

to Congress as President, to catechize the legislative branch on the principles of democratic government. In the course of his message he laid bare the major assumptions of his democratic faith and provided us with a characteristic statement of "the first principle" of Jacksonian democracy, "*the majority is to govern.*"[12]

When Jackson asserts the rule of the majority to be the first principle of "our system," he is on uncertain historical ground. True, even Alexander Hamilton, who was not greatly enamored with the prospect of rule by the people, defended the principle as primary, but the Constitution to which Jackson appeals is not a document devised to implement a thoroughgoing domination by the majority in politics. Jackson, in saying it does, seems to verge on the tyranny of the majority, which so concerned Tocqueville in his analysis of an equalitarian society. But as one watches the development of Jackson's argument, one sees him avoid in an astonishing way the power of the majority, which seems at first to be the conclusion toward which he is moving.

"To the People," said Jackson, "belongs the right of electing their Chief Magistrate." Neither the electoral college nor the House were ever meant to frustrate the people's choice. "Experience proves," as for Jackson it clearly did in 1824, "that in proportion as agents to execute the will of the People are multiplied there is danger of their wishes being frustrated. Some may be unfaithful; all are liable to err. So far, therefore, as the People can with convenience speak, it is safer for them to express their own will."[13] So Jackson spoke for the obliteration of "all intermediate agency" in the election of the President.

The premise of Jackson's message is a trust in the will of a virtuous and competent people. But agents trusted with the power of translating the will of a virtuous people into reality will inevitably be corrupted by that power: "There are, perhaps, few men who can for any great length of time enjoy office and power without being more or less under the influence of feelings unfavorable to the faithful discharge of their public duties. . . . They are apt to acquire a habit of looking with indifference upon the public interests, and of tolerating conduct from which an unpracticed man would revolt. Office is considered as a species of property, and government rather as a means of promoting individual inter-

[12]James D. Richardson, *A Compilation of the Messages and Papers of the Presidents, 1789–1907* (n.p., 1908), II, 448.

[13]Richardson, *Messages and Papers,* II, 447.

ests than as an instrument created solely for the service of the people."[14]

The negation of Jackson's premise is the corruption of the will of a virtuous people by the selfish instincts brought into play by power. At this point in his message, Jackson stands at the edge of the world of practical politics. He has already summarily solved the theoretical problem of identifying "the People." "The People" are the majority of the people. If "the People" could act directly, there would be no problem because there would be no need for refractory intermediate institutions. The problem arises because "the People" must rely on agents, the body of legislators, to translate their will into reality; but, by that very fact, "corruption" and a "perversion of correct feelings and principles" threaten constantly to divert government from its "legitimate" ends and "make it an engine for the support of the few at the expense of the many."[15] Having identified the will of the people with the will of the majority outside the institutions of government, Jackson's task becomes, then, to show how it is possible to pattern the institutions of government so the governors are made responsible to the power that creates them. In other words, if the seductions of power threaten constantly to make the political state the enemy of the general society, then the first job of politics is to circumvent the danger.

Jackson's solution is, however, to deny the very antithesis he has just developed; that is, he tries to obliterate the distinction between the government and the people. "The duties of all public officers are, or at least admit of being made, so plain and simple that men of intelligence may readily qualify themselves for their performance; and I can not but believe that more is lost by the long continuance of men in office than is generally to be gained by their experience."[16] So Jackson spoke for limited tenure in elective offices and rotation in all appointive offices. Later generations would stigmatize the principle by remembering it only as the "spoils system." It is true that, under the tutelage of professional politicians like Martin Van Buren who saw the need and the advantages of party organization, Jackson recognized the uses of patronage in building a national political party, but Jackson's

[14]Richardson, *Messages and Papers*, II, 448–49.
[15]Richardson, *Messages and Papers*, II, 449.
[16]Richardson, *Messages and Papers*, II, 449.

rejection of a trained and experienced class of legislators and civil servants was, much more importantly, a species of reform.

Jackson's solution to the paradox of politics, the corruption of the selfless will of the people by the power necessary to implement that will, was no less than to try to dismiss the need for politics at all, that is, to abolish the distinction between "the People" and the government. If power corrupts, then America was in the happy state of having no need for power. Jackson could say so only on the assumption that the work of government was essentially so plain and simple that the average intelligent man could do the job. The assumption of simplicity made it possible to reject the need for training and experience, to dismiss the existence of a governing class, and to argue that the people could act directly by being rotated through the offices of government and performing the simple tasks that were the legitimate ends of government. The task of government was to see to the minimal preservation of law and order and to leave the business of society "to flow in those channels to which individual enterprise, always its surest guide, might direct it."[17] The danger of the tyranny of the majority vanishes in a world where each individual is busy about his own business.

The abortive dialectic, the refusal to attempt a synthesis that would resolve the antithesis between the will of a virtuous people and the corruption of political power, was not Jackson's alone. It suffused the political thought of the period. Jackson's message comes at the beginning of his tenure of office. At the end of that tenure, in 1838, the *United States Magazine and Democratic Review*, founded to advocate the "high and holy DEMOCRATIC PRINCIPLE which was designed to be the fundamental element of the new social and political system created by the 'American experiment,' " introduced itself to the public with a presentation of the nature of that democratic principle.[18] The argument of the "Introduction" to the *Democratic Review* is longer and more ambitious than Jackson's *obiter dicta* to the Congress, but the underlying structure of the argument is precisely the same. Because the article is an attempt to present a reasoned account of the democratic faith, it becomes involved in a crucial dilemma concerning

[17]Richardson, *Messages and Papers*, II, 449.

[18]*The United States Magazine and Democratic Review*, I (October–December, 1837), 1. Although carrying the date "October–December, 1837," the first volume was actually published in January, 1838; see the publisher's note at the front of the first volume.

the relation of the individual to society and points, by its solution, to the vital source of a democratic faith that staked its all on the self-sufficiency of the individual.

The author of the "Introduction" to the *Democratic Review*, presumably John L. O'Sullivan, who was part owner and political editor of the magazine, begins on a characteristic Jacksonian note. His task is the "purification" of the democratic creed "from those corruptions" that have prevented its glorious tendencies. He proclaims his "abiding confidence in the virtue, intelligence, and full capacity for self-government, of the great mass of our people, our industrious, honest, manly, intelligent millions of freemen." The premise, put with somewhat greater rhetorical flourish, is the same as Jackson's in his message to Congress: the people are virtuous and capable, but somehow corruption has entered the populist heaven.

"We are opposed," O'Sullivan continues, "to all self-styled 'wholesome restraints' on the free action of the popular opinion and will, other than those which have for their sole object the prevention of precipitate legislation." To assure that the speed with which the popular will is translated into action is deliberate enough, O'Sullivan accepts "the expedient of the division of power, and by causing all legislation to pass through the ordeal of successive forms; to be sifted through the discussions of coördinate legislative branches with mutual suspensive veto powers." O'Sullivan speaks, of course, of what we call the system of checks and balances, the ordering of the institution of government into separate departments that check each other. But he does not mean to say that such a system of countervailing power acts against the will of the people, only against other departments, and he stresses his point immediately. "Yet all should be dependent with equal directness and promptness on the influence of public opinion; the popular will should be equally the animating and moving spirit of them all, and ought never to find in any of its own creatures a self-imposed power, capable (when misused either by corrupt ambition or honest error) of resisting itself, and defeating its own determined object. We cannot, therefore, look with an eye of favor on any such forms of representation as, by length of tenure of delegated power, tend to weaken that universal and unrelaxing responsibility to the vigilance of public opinion, which is the true conservative principle of our institutions."[19]

O'Sullivan has here compressed an extremely long and com-

[19]*Democratic Review*, I, 2.

plicated problem in American constitutional thought into a short statement. There are many issues lurking in his few words. One is the uneasy tension between the "true" conservatism of responsiveness to public opinion and the acceptance of institutional arrangements that will prevent "precipitate" legislation: the latter strategy implies that public opinion is sometimes hastily wrong. But beneath such obvious problems lies a much more complex one. Two opposing traditions of American constitutional thought coexist awkwardly in O'Sullivan's paragraph.

From the beginning, American political thought has developed two antithetical views of the nature of a proper constitution. One places emphasis on the form of government created by a constitution, on the institutional arrangement of the organs of government. That is, responsible government is to be achieved by distributing power throughout the various governmental parts in order to check undue power by a particular branch in the whole, finely articulated, self-regulating system. A good constitution is one that sets up a specific form of government. The other view of the nature of a proper constitution places emphasis on the process by which constitutions are made, and unmade, and insists that the true check on the power of government, or on any of the particular, institutionalized branches of government, lies in the power of the people outside the doors of the government. Here, a good constitution rests not so much in a form of government as in the effectiveness of the process by which the people out of government are constantly able to discipline government by exercising the inalienable power that ultimately sanctions all governments.

In the first, the language of the constitution that creates the government is the will of the people. Having spoken once, the people are excluded, except through the unwieldy amendment process, from speaking again, and the organ of the government that is given the final say on the meaning of the constitution, which embodies the will of the people, is that department of government most removed from the people in their electoral capacity, the Supreme Court. In the second, the will of the people is always alive and potent. The people never exclude themselves from exercising the power that is always, by definition, invested in them: changing or abolishing the present form of government. Other than revolution, of course, the only way the people can act in such a sovereign capacity is through what O'Sullivan refers to as "public opinion," and it was to give institutional structure to the amorphous shape of public opinion that political parties came into being in our national politics. The first strain of constitutional thought, the emphasis on constitution as institutional form, is best associated with John Adams; the second, the emphasis on constitution as process, the process by which people constitute and control government, is best associated with Thomas Jefferson.

O'Sullivan's acceptance, in his compact statement, of both the division of power and the will of the people outside the government indicates his avoidance of the subtle and sophisticated political terms of his problem. Both versions of constitutionalism raise difficult problems concerning the relation of the individual to society. In one, the will of the individual is somehow supposed to be represented in the order of government created by the language of the constitution; in the other, the will of the individual is somehow supposed to be represented by the will of the majority of his equal fellows in society. O'Sullivan recognizes that either view of politics will land him in a dilemma concerning the uninhibited freedom of the individual. He sees in any check on the will of the people the danger of rule by a minority; he is also uneasy about the extinction of minority rights under rule by the majority. If pushed to choose, he will pragmatically accept the lesser evil of majority rule but asks, "Have we but a choice of evils? Is there, then, such a radical deficiency in the moral elements implanted by its Creator in human society, that no other alternative can be devised by which both evils shall be avoided, and a result attained more analogous to the beautiful and glorious harmony of the rest of his creation?"[20] The tone, of course, suggests surely not.

O'Sullivan answers his own rhetorical question by pointing out that "it is under the word *government*, that the subtle danger lurks." Like Jackson, rather than pursue the problem he has defined, O'Sullivan proceeds to abolish it. "All government is evil, and the parent of evil. A strong and active democratic *government*, in the common sense of the term, is an evil, differing only in degree and mode of operation, and not in nature, from a strong despotism." If government presents the dilemma of the power of a minority in office on one hand, or the tyranny of the majority outside of office on the other, the dilemma is to be avoided by denying the need for government. "The best government is that which governs least."[21]

[20]*Democratic Review*, I, 5.

[21]*Democratic Review*, I, 6.

The reason O'Sullivan gives seems, at first glance, perverse: "No human depositories can, with safety, be trusted with the power of legislation upon the general interests of society. . . . Such power must be perpetually liable to the most pernicious abuse, from the natural imperfection, both in wisdom of judgment and purity of purpose, of all human legislation." So sour a view of human nature leads O'Sullivan to the drastic conclusion that "government should have as little as possible to do with the general business and interests of the people." Since the general interests of the people define the whole business of government, nothing is left when O'Sullivan finishes but a bare administrative state: "the administration of justice, for the protection of the natural equal rights of the citizen, and preservation of social order."[22]

As one follows O'Sullivan's argument with its distrust of "human depositories" and its assertion of the "natural imperfection . . . of all human legislation," one wonders what ever happened to that great mass of "industrious, honest, manly, intelligent millions of freemen" who, at the outset, provided support for his buoyant faith in democracy. There are, rationally, two views of human nature that will support a dismissal of the power of government. Anarchism can, logically, find a basis in two opposing views of human nature. One is optimistic: people are so honest and manly that they need no government. The other is pessimistic: people are so naturally depraved that, whatever the other inconveniences, none of them had best be trusted with the power of ruling. O'Sullivan seems to be having it both ways, arguing for the abolition of government from two antithetical conceptions of human nature. But his position is a bit more sophisticated than such blatant self-contradiction. His premise is, like Jackson's, "an abiding confidence in the virtue, intelligence, and full capacity for self-government, of the great mass of our people." The accent falls on "self-government." As long as the virtuous, manly American democrat has only his own interests in hand, there is no cause for hesitation or doubt. But give him power and he will, all too humanly, read his own interests as the general interest and become "selfish and tyrannical . . . vigilant, persevering, and subtle in all the arts of deception and corruption." It is the power made possible by the awful power of legislation "by which human nature has been self-degraded."[23]

[22]*Democratic Review*, I, 7.

[23]*Democratic Review*, I, 6.

To repeat, then: the same dialectic, or aborted dialectic, provides the structure for both Jackson's few words and O'Sullivan's long article. Both subscribe to the thesis of the will of the people by power. The synthesis, or better, the absence of a synthesis, is astonishingly simple: there is no need for power, for government. Do away with it.

II

The key words in the political vocabulary of the period of the early nineteenth century were "simple" and "corruption." Not only were the principles of democracy simple enough to be easily and universally comprehended, but the practice of democracy, the duties of public officers, involved tasks so simple that they could be entrusted to the average citizen for execution. Jacksonian political thought can best be understood as an attempt to celebrate the capacity of a virtuous people by insisting that the intricacies of government were essentially so plain and simple that there was no need to admit a distinction between the governors and the governed. The result was to abolish the distinction between government and society, to deny the problem of politics by refusing to define a general interest at all. Society was no more than the sum of individual interests. Corruption was to be avoided by denying any individual, or group of individuals, power over others. Leave each man free from external restraint and the good society would emerge spontaneously.

In discussing a political movement so thoroughly dedicated to the denial of power, historians ever since have been bemused by Jackson's vigorous Presidency. He was one of our few "strong" Presidents. Nearly every important issue Jackson confronted in office led to an enlargement of the powers of the office of the President. His major actions—his extensive use of the veto power, his removals from office, his veto of internal improvements in the Maysville Road Bill, his attack on and destruction of the second Bank of the United States, and his assertion of federal supremacy over the threat of nullification in South Carolina—all demonstrated the variety of sources of power at the disposal of the Chief Executive. After Jackson and because of Jackson, the Presidency was a far more potent element in the system of organized power we call the government.

Yet whatever consequences Jackson's Presidency had for the

expansion of the power of the office, Jackson's whole intention was to strip government of power. He may have acted power-fully to achieve his ends, but his ends were negative in the sense of attempting to deny positive power to the national govern-ment. The rationale underlying removals from those offices within the power of the President's appointment was to destroy the possibility of the existence of a corps of permanent profes-sionals who would have a vested interest in the offices of govern-ment. The veto, by definition, was to prevent action by the legis-lative branch. The Maysville Road veto was to get the national government out of the business of internal improvements within the particular states. The attack on the Bank of the United States was to separate the government from the business of banking as well as to see to it that the government did not create an artificial monopoly in a trade that, the Jacksonians thought, should be open to entry and competition like any other business. The only positive action Jackson took on a major issue was the elemental one of preserving the Union, the nation itself, against the threat of dissolution into the petty principalities of the separate states.

The paradox of Jackson's administration appears whenever power is used to destroy power. In acting to whittle away the power of the national government, Jackson greatly enlarged the power of his office and schooled subsequent presidents on the potent dimensions of their place in government. Analogies are always dangerous, but the Jacksonian program is analogous to the communist theory of the dictatorship in behalf of the prole-tariat where, ideally, the power of the state is seized and used with intense vigor in order to realize the harmonious society, free from social conflict, in which the state then withers away because it has achieved its mission. One is, of course, rightly uneasy with the analogy because there is a basic difference between Marxist ideology and Jacksonian democratic ideology. For the Marxist, the ideal community in which the free development of each indi-vidual is compatible with the development of all individuals is to be arrived at, to be won, only at the end of the unfolding of history. A disciplined group seizes the power of the state to create the conditions in which the state is unnecessary. What remains after success is what the Jacksonians dreamed of: simple admin-istration of a few essentials. But for the Jacksonians, as for all classical liberals, the ideal community was to be recovered. The ideal society of individuals free from external restraint was the premise of history, not its conclusion.[24] The world was not to be made simple and harmonious. It *was* simple and harmonious. The job of government was negative in the sense that it need not act to create the good society; it needed only keep a sharp eye on and check those who might corrupt the good society.

In the history of American political thought, the Jacksonians are rightly placed in the Jeffersonian tradition of strict construction of the Constitution. If only Americans would remain true to the wisdom of the founding fathers, if only Americans would resist the seductions of power, public or private, if only Americans would purify their system from the corruptions that tend to stain it, then American democracy would last "through countless ages of the future."[25] The accent has persisted in American politics: looking nostalgically backward to a golden past, Americans press energetically into an auspicious future. But the animating source of the Jacksonian faith was not simply the fundamental law of a political constitution made by human beings; it was no less than a cosmic constitutionalism, a belief in a fundamental law that pervaded all reality, natural and social, that was made not by human beings but was an integral part of the universe and that would manifest itself inevitably if human beings did not pervert it by their actions.

"Afford but the single nucleus of a system of administration of justice between man and man," O'Sullivan argued in support of his principle of freedom from the coercive power of the state, "and, under the sure operation of this principle, the floating atoms will distribute and combine themselves, as we see in the beautiful natural process of crystallization, into a far more perfect and harmonious result than if government, with its 'fostering hand,' undertake to disturb, under the plea of directing, the process. The natural laws which will establish themselves and find their own level are the best laws. The same hand was the Author of the moral, as of the physical world; and we feel clear and strong in the assurance that we cannot err in trusting, in the former, to the same fundamental principles of spontaneous action and self-regulation which produce the beautiful order of the latter."

This was the "principle" that constituted the Jacksonian "point of departure": "This is the fundamental principle of the

---

[24]For further discussion of the point, see my article, "Mill, Marx, and Modern Individualism," *Virginia Quarterly Review*, XXXV (Autumn, 1959), 527–39.

[25]*Democratic Review*, I, 1.

philosophy of democracy, to furnish a system of administration of justice, and then leave all the business and interests of society to themselves, to free competition and association—in a word, to the VOLUNTARY PRINCIPLE." What had worked so well in religion would work just as well in all areas of social life. If government refused to intervene, if government were "sifted and analyzed down to the lowest point of simplicity consistent with the preservation of some degree [!] of national organization," then the result would be "the best possible result of general order and happiness."[26]

In O'Sullivan's argument, the imagery of the perfect crystal is Newtonian. When he writes that the principle of freedom from government "is borrowed from the example of the perfect self-government of the physical universe, being written in letters of light on every page of the great bible of Nature," he is reading from a different book of nature than, say, his contemporaries, Emerson and Thoreau. But he agrees with them in believing that the utmost freedom for each individual is a "great moral truth," and, even more importantly, he agrees with them in believing that spontaneous action and self-regulation by each member in society is the only and proper road to the good society.[27]

Alfred North Whitehead has written that "every philosophy is tinged with the coloring of some secret imaginative background, which never emerges explicitly into its train of reasoning."[28] The secret imaginative background that made it possible for Jacksonian political philosophy to come to the astonishing conclusion that America had no need for politics was a fervent belief in a fundamental law in the universe, a cosmic constitutionalism, which made it unnecessary for man to plan for, create, and achieve the good society. Further, this fundamental law was reached by the "instinctive perception" of the mass of the people.[29] Once man was freed from the "artificial institutions" of society, he would "walk abroad through the free creation in [his] own majesty."[30] As George Sidney Camp put it, "a republic is not so correctly a form of government as it is the supremacy of principle. Forms of govern-

---

[26]*Democratic Review*, I, 7.

[27]*Democratic Review*, I, 8.

[28]Alfred North Whitehead, *Science and the Modern World* (New York: Signet edition, n.d.), pp. 49–50.

[29]*Democratic Review*, I, 13.

[30]*Democratic Review*, I, 11.

ment have been, for the most part, only so many various modes of tyranny. Where the people are everything, and political forms, establishments, institutions, as opposed to the people, nothing, there and there only is liberty; such a state, and such a state only, constitutes republican government, the fundamental principle of which is not a human invention, but results from the leaving untrammelled by human devices the just and natural relations of man to man."[31] No less than with transcendentalism and Protestant evangelical revivalism, the secret spring of the political faith of the early nineteenth century lay in the trust that the ideal society was to be reached by turning away from the actual institutions of society and allowing the "just and natural" relations of man to man to appear.

III

Democratic thought of the early nineteenth century has many curious turnings. The constant celebration of "the People" and the instinctive wisdom of the average man seems to point toward what Tocqueville called the "tyranny of the majority," an egalitarian populism in which the many run roughshod over the one. But the conclusion turns out to be a world in which power, even the power of the many, disappears, and in its place we have the happy concourse of the individual wills of manly, independent American Democrats acting on the "natural moral principles" infused into them by their creator for their own "self-development and self-regulation."[32] Similarly, the ideology of simplicity would seem to imply a sociology of simplicity, that is, a relatively uncomplicated social world of self-sufficient individuals living in a providentially determined and easy harmony one with another. But that is not the conclusion reached.

At one point in his exposition of the democratic principle of freedom from the restraint of government, John L. O'Sullivan speaks with an "honest, manly contempt" of "the pretensions of those self-styled 'better classes' to the sole possession of the requisite intelligence for the management of public affairs." He based his contempt, first, on the pragmatic ground that the "general diffusion of education" in the United States makes the requisite

[31]Camp, *Democracy*, pp. 161–62.

[32]*Democratic Review*, I, 11.

intelligence available to all classes of men. Then, however, he goes on to say: "As far as superior knowledge and talent confer on their possessor a natural charter of privilege to control his associates, and exert an influence on the direction of the general affairs of the community, the free and natural action of that privilege is best secured by a perfectly free democratic system, which will abolish all artificial distinctions, and, preventing the accumulation of any social obstacles to advancement, will permit the free development of every germ of talent, wherever it may chance to exist, whether on the proud mountain summit, in the humble valley, or by the wayside of common life."[33] As always in Jacksonian rhetoric, the critical words here are "natural" and "artificial." If the organization and institutions of society do not confer on some an "artificial" advantage, such as legislative charters that grant a favored position in the market, there will still be privilege, but it will be a "natural" charter of privilege to wield power, to "control" one's associates and direct the affairs of the community. Having wiped the social slate clean of artificial lines of distinction, the American Democrat begins an anxious race to prove he is naturally a good deal more equal than his fellows.

George Sidney Camp, in his definition of liberty as that society in which the people are everything and "political forms, establishments, institutions" nothing, was careful to avoid the suggestion that those who held his view were "levellers." On the contrary, as he insisted more than once, "Republicans do not contend for the annihilation of social distinctions"; "Republicans are . . . for distinctions and inequalities."[34] Camp thought the "I'm-as-good-as-you principle" was not correctly understood. "When we say that all men are by nature equal," he explained, "we mean nothing more than that all are by nature equal in their moral attributes—equally moral and accountable beings—and, therefore, equally entitled to the regulation of their own conduct, as that is the basis of moral accountability; therefore, all by nature equally entitled to exercise their own government, privately and publicly, socially and politically."[35] But there would still be "just distinctions" among men. "If one man has a more inventive genius, a more comprehensive prudence, a more enlarged experience, a more scrupulous integrity than another, what is the nat-

[33]*Democratic Review*, I, 4–5.

[34]Camp, *Democracy*, pp. 133, 136.

[35]Camp, *Democracy*, p. 133.

ural, I may say, the inevitable consequence, from the possession of such superior qualities? He possesses superior power and influence." He has, in O'Sullivan's words, "a natural charter of privilege" but not, as Camp put it, "from the arbitrary force of circumstances, or the coercive power of human laws."[36] "Nature" would, by "her own means, effect the same harmony of ranks and orders in society which she has so successfully achieved in the vegetable and animal creation." So, a republican government was to achieve "the proper divisions of rank and grade in society" by leaving "the matter entirely to the regulation of itself." It was by assuming the moral equality of all men and then leaving them to their own devices that "you increase, as much as human means can, the force of [a man's] moral motives and the energy of his active powers."[37]

In a chapter devoted to "Aristocratic Society in America," Camp pointed out that there was, properly speaking, no aristocracy in the strict sense of government by the few in the United States; he preferred not even to use the word to describe American society but did so, grudgingly, since it was "in use." If by aristocracy, however, one meant, in the more general sense of the word, "discrimination of ranks in society," there was nothing in democracy incompatible with the notion, "so long as that discrimination is voluntarily made by individuals." Democracy has borne the "obloquy of cherishing a levelling spirit and aiming at agrarian measures," but this was, one "cannot too often repeat, a mistaken notion as to the kind of equality that a democracy demands, which is not an equality in the circumstances, but an equality in the rights of mankind. In utterly repudiating all distinction in political rights, it admits freely of every other distinction, to the most absolute and unqualified extent. It destroys arbitrary and fictitious, to make room for real rank."[38]

It is a commonplace in the history of political ideas to draw a sharp distinction between equality and liberty. To maintain the equality of all people implies an abridgement of the liberty to some people; to allow the liberty of all people implies an eventual inequality between some people. Democratic political thought of the early nineteenth century attempted to yoke the two, to maintain what analytically may seem a contradiction, by confining the

[36]Camp, *Democracy*, p. 135.

[37]Camp, *Democracy*, p. 136–38.

[38]Camp, *Democracy*, p. 220–21.

notion of equality to the political dimension of life on the ground that it created the greatest possible liberty in the social dimension of life. Whether the political and social dimensions can be so neatly isolated one from the other can reasonably be doubted, but the Jacksonian notion ran that if each individual was made equal before the law, and if organized power in the form of governmental intervention in the society did not create artificial advantages, then each individual was set free to make what he could of himself. If, at first glance, the democratic thought of the time seems to offer the ideal of a simple, naturally harmonious society, at second glance, it reveals an intensely busy, competitive society.

To a later generation, accustomed to the assumption that a rough degree of social and economic equality must exist to make democracy a viable form of government, it is hard to catch the accent of political idealism in early American democratic thought. The argument did not run that economic and social conditions create a certain kind of personality, which, in turn, makes possible a characteristic form of government. Quite the opposite. The form of government, rather than an epiphenomenon of the material base of society, was itself the dynamic source of change that transformed the rest of society. "The liberty that republics afford to all men of every rank of governing themselves," asserted Camp, "elevates their characters, and qualifies them for self-government. The elevation which this freedom confers on people of the lowest station, stimulates to a degree of self-improvement."[39] Freedom would create the personality appropriate to the conditions of freedom and, as a by-blow, release the energies that would lead to self-improvement and industrious activity.

The notion was a common one. Frederick Grimke, in the best single contemporary book on the political thought of the period, *Considerations Upon the Nature and Tendency of Free Institutions* (1848), pointed out that "even in America we can discern a well-defined line between the higher and lower orders of men. Free institutions do not obliterate the distinctions; on the contrary, they are eminently favorable to the accumulation of wealth in private hands, since they add to the natural gifts of some, the further advantage of opportunity, and the protection of a system of laws which is equal and invariable in its operation. It is like the addition of a new faculty to some men." Grimke, speaking out

[39]Camp, *Democracy*, p. 141.

of the tradition of Lockean faculty psychology, is making an extravagant analogy here. Free institutions create new personalities by calling into being new "faculties" among men. The result is that "the resolute, the enterprising, and the industrious, move forward with rapidity."[40] Grimke argued that "the principle of equality may very well be recognized as the rule among men as citizens—as members of a political community, although as individuals there may be very great and numerous inequalities between them. The utmost which the citizen can demand is that no law shall be passed to obstruct his rise, and to impede his progress through life. He has then an even chance with all his fellows. If he does not become their equal his case is beyond the reach of society, and to complain would be to quarrel with his own nature."[41] Free institutions had the double merit of stirring men into activity and then refusing to intervene to erase the natural distinctions that would arise. Government was to be limited in its activity to the role of umpire in an equal contest on an open field because of the belief that "the improvement of our condition, whether intellectual or physical, depends infinitely more upon our own independent exertions, than upon all other circumstances put together."[42]

IV

The appropriate symbol for the political thought of the early nineteenth century would be Janus, the god who faces both ways, looking backward and forward. With one face, early democratic thought looks backward in time to a simple order of society, free from the unnecessary institutions that corrupt the arcadian world of independent individuals related one to another only through the moral order in which each participates. With the other face, it looks forward to a busy, competitive, expansive society of energetic individuals. Yet, despite the different worlds that the faces look upon, in each the solitary, self-reliant individual stands at the center of the social order.

In his Farewell Address to the American people on March 4,

[40]Frederick Grimke, *Considerations Upon the Nature and Tendency of Free Institutions* (Cincinnati and New York, 1848), p. 459.

[41]Grimke, *Free Institutions*, p. 53.

[42]Grimke, *Free Institutions*, p. 459.

1837, Andrew Jackson spoke to the great mass of the people who constituted his following and for whom he had acted: "The planter, the farmer, the mechanic, and the laborer all know that their success depends upon their own industry and economy and that they must not expect to become suddenly rich by the fruits of their toil. Yet these classes of society form the great body of the people of the country; they are the bone and sinew of the country—men who love liberty and desire nothing but equal rights and equal laws, and who, moreover, hold the great mass of our national wealth, although it is distributed in moderate amounts among the millions of freemen who possess it."[43] It was for a world defined by these millions of simple, hard-working folk that Jackson had restricted government to its limited tasks, attacked artificial monopolies of wealth, and resisted "extravagant schemes" of governmental action. Speaking to them directly, Jackson's last counsel as their leader was to say, "If you are true to yourselves nothing can impede your march to the highest point of national prosperity."[44] The worth of the Constitution, Jackson thought, was "in the security it gives to life, liberty, character and property."[45] To the conventional trinity, Jackson added "character." If the great mass of manly, independent American Democrats, acting for themselves, were not seduced by the expectation of becoming "suddenly rich," if the people did not "withdraw their attention from the sober pursuits of honest industry,"[46] then a pure and simple government would be sufficient for a pure and simple people.

But they were a people, in Jackson's words, pressing forward in the "march to the highest point of national prosperity." There are many ironies in American history, but surely one of the most massive is that the ideal of a simple, uncomplicated society, based solely upon the character of men strong enough to remain true to their best selves, found its most persuasive political voice at precisely the moment of economic and industrial growth, which preceded the full emergence of a society committed to wealth and power. The hero of that enterprise, too, was a self-reliant man. "Ours is a country," wrote Calvin Colton, speaking for the Whigs in 1844, "where men start from an humble origin . . . and where they

[43]Richardson, *Messages and Papers*, III, 305.

[44]Richardson, *Messages and Papers*, III, 294.

[45]Richardson, *Messages and Papers*, III, 297.

[46]Richardson, *Messages and Papers*, III, 302.

can attain to the most elevated positions, or acquire a large amount of wealth, according to the pursuits they elect for themselves. No exclusive privileges of birth, no entailment of estates, no civil or political disqualifications, stand in their path; but one has as good a chance as another, according to his talents, prudence or personal exertions. This is a country of self-made men, than which nothing better could be said of any society."[47] The enigma that lies at the heart of the political thought of the early nineteenth century is whether the American Democrat it had in view was the self-sufficient character of Emerson's ideal and Jackson's rhetoric or the self-made man, desiring only a natural charter of privilege that would not impede his march to great wealth. Or was he one and the same person?

[47]Calvin Colton, *The Junius Tracts*, VII (1844), 15.

THE REFORMER AS CONSERVATIVE: PROTESTANT COUNTER-SUBVERSION IN THE EARLY REPUBLIC

W. David Lewis / AUBURN UNIVERSITY

One of the most striking features to be observed in the history of American reform movements is the great diversity of ideas and impulses by which the reformers have been impelled. It is sometimes tempting, however, to lose sight of this fundamental complexity and think of reformers in terms of stereotypes. At one extreme is the selfless humanitarian, willing to brave any danger for a worthy cause. At the other is the deluded fanatic or impractical dreamer, creating all sorts of difficulties for sensible people who must bear the burden of managing affairs in an inevitably imperfect world. Or there is the reformer who acts as the conscious or unconscious agent of selfish interests. However valid such facile impressions may be in individual cases, they can seriously distort the past if carelessly applied, for human motives are seldom—if ever—simple. This is as true in evaluating the influence of religion upon reform, the primary concern in this essay, as it is in other cases.

In examining the history of reform movements, therefore, it is well to analyze the influence of specific impulses and beware of hasty generalizations. Yet, if it is dangerous to oversimplify the aims and motives of reformers, it is also desirable and fruitful to look for common ideas and traditions that have been shared by like-minded people or for recurrent impulses at work in a particular nation or culture over extended periods of time. Perhaps more deeply than most people, reformers are strongly influenced by what is going on around them. Indeed, it is because they perceive—or think they perceive—certain conditions or trends with abnormal clarity that they are impelled to take part in various ameliorative causes. In view of this receptivity, it is logical to suppose that the existence of broad patterns of thought or climates of opinion in given historical eras will be reflected in the activities and pronouncements of individual reformers, each manifesting in a particular way certain paramount ideas or concerns of the time. This approach does not deny the existence of diverse aims and motives in any period, nor does it overlook continuities between one era and the next. It merely suggests that some impulses may appear more strongly in certain historical contexts than in others.

Like various other historical phenomena, reform movements can be seen to occur in cycles, each of which manifests a characteristic pattern. For example, some periods have been deeply affected by a concern for the individual, while others show the influence of organic group consciousness.[1] Similarly, some eras display a strong receptivity to change, while others reveal a desire for stability and order. This essay lends support to the views of recent scholars who have seen that reform efforts can stem from what are customarily called "conservative" impulses as well as from what might be considered "liberal" or "radical" ones.

[1]For an interesting analysis in this regard, see John L. Thomas, "Romantic Reform in America, 1815–1865," *American Quarterly*, XVII, 4 (Winter, 1965), 656–81. The cyclical view of American history, especially in political matters, is perhaps most closely associated with the work of the late Arthur M. Schlesinger, Sr.; see particularly his book *Paths to the Present* (New York, 1949), pp. 77–92. However, Schlesinger's book *The American As Reformer* (Cambridge, Mass., 1951), as well as Alice Felt Tyler's *Freedom's Ferment: Phases of American Social History to 1860* (Minneapolis, 1944), suffers from a tendency to see reformers only in a "liberal" perspective, without realizing that "reformer" and "conservative" are not necessarily antithetical terms. The same deficiency exists in the introduction to Henry Steele Commager's book of source materials entitled *The Era of Reform, 1830–1860* (Princeton, N.J., 1960), except that the "liberal" view does happen to fit that particular three-decade period better than it does some other eras.

Cyclical trends are observable in the reform movements that flourished in antebellum America. The era of the American Revolution, for example, manifests the impact of closely associated impulses. The idea of natural rights had obvious applications in various areas of life, as did the doctrine that all men are created equal, with its corollary that artificial distinctions among human beings are wrong. The full implications of these concepts were not quickly or completely translated into action, but their influence was clearly evident in measures taken to separate church and state, to abolish primogeniture and entail, and to outlaw slavery.[2] Reforms like these also drew upon the ideas of eighteenth-century rationalists, who demanded an end to social practices based upon mere superstition and credulity or blind reverence for the past. In addition, this era witnessed the flowering of a religious and humanitarian outlook that had been gaining strength in England among members of the Society of Friends, the followers of John Wesley, and the associates of the noted Anglican minister Dr. Thomas Bray. Exemplified in the work of such men as the great prison reformer John Howard, this type of Christian concern provided much of the impetus for efforts in America by men like Thomas Eddy and Episcopal bishop William White to improve the treatment of criminals and the mentally ill.[3] And although strong conservative trends were evident during the 1790s, the outbreak and progress of the French Revolution inspired sympathetic Americans to struggle for a wider application of civil liberties and to intensify their efforts for such objectives as women's rights and equal educational oportunities for the poor.[4]

[2] J. Franklin Jameson, *The American Revolution Considered as a Social Movement* (Princeton, N.J., 1940), pp. 21–26, 37, 83–91, and passim. In his article, "The American Revolution Considered as a Social Movement: A Re-Evaluation," *American Historical Review*, LX, 1 (October, 1954), 1–12, Frederick B. Tolles points out that the significance of such reforms can be exaggerated, especially because some of the institutions that were abolished or attacked were of only vestigial importance by the time of the Revolution. Nevertheless, it is pertinent to note that some of these changes were effected only after protracted struggles in the states involved. See for example Merrill Jensen, *The New Nation: A History of the United States During the Confederation, 1781–1789,* Vintage ed. (New York, 1965), pp. 131–36.

[3] See especially W. David Lewis, *From Newgate to Dannemora: The Rise of the Penitentiary in New York, 1796–1848* (Ithaca, N.Y., 1965), pp. 1–28.

[4] Eugene Perry Link, *Democratic-Republican Societies, 1790–1800* (New York, 1942), passim, particularly pp. 156–74.

Turning from the late eighteenth century to the decades just before the Civil War, one can observe various similarities in the reforms that flourished during these two eras, as well as equally important differences. Certainly a deep concern for human equality helped motivate the antislavery efforts of people like William Lloyd Garrison and the feminist crusade of Elizabeth Cady Stanton and Susan B. Anthony. The struggle for free public education carried on by such leaders as Stephen Simpson, Horace Mann, and Robert Rantoul, Jr., can be seen in part as a logical extension of principles espoused in an earlier day by Thomas Jefferson. The activities of Dorothea Dix on behalf of the insane and other social deviates remind one of previous efforts by such men as Thomas Eddy. The fact that Eddy belonged to the Society of Friends suggests another similarity between the two periods, for Quakers like James and Lucretia Mott, Dr. Thomas Kirkbride, and Richard Vaux were active in pre–Civil War attempts to free the slaves, elevate the status of women, improve the treatment of the mentally ill, and provide better care for prisoners.[5] Yet the reform activities of the late antebellum period also show the impact of new influences, like romanticism, transcendentalism, Christian perfectionism, anarchism, and utopianism, which were either totally absent or only weakly felt in the late eighteenth century. Nor are these differences surprising, for the dynamic, mobile, and rapidly growing America of the 1840s and 1850s was hardly the same as the young republic that had existed two generations before.

In the broadest sense, however, the reform currents of the revolutionary era and the late antebellum period were similar in that they revealed strong impulses to question previous ways of doing things, to experiment with radical ideas, and to welcome

[5]Citations from the vast literature on the abolitionist movement in general and Garrison in particular would be superfluous here, but for a useful general survey see Louis Filler, *The Crusade Against Slavery, 1830–1860* (New York, 1960). For varying points of view on the female-rights movement, see Eleanor Flexner, *Century of Struggle* (Cambridge, Mass., 1959); Robert E. Riegel, *American Feminists* (Lawrence, Kansas, 1963); and Andrew Sinclair, *The Better Half: The Emancipation of the American Woman* (New York, 1965). Selections from the writings and speeches on free public education by Simpson, Mann, and Rantoul can be conveniently found in George E. Probst, ed., *The Happy Republic: A Reader in Tocqueville's America* (New York, 1962), pp. 419–39. On the activities of the Motts, Kirkbride, and Richard Vaux, see Ira V. Brown, *Pennsylvania Reformers from Penn to Pinchot* (University Park, Pa., 1966), pp. 7, 31, and 34. Vaux was the son of Roberts Vaux, an important penal reformer of the late eighteenth and early nineteenth centuries.

social change. But reformers are not always so receptive to the unfamiliar. As scholars like Clifford S. Griffin and Charles I. Foster have shown, they can be animated by doubts and fears as well as by hopes, by desires to preserve as well as propensities toward change, by yearnings for the past as well as visions of the future.[6] The existence of reform cycles dominated by such impulses is readily understandable, for periods of marked change and upheaval lead naturally to desires for a return to stability and order. The influence of such desires can be observed by examining in detail the period between the revolutionary era and the onset of the Jacksonian age.

I

During the closing years of the eighteenth century, a number of Protestant clergymen and lay leaders launched a vigorous effort to overcome forces of immorality, infidelity, and instability that they believed to be widespread throughout the United States. The relatively large number of books and articles by recent historians who have studied this phenomenon makes it possible to examine the movement in detail and to assess its importance in the development of American culture. Viewed from one perspective, it can be seen as a stage in the long and sometimes painful process of adjustment that took place as church and state were separated in a democratic society. In yet another light, it illustrates the influence of mingled hopes, doubts, and fears fostered by the rapid internal development of a young nation striking out on new political, social, and economic paths. And it helps illuminate the long-range impact of certain moral and religious beliefs deeply embedded in America's colonial past.

[6]The works toward which attention is chiefly directed here are Clifford S. Griffin, *Their Brothers' Keepers: Moral Stewardship in the United States, 1800–1850* (New Brunswick, N.J., 1960), and Charles I. Foster, *An Errand of Mercy: The Evangelical United Front, 1790–1837* (Chapel Hill, N.C., 1960). See also Griffin's article, "Religious Benevolence as Social Control, 1815–1860," *Mississippi Valley Historical Review*, XLIV, 3 (December, 1957), 423–44. I greatly admire Griffin's work but believe that the social-control motivations he describes are less helpful for understanding reform developments after about 1830 than they are for explaining prevailing tendencies before that time. Foster shows acute perception in ending his study in the 1830s, which I regard as a decade of transition into a period dominated by new reform impulses. Although my essay had been substantially completed before the appearance of a book of readings on pre–Civil War reform re-

To be properly understood, therefore, this movement must be seen from a broad cultural perspective. This poses problems, for it must be acknowledged at the outset that the relationship of religion to social reform is a subject surrounded by potential pitfalls. It is deceptively easy, for example, to assume a crudely functional position that makes religious ideas and practices mere tools in the hands of self-interested groups or classes and to ignore the possibility that the religious life possesses an inner vitality of its own. As David B. Davis has pointed out, "the great object of American revivalists from Jonathan Edwards to Billy Graham has not been to perfect society but to save men's souls by arousing them to full awareness of their involvement in sin."[7] And Sidney Mead has reminded us that, in a modern world deeply permeated by skepticism on religious matters, it is misleadingly tempting to impute ulterior motives to people who, in an age of belief, were capable of actions stemming from a sincere and overpowering "experience of God."[8]

On the other hand, it would be completely unrealistic to maintain that religious and secular ideas have existed in sealed compartments and exerted no influence upon one another. The gospel emphasis upon loving one's neighbor has been a potent source of reform ideas, as has the Quaker conviction that all men possess a share of the divine "inner light," which can be reached and nurtured in the worst of human beings. In another vein, the Judeo-Christian concept of a just God has periodically inspired victims of oppression, whether individually or in groups, to rebel against conditions that seemed plainly at variance with Biblical precepts. Christian millennialism has also had an important bearing upon reform. Ernst Troeltsch has indicated that a belief in the imminence of Christ's return weakened the desire of the early church

---

cently published by David B. Davis, I concur with the implications of his statement that "Few subjects in American history are in such need of rigorous analysis as the interrelationship of specific reform movements and the transition from an evangelical drive for social control to a romantic and humanitarian crusade for liberty, uplift, and social justice." See Davis, ed., *Ante-Bellum Reform* (New York, 1967), Introduction, p. 9. Like Davis, I also recognize the conceptual inadequacies of terms like "conservative," "liberal," and "radical" in analyzing reform movements, but I have no better ones to propose.

[7] Davis, *Ante-Bellum Reform*, Introduction, p. 6.

[8] Sidney E. Mead, *Nathaniel William Taylor, 1786–1858: A Connecticut Liberal* (Chicago, 1942), pp. 58–9.

to rectify earthly conditions, which were destined soon to pass away; he has also shown that a far different result was produced in later times by a belief that people could prepare the way for the second coming by establishing, so far as lay within their ability, a secular order consistent with the Savior's teachings.[9]

For a proper understanding of reform efforts by American Protestants in the late eighteenth and early nineteenth centuries, however, it is especially pertinent to note the impact of influences associated with New England Puritanism. Calvinist in theology, Puritans believed in an all-powerful and all-sovereign God who before time began had arbitrarily predestined certain individuals to salvation and others to eternal damnation. Although determining who belonged to the elect and who did not was difficult, the Puritans believed that one might gain reasonably conclusive evidence by examining one's life and behavior for signs of a conscious willingness to serve as an instrument for the realization of divine purposes. People who were desperately eager to believe themselves among the saved endured an agony of mind and spirit that could produce an intense, driving activism in everyday affairs. It was logical to believe that people who had been singled out by God to be special recipients of His grace also had a mandate to govern the affairs of men, and this attitude was therefore capable of producing a distinctively paternalistic reform impulse.

Yet to see only the authoritarian aspects of Puritanism in its bearing upon social reform would be to oversimplify and distort the past. One must also acknowledge that many elements of Calvinist thought in early New England, such as individualism, an emphasis upon a higher law superior to the claims of earthly powers and institutions, and a belief that divine grace was visited upon people irrespective of social class or station, produced a liberalizing and democratic effect. Similarly, the idea that education must be available to all citizens in a Bible-reading commonwealth was shared by many Puritan leaders. Nor should it be forgotten that, although many aspects of Puritanism may seem harsh by modern standards, it possessed a "moral vigor," to use Clinton Rossiter's words, that contributed a healthy sense of communal responsibility to the development of American democracy.[10]

Although the moral earnestness characteristic of Calvinism

[9]Ernst Troeltsch, *The Social Teaching of the Christian Churches*, Olive Wyon, trans. (2 vols.: New York, 1931), passim.

[10]Clinton Rossiter, *The First American Revolution* (New York, 1956), p. 94.

was manifested in the Middle Atlantic and southern colonies by Scotch-Irish Presbyterians and others, these groups never brought about a church-state alliance, in part because of the prior arrival of other settlers and the fact that Anglicanism was already established in many colonies. The case was different in New England, however, where Puritan Congregationalists were first on the scene and able to implement their plans for a model Biblical commonwealth in the American wilderness.

In such colonies as Connecticut and Massachusetts, church and state were tightly connected. Political power was reserved for those who possessed membership in a congregation, and membership in turn was extended only to "visible saints" who could give satisfactory evidence of having experienced saving grace.[11] The connection between religion and the secular order was rationalized at every level in terms of a complicated "federal theology" involving a series of covenants between believers and God on an individual plane, between congregations and God on a group basis, and between the entire commonwealth and God on a still broader scale.[12] These New Englanders believed that God had chosen their settlements for the realization of special purposes, just as He had once set apart the Hebrew nation. The faithful were urged constantly to examine not only their own lives, but also those of their neighbors, in an effort to ensure that the conduct of the community would conform as closely as possible to Scriptural teaching.

Despite the tightly knit character of the theocracy that Puritan leaders had thus established, they had difficulty maintaining the type of piety they desired indefinitely. This was particularly true after the first generation, when settlers' common recollections of persecution in the mother country and shared hardships of emigration had promoted a degree of group cohesion that was never fully recaptured. Anxiety about sinful behavior among the inhabitants mounted as worldliness became more widespread and fewer people sought congregational memberships; in turn, worried ministers developed a distinctive type of sermon known as the "jeremiad," which warned that a chosen people who became guilty of backsliding could expect visitations of divine wrath. In

[11]For an illuminating discussion of this particular aspect of Puritan thought, see Edmund Morgan, *Visible Saints: The History of A Puritan Idea* (New York, 1963).

[12]The covenant theology is analyzed at length in Perry Miller, *The New England Mind: The Seventeenth Century* (New York, 1939), pp. 365–462.

addition, some clergymen, like Solomon Stoddard, deliberately relaxed standards of admission to the church, reasoning that if people were to be awakened spiritually it was necessary to keep as many of them as possible fully affiliated and thus potentially susceptible to religious teaching.[13]

With the spreading of special efforts to induce repentance and public rededication, a pattern of American revivalism gradually took shape, appearing sporadically from the late seventeenth century onward and bursting into flame during the celebrated Great Awakening, which began in the 1730s. Seasons of mass anxiety and conversion heartened many religious leaders but caused others to recoil when they observed that excesses of enthusiasm posed no less of a danger to established institutions than had the indifference of an earlier day. Some groups of "awakened" people split away from their congregations to join sectarian denominations or set up schismatic bodies of their own, often emphasizing the direct operation of divine grace to the point of denying the need for an educated clergy. The sermons of incendiary preachers, notably James Davenport, led to outbursts of mob action, such as a book burning in Connecticut, that seemed to presage assaults by the rabble upon existing social and economic arrangements. Endeavoring to shut what had proved to be a Pandora's box, various ministers wrote antirevival treatises and succeeded in dampening the fires of excitement at least temporarily.[14] In the future, the standing clergy would have to learn how to arouse spiritual renewal without endangering the security of the established order.

This dilemma, which is important for an understanding of the conservative reform efforts of the early national period, became ever more critical throughout the remainder of the eighteenth century, for spiritual indifference and ungodly behavior increased while the church became less and less capable of preserving its

[13]These and other developments are discussed in Perry Miller, *The New England Mind from Colony to Province* (Cambridge, Mass., 1953). For a work challenging the traditional interpretation of declension in New England churches and discussing more fully the innovations in church membership made in the second half of the seventeenth century, see Robert G. Pope, *The Half-Way Covenant: Church Membership in Puritan New England* (Princeton, N.J., 1969).

[14]See especially Edwin S. Gaustad, *The Great Awakening in New England* (New York, 1957), and C. C. Goen, *Revivalism and Separatism in New England, 1740–1800: Strict Congregationalists and Separate Baptists in the Great Awakening* (New Haven, Conn., 1962), passim.

traditional role in society. Attendance at divine worship fell off in the late colonial era, and ministers worried about the growing influence of Deism in popular thought. Then came the revolutionary years, accompanied by governmental instability, economic confusion, and complaints of excessive gambling, drinking, cursing, and lewdness amid the unsettling conditions that inevitably followed the movements of armed forces about the countryside. Next appeared the troubled postwar period, with depression stimulating discontent among the lower class and debtors, while further evidence of declining public morality aroused bitter complaints among clergymen like Timothy Dwight of Connecticut and Jedediah Morse of Massachusetts. The outbreak of the French Revolution intensified such anxieties, for it was now feared that subversive groups influenced by Jacobinism and other alien doctrines were plotting the overthrow of American institutions and poisoning the country with insidious propaganda. The growing strength of the Republican party under Thomas Jefferson also contributed to clerical concern, especially in New England. Considered a vehicle for atheism and French ideas, its Presidential victory in 1800 seemed to many pious citizens to indicate that a veritable day of doom was at hand.[15]

Imbued with ever mounting apprehensions, various Protestant leaders in New England and elsewhere began, during the closing years of the eighteenth century, to organize a powerful reform movement to counter the undesirable influences that they detected in American life. The task was not easy, for in some parts of the country certain denominations were engaged in a difficult process of reorganization following the breaking of former administrative ties with parent European bodies as a result of national independence. Anglicanism, though established by law in a number of colonies, had become increasingly enfeebled in the pre-revolutionary years, and the Protestant Episcopal Church, which

[15]Among older sources on the growth of ministerial fears during the Revolutionary and post-Revolutionary periods, see especially Charles E. Cuningham, *Timothy Dwight, 1752–1817* (New York, 1942), pp. 294–300, and Vernon Stauffer, *New England and the Bavarian Illuminati* (New York, 1918), pp. 13–141. For a more recent analysis, see Gary B. Nash, "The American Clergy and the French Revolution," *William and Mary Quarterly*, 3rd Ser., XXII, 3 (July, 1965), 392–412. Nash argues cogently that vehement clerical attacks upon the French Revolution did not appear in the United States until 1794 and 1795 and were then prompted by rising tides of irreligion, social disorder, and Jeffersonian political activity in America itself rather than by the actual situation prevailing in Europe.

succeeded it after independence, struggled both with organizational problems and with popular prejudice in areas where Tories had been especially prominent among its members. Furthermore, not all denominations were strongly imbued with a sense of need for involvement in secular affairs or identified with classes likely to lose from the weakening of established institutions. It is therefore not surprising that although the Protestant counteroffensive found support among prominent citizens in various parts of the country, it derived its main thrust from New England, where the tradition of an established church still survived and where the clergy still enjoyed considerable power and prestige in secular, as well as sacred, concerns.

By the late eighteenth century, the religious tenets characteristic of New England in the period preceding the Great Awakening had been modified in various ways. Some clerical leaders deemphasized strict predestinarian doctrines and were approaching a belief that God's grace was available to all who would earnestly seek it. Others, however, followed the preaching of Samuel Hopkins in stressing God's total sovereignty so much as to postulate that one must love Him to the point of glorying in one's own damnation if this proved to be His will. This concept of "disinterested benevolence" had an important bearing upon later reform movements, arousing an almost pathological self-abnegation among some converts. As Whitney Cross has pointed out, revivalists were to draw on both of these new tendencies and breed from them "an illogical, but effective, doctrine."[16] To men like Dwight, it made tactical sense to overlook "fine theological distinctions and subtleties" if this enabled conservatives to unite more effectively against such menacing forces as Jacobinism and infidelity.[17] Nevertheless, doctrinal differences, though submerged, remained latent among defenders of the standing order and would return to plague the conservatives in the future.

Though clinging to an official church-state connection in New England, leaders of the Protestant reform movement had no thought of attempting to secure such an arrangement in other parts of the country, which would have been impossible anyway in view of adverse popular sentiment and various constitutional safe-

[16]Whitney Cross, *The Burned-over District: The Social and Intellectual History of Enthusiastic Religion in Western New York, 1800–1850* (Ithaca, N.Y., 1950), pp. 27–28.

[17]Mead, *Nathaniel William Taylor*, p. 48.

guards. This did not mean, however, that there might not be achieved a strong unofficial alliance between organized religion and the several levels of government, particularly if political leaders who sympathized with the objectives of Protestant spokesmen could be maintained in power. Indeed, such an alliance seemed almost imperative to some clerical leaders, whose dislike of certain trends taking place in America did not prevent them from sharing a good deal of the nationalism that was emerging throughout the country at the time. From the venerable ideas of the federal-covenant theology, it was but a short step to the conviction that the United States had been chosen by God for the achievement of special purposes, but this meant also that it would feel the full force of His displeasure if it failed to live up to its divine commission. To minds influenced by such beliefs, it was inconceivable that organized religion should not have an important part to play in guiding the secular development of the young republic.[18]

II

Though confident that they were in league with the Almighty, Protestant reform leaders were under no illusions about the difficulties that lay in their path. For the better part of a generation, until the final downfall of Napolean in 1815, they were acutely conscious of a grave international threat to the principles in which they believed. During this period and for some time afterward, they were also intensely aware of the growth of egalitarian democracy at home, unrestrained by many of the barriers that existed in older, more aristocratic cultures. If this force could not be arrested—and it became increasingly clear that it could not— every effort would have to be made to inculcate in Americans a respect for order and propriety. This reform activity, if successful, would produce "inner controls" that might compensate for the wide external freedoms enjoyed by citizens of the United States. Otherwise, the result of unbridled popular rule could well be catastrophic.

---

[18] A useful book on ministerial attitudes toward social problems during this period is John R. Bodo, *The Protestant Clergy and Public Issues, 1812–1848* (Princeton, N.J., 1954), on which I have drawn at a number of points. See also Charles C. Cole, Jr., *The Social Ideas of the Northern Evangelists, 1826–1860* (New York, 1954).

These issues were portentous in the well-established and long-civilized areas along the Atlantic seaboard, but they were even more pressing in western regions to which increasing numbers of people were migrating during the late eighteenth and early nineteenth centuries. New England was experiencing such an outpouring as early as the 1780s, and the exodus accelerated in the years that followed. Protestant leaders recognized that life in the newly opened areas lacked the restraining influence of many institutions that were taken for granted in the better-settled parts of the country and feared a complete breakdown of established morals and amenities on the frontier unless immediate attempts were made to forestall it. A conviction that the fate of American democracy might well be decided by the outcome lent additional urgency to the struggle, accounting in large measure for the intensity with which western missionary ventures were organized and propagated by eastern congregations. Being adjacent to New England, upstate New York was a particularly favored target for such endeavors and became the scene of so many enthusiasms and revivals that it earned the name of the "burned-over district."[19]

The task of promoting civilization on the frontier, however, could hardly be performed if there was a further deterioration of manners and morals in the very citadels of organized Protestantism. To insure that this would not happen, religious leaders along the east coast launched a revival movement reminiscent of the earlier Great Awakening. In Connecticut, for example, Congregationalist ministers turned to the tactics of their Puritan predecessors and preached somber jeremiads about prevailing wickedness, resulting in an early wave of revivals that reached its peak in the years between 1797 and 1801. The desire to enkindle a moral renewal, however, was tempered by a remembrance of dangers that had appeared in the past. Mindful of the excesses that had taken place under such men as James Davenport, Connecticut clergymen made every effort to see that a desirable spiritual reinvigoration did not get out of bounds, to guard against the splintering of congregations, and to discourage violent outbursts of emotion. Whenever possible, revivals were conducted by resident pastors among their own flocks; when itinerant evangelists were needed, the choice fell upon sober,

[19]Cross, *Burned-over District*, passim. Chapters I–VII, pp. 3–137, are particularly relevant to the concerns and activities here described.

dignified men like Nathaniel Emmons and Asahel Nettleton. Under this careful approach, seasons of repentance and conversion took place regularly throughout the first three decades of the nineteenth century.[20]

Because of their realization that theological bickering would only weaken them in their fight against evil and subversive influences, Protestant reformers made a variety of moves to end unnecessary divisions and coordinate the activities of like-minded men on a national basis. The most significant step in this direction was the adoption of the widely hailed Plan of Union by New England Congregationalists and Presbyterians in other parts of the country beginning in 1801. Negotiated by two groups that differed over organizational methods but shared a Calvinist heritage, this arrangement applied to western areas into which Congregationalists and Presbyterians migrated, thus preventing wasteful duplication of effort. Another move toward unity took place in New England itself, where schisms within Calvinist ranks had facilitated the spread of Unitarianism. Bitterly hostile toward the latter, conservative leaders like Jedediah Morse were deeply chagrined when a lack of effective cooperation between Hopkinsians and "Old Calvinists" enabled the Unitarians to win the coveted Hollis professorship of divinity at Harvard in 1805. Partly as a result of this lesson, the two traditionalist groups joined forces by 1808 in the establishment of Andover Seminary in Massachusetts, which quickly became a leading center of conservative reform activity.[21] Princeton Seminary, founded shortly thereafter in New Jersey, and Auburn Theological Seminary, located in upstate New York, were similarly oriented.

The trend toward cooperation among Protestant groups, especially those of a conservative variety, was also exemplified in the formation of interdenominational societies patterned after English counterparts, which had been organized to combat the spread of French revolutionary ideas. Centered in the Anglican church, but maintaining a cooperative attitude toward various

[20]For a detailed account of revivalism in Connecticut during this period, see Charles R. Keller, *The Second Great Awakening in Connecticut* (New Haven, Conn., 1942), pp. 36–69. On the consciously conservative nature of the tactics used, see also Bernard Weisberger, *They Gathered at the River: The Story of the Great Revivalists and Their Impact Upon Religion in America* (Boston, 1958), pp. 53–86.

[21]William W. Sweet, *Religion in the Development of American Culture, 1765–1840* (New York, 1952), pp. 99–102; Mead, *Nathaniel William Taylor*, pp. 129–30.

nonconformist denominations, a strong counter-subversionist movement had emerged in Britain during the late eighteenth century, attacking radical influences through such organizations as the Religious Tract Society, which issued inexpensive devotional literature to the masses; the British and Foreign Bible Society, which distributed copies of the Scriptures; the London Sunday-School Union, which helped overcome illiteracy and thus promoted the reading of religious materials; and the London Missionary Society, which spread the Gospel abroad and gave supporters the invigorating feeling of participating in a worldwide crusade. The example of these societies was quickly emulated in the New World by Protestant organizations that first appeared on the state and local levels and we_e ultimately transformed into such large national ventures as the American Tract Society, the American Sunday School Union, the American Bible Society, and the American Home Missionary Society.[22]

Although these organizations welcomed members from various denominations, they were dominated by conservative leadership as represented by the Congregational, Presbyterian, Dutch Reformed, and Associated Reformed churches. In most of them, the bulk of official duties were performed by laymen, especially prominent politicians like Theodore Frelinghuysen of New Jersey and wealthy merchants like Robert Ralston of Philadelphia or Arthur and Lewis Tappan of New York. In some cases, the piety of Protestant businessmen was buttressed by a realization of the need for inculcating such virtues as sobriety, frugality, and diligence among the citizens of a country that was in the beginning stages of industrialization and that needed a dependable labor force as well as a maximum of saving in order to release capital for purposes of economic expansion. It is evident, too, that participation in the work of interdenominational societies and the reform organizations that came to be associated with them provided an outlet for the energies of people who yearned to accomplish something of transcedent worth but found this impulse difficult to satisfy in an increasingly secularized social order. The growth of egalitarianism and the erosion of traditional class lines, though feared by conservatives, also stimulated the development of benevolent and religious societies, for membership in these

[22]Foster, *An Errand of Mercy*, is particularly informative and detailed on the British counter-subversive movement and its influence upon similar developments in America.

groups and collaboration with like-minded people in a common cause created a sense of belonging that appealed strongly to individuals who felt uncertain about their status in the community at large. For various reasons, therefore, the Protestant campaign attracted widespread support among different types of people and quickly became a force of considerable power.[23]

II

The rise of tract, Bible, Sunday School, and missionary societies afforded means by which conservative reformers could inculcate piety among Americans in a general way. To such men, however, it was not sufficient merely to disseminate the Gospel, important as that objective might be; it was also necessary to apply Christian teachings to specific social evils and problems in an organized, effective manner. Accordingly, the Protestant offensive soon branched out into a variety of reform activities. These were promoted through the use of various techniques, ranging from subtle persuasion to outright coercion, but the end remained constant. If the United States were to achieve its God-given mission, if order and stability were to be preserved in a democratic nation, action was needed to bring social behavior into line with proper standards and values.

The implications of this attitude were quickly borne out in various aspects of American life, minor as well as major. Card playing, dancing, the use of tobacco, horse racing, and other practices that had earlier been regarded as harmless diversions were now branded as frivolous or hurtful forms of self-indulgence that had no place in a God-fearing nation.[24] The social effects of such beliefs were pervasive in many sections of the country for generations, especially in villages and small towns where the strictures

[23]The fullest account of the development and activities of American tract, Bible, Sunday School, and missionary societies is provided by Griffin, *Their Brothers' Keepers.* See also Cross, *Burned-over District,* pp. 126–30; Foster, *An Errand of Mercy,* passim; Colin B. Goodykoontz, *Home Missions on the American Frontier* (Caldwell, Idaho, 1939), passim; Keller, *Second Great Awakening,* pp. 94–130; and George M. Stephenson, *The Puritan Heritage* (New York, 1952), pp. 141–80.

[24]See particularly Dixon Ryan Fox, "The Protestant Counter-Reformation in America," *New York History,* XVI, 1 (January, 1935), 31. This short, well-written article anticipates some of the themes that were later to be developed systematically by Foster, Griffin, and other historians.

of Protestant conservatism retained force long after their influence had been weakened in urban centers. These standards of
behavior became badges of middle-class respectability for many
people and were accepted not only by believers with a Calvinist
heritage, but also by members of various sectarian groups whose
growth in numbers was accompanied by desires to escape previous lower-class associations. They were also vigorously inculcated among aspiring young businessmen who could keep their
eyes more firmly fixed upon the goal of financial success if their
attention was not diverted by various forms of extravagance and
dissipation.[25]

Many of the pressures exerted in behalf of social order and
decorum were applied in an undramatic, but nevertheless effective, manner through everyday discourse, the exhortations of
teachers and preachers, and the admonitions and disciplinary
tactics of parents imbued with the strict standards of conduct
propagated by conservative reformers. In other cases, however,
well-organized societies were created to reinforce conventional
methods of securing conformity with the power of systematic
group effort, leading, if necessary, to the enactment of legislation
aimed at specific evils. Such action was frequently manifested at
the town or village level in the form of blue laws prohibiting
certain minor practices deemed objectionable by local religious
leaders, but it was also exemplified on a state or national basis by
the appearance of concerted drives against forms of behavior
about which conservative spokesmen were particularly concerned, such as dueling, Sabbath-breaking, intemperance, and
outright crime. Although the societies that were formed to combat such evils enlisted members from various religious groups,
the influence of New England was again pronounced, especially
during the early stages of the attack.

One of the most noteworthy leaders in the Protestant reform
efforts of the early nineteenth century was Lyman Beecher, a
native of Connecticut. During his college years at Yale in the
mid-1790s, Beecher came under the influence of Timothy Dwight,
who had launched a revival movement among the students after
assuming the presidency of that institution in 1795. After gradua-
tion, Beecher entered the Congregational ministry and held a pas-

---

[25]On the place of such ideas in the nineteenth-century American business tradition, see especially Irvin G. Wyllie, *The Self-Made Man in America* (New Brunswick, N.J., 1954), passim.

torate on nearby Long Island, returning after a few years to his home state to take charge of the church at Litchfield. Here in 1806 he launched an attack upon the practice of dueling in a New Year's Day sermon cast in the best traditions of the New England jeremiad. Terming the custom, which had recently taken the life of conservative idol Alexander Hamilton, "a great national sin," he warned that God's judgment would surely be visited upon a country that tolerated its continuance. The sermon was published widely, and at a subsequent ecclesiastical meeting in New Jersey, Beecher urged the formation of antidueling societies, which were soon flourishing in a number of states. By 1818 Connecticut had become the first state to take legal action against the practice when its new constitution disqualified from voting any person convicted of participating in a duel. From this time onward, other states passed laws against the custom, leading to its ultimate disappearance from the American scene.[26]

Not all of the practices against which conservative reformers directed their fire, however, seemed as pernicious to their fellow citizens as that of dueling. Taking part in various light diversions on Sundays, for example, did not appear especially heinous to many persons who worked long and grueling hours on the other six days of the week. Nevertheless, to many ministers and laymen a strict observance of the Sabbath was a matter of vital concern if the United States was to set a proper example as a truly Christian nation. Laws demanding the cessation of many ordinary weekday activities on Sunday had existed in New England from colonial days and were also on the books in other parts of the Union. In this respect, a proper discharge of Protestant duty seemed to some degree to require the mere enforcement of statutes already in being rather than the enactment of new coercive measures, but Sabbatarians also seized upon new issues to dramatize their case.

At the local level, the fight for a strict observance of the Sabbath consisted, for the most part, of using various social pressures to see that citizens observed Sunday in a quiet and decorous manner, encouraging attendance at public worship, and employing legal or other means to prevent business transactions or other activities—especially recreations and amusements. One aspect of the movement, however, was national in scope and drew much attention to the cause. Sunday mail deliveries by federal post

[26]Anson P. Stokes, *Church and State in the United States* (3 vols.: New York, 1950), II, 5–12.

offices had stirred controversy in Massachusetts as early as the 1790s, and when Congress passed a law in 1810 requiring postal employees to process mail on every day of the week, a number of Protestant groups began to remonstrate vigorously. Beginning in 1814, Lyman Beecher organized a campaign of petitions to Washington on the issue; this movement spread rapidly and culminated in 1828 with the formation, at a large meeting in New York City, of the General Union for Promoting the Observance of the Christian Sabbath. Petitions bearing thousands of signatures were dispatched to the national capital from such places as New York, Boston, Albany, and Charleston, demanding the repeal of laws requiring post offices to stay open on Sundays, while in upstate New York boycotts were organized against transportation enterprises that ran on the sacred day. The crusade backfired, however, by arousing determined opposition from citizens who prized Sunday as a time of diversion from the grinding routine of weekday labor and resented what they regarded as theocratic attempts to dictate how it should be spent. In addition, liberal groups and such religious denominations as the Baptists assailed the effort to halt Sunday mail delivery as a blatant attempt to violate the separation of church and state. The controversy finally resulted in the submission of a report to Congress by Senator Richard M. Johnson of Kentucky roundly condemning religious interference with civil institutions. This document secured widespread endorsement throughout the country by state legislatures and private citizens alike. Thus one conservative reform effort encountered a humiliating defeat.[27]

By all odds the most intensive campaign to impose rigid new standards of behavior upon American society was the drive that began late in the eighteenth century to diminish, and ultimately to abolish, the use of alcoholic beverages.[28] During the colonial period, such drinks had been widely regarded as products of

[27]*Ibid.*, II, 12–30; Bodo, *Protestant Clergy and Public Issues*, pp. 39–43; Cross, *Burned-over District*, pp. 131–34.

[28]The following account of the temperance movement is based chiefly upon John A. Krout, *The Origins of Prohibition* (New York, 1925). Despite the continuing usefulness of Krout's book, an up-to-date historical analysis of the antebellum temperance movement would, I believe, be a worthwhile undertaking. Andrew Sinclair's excellent *Era of Excess: A Social History of the Prohibition Movement*, Colophon ed. (New York, 1964), deals chiefly with the post–Civil War era. For a commendable work on one particular antebellum temperance reformer, see Frank L. Byrne, *Prophet of Prohibition: Neal Dow and His Crusade* (Madison, Wis., 1961).

God's bounty, though subject to possible abuse. Nevertheless, a number of religious leaders like Increase and Cotton Mather, Jonathan Edwards, Anthony Benezet, and John Woolman had become greatly concerned about the sinfulness of imbibing to excess, while during the Revolution the physician-general of the Continental forces in the Middle Atlantic area, Benjamin Rush, had become convinced that many camp illnesses were aggravated by the use of liquor. After the war, Rush came to the conclusion that even the moderate use of ardent spirits was harmful, and he wrote a widely circulated treatise urging Americans to substitute malt drinks like beer and ale for distilled beverages. As the incidence of hard drinking continued to climb throughout the country despite such warnings, an organized campaign eventually got underway to combat it. The first temperance society in the United States was founded in 1808 by residents of the small community of Moreau in eastern New York under the leadership of a Congregationalist minister and a physician who had read Rush's writings. From this beginning there quickly flowered a movement that became a key element in the Protestant drive for a stable and virtuous America.

Throughout the growth of the temperance movement, there was much evidence of the fear that political democracy would degenerate into chaos unless means were taken to control the baser instincts of classes that were gaining powers once reserved for the privileged few. Drunkenness served to accentuate those aspects of irresponsible behavior that conservative reformers dreaded among elements of the population referred to by Lyman Beecher as the "ruff-scuff." As Joseph R. Gusfield has pointed out, the espousal of temperance also enabled upper-class elements to sharpen their feelings of difference from groups lower in society, serving to buttress a sense of status that was, in reality, already being eroded by the social changes that men like Beecher feared.[29] The Connecticut Society for the Promotion of Good Morals, founded by Beecher and others in 1813, was primarily devoted to temperance. The Massachusetts Society for the Suppression of

[29]Joseph R. Gusfield, *Symbolic Crusade: Status Politics and the American Temperance Movement* (Urbana, Ill., 1963), pp. 36–44 and passim. This is a valuable book, which, among other things, comments perceptively on many of the new elements and motives that appeared in the temperance movement during the 1830s and 1840s. However, it is essentially a sociological treatise based upon historical evidence that, through no fault of Gusfield, is in some spots relatively thin, underscoring once more the need for some fresh work in the field.

Intemperance, organized during the same period, performed similar work under the direction of prominent clergymen and wealthy merchants. Beecher gave the cause great impetus in a series of six sermons preached at Litchfield in 1825 and subsequently published throughout the country. Defining intemperance as any use—however moderate—of distilled liquors, and rejecting the idea of gradual withdrawal from the drinking habit through the use of such substitutes as wine, he called for "the banishment of ardent spirits from the list of lawful articles of commerce, by a correct and efficient public sentiment." The following year witnessed the formation of the American Society for the Promotion of Temperance, and by 1833 it was estimated that there were over four thousand societies devoted to the cause throughout the nation, with more than one-half-million members. The heart of the movement, however, remained in New England and upstate New York, while other centers of strength were particularly evident in areas to which Yankee settlers had migrated.

Space does not permit a detailed treatment of the later evolution of the temperance crusade, which ultimately became more strongly associated with such denominations as the Methodists than with the religious denominations that had originally been its strongest champions. This suggests a pronounced urge for middle-class status on the part of sectarian groups that had at first drawn most of their membership from the humbler elements of society. As Samuel P. Hays has shown, opposition to the sale of alcoholic beverages also became part of a rural attack upon the values of an increasingly urban society in the late nineteenth and early twentieth centuries.[30] If the movement derived its strength from a variety of impulses, however, it is important to note that even in its early stages, as Beecher's sermons indicate, it began to manifest strongly coercive strains that had been latent from the beginning in the attitudes of many conservative reformers. Initially confining themselves to the use of moral suasion, proponents of the cause eventually campaigned for laws banning the sale of all alcoholic beverages, resulting in prohibition statutes at the state, and ultimately the national, level. If people would not willingly listen to the advice of those who knew what was best for them, self-appointed custodians of their moral welfare were prepared to resort to naked force.

[30]Samuel P. Hays, *The Response to Industrialism, 1885–1914* (Chicago, 1957), pp. 114–15.

This spirit, which was implemented in the temperance drive only after considerable hesitation on the part of reformers who recognized the extent to which it conflicted with individual liberty, was manifested somewhat earlier in another variety of meliorative activity, involving the care and treatment of criminals.[31] America had been the scene of important correctional developments during the Revolutionary era, with Quakers playing an especially prominent role in securing the establishment of penitentiaries in which felons were confined over protracted periods of time instead of being subjected to the brutal methods of lashing, branding, ear cropping, and pillorying that formerly had been used. In the new institutions, disciplinary methods were generally mild, and the professed aim of treatment was to produce repentance and amendment of life.

These changes, however, did not fulfill the sometimes extravagant hopes of reformers who had expected the penitentiary to lessen the incidence of crime to a significant degree. Furthermore, a number of the prisons that were constructed in the first flush of enthusiasm for the new correctional techniques proved seriously defective in design. During the early nineteenth century, mounting crime rates in various parts of the country, coupled with lax discipline and internal disorder prevailing in many penitentiaries, led to increasing exasperation among private citizens and public officials alike. These conditions also contributed to the alarm of conservative reformers, who, not surprisingly, viewed lawbreaking and prison disturbances as further indications of the social unrest that they so greatly feared.

Thus the stage was set for a new type of prison reform, which contrasted sharply with the humanitarian efforts that had characterized the Revolutionary era. Vividly demonstrating the impact of impulses far different from those that had animated earlier penal experiments, the approach that now prevailed was best characterized at Auburn, a community located in the heart of the "burned-over district." Here, under a harsh, repressive despotism, convicts were kept in solitary confinement at night and forced to work together in absolute silence by day. Their lives were regulated to the tiniest detail, and any breach of discipline was immediately punished by flogging. Some officials at Auburn went so far as to ridicule the very idea of rehabilitation and based

[31]For a more extended discussion of the developments that follow, see Lewis, *From Newgate to Dannemora*, Chapters I–IV, pp. 1–110.

their practices exclusively upon a philosophy of deterrence, but others, like Gershom Powers, a native of New Hampshire who became warden in 1827, held that convicts could be reformed through hard work and religious influences after they had been thoroughly humbled and subdued by an initial "breaking" process. However it was justified in theory, the Auburn system spread rapidly throughout the United States and soon became the country's most widely used method of penal discipline.

The popularity of the Auburn system resulted partly from its relatively low cost of administration but was also enhanced by the support of conservative reformers who saw in it an ideal vehicle for the implementation of their beliefs. Chief among these spokesmen was Louis Dwight, a zealous New England Congregationalist who founded the Boston Prison Discipline Society and made it a powerful agent for disseminating propaganda concerning the new correctional methods developed in New York. An ardent exponent of temperance and Sabbatarianism, Dwight was attracted by the various features of a system that produced the tightest form of order and literally compelled men to be abstemious and industrious. Indeed, he was so impressed that he wanted to see the Auburn techniques applied not only in the treatment of convicts but also in the management of schools, orphanages, workshops, factories, and even private homes, where he believed such methods would promote "order, seriousness, and purity." Although the extent to which this advice was taken would be impossible to determine, it provides an excellent illustration of the lengths to which some conservative leaders were willing to go in imposing regimentation upon their fellow citizens.

Men like Louis Dwight were also concerned about another social evil, slavery, but seldom could bring themselves to propose its outright abolition. Although some people like Arthur and Lewis Tappan became abolitionists, most leaders of Protestant counter-subversion devoted themselves to the colonization movement, which aimed to solve the problem by removing Negroes, both slave and free, from America and transporting them back to Africa. This approach was particularly attractive to some Protestant reformers because it was assumed that the blacks, having been converted to Christianity in the United States, would form a powerful missionary spearhead when returned to their native continent. In addition, the colonization idea was easily reconciled with a belief in the slaveowner's property right in his human chattels until he had voluntarily emancipated them, and it skirted the difficult question of how American society could absorb large numbers of free Negroes in the event of widespread manumission. For such reasons, deportation retained considerable support among conservative leaders long after its impracticability had been demonstrated and its tenets rejected by slaveholders and abolitionists alike.[32]

In view of the circumstances that had inspired the Protestant offensive against unsettling influences in American society and the antisubversive attitudes of many of its proponents, it is not surprising that movements to protect the United States from allegedly dangerous foreign ideologies and other alien influences found willing recruits within the ranks of conservative reformers. The antimasonic crusade that began in upstate New York in 1826, after the abduction of William Morgan, drew much of its strength from the same denominations that supported other Protestant reform causes during the same period. During the late eighteenth century, Masonry had been popularly associated with the doctrines of the French Revolution, and one offshoot, the Order of the Bavarian Illuminati, had been particularly feared by the New England clergy. The antimasonic impulse was present in many Protestant groups, but, as Whitney Cross has shown in his pioneering study of religious enthusiasm in western New York, emigrant Yankees were among those most susceptible to its influence. The rhetoric of the cause was trenchantly exemplified in the writings of Lebbeus Armstrong, a minister whose treatise, *Masonry Proved to be a Work of Darkness*, was widely circulated throughout the country. The frequency with which devotees of Sabbatarianism and other conservative reform efforts were found among antimasons gave the movement a semireligious aura and led opponents to claim that it sought to reestablish a strong connection between church and state in America.[33]

---

[32]P. J. Staudenraus, *The African Colonization Movement, 1816–1865* (New York, 1961), is the standard general work on this subject, superseding previous accounts. See also Bodo, *Protestant Clergy and Public Issues*, pp. 112–51, for helpful supplementary information on ministerial attitudes.

[33]Stokes, *Church and State*, II, 20–25; Lorman A. Ratner, "Antimasonry in New York State: A Study in Pre–Civil War Reform" (unpublished M.A. thesis, Cornell University, 1958), passim; Cross, *Burned-over District*, pp. 74, 113–25, 135. On the "quasi-religious" nature of antimasonry, its church-and-state orientation, and its identification with such causes as Sabbatarianism, see also Lee Benson, *The Concept of Jacksonian Democracy: New York as a Test Case* (Princeton, N.J., 1961), p. 35. I am, however, skeptical about some of Benson's theories on the "leveling"

The same fears that contributed to the spread of antimasonry were also evident in the progress of hostility toward Roman Catholicism in the United States during the early nineteenth century. As the country experienced a rapid rise in immigration from Catholic sections of Europe after 1815, many Protestant leaders became convinced that a Papist conspiracy was endangering the security of American institutions. The "trusteeship controversy" of the 1820s, during which a number of Catholic laymen attempted unsuccessfully to wrest control of church property from the hierarchy, highlighted differences between Catholics and Protestants, and animosities were intensified by public debates and journalistic controversies that became increasingly common between spokesmen for the two groups. Leaders of conservative Protestant reform activity willingly enlisted in such hostilities; Lyman Beecher, for example, preached a series of bitterly anti-Catholic sermons in Boston in 1830 and returned in 1834 to deliver another set of addresses that helped fan the type of public animosity that led to the burning of the Ursuline convent in Charlestown later in the same year. Some Protestant spokesmen were also greatly alarmed about a supposed plot by Catholics to gain control of the Mississippi Valley through the activities of such European missionary societies as the Association for the Propagation of the Faith, prompting Beecher to write an inflammatory *Plea for the West* in 1835. To combat the alleged Papist menace, the interdenominational American Protestant Association ultimately was formed in 1842, paralleling earlier joint efforts in other spheres of concern.[34]

---

characteristics that he attributes to the antimasonic impulse. For a lucid discussion about the place of antimasonry among the counter-subversionist movements of the antebellum era, see David B. Davis, "Some Themes of Counter-Subversion: An Analysis of Anti-Masonic, Anti-Catholic, and Anti-Mormon Literature," *Mississippi Valley Historical Review*, XLVII, 2 (September, 1960), 205–24. Professor Ratner's *Antimasonry: The Crusade and the Party* (New York, 1969), based in part upon his unpublished M.A. thesis mentioned above, should be consulted by students interested in the movement. It contains valuable primary sources as well as an able introduction discussing the antimasonic crusade generally.

[34]This summary treatment is based chiefly upon Ray A. Billington, *The Protestant Crusade: A Study in the Origins of American Nativism* (New York, 1938), passim. See also Bodo, *Protestant Clergy and Public Issues*, pp. 61–84. Although nativist anti-Catholicism enlisted the support of people whose reform impulses were of a conservative nature, it also drew upon a radical anticlerical tradition whose influence has been underplayed in scholarly treatments of the subject. A fresh study of the extent to which this motivation was present, particularly in the latter decades of the antebellum period, would be a worthwhile project.

In assaying the impulses that underlay the Protestant reform activities of the early nineteenth century, it is instructive to examine not only the causes to which many clergymen and lay leaders gave vigorous support, but also the movements in which their energies were enlisted only weakly or not at all. In view of the fact that criticism of the War of 1812 had been widespread throughout New England, it is not surprising that some Congregationalists were temporarily active in the peace crusade shortly after the second conflict with Britain came to an end in 1815. Although a number of peace societies were formed throughout the country, however, apathy quickly set in and the movement would have collapsed but for the efforts of a handful of zealots who barely managed to keep it alive. Conservative religious leaders were especially quick to defect; in general, they were too heavily influenced by Old Testament concepts to endorse pacifism and ultimately came to feel that military conquest might provide one means of spreading the Gospel into unconverted regions. Thus, while the peace movement was strong for a time in Connecticut and a society was even formed at Andover Seminary, the cause never commanded the support given to tract, Bible, missionary, Sabbatarian, and temperance efforts.[35]

Even less popular among many conservative reformers were movements devoted to female rights, abolitionism, the elimination of capital punishment, and the rights of the working classes. Although such causes as temperance unquestionably provided outlets for female activity, it was impossible for counter-subversionist spokesmen to endorse the radical ideas of such people as Mary Wollstonecraft and Frances Wright, who argued for basic changes in the status of women and even for a modified approach to such institutions as marriage.[36] Similarly, abolitionism challenged deeply ingrained concepts of private property and threatened to split the Union itself, thus endangering the national destiny envisioned by many Protestant leaders. The use of capital punishment appealed to most conservatives as an excellent means of social control for intimidating would-be lawbreakers.[37] So far as the

[35]Merle Curti, *The American Peace Crusade, 1815–1860* (Durham, N.C., 1929), pp. 3–66; Bodo, *Protestant Clergy and Public Issues*, pp. 226–32.

[36]For perceptive insights on the ambivalence felt by many Protestant ministers toward the participation of women in charitable and reform activities at this time, see Keith Melder, "Ladies Bountiful: Organized Women's Benevolence in Early 19th Century America," *New York History*, XLVIII, 3 (July, 1967), 240–42.

[37]Opposition by the conservative clergy to the abolition of capital punishment was particularly intense during the 1840s, when the antigallows movement was

workingmen's movement was concerned, people like Beecher and his associates were too firmly committed to an aristocratic conception of society and too fearful of class struggle to countenance the activities of most labor leaders and found it easy instead to attribute the troubles of craftsmen and artisans to such causes as laziness, intemperance, and lack of thrift.[38]

However selective in its approach to social reform, the drive for an orderly and God-fearing nation was clearly a force of great significance in the development of American culture during the early nineteenth century. Representing what was left of a once powerful theocratic tradition, and exemplifying the conviction that the church still had a vital part to play in the conduct of secular affairs, a conservative reform coalition attempted through the use of voluntary associations and other means to protect social order and play the traditional role of an ecclesiastical establishment in a country that was rapidly abandoning all vestiges of the time-honored connection between church and state.

III

Despite the vigor with which this movement was prosecuted, however, and even though church membership in the United States increased greatly during the early nineteenth century, it was clear by the 1830s that the course of developments in America had shattered many of the ideas most deeply cherished by the champions of conservative reformism. Instead of providing an environment in which a traditionalist church could guide the destinies of an orderly commonwealth, conditions in the young republic had nourished ever greater tendencies toward competitive denominationalism in a society characterized by ceaseless and

---

reaching its crest on waves of romanticism and humanitarianism that had been unleashed in the United States by that time. See David B. Davis, "The Movement to Abolish Capital Punishment in America, 1787–1861," *American Historical Review*, LXIII, I (October, 1957), 23–46. Like some other types of conservative activity stemming from social-control motivations that persisted in the late antebellum period, this ministerial effort in my opinion has something of a "rear guard" character in an age when the dominant reform impulses were considerably different from those that had prevailed during the earlier heyday of the Protestant counter-offensive.

[38]Bodo, *Protestant Clergy and Public Issues*, pp. 175–76.

often bewildering change. Conservative teachings still tinged to some extent with a predestinarian heritage were proving less and less attractive to the citizens of a democratic nation, who preferred instead to identify themselves with religious groups preaching that grace was freely available to all. Voluntary societies, employed with great effect by orthodox spokesmen, were also organized by reformers who operated on different premises and often turned bitterly on church leaders for their unwillingness to endorse radical solutions to such problems as slavery. Class distinctions that had once seemed fundamental were overwhelmed in a rising tide of egalitarianism, and the maintenance of traditional ethical standards was complicated by the emergence of a highly speculative economy toward which the government took an increasingly laissez-faire attitude. Despite a generation of concerted effort by various Protestant reformers, events were still moving in a direction calculated to arouse alarm among conservatives.

Although space will not permit a detailed examination of these trends, some aspects deserve brief attention. One of these was the final collapse in New England of the church-state connection that had survived there despite being swept away elsewhere in the Revolutionary era. In Connecticut, a mounting campaign against the Congregational establishment by Methodists, Baptists, Episcopalians, and other dissenting groups culminated in the adoption by 1818 of a new state constitution making the support of religion a voluntary matter. In 1819 legislation was enacted in New Hampshire making it impossible to coerce dissenters to pay for the support of a standing clergy, as had previously been done in some localities. In Massachusetts, the struggle between Unitarians and more theologically conservative elements so weakened what was left of the church-state connection that a constitutional amendment was overwhelmingly passed in 1833 ending the establishment and leaving a voluntary system in its place. Along with the demise of the Federalist party in the 1820s, these events eliminated any hope for an effective coalition between conservative religious leaders and political authorities in the supervision of public affairs at the state level.[39]

_____

[39]Keller, *Second Great Awakening*, pp. 188–89; Charles B. Kimmey, Jr., *Church and State: The Struggle for Separation in New Hampshire* (New York, 1955), pp. 107–18; Jacob C. Meyer, *Church and State in Massachusetts from 1740 to 1833* (Cleveland, 1930), pp. 201–20.

If the church of the Puritan fathers was now only one of many competing denominations in New England, divided within itself and forming a minority caught between growing Protestant sects on the one hand and a rapidly increasing Roman Catholic population on the other, its position was certainly no better elsewhere in the country. Despite the Plan of Union and other tactical measures, the Congregational and Presbyterian churches lacked the growth potential of other varieties of Protestantism in a nation in which power was ever more closely associated with numbers. The chief beneficiaries of the religious harvest in the west, and in other parts of the country as well, were the Methodists and Baptists, who had no fear of the common masses, did not emphasize an educated clergy, and welcomed excesses of emotionalism in revivals that repelled many traditionalists.[40]

Furthermore, by the 1830s it was clear that many who still remained within the organizational confines of the Calvinist churches were badly infected with unorthodox ideas. This was especially true in upstate New York, where Charles G. Finney had enjoyed spectacular success conducting revivals far different from those presided over by people like Asahel Nettleton and Nathaniel Emmons. Finney's "New Measures," as they came to be called, included the use of protracted and spiritually agonizing prayer meetings, the singling out of unconverted sinners by name, the use of an "anxious bench" where people in a state of near-conversion could obtain special assistance from the preacher and his helpers, the encouragement of speaking by women, and the employment of other techniques for the production of emotional conversion. Although theoretically within the fold of the Congregationalist-Presbyterian alliance established by the Plan of Union, Finney openly flouted various Calvinist tenets, repudiating the doctrine of predestination altogether and declaring that any man could lay hold of salvation if he were willing to accept the redemption that God freely offered him.[41]

Despite the controversy that they aroused, Finney's practices

[40]See Winthrop S. Hudson, *American Protestantism* (Chicago, 1961), pp. 97 ff. Calvinist doctrines were still widespread among Baptists in 1830 but became steadily less so. As Hudson comments, "by 1850 Evangelical Protestantism had become defined almost wholly in Methodist terms" (p. 99).

[41]Among various treatments of Finney and his "New Measures," see especially Cross, *Burned-over District*, pp. 151–84; William G. McLoughlin, Jr., *Modern Revivalism: Charles Grandison Finney to Billy Graham* (New York, 1959), pp. 11–121; and Weisberger, *They Gathered at the River*, pp. 87–126.

and ideas were not really as revolutionary as they seemed.[42] In areas like western New York, as Whitney Cross has pointed out, some of the "New Measures" had already appeared before Finney started conducting his revivals. And in New England, the disciples of Timothy Dwight had fallen increasingly under the influence of ideas that Finney merely preached in unequivocal form and with greater dramatic flair. In the conservative Connecticut bastion of New Haven, Nathaniel W. Taylor, a Congregationalist minister who had at one time been Dwight's personal secretary, developed a theology that was ostensibly Calvinist but nevertheless conceded a degree of human ability to lay hold of divine grace, which ill comported with rigid predestinarianism. Lyman Beecher, a close friend of Taylor's, was in sympathy with his ideas. But other conservative clerical leaders in the Nutmeg State were not and began a revolt that exposed some of the theological differences that Timothy Dwight had tried to deemphasize. The news of Finney's revivals helped to trigger this important development, with divisive consequences for the Protestant reform front.

Lyman Beecher himself was somewhat disturbed by reports of the sensationalism and emotional upheaval that accompanied Finney's revivals, but men like Asahel Nettleton were horrified by them and demanded some form of action by New England clergymen against the spread of the "New Measures." Finney's methods seemed reminiscent of those adopted by such preachers as James Davenport at the time of the Great Awakening and furthermore smacked of the rising turbulence of Jacksonian democracy. The fact that Finney was neither a college graduate nor a trained theologian was an additional source of alarm to settled clergymen who clung to traditional ways.[43] Beecher was sensitive to

[42]The analysis that follows is drawn principally from Cross, *Burned-over District*, passim, and Mead, *Nathaniel William Taylor*, pp. 200–21.

[43]On the congruence between Finney's outlook and various currents of popular thought and ideology that were beginning to appear strongly in America at this time, including those associated with the rise of Andrew Jackson, see especially the portions of McLoughlin's introduction to Finney's *Lectures on Revivals of Religion* (Cambridge, Mass., 1960), reprinted in Davis, *Ante-Bellum Reform*, pp. 97–107. As Davis notes, this congruence does not indicate that Finney himself was one of Jackson's followers or was any less conservative in many of his social and economic beliefs than the New Englanders who responded to his sudden rise to prominence with a measure of alarm; rather, it helps us to see how Finney's thought "could inspire far more radical reformers than himself" (p. 97). For another assessment of the differences between Finney and his predecessors and of

these fears but found himself in a tight spot. He was trying to keep the conservative coalition alive, particularly against the spread of such dangers as Unitarianism, which had been making alarming strides in New England, and he badly needed the support of Nettleton and his associates. On the other hand, he felt that he could not support drastic action against Finney without giving aid and comfort to the enemies of revivalism and impugning some of his own theological beliefs in the process.

It was not surprising, therefore, that when a face-to-face encounter with Finney and a delegation of his followers was arranged in 1827 at New Lebanon in eastern New York at Nettleton's behest, Beecher and his New England supporters disappointed Nettleton by temporizing with the upstart revivalist and settling for a truce rather than risking an open break with him. Finney's behavior did become somewhat more moderate over the course of the next few years, but many western preachers who followed his leadership were even more quick than he once had been to resort to new techniques for stimulating mass conversions; during the 1830s the worst fears of people like Nettleton were realized when such areas as upstate New York became hotbeds of "ultraist" beliefs among those whom Finney had helped to evangelize. Within a decade of the New Lebanon meeting, differences between Finneyite "New Lights" and more traditionalist Presbyterian-Congregational elements became so pronounced as to undo the Plan of Union and create factions that were to struggle bitterly with one another until after the Civil War. Meanwhile, Finney's beliefs led him into a type of Christian perfectionism that proved far more amenable to such radical causes as abolitionism than the ideas of the conservative reformers ever had been and that was in time drawn upon as a source of inspiration by American labor leaders in the late nineteenth century.[44]

In brief, although some continuities can be observed between the antisubversive crusades of the post-Revolutionary period and

---

the reasons why his tactics aroused fear in some quarters, see Perry Miller, *The Life of the Mind in America from the Revolution to the Civil War* (New York, 1965), pp. 22–35.

[44]See especially Herbert G. Gutman, "Protestantism and the American Labor Movement: The Christian Spirit in the Gilded Age," *American Historical Review*, LXXII, No. 1 (October, 1966), 83.

developments transpiring after the dawn of the Jacksonian age, it is clear that by the 1830s the crest of conservative Protestant reform activity had been reached.[45] The work of interdenominational, Bible, and missionary societies went on, but money was increasingly drained off into strictly sectarian, competitive enterprises, and the Panic of 1837 also dried up some sources of funds upon which previous conservative efforts had depended. The temperance movement enjoyed a growing influence, but the failure of the attempt to halt Sunday mail delivery had already dealt Sabbatarianism a heavy blow. In the field of penal reform, the heyday of the Auburn system was past by the mid-1830s, and developments in New York and elsewhere entered a new phase marked by the emergence of environmental concepts of criminality that alarmed traditionalists because they threatened long-accepted ideas about human guilt and freedom of the will. The colonization movement had entered a moribund state and was rapidly giving way to abolitionism, which most conservative religious leaders could not endorse. Above all, the development of a democratic society in an age of emergent laissez-faire capitalism had destroyed whatever hope had once existed for a stable commonwealth evolving in an orderly manner under the restraining hands of a paternalist government in open alliance with established religious institutions. In such respects as these, American life continued to produce a distinctively pluralistic culture that, however extensive its borrowings from other sources, possessed a vitality uniquely its own.

[45]Clifford S. Griffin's brief interpretative study, *The Ferment of Reform, 1830–1860* (New York, 1967), contains the best summary in print of the historiography of antebellum social reform movements and presents a number of acute and cogent insights about the varieties and consequences of reform activity. Despite its very considerable merits, however, it fails to perceive the crucial differences between the dominant reform impulses of the late antebellum era, which usually manifested a receptive attitude toward fundamental social change, and the conservative impulses that characterized the period from about 1795 to about 1830.

NORTHERN AND SOUTHERN WAYS OF LIFE AND THE CIVIL WAR

Carl N. Degler / **STANFORD UNIVERSITY**

The United States is the only country that required a civil war to eradicate slavery. It is true that the slaves emancipated by the European nations were to be found only in the colonies, a fact that certainly made emancipation politically and socially easier than it would otherwise have been. Yet imperial Russia managed to emancipate the serfs in 1861 without civil war, even though great economic and social interests were at stake. More pertinent still are the examples of abolition in Latin America, where the social and racial circumstances were analogous to those in the United States. Of all the comparisons with the experience of the United States with slavery, that of Brazil is probably the closest. Brazilian slavery, like that in the Southern states of the United States, was an integral and important part of the economy, providing the principal labor supply for the production of the chief exports of the country. Also, in Brazil, as in the United States, there was an aggressive abolitionist movement that carried on its campaign for years. In fact, abolition in Brazil was not finally achieved until 1888, some two decades after emancipation in the United States. Yet, unlike the United States, Brazil managed to rid itself of slavery without civil war.

There are at least two inferences that might be drawn from the uniquely violent conclusion to slavery in the United States.

One is that slavery was more deeply and firmly established in the United States than anywhere else and hence required more strenuous efforts to remove it. The other is that the necessity for civil violence was a measure of the weakness of American nationalism. For no matter how else one might view the Civil War in the United States, it was at least a failure in the building of a nation.

The first inference can be disposed of rather quickly. It is not really possible, of course, to measure precisely the relative firmness with which slavery was embedded in American and Brazilian society. But the general measures that might be used suggest that, if anything, slavery was more firmly established in Brazil than in the United States. Slaves made up a larger proportion of the laboring force in Brazil, slavery lasted longer there, and the importance of slave labor in the total economy was at least as great as in the United States. The ending of slavery, moreover, was one of the principal causes for the bloodless fall of the monarchy and the establishment of the republic the following year.

Why then was a civil war necessary only in the United States? Certainly it was not that slavery was shored up by public opinion at home or abroad. Indeed, by the middle of the nineteenth century all European nations not only had abolished the institution but looked upon it as outmoded and cruel. In the United States and wherever else it existed, it was under attack from every angle, being denounced as un-Christian, inefficient, undemocratic, and contrary to natural law. Why, we ask again, was American nationalism so fragile that it could not accommodate a social change that all the civilized world supported and peacefully carried out? The answer to the question goes to the heart of American cultural development in the generation prior to 1860.

The explanation must begin with the size of the country and the rapidity with which it was settled. For half a century or more prior to 1860, Americans were a people in motion. As they moved west of the Appalachians they created, in less than a person's lifetime, not only several countries, as measured by European standards, but several cultures as well. As early as the 1820s Americans recognized that their sprawling country was divided into three quite distinct regions—East, West, and South. The nationalism aroused by the War of 1812 soon proved to be premature; the Era of Good Feelings dissolved in the face of Eastern demands for a protective tariff, Western demands for internal improvements, and Southern objections to both. The three sections did not quite follow Thomas Cooper's cynical advice to "calculate the value of the Union," but each clearly consulted its own interests and rejected any others that seemed to limit its freedom of development. Moreover, the traditional forces of national cohesion so evident in Europe were few in the United States. In fact there were no really national organizations of any strength to knit together a country spread across great distances in an age of slow, uncertain travel and overland communication. There was no national bench or bar, no established church, no labor organization or business group of national extent. Even the major Protestant churches split apart in the 1840s.

But the customary emphasis upon a tripartite division obscures a deeper social cleavage in American culture. Southerners and Westerners, it is true, in the 1830s and 1840s spoke of their common agricultural interest as distinguished from the growing commercial and industrial interest of the East. Hindsight, however, now allows us to see that the West was not essentially different from the East. In the years between 1820 and 1860 the social and economic differences between the East and West gradually, yet significantly, lessened. Part of the weakening of differences is attributable to improved communications, like the Erie and other canals in the 1820s and 1830s and the extensive east-west railroad construction in the 1850s. But the most important reason was less measurable. It was that the two regions were divided by little except time. Give the West a generation and it would reproduce the social and cultural forms and values of the East, as in fact it did. Its small towns became cities, its shops factories, its river and lake ports bustling centers of commerce, and its agriculture increasingly commercial and scientific. The West's cultural values and economy were modeled after those of the East. By the 1850s, there were only two sections, culturally speaking, the North and the South. And the most obvious difference between them was that in one slavery and the plantation flourished while in the other the plantation was absent and slavery was almost gone.

I

The slave plantation originated in the tobacco areas of seventeenth-century Virginia and Maryland and in the eighteenth-century rice and indigo regions of South Carolina and Georgia. When the plantation with its slave labor force was adapted to cotton culture in the early nineteenth century it spread westward, for climate prevented cotton from being grown in the northwest. Thus new Southern states like Alabama, Mississippi, and Tennessee drew their values, not from the commercializing and industrializing East, but from the rural, slave society of the Southern seaboard states.

It is debatable when Southerners first began to be viewed as different from other Americans, but certainly differences were already being noticed and commented upon early in the nineteenth century. At the time of the Missouri Compromise debates in 1820, for instance, both Northerners and Southerners recognized that slavery set the South apart. It is possible, of course, to exaggerate the cultural differences between the North and the South before the Civil War, as some historians have warned. For even at the height of the sectional conflicts of the 1850s, Southerners and Northerners still spoke the same tongue, read the same literature, looked back upon a common past, worshipped in the same Protestant manner, and praised the same Constitution. But these shared interests are broad categories; within virtually all of them, as we shall see, there were differences between Northerners and Southerners that in truth resulted in two ways of life.

The mere fact that slavery and the plantation flourished in one region and not in the other was only the beginning of the divergence. For, as we shall see, the differences in labor system (slavery) and agricultural organization (plantation) produced still other, and more enduring, cultural differences. Even after slavery was gone those cultural values and traits would remain, much as the waves of a pond lap the shore long after the stone that produced them has sunk below the surface. The ways of life that a society evolves may begin with one set of circumstances, but they find justification and perpetuation through long familiarity, usefulness, and sheer habit. And so it was with the Southern tradition that grew up around the slave plantation.

Let us look now at some of the immediate ways in which slavery set off the South from the North; later, we will examine some of the more remote cultural effects of the South's "peculiar institution." Whether slavery existed or not, Southerners probably would have grown their distinctive crops of cotton and tobacco, though probably not sugar and rice, since the latter two required large work forces. The importance of slavery is that it wedded the South to the extensive cultivation of these staples. Slavery provided an agricultural labor supply that was otherwise difficult, if not impossible, to secure in a new country where land was plentiful and cheap and labor was scarce and expensive. By providing a ready labor supply, slavery made the plantation possible, thereby providing a source of quick wealth and perpetuating a rural society.

There were other ways in which the peculiar agriculture of the South set the region apart from the North. The very crops that the slaves produced were uniquely Southern, for cotton, sugar, and rice could be grown only in the South and tobacco and hemp found their best localities there. Moreover, cotton was almost entirely sold abroad; indeed, Southern crops as a whole constituted about two-thirds of the total exports of the United States in the antebellum years. The market for Western wheat and pork, on the other hand, was primarily domestic. Thus the facts of trade compelled the South to look outside the country, while the same facts of trade brought the East and West together.

Furthermore, the very concentration of slaves in one section, which was largely the accident of geography and the world demand for cotton, made it inescapable that once slavery became a social and political issue, it would also be a sectional bone of contention. As such it could not help but threaten the unity of the nation as it would not if it had been spread throughout the country. In Brazil, for example, where slavery was legal in all states until within four years of final emancipation in 1888, sectional conflict over abolition was late in developing and therefore constituted no threat to national unity.

But slavery did more than polarize political and moral opinion; it encouraged Southerners to build a system of values and a society that were different from those of the North. What began often as defenses of slavery ended as cherished parts of a Southern tradition that came to be defended for their own sake, regardless of origins.

As an anachronism in the middle of the nineteenth century, slavery naturally provoked attacks from many quarters. Just as naturally, such criticism evoked defensive measures by Southerners to protect their "peculiar institution," as they aptly referred to slavery. Sometimes it is argued that Southerners defended slavery only because it was attacked by outsiders, that if left alone Southerners would have found the institution unworthy of defense. Undoubtedly much of the animus and bitterness evident in the developed proslavery argument of Southerners stemmed from those alien criticisms. But the roots of the Southern defense of slavery go deeper than simple resentment of criticism. For one thing, slavery was economically important to the prosperity of the region, a fact that in itself generated a strong defense. Perhaps as much as 75 percent of the Southern cotton crop was produced by slave labor; virtually all of the sugar, rice, and hemp crops and most of the tobacco came from the labor of slaves. In short, despite the fact that about three-quarters of Southern families did not own a single slave and that plantations made up less than 20 percent of the agricultural units of the region in 1860, slavery was central to the production of Southern wealth. The rising price curve for slaves during the last antebellum decade further attests to the economic value that Southerners placed upon slavery.

The peculiar institution provided more than wealth for the South; it also helped to preserve the supremacy of the white man. Southerners did not need slavery to make them believe that blacks were inferior to white men. That prejudice antedated slavery. But slavery certainly reinforced the Southerner's sense of superiority by making the typical black man a legal chattel. It served the additional end of providing the means for keeping the white man on top. Whether slaveholder or not, most Southern whites defended slavery because it controlled and subordinated blacks. Even Southern white men who opposed slavery could not really imagine what to do with blacks if they were not slaves. As one back-country Southerner confessed to Frederick Olmsted, the northern traveler in the South during the 1850s: "I wouldn't like to hev 'em free, if they gwine to hang around . . . because they is so monstrous lazy." Besides, he continued, "How'd you like to hev a nigger steppin' up to your darter? Of course you wouldn't; and that's the reason that I wouldn't like to hev 'em free; but I tell you, I don't think it's right to hev 'em slaves so; that's the fac—taant right to keep 'em as they is."[1]

As will be evident a little later, a belief in Negro inferiority was not peculiar to Southerners; Northerners held similar views. What made the South distinctive was its defense of slavery as the proper status for blacks. In advancing that defense against the criticisms, not only of Northern antislavery people, but of the modern world as well, the South differentiated itself from the rest of the western world. In fact, by defending slavery as a desirable thing, South-erners sacrificed cultural values they had once shared with the rest

[1]Frederick Law Olmsted, *The Cotton Kingdom* (Arthur M. Schlesinger, ed., New York, 1953), p. 225.

of the country, like freedom of speech, the right to dissent in politics and religion, and toleration of the opinions of outsiders. In North Carolina, for example, a Southern professor at the university who dared to say he intended to vote Republican in 1856 was dismissed and forced to leave the state; in Kentucky, a Southern newspaper editor who publicly opposed slavery saw his press destroyed. Farther south, in South Carolina, where there was no local dissent, postmasters destroyed any abolitionist literature that came through the mails. In Congress in the 1830s Southern representatives insisted that all Northern abolitionist petitions be barred because of their hostility toward a cherished Southern institution. Freedom of inquiry and dissent stopped in the antebellum South where the security of slavery began. Moreover, the beatings and mob action that accompanied this search for security bequeathed to the region, even down to our own time, a tradition of violence and extralegal action that has been a burden and a characteristic of the South.

In the early years of the nineteenth century, it was New England that was the conservative region while the South was the home of free-thinking Thomas Jefferson and social progress. (Before 1820, for example, most antislavery societies were in the South.) But in the middle of the nineteenth century a society organized around slavery and the plantation could not be progressive and flexible; its ways were too much at odds with those of the rest of the world. Reform and change, which had been cherished words for Jefferson, became dangerous ones in the South of John C. Calhoun. During the 1830s and 1840s all kinds of reforms, from women's rights to phrenology, engaged the restless minds of Northerners, but in the South reform was shunned, for it might endanger slavery. Some Southerners even took public pride, as one North Carolina editor wrote, in being free from "the isms which infest Europe and the Eastern and Western states of the country." In this connection, it is significant that only two of the one hundred or more utopian communities that were established as a result of the reform outburst of the early nineteenth century were located in the South. Utopias were not for down-to-earth, realistic Southerners.

Southerners may have been Protestants like most other Americans, but as the need to defend slavery mounted in the 1830s and 1840s, Southern Protestantism became increasingly conservative. At one time, Jefferson had supported and urged upon his fellow Southerners the widespread acceptance of the radical Unitarian church. But by 1860 that church was no longer to be found in the conservative South, though it flourished in New England. Instead, Southerners turned to a narrow and literal interpretation of the Bible, just as in politics they turned to a literal interpretation of the Constitution. In 1817, when he was still a nationalist, John C. Calhoun told Congress, "I am no advocate for refined arguments on the Constitution. The instrument was not intended as a thesis for the logician to exercise his ingenuity on. It ought to be construed with plain, good sense."[2] But, as is well known, by the 1840s and 1850s Southerners were construing the Constitution narrowly and literally.

A literal interpretation of a traditional document, whether the Constitution or the Bible, is typical of a conservative cast of mind, for insistence upon the letter of the law discourages innovations that might be introduced by interpretation. The narrow interpretation of the Constitution that Calhoun used to defend slavery, other Southerners used later to frustrate reform in other areas. Southern religious leaders followed the same path, first looking to a literal interpretation of the Bible to defend slavery and then moving on to a fundamentalist position on questions of theology as well. Ever since, the South has been the principal locale of religious fundamentalism in the United States.

Earlier it was suggested that the South differed from the rest of the United States in its predominately rural character. Let us look more closely now at the causal connection between that fact and the slave-plantation system. In the 1850s the South was the least urbanized of any section of the country, its only large cities being ports around its periphery, like Baltimore, New Orleans, St. Louis, and Louisville. Even when the region was compared with the agricultural West, it was conspicuously rural. In 1860, only 7 percent of all Southerners lived in cities as compared with twice that proportion in the West. In 1850 there were more cities over three thousand population in Indiana and Illinois alone than there were in the nine states south of Kentucky and Virginia. Arkansas counted not a single city of twenty-five hundred or more and Mississippi contained only two, each of which was less than five thousand.

One of the direct consequences of the rural character of the South was that the proportion of illiteracy among Southern white people was the highest of the three sections. The concentration of

[2]John C. Calhoun, *Works* (Richard K. Crallé, ed., New York, 1883), II, 192.

population necessary for a good school system was simply lacking. In 1850 one out of every five white Southerners was unable to read as compared with one out of ten in the Western states and one out of thirty-five in the Middle Atlantic states. (That these proportions were more a function of the rural character of the region than of hostility toward education was shown by the greater proportion of college students in the South than in either of the other two sections.)

The lack of cities in the South was largely the result of the failure to develop manufacturing in the region. There was some cotton textile manufacturing in Georgia, as well as the impressive Tredegar Iron Works and extensive tobacco manufacturing in Richmond, which were well known, but the region as a whole lagged behind even the new West in manufacturing. Again, the two western states of Illinois and Indiana in 1860 counted more capital invested in manufacturing than all seven states of the deep South combined. Basically, Southerners found staple agriculture a more profitable and a more socially rewarding field of activity than manufacturing or trade. The reason they did can be explained by slavery and the plantation. One of the necessary bases for the growth of manufactures is an adequate market. A society in which a quarter of the producing population is slaves does not provide a wide market since the slaves consume only the barest necessities. It is not surprising, for example, that Southern states with few slaves, like Kentucky, Missouri, and western Virginia, were the largest producers of manufactures in the South.

The narrowness of the Southern market also helps to account for the inability of Southern ports to maintain direct trade with Europe. Most foreign imports to the South came through New York and other Northern ports. Southerners resented the fact that few ships came to Charleston or New Orleans directly from Europe though Southern cotton paid for half of all United States imports. Southern importers had to pay for extra handling in New York as well as higher shipping charges because of the circuitous routing. This dependence on the North aroused Southern resentment; complaints about it appeared in all Southern demands for political independence. The lack of direct trade with Europe, however, was not the result of Northern conspiracy, as many Southerners contended; it was simply the economics of trade. It was unprofitable to run shipping lines to Southern ports when the markets there, because of slavery, were so meager.

The South's failure to develop manufacturing, however, was

not only a question of economics. As Southern society perpetuated its rural character through its commitment to slavery and the plantation, it also perpetuated and elaborated rural hostility toward industrial and commercial pursuits. As Southerners at the time pridefully said, the Southern gentleman was a landed man with slaves. Even a Southerner like William Gregg, the South Carolina cotton-mill owner, who wanted the South to do more manufacturing, feared the social changes industry would introduce. He advised, for example, that cotton mills be located in the country rather than in the cities, for Southern workers, he warned, would be corrupted by urban life.[3]

By retarding the growth of cities and manufacturing, the slave-plantation system shaped still further a distinctively Southern culture. The 1840s and 1850s witnessed a flood of German and Irish immigration into the United States, but the South saw few of the newcomers. There simply was little need for them on the plantations, and there were few cities to provide work for them. In 1860 less than 7 percent of the South's population was foreign born at a time when 12 percent of Ohio's and 33 percent of Wisconsin's were. No Southern state in 1860 counted as high a proportion as Ohio, and most were considerably below that figure. Thus, during the 1850s the South avoided both the negative and the positive effects of immigration that were then transforming the North. Socially, the South was fortunate in avoiding the nativist violence born of fear of the immigrant that erupted in Northern cities. But, more important, its economy lacked the skills and labor of the new arrivals, which gave an impetus to Northern economic growth in these same years.

The relative dearth of immigrants in the South, except in a few seaports like New Orleans and Baltimore, helped to make the already rural region still more provincial and isolated from world intellectual currents. That provinciality was further enhanced by the South's need to draw away from any outside contacts that might endanger the security of the slave system. Increasingly, connections with the North aroused suspicion, and opinion from abroad was stigmatized as irrelevant if it entailed adverse criticisms of Southern institutions. William Gilmore Simms, the South Carolina novelist, complained in 1846 that he was in danger of being defeated for public office in the coming election

[3]Quoted in Clement Eaton, *The Growth of Southern Civilization, 1790–1860* (New York, 1961), p. 229.

because of his frequent visits to the North. "The cry is that I am a Northern man," he despairingly wrote a friend, "that my affinities are with the North etc."[4] And defeated he was, even though the period of intense suspicion of Northern ties had not yet begun. By the late fifties a defender of the proposal to reopen the slave trade argued that the opinion "of the outside world on slavery is entitled to less weight than upon almost any other subject, being destitute of every foundation which renders opinion respectable."[5] His point was that no one was entitled to comment on the merits of slavery unless he or she lived under the system. To many Southerners by the close of the antebellum period, the world was out of step with the South.

Around slavery and the plantation, Southerners erected a distinctive way of life that reached its height in the Southern gentleman, whose charming manner, genteel and gracious style of living, and conservative leadership of the community became the ideal of the region. It is true that the so-called aristocrats of new states like Mississippi and Alabama were more often first-generation nabobs rather than the descendants of cavaliers, as the myths of the region asserted. But new and even crude as the society as a whole may have been—much of the Southwest was still frontier in the 1850s—the Southern planter was the social ideal. For despite the lowly origins of many of the great planters, the fact was that as owners of land and slaves they affected a way of life that fitted the classic ideal of the country gentleman and man of affairs. The semiliterate overseer who hoped one day to own a farm and slaves, the small commercial farmer who was saving for his second or third slave, or the village merchant who worked long hours to gain a competence for his old age, all looked to life on a plantation with a great house as the measure of ultimate success.

It is true that manufacturers, cotton factors, and storekeepers, all of whom were significant elements in the Southern economy, were generally not among the leaders of Southern life. Yet it would be a mistake to conclude from that fact that the South was dominated by a value system that scorned profit making or traditional business success. Perhaps the most striking single piece of evidence for rejecting that view is that, on the average, cotton planting produced a rate of profit for the planter that was fully comparable to what a similar investment would have earned in

[4]*Ibid.*, p. 297.
[5]*Ibid.*, p. 323.

the North. In short, planters averaged as good a return on their efforts as Northern businessmen, suggesting that Southerners were concerned with efficient business practices and the making of money. Rather than seeing the planters as inefficient operators, it would be more accurate to view them as among the best entrepreneurs of their region.

As the owner of many slaves, a great planter often developed a relationship to his workers that was foreign, if not distasteful, to a Northern manufacturer who dealt differently with his employees. But that difference was due less to noncapitalistic paternalism on the part of the planter and more to a rural man's method of dealing with the people who worked his land and who lived in close proximity to him—a situation that rarely occurred among factory owners and their workers in the North. Insofar as the outlook of a Southern planter and a Northern businessman differed, it was a difference of emphases rather than of kind. It was the difference between the outlook of a rural and an urban dweller, rather than the disparity between two sharply differentiated systems of values. At bottom what separated them, of course, was slavery. That was the source of the South's commitment to agriculture and the root of its social and economic divergences from the North. But the Southerner employed his slaves in a capitalistic way for capitalistic ends; in regard to fundamental social and political values, South and North were not at odds. The truth of that assertion is brought home when it is recalled that slavery was abolished by force in 1865 but the South accepted that result of war without resistance and even without protest. No significant figure in the postbellum South ever called for the restoration of slavery; in fact, many leading postbellum Southerners, themselves once slaveholders, publicly contended that the abolition of slavery had been a blessing for the region. Yet if slavery had been deeply engrained in a value system that was fundamentally different from the North's, the elimination of slavery would certainly have been lamented and resisted. Significantly, as we shall see a little later, the South did not acquiesce so easily to another decree from the North, also backed by military power, namely, the command to accept blacks as voters and civil equals. That attempt to overturn Southern values was resisted vehemently during the ten years of Radical Reconstruction.

The rurality to which slavery held the South encouraged Southerners to develop a way of life that set them apart in other ways besides the differences in the relationships between a master and his "people" on the one hand and between a factory owner and his "hands" on the other. The planter ideal looked back to earlier rural societies and traditions, causing some Southerners to emulate practices that were feudal in both origin and tone. Reenactments of medieval joustings, in full knightly regalia, were not unknown in the Old South, for Sir Walter Scott and his medieval romances were highly thought of since they extolled a hierarchical, rural society, which Southerners liked to think was similar to their own slave society. The chivalric ideal also carried over into Southern attitudes toward women, who were accorded an exaggerated deference for their delicacy and innocence, despite the undeniably hard labor that was the daily routine of the wife of the average planter. Not surprisingly, the women's rights movement, which gained attention in the North in the 1850s, found no echo in the South. Or if it did, as in the example of the Grimké sisters of South Carolina, the proponents felt compelled to leave the region for the more congenial North.

If women were expected to remain in the home, the men were expected to be forthright and even aggressive leaders in politics and war. Southern interest in military education and the military life was well recognized. There were more military academies in the South than in any other section, and in 1850 Southerners made up 47 percent of the members of the West Point graduating class that year, but only 35 percent of the population of the country. The prevalence of military titles in the South was both a reflection of the military interests and the romantic outlook of Southerners. "Almost every person of the better class is at least a Colonel, and every tavern-keeper is at least a Major," reported one astonished English visitor to the South in 1834.[6] The addiction of Southerners to dueling was widely acknowledged as a regional characteristic. Dueling occurred at times in the North, to be sure, but it was illegal and carried out in secret. In the South, legal prohibitions, where there were any, were openly flouted and the niceties of the *code duello* both adhered to and appreciated. When Congressman Preston Brooks decided in 1856 to punish Senator Charles Sumner for his public insult to a relative, he carefully chose a cane rather than a whip or a challenge with pistols, for a cane conveyed precisely his low opinion of Sumner while acknowledging Sumner's high station.

---

[6]Quoted in Rollin G. Osterweis, *Romanticism and Nationalism in the Old South* (New Haven, Conn., 1949), p. 105.

Southern social values were at once individualistic and communal. The justification for dueling, for example, was that a man did not expect society to give him satisfaction for an insult; that was a personal matter to be settled by individuals. David Donald has been so impressed by the Southern lack of social obligation and discipline that he named it a significant contributory cause for the defeat of the Confederacy.[7] The world of the Southerner was bounded by the family and his immediate locality; it did not extend to society at large. To that closer and smaller society he owed his primary obligation and from the more detached and larger society he expected little.

II

By the 1850s Southerners and Northerners alike recognized that they were different, that two civilizations now existed within the United States. (In June 1860 the *Southern Literary Messenger*, published in Richmond, carried an article entitled, "The Difference of Race Between the Northern People and the Southern People.") But these differences in themselves cannot account for the failure of nationalism that took place in 1861. In fact there is some reason to believe, as David Potter has written, that Southerners and Northerners are as different today as they were in 1860, yet separation is not likely.[8] Moreover, other societies have developed divergent cultural patterns without splitting apart. One can think of Switzerland in the nineteenth century along with northern and southern Italy, and French and English Canada in the twentieth century. Countries can often survive deep differences in cultural patterns and even different sectional rates of economic growth, if the political ties are sufficiently strong. In the case of the United States, however, strong political ties were not only absent, but as the cultural differences developed, political ties weakened.

One reason they weakened was that almost from the beginning of the Union the doctrine of states' rights was ready for use.

[7]See the essay "An Excess of Democracy: The American Civil War and the Social Process," in David Donald, *Lincoln Reconsidered* (2nd ed., enlarged, New York, 1961), pp. 209–35.

[8]David M. Potter, "The Historian's Use of Nationalism and Vice Versa," *American Historical Review*, LXVII (July, 1962), 924–50.

The significance of this doctrine is not that a Southerner, Thomas Jefferson, introduced it with his Kentucky resolutions or that another Southerner, John C. Calhoun, raised it to a sectional principle; New Englanders in 1804 and 1814, after all, also had recourse to it. Its importance lies in the fact that states' rights provided a *constitutional* or legal basis for the disruption of the Union. For a region as traditional and conservative as the South such a means of protest was necessary as well as congenial. As the rhetoric and facts of Southern secession now make clear, an appeal to revolution would not have carried the South out of the Union in 1860/61. Even in the heated atmosphere of 1860 the average Southerner, who was also conservative, required a legal, constitutional justification for his strike for independence.

But the formal argument of states' rights and constitutional secession was not as important in accounting for the breakdown of American nationalism as the conception of the Union that Southerners and many other Americans had come to accept by the 1850s. In part, to be sure, this conception of the Union was an outgrowth of the increasing Southern emphasis upon states' rights in the 1830s and 1840s. But to a much greater extent it was the result of American social and cultural development over the preceding half century. The very looseness and mobility of American society, as well as its individualism and lack of traditional institutions like a national church, a national aristocracy, or a dominating national capital, predisposed Americans to define the Union in similarly loose and individualistic terms. It was to them a Union freely entered into and freely adhered to. Unlike other countries, Americans believed, the Union was composed of states that linked their fates out of the self-interest of their citizens, not out of military force or fear. Americans regarded their country as the freest in the world simply because its continued existence rested upon the free choice of its inhabitants. Conversely, to maintain the Union through force was to destroy the liberty that justified it. As even a Northerner like Wendell Phillips said during the secession crisis, "A Union is made up of willing states, not of conquered provinces. There are some rights, quite perfect, yet wholly incapable of being enforced. A husband or wife who can only keep the partner within the bond by locking the doors and standing armed before them, had better submit to peaceable separation."[9] By the 1850s Northerners as well as Southerners

[9]Quoted in Paul C. Nagel, *One Nation Indivisible: The Union in American Thought 1776–1861* (New York, 1964), p. 257.

spoke of "this confederacy" when they meant the Union and in doing so they gave popular voice to Calhoun's view that there was no nation, but only a collection of states joined in convenient and free Union. Indeed, few men spoke of the nation at all; almost invariably it was simply the Union.

At no time was the dilemma of American nationhood more clearly delineated than in President James Buchanan's response to the secession of the lower South during the winter of 1860–61. A staunch Jacksonian Democrat who had witnessed the firm Unionist stand of his predecessor in the crisis of 1832, Buchanan in 1861 was nonetheless acutely aware of the popular conviction that the United States was not held together by force. As a result he could not bring himself to resist secession by arms, but neither could he, as an old Jacksonian, countenance secession as a legal remedy under the Constitution. In retrospect and despite the criticism that historians have heaped upon Buchanan's "indecision," the truth seems to be that probably a majority of Americans—taking Southerners into the count—agreed with Buchanan's view. The idea of a centralized state maintaining itself by force simply was not, to most Americans, the proper basis of Union.

If most Americans, North and South, in 1860 emphasized a Union of limited authority, there was still a large—and as events would show, a growing—minority who envisioned the United States as a nation, a people united by ties of tradition, history, and emotion. (Ironically enough, many of these people drew their inspiration from Southern leaders of an earlier and more nationalistic time, like Jefferson, Andrew Jackson, and Henry Clay.) To this romantic nationalism Lincoln appealed in his first inaugural address when he spoke of "the mystic chords of memory, stretching from every battlefield and patriot grave to every living heart and hearthstone all over this broad land." His decision to sustain Fort Sumter tested which view of the Union would prevail, for, as Southern Unionists had warned, to use coercion would cause the upper South to join the new Confederacy. One North Carolina Unionist editor wrote in January 1861 that he did not believe in secession, but he "would never, as a Southern man, suffer a Southern state to be driven into subjection by armed force, as long as we could stagger under a musket."[10] Even some ardent Northern Republicans, like Horace Greeley, at first counseled

[10]Dwight Lowell Dumond, ed., *Southern Editorials on Secession* (New York, 1931), p. 386.

that the "erring sisters" be permitted to go in peace, rather than use coercion. Lincoln's decision to hold the Union together by military power marked a new stage in the evolution of American nationhood.

III

From the war that followed upon Lincoln's decision, a nation emerged where none had existed before. Both Lincoln and his successor Andrew Johnson contended that the war was fought to preserve the Union, but the fact of the matter was that the old Union died when the war began. The old Union had left a loophole for secession; the new Union made secession hereafter intellectually unthinkable and politically impossible.

It was more than a nationalistic conception of the Union that made the change. Of great importance were the nationalizing demands that the war placed upon the institutions of the country. When the Lincoln government undertook to suppress the rebellion, the country was like a jellyfish in organizational structure and internal skeleton. England, Allan Nevins points out, was better organized to fight Napoleon half a century earlier than the United States was to suppress secession.[11] This invertebrate character was even more evident than at the time of the Revolution, for in the interim the country had tripled in extent and seventy-five years of rapid economic growth and democratic individualism had watered down, rather than strengthened, social cohesion. In 1860 there were no large business enterprises, yet massive amounts of goods had to be produced quickly to equip the great army and navy that would be needed; railroads were still primitive by European standards and differences in gauges made them less useful as long-distance haulers than the lines on maps would suggest. There were no medical or legal societies, no business organizations, no farmers' or workers' groups to which the government could turn for advice, assistance, or much-needed expert personnel. The complicated organization required to fight a major war had to be constructed from the ground up. And when it was done a new nation emerged, tied together by the communications, organizations, and bureaucracy generated by the demands of war.

[11]Allan Nevins, *The War for the Union* (New York, 1959), I. 243.

The new nationalism was evident even as the war was being fought. Americans had always been proud of their freedom and prosperity, but few of them had thought in modern nationalistic terms. Loyalty to the Union was common, but loyalty to the nation was a new idea. As Ralph Waldo Emerson said in 1864, "Before the War our patriotism was a firework, a salute, a serenade for holidays and summer evenings. . . . Now the deaths of thousands and the determination of millions of men and women show that it is real."[12] The measure of that reality was the evocation of an emotional attachment to the nation—that is, the creation of a modern sense of nationhood. It is not accidental that Edward Everett Hale's emotionally nationalistic story "A Man Without a Country" appeared in 1863, just when many Americans were feeling for the first time the emotion of nationalistic fervor. At the close of the war James Russell Lowell commented that before 1860 there had not been "that conscious feeling of nationality, the ideal abstract of history and tradition, which belong to older countries," but now the war had changed that. "Here at last is a state whose life is not narrowly concentered in a despot or a class, but feels itself in every limb; a government which is not a mere application of force from without, but dwells as a vital principle in the will of every citizen. . . . Loyalty has hitherto been a sentiment rather than a virtue."[13]

The marks of a new government of strength to which Lowell referred were all around. In prosecuting the war, the Lincoln administration was compelled to take measures that no federal government before had dared to assume, but that thereafter no national government could fail to use. Issues that had been sources of deep constitutional dispute in the years before 1861 now became matters of mere expediency. During the war the protective tariff was raised to new levels, to become a standard Republican campaign plank. Though Democrats in later years, as during the war, would challenge the wisdom of protection, they no longer argued, as they had before 1860, that it violated the constitutional limits on federal power. In the name of winning the war, the finances of the nation felt the centralizing power of the new, vigorous federal government. Congress authorized the printing of almost $400 million worth of "greenbacks" to help pay for the war. This currency was the first paper money issued

[12]Quoted in Merle Curti, *The Roots of American Loyalty* (New York, 1946), p. 169.
[13]*Ibid.*, p. 170.

by the federal government in its history, the backing of which was only the credit and prestige of the government. A national banking system was established to replace the unsystematic state banks; a newly imposed federal tax virtually drove out of circulation the paper money issued by the state banks. The nation's first income tax was enacted along with the first conscription law. Never before had the federal government resorted to such a denial of individual liberty as when it enacted conscription. And the bloody riots that broke out in protest in a number of Northern cities measured in violence the novelty of the experience for Americans.

Undoubtedly the most telling instance of the new nationalism was the destruction of slavery itself. Only a few years before, almost all Americans agreed that slavery in the Southern states enjoyed a constitutional sanctuary forever. Lincoln himself, in his inaugural address, as a means of forestalling the secession of the upper South, reiterated his conviction that the federal government had no constitutional authority to deal with slavery in the South. Yet within two years, under the exigencies of the war, Congress and then the President abolished slavery in those states in rebellion. The immediate practical effect was nil, to be sure, since federal forces did not yet control affairs in those states. But in the long perspective, those first blows against slavery determined the future and provided yet another instance of the new national power in Washington.

If the war produced a revolutionary effect upon federal power, in other ways it made Americans less radical. For one thing, the new emphasis upon organization, system, and institutions as means for preserving the Union constituted a repudiation of the individualistic, anti-institutional, almost anarchistic outlook exhibited by many reformers of the antebellum years. Men like Emerson and Theodore Parker and movements like transcendentalism had sung the praises of the individual while questioning the value of organized society with its emphasis upon conformity. Tradition, these reformers proclaimed, was the enemy of progress. The abolitionists, too, had found established institutions faulty if only because they justified the bondage of the slave. Some of the more radical antislavery men had even repudiated the Constitution itself as a "covenant with death and an agreement with hell," because it sanctioned slavery.

But when the war became an antislavery struggle, organization and established institutions of society were no longer to be scorned. Reformers and social critics who for years had believed that reform could be achieved only by the disruption of institutions suddenly found themselves, perforce, working to strengthen them in order to preserve the Union and eradicate slavery. After the Civil War American reform lost much of the semianarchistic, anti-institutional outlook, which had been so striking in the pre-war years.

To make that observation is only to say that reform now became respectable. During the 1850s many Northern and Southern conservatives had despaired for the future of the Republic as they witnessed unrestrained individualism attacking the organizations and institutions of society. Some, like Francis Lieber, a professor of political science at Columbia College, actually hoped for a war in order to stun the nation back to its senses and social responsibility. The war had the further effect of making clear to conservatives that reform and social change could be supported without at the same time seeming to advocate anarchy or repudiating social institutions. It was not accidental, as George Fredrickson has pointed out, that the conservative elite of the North wholeheartedly supported the Sanitary Commission.[14] The commission was organized early in the war to provide medical and other aid to the Union soldiers. Like the army, the Sanitary Commission was one of the new nationwide organizations that sought to achieve reform *through* institutions, rather than by repudiating them. It also demonstrated that reform could be tough minded, practical, and devoid of the sentimentality that many conservatives had found objectionable in the reform activities of the 1840s and 1850s. Some of the older reformers, on the other hand, found the new humanitarianism of the Sanitary Commission overly organized and lacking in concern for individuals. Walt Whitman, for example, whose primary drive as a volunteer army nurse was compassion for the soldiers, loathed the male nurses of the commission, whom he called "hirelings." The purpose of the Sanitary Commission was eminently practical—to return the men to battle as soon as possible, for the winning of the war was the commissioners' principal object. The means was the institutionalization of medical care and the bringing of efficiency to a hitherto haphazard service. As a consequence, the commission usually resented the "meddling" and sentimentality of a Clara Barton or a Walt Whitman.

[14]George M. Fredrickson, *The Inner Civil War: Northern Intellectuals and the Crisis of the Union* (New York, 1965), Chap. 7.

In another way the war moderated the American revolutionary tradition. It destroyed the simple connection between revolution and the Good that Americans had assumed ever since 1776. Down through the years since their own revolution most Americans, both Northern and Southern, had applauded each effort of a suppressed European nationality to be free of its alien master. Thus Americans supported the Greeks and the Latin Americans in the 1820s and the Hungarians in 1848 when they revolted against their oppressors. For many Americans, especially Democrats, who constituted a majority of the voters in the North, and for many Southerners, of course, the secession of the South was 1776 all over again. Among European liberals, too, it was commonplace to regard the secession of the South as an effort by a new people to achieve self-determination and freedom. Such liberals wished success to the Confederacy just as they had wished success to similar struggles for self-determination in central and eastern Europe. Indeed, it was just that analogy that proved embarrassing to many Northerners, when, in 1863, the Poles rose in rebellion against their Russian overlords. It was difficult for some Northern newspapers that supported the war against the South to explain how they could, at the same time, support the Polish revolt in the name of self-determination. When the Russian fleet arrived at New York, the *New York Times,* an ardent supporter of the Lincoln administration, abandoned the Polish cause entirely in the interest of friendship with the Russians. After the secession of the Southern states it was no longer possible to assume that a people who declared themselves a separate nation should automatically be granted the right of self-determination.

Some political thinkers, like Francis Lieber, argued that Southern secession was illegitimate because it was against a democratic government, against which there was never any justification for violence. In making his point, however, Lieber was compelled to repudiate the Jeffersonian justification for revolution, for Jefferson had drawn no distinction between forms of government in his advocacy of periodic revolutions. The old Jeffersonian love of revolution was undoubtedly romantic as well as impractical, but it had been a symbol of the more profound idea that all governments tend to become rigid and unresponsive to the will of the people (regardless of their form or origin). After the Civil War Americans would never again exhibit that insouciant attitude toward revolution that Jefferson and his generation had exemplified.

"The Civil War," wrote Henry James in 1879, "marks an era in the history of the American mind. It introduced into the national consciousness a certain sense of proportion and relation, of the world being a more complicated place than it had hitherto seemed, the future more treacherous, success more difficult. At the rate at which things are going, it is obvious that good Americans will be more numerous than ever; but the good American, in days to come, will be a more critical person than his complacent and confident grandfather. He has eaten of the tree of knowledge."[15] Other men, too, who lived through the war found the world and their fellow men changed by the conflict. The devotion and courage of the soldiers, the sacrifices of the civilians, and the martyrdom of Lincoln provided a new dimension of human experience as well as setting a new standard of loyalty that transcended self and family. Twenty years after the war, Oliver Wendell Holmes, Jr., vividly recalled that "through our great good fortune in our youth our hearts were touched with fire. It was given us to learn at the outset that life is a profound and passionate thing."[16] A half century after the war, William James, the brother of the novelist, talked of the need for a "moral equivalent of war" in times of peace. James thought he found that equivalent in a new form of service by youth to the nation, analogous to the Civilian Conservation Corps of the New Deal or the Peace Corps and Vista of the 1960s. Still other men, also unable to forget the courage, manliness, and discipline that the war evoked, cast about for ways to call forth those virtues again. One way was through competitive athletics, which became common for the first time on college and university campuses in the 1880s. Henry Lee Higginson, a Boston philanthropist, hoped to rekindle the fire to which Holmes referred when he gave an athletic field to Harvard to be called, appropriately enough, Soldiers Field.

Southerners, too, found the war a sobering experience, for they had lost it. As C. Vann Woodward has pointed out,[17] no other Americans had suffered defeat on the battlefield. Defeat was to make them a little less sure of the future, a little less confident that things would turn out all right, a little less assured that people could control their destiny. The war for them reinforced

[15]Henry James, *Hawthorne* (New York, 1879), p. 144.

[16]Quoted in Frederickson, *Inner Civil War*, p. 219.

[17]C. Vann Woodward, *The Burden of Southern History* (Baton Rouge, La., 1960), pp. 19–21.

rather than effaced the differences between the Southerner and the Northerner even as it forced the sections together again under the old flag.

IV

The new nationalism bred by the war displayed its power in the Reconstruction of the South. In swift, clean strokes the Fourteenth Amendment cut down the states and destroyed the old Union. Its very first clause, in which blacks were made citizens, not only repudiated the Dred Scott decision of 1857, but also for the first time clearly specified United States as well as state citizenship. In its potent second clause, the amendment prohibited the states from depriving any citizen of the United States of his rights or privileges, thereby erecting a whole new series of rights that were derived from the nation's, as distinct from the states', authority. In the twentieth century this single clause has been the textual basis of a whole body of judicial interpretation protecting citizens against state power. Freedom of religion, freedom of speech, and freedom for black children to attend schools with white have all been shielded against contrary state action by this one clause. The decline of the states in the federal system can be dated from the Fourteenth Amendment.

The very idea of a reconstruction of the South was a manifestation of a new view of the American Union. At the time of his death Lincoln still talked of restoring the South to the Union as rapidly as possible, with no other social and political changes than the abolition of slavery and the repudiation of secession. His successor, Andrew Johnson, less flexible and more Southern than he, almost achieved that goal at the end of 1865. But for most Northerners the war, in destroying the old Union, made it impossible for the South to return unchanged to political and constitutional power. The underlying assumption of Radical Reconstruction policy as it evolved in 1866 and 1867 was that only by a social revolution in the South could a repetition of secession be averted. Since it had been the different society of the South that was the seedbed of the rebellion, only by transforming that society could the old Union be reconstituted as "One Nation," as Charles Sumner phrased the goal.[18] Most Radicals, it is true, did

[18]The words appear in Charles Sumner's essay, "Are We a Nation?" quoted in Hans Kohn, *American Nationalism: An Interpretive Essay* (New York, 1957), p. 127.

not accept Wendell Phillips's plan for an indefinite occupation of the South. But they followed his conception of reconstruction when he described it as "primarily a social revolution. You must plant at the South," he advised, "the elements which make a different society."[19]

Under the Radical program the slave system was to be replaced by civic equality for blacks and the removal of the great planters and Confederates from the political leadership of the region. Loyal Southern whites and blacks and Northerners, it was hoped, would create a new society modeled after that of the North. And the constitutions that these Reconstruction leaders in the South drew up for the Southern states reflected their revolutionary intent as well as their Northern bias. Popular education was introduced, women's rights over their property expanded, many local officials for the first time made subject to popular election, and railroad and industrial development encouraged. Moreover, many of the carpetbaggers who went South after the war saw themselves engaged in a mission to a benighted and undemocratic South, long retarded by slavery. One carpetbagger, Adelbert Ames, who became Governor of Mississippi, recalled later: "That I should have taken a political office seems almost inexplicable. My explanation may seem ludicrous now, but then it seemed to me that I had a Mission, with a large M. Because of my course as military governor, the colored men of the state had confidence in me, and I was convinced that I could help to guide them successfully, keep men of doubtful integrity from control, and the more certainly accomplish what was every patriot's wish—the enfranchisement of the colored men and the pacification of the country."[20]

What better way to remove the source of national disruption forever than to bring the Republican Party into the South, based upon the votes of the former slaves? With such a political revolution the conservative and unprogressive plantation society of the antebellum years would be beyond restoration. Not until the Second World War, when Americans determined to remake German and Japanese society in the image of western political and social democracy, would Americans undertake as thoroughgoing a social transformation as they sought to achieve in the South after

[19]Quoted in James McPherson, *The Struggle for Equality: Abolitionists and the Negro in the Civil War and Reconstruction* (Princeton, N.J., 1964), p. 370.

[20]Quoted in James W. Garner, *Reconstruction in Mississippi* (New York, 1901), p. 290n.

1865. Ironically enough, the demand made upon the South that attracted the most attention then and later—equality for the Negro—was the one least derived from Northern experience.

Prior to the Civil War Americans differed profoundly as to the merits of slavery and the nature of the Union. But many antislavery Northerners in seeking to end slavery gave little thought to what should be the status of the freed blacks. Undoubtedly one reason the future was so little anticipated was that in the North, where slavery no longer existed, blacks were neither numerous nor economically important. For Southerners, however, the institution of slavery was the principal means of keeping in subordination a people who constituted a quarter of the population of the South. Abolition would strike not only at their pocketbooks, but at their conception of social order as well. Northerners prior to 1861 would not engage in the debate over slavery on these terms, but when the war brought slavery to an end, it was evident that all along the basic question had been the future of blacks in American society.

Some of the leading abolitionists like William Lloyd Garrison, Theodore Weld, and Angelina and Sarah Grimké, it is true, left no doubt that they believed in the complete equality of blacks and whites. But their views were not representative of the millions of Northerners who supported the war against slavery, either in 1868 or after. More typical was the view of a man like James Pike, a Republican journalist and vociferous antebellum opponent of slavery. Pike believed blacks to be racially inferior and unworthy of inclusion in a white man's society. He advocated that they be herded together into some remote corner of the country and denied any influence. Other antislavery men thought the only solution was colonization abroad—usually in Africa—though thirty years of the experiment in Liberia had shown that most blacks refused to leave their native soil in America for an unknown life on an alien continent. Even Abraham Lincoln was unwilling to grant equality to blacks, despite his conviction that slavery was wrong. While President he continued to seek places and means to colonize the freed slaves outside the country, on the assumption, as he told a group of blacks in 1862, that black men would never be accepted as equals by white Americans. Ultimately, Lincoln's practical outlook compelled him to abandon his attempts at colonization, but his frequently expressed doubts that blacks could live in equality with whites in the United States accurately reflected the attitudes of millions of his fellow citizens in the North.

Lincoln's doubts rested on the undeniable social fact that the North, like the South, did not treat blacks equally. All the Northern states, it is true, had abolished slavery by the 1850s; yet only six states permitted blacks to vote and only Massachusetts allowed blacks to attend the same schools as whites. In fact, in most of the states of the North, blacks received no public education at all, though they were expected to pay taxes, obey the laws, and live peacefully. Throughout the North blacks were relegated to special sections in or excluded entirely from omnibuses, trains, hotels, restaurants, theaters, and other public places. Moreover, in times of tension blacks were the objects of vicious physical assaults, usually without any provocation except their color, as during the draft riots in New York City in 1863, when scores of blacks were maimed and dozens murdered by mobs. Although two hundred thousand blacks served honorably in the Union army and navy during the war, resentment against blacks ran high in the military services. Soon after the Emancipation Proclamation was issued, one Indiana soldier wrote: "As soon as I get my money . . . i am coming home let it be deserting or not, but if they dont quit freeing the niggers and putting them in the North i won't go back any more . . . it is very wrong to live with niggers in freedom."[21] Northern public figures during the war, as before, did not hesitate to express their conviction that blacks could not be accorded equal rights with whites. Indeed, as late as January 1865 the Democrats in the House of Representatives fought hard to prevent the passage of the Thirteenth Amendment, which would finally abolish slavery throughout the Union. As it was, the amendment passed by only two more votes than the necessary two-thirds. In 1867, the very same year that the radical Republican Congress was imposing Negro suffrage upon the South, the states of Ohio and Kansas turned down proposals for Negro suffrage, though the number of blacks in both states was politically inconsequential. When blacks were voting in the South as a result of the Radical Reconstruction policy, more than half of the Northern states still withheld the ballot from blacks.

In the context of these Northern attitudes and practices, the revolution in public policy that took place between 1865 and 1870 is all the more remarkable. For in the course of those five years the American people wrote into the Constitution, with the Fourteenth and Fifteenth Amendments, the complete equality of black and white both at the polls and in civil rights.

[21]Quoted in Bell Irvin Wiley, *Life of Billy Yank* (Indianapolis, 1952), p. 112.

How was such a revolution in law and outlook effected? Part of the explanation is undoubtedly to be found in the desire of Republicans to have their party be the agency for the remolding of the South. For if that party was to remain in power and to consummate the revolution it thought necessary in the South, it would have to secure votes there. As Thaddeus Stevens, one of the leaders of Radical Reconstruction, told the House in January 1867, unless blacks received the right to vote, loyal whites in the South would be outvoted. Furthermore, he pointed out, Negro suffrage was necessary to "assure the ascendancy of the Union party. . . . I believe that on the continued ascendancy of the party depends the safety of this great nation."[22]

But those who believed in and worked for the idea of Negro equality had a second reason for their espousal of Reconstruction. They drew inspiration from the traditional American belief in equality. When Americans spoke of equality, they had in mind at least two meanings. The most familiar kind was equality of opportunity; indeed, it was this form of equality that Lincoln invoked when he opposed slavery because it set limits to the opportunities open to blacks. But along with equality of opportunity Americans also cherished a belief in the equality of worth of each individual. Alexis de Tocqueville saw this form of equality being practiced in the age of Jackson when he reported that Americans could not abide invidious social distinctions. They will accept many things, he said, but they will not accept aristocracy. Mrs. Trollope also noticed the same attitude, though with more distaste. She reported that Americans disliked being domestic servants because such a station implied servility and denied equality. Politically the American idea of equality of worth expressed itself in the drive for universal manhood suffrage, in which each man's vote was equal, regardless of his wealth, education, or any other personal qualification.

Historically, to be sure, Americans have not applied the idea of equality, of either kind, to all people. Nativists during the 1850s, for example, tried to prevent immigrants from being treated equally with the native born, but that attempt was scotched before the decade was out. For most of the nineteenth century, however, Indians, blacks, and women were all denied equality of both kinds, just as in earlier years men without property had been denied the suffrage or the opportunity to hold office. Yet, despite the unevenness with which Americans have in-

[22]Quoted in Ralph Korngold, *Thaddeus Stevens* (New York, 1955), p. 382.

terpreted equality, it is clear that the principle has always carried great persuasive power for them. Appeals to it cannot be easily brushed aside. During and immediately after the Civil War, abolitionists and other advocates of Negro equality successfully appealed to that egalitarian tradition. The stirring war against slavery and the need to make the results of the war permanent coincided with great tradition. As a consequence, equality for blacks was written into the Constitution.

As events turned out, though, the inclusion of blacks in the doctrine of equality was a vague promise rather than a firm commitment. Considering the long history of the American belief in Negro inferiority, any other result would have been a miracle. Even for abolitionists the conception of full equality for blacks was essentially a matter of faith, for there was little social evidence to support it. In both North and South blacks were at the bottom of the social and economic scale. The abolitionists, however, began with the assumption that blacks were human beings who had been ruthlessly suppressed for generations. In spite of blacks' low position, the abolitionists possessed the faith that once slavery was removed the human potentiality of blacks would realize itself in tangible social achievement. One abolitionist, appalled at the ignorance and lack of morals he found among the newly freed slaves of the South, clearly expressed both that faith and the social obstacles to its realization. "They, the freedmen, are not angels," he wrote to a fellow abolitionist in 1863, "they are not even civilized men. . . . We must deal with them as children in intellect, but men in instincts and passions. . . . It is useless to disguise the difficulties, or to throw a false halo of romance about the negro. It is the highest proof of genuine sympathy and interest, to admit all the disagreeable features of the work, to realize all the difficulties and *still to go on.*"[23]

Although abolitionists might have faith in the human potentialities of blacks, most pragmatic Americans did not. For them to be convinced required tangible proof—that is, social achievement. For many reasons the requisite achievement did not come. The burden of slavery was too heavy to be quickly overcome, the opposition of white Southerners too consistent and determined, and the support from Northern Republicans too meager. In fact, as early as 1872 liberal members of the Republican Party in the North were already calling for the abandonment of the social

[23]Quoted in McPherson, *Struggle for Equality*, pp. 174–75. Emphasis in original.

revolution in the South on the ground that it had failed. Men like
Horace Greeley and Carl Schurz, who had been strong supporters
of early Reconstruction policy, now turned against it. By 1876 the
Republican Party as a whole reached much the same conclusion
as it became evident that the North was not prepared to force
equality of blacks upon the South.

V

The Radical experiment in social revolution was abandoned for
another reason besides the weakness of the Northern commitment to Negro equality. Just as in the full flush of the war, Americans had taken up a new position on blacks, so they had assumed,
as we have seen, an extremely nationalistic position in regard to
the power of the federal government. Together, these had constituted the Radical experiment to remold Southern society. By the
middle seventies the war was ten years in the past, yet the Radical experiment had produced few results. The Southern whites
were more adamantly set against Reconstruction policy than
ever; by 1874 over half of the former Confederate states were
already under Democratic regimes. Only by a persistent exertion
of federal power in the South for an indefinite length of time
could the few remaining Radical regimes be sustained. This unprecedented road, however, the country was not prepared to take.
Not even the great majority of Northern Republicans cared to
defend the degree and duration of centralized control that would
be necessary for the full carrying out of the Radical policy in the
South. The end came in 1877 with the withdrawal of the last
federal troops from the South, much to the relief of most Northerners as well as white Southerners.

When faced with a choice between a federal government that
would dominate the internal affairs of the states for an indefinite
period and one under which local self-government by Southern
whites would be restored, Americans chose the latter. Local self-
government, Americans were saying, was a more important social
and political value than the renovation of the South or the civic
equality of blacks. They also were announcing that there were
limits to the new war-born powers of the federal government.

In cultural terms the ending of Radical Reconstruction meant
that the United States was not to be a unified, homogeneous
nation but a federation of regions still, in which each section

would be free to pursue its own social patterns. Indeed, it was the decision to limit the national authority and to permit cultural diversity that explains the rapidity and ease with which "The Road to Reunion" was traveled after 1876. Since, for the remainder of the century, the dominant Northern attitude was that white Southerners ought to be permitted to shape their society without interference, Southerners could fit their divergent culture into the national framework without strain.

One consequence of the South's freedom from national interference was the removal of blacks from the mainstream of Southern life through disfranchisement, segregation, and confinement to the occupation of farm laborer. The acceptance of that consequence by the nation was symbolized by the decision of the Supreme Court in *Plessy* v. *Ferguson* in 1896. In that decision the court accepted segregation in public facilities so long as the accommodations were equal, arguing that "legislation is powerless to eradicate racial instincts or to abolish distinctions based upon physical differences, and the attempt to do so can only result in accentuating the difficulties of the present situation."[24]

The imprimatur of a Northern-dominated Supreme Court upon Southern segregation, ironically enough, only deepened the division between the two cultures. Northern society, to be sure, did not accept the Negro as an equal any more than Southern society did. The social practices of the North denied blacks equal access to public places like bathing beaches, hotels, and restaurants. Moreover, blacks held the lowliest jobs there too because white men would neither hire them for anything better nor work beside them. But it is significant that the North did not follow the Southern states in writing segregation into law. Indeed, some of the Northern states actually enacted civil-rights acts as gestures—they were little more than that—in support of Negro equality. More important, blacks continued to vote freely in the North, and legally segregated schools gradually disappeared. In the South, on the other hand, the tendency was in the opposite direction: to separate white and black as much as possible by law.

It is quite true that to blacks then and later the difference between legal and practical segregation may not have been great. But from the standpoint of the historian attempting to discern the social values of a society, a legal commitment is a significant statement. There is surely a difference in values between a society

[24]163 *U.S. Reports* 551.

that legally discriminates against blacks, as was true in the South, and one that legally proclaims equality even though it practices discrimination, as happened in the North. For law is an expression of social values; it sets social goals and by its very existence influences the direction in which the society will move. In fact, without the enactment of the Fourteenth and Fifteenth Amendments during the Reconstruction period, the movement for real equality for blacks in practice as well as in law would have been constitutionally without foundation in our own time. By the close of the nineteenth century the South still held out against the inclusion of blacks within the meaning of equality.

The disfranchisement and segregation of blacks by law in the South was not the only manifestation of the persistence of the two ways of life. Less ambiguous evidence is to be found in the failure of the movement to create a "New South." After Reconstruction enterprising Southerners like Henry Grady, Daniel Tompkins, Richard Edmonds, and many others campaigned vigorously and unceasingly for the industrialization of their region. Although there was a quickening of industrial activity in the South in the 1880s, the results by 1900 were disappointing. At the opening of the new century Dixie was still an agricultural region, beset by a growing burden of farm tenancy, both black and white, and falling even further behind the North in industrial growth. Indeed, as Clement Eaton has pointed out, in 1900 the South produced a smaller proportion of the nation's manufactures than it had in 1860.

The devastation of the war undoubtedly accounted in part for the slow economic growth of the South. But modern examples of rapid recovery from even more extensive destruction, as in Germany and Japan after World War II, suggest that war damage alone is not enough to account for the retardation. A more convincing explanation is to be found in the persistence of those attitudes and circumstances that had set the South apart from the rest of the nation in the days of slavery. Slaves may have constituted a poor market for manufactures, but poverty-stricken black tenant farmers did not provide a much better one. And a segregated, uneducated black population and a poorly educated white population offered little hope for a changed situation in the future. As before the war, the South found itself caught in a vicious economic circle. The limited economic opportunities of the region meant that the efforts of the leaders of the New South to attract immigrants into the region came to nothing, though the incoming tide of newcomers reached new heights in the North during the 1880s. Socially and religiously the South remained outside the mainstream of American society; it had few immigrants, few Jews, and few Catholics. Furthermore, without substantial industrial growth the South continued to be without many large cities, though the decade of the 1880s saw spectacular urban growth in the Middle West and on the Pacific coast. Although advocates of a New South were articulate and could capture the attention of Northerners, the fact of the matter seems to be that the great majority of Southerners were simply not convinced of the virtues of an industrial order. This lack of conviction is evident, for example, in the attacks by Populists and other leaders of farmers upon the advocates of a New South and Northern capitalists and upon the whole idea of an industrial South. Moreover, as late as the 1920s a group of Southern intellectuals like the Vanderbilt Agrarians could still get a hearing for their forthright repudiation of industrialization for the South.[25]

The divergence between North and South may have originated in the fact that slavery and the plantation existed in only one of the two regions, but a generation after slavery had been abolished completely the old differences still persisted. Indeed, by the close of the nineteenth century the gulf between the two sections may well have been wider than ever because of the South's military defeat and the "angry scar" left on Southerners by the experience of Reconstruction. Much later, in the middle of the twentieth century, the task of reducing the differences would be taken up again. This time the forces at work would be more powerful than earlier: World War II introduced massive federal-government and private investment in the South, helping to diversify the region's heavily agricultural economy, while mass communications media like the movies, radio, and television brought a national culture to the South. Along with these long-term influences came the second Reconstruction, which the Supreme Court initiated with its antisegregation decision in 1954 and which the administrations of John F. Kennedy and Lyndon Johnson implemented and advanced. One measure of the reduction in the sense of difference between the sections by the 1970s was the election in 1976 of Jimmy Carter, the first President elected from the Deep South since Zachary Taylor in 1848.

---

[25]See *I'll Take My Stand* by Twelve Southerners (New York, 1930), which is the manifesto of the group.

THE
PROGRESSIVE
ETHOS

Clyde Griffen / **VASSAR COLLEGE**

During the past decade, proponents of the "organizational synthesis," such as Robert Wiebe and Samuel Hays, have interpreted progressivism primarily as an expression of the "modernization" of American society. They have emphasized the extent to which newer rather than older values predominated among reformers. Wiebe has claimed that most of the reformers "lived and worked in the midst of modern society and accepting its major thrust drew both their inspiration and their programs from its peculiar traits."[1]

My purpose in this essay is to suggest how much the progressive ethos owed to tendencies in American Protestantism during the nineteenth century. I do not regard these tendencies as reducible to expressions of "modernization," however defined. I do emphasize that ethos's vulnerability in presuming a common social ideal and recognize the varying accommodations among progressives to the values, interests, and techniques of a more specialized society. But my view stands closer to the work of Richard Hofstadter and especially of Henry May in interpreting the progressives' mood as one of new hope that old values might finally be realized. The simple virtues they identified with the small community remained for them profoundly relevant to a world of large-scale organization.

[1]The quotation is from Robert H. Wiebe, *The Search for Order, 1877–1920* (New York, 1967), p. 165.

The work of historians like Herbert Gutman and Morton Keller has emphasized the persistence of older values during periods of rapid social change. Sometimes these values—notably preindustrial attitudes among workers—survived through fresh infusions of people from outside the mainstream of change. Sometimes they survived through restatements that made the older values seem fresh and contemporary to a younger generation. Progressivism among middle-class native white Protestants still seems to me a notable example of this kind of survival. I also remain persuaded that progressivism must be distinguished from other contemporary reform movements, which Richard Abrams has described recently in *The Burdens of Progress, 1900–1929* as the corporate-reform, socialist, labor-union, ethnic, and agrarian-radicalism movements.

I

From the vantage of the 1920s, the distinguishing feature of reform in the progressive era seems to have been an ethos, a unifying spirit, that did not long survive the First World War. Secular and religious versions of the nineteenth-century evangelical Protestant hope of realizing the Kingdom of God on earth permitted prewar Americans seeking different kinds of change to think of themselves as sharing in a larger crusade. At the height of progressive enthusiasm in 1912, the journalist Walter Weyl described a new social spirit that "in a curiously cautious, conservative way, is profoundly revolutionary. . . . Reform is piecemeal and yet rapid. It is carried along divergent lines by people holding separate interests, and yet it moves toward a common end. It combines into a general movement toward a new democracy."[2]

Contrasts between the progressive era and the twenties are dramatic. The chief casualty of disillusionment following the war "to make the world safe for democracy" was the ethos that allowed reformers with separate interests to learn from each other and to cooperate in pushing particular measures. In 1912 Theodore Roosevelt—no stranger to paranoia about danger from the Left—could say, "Many of the men who call themselves Socialists to-day are in reality merely radical social reformers, with whom on many points good citizens can and ought to work in

[2]Walter Weyl, *The New Democracy* (New York, 1964), pp. 165, 167.

hearty general agreement, and whom in many practical matters of government good citizens can well afford to follow."[3] But after the Bolshevik Revolution and the American "Red Scare" of 1919, Christian Socialists and other proponents of welfarism were suspect. As early as 1919, settlement worker Lillian Wald reported that old and generous friends were withdrawing financial support because she was " 'socialistically inclined.' Poor things I am sorry for them—they are so scared. It is foolish since . . . I am at least one insurance against unreasonable revolution in New York."[4] By 1920 some erstwhile progressives were joining businessmen in campaigns, such as that of the National Civic Federation, to root out radicalism within the churches, labor unions, and organizations of the foreign born.

The dissipation of support for reform was more rapid than awareness of it, however. In the immediate aftermath of war everything seemed possible to the dedicated minority of professional social workers, social-gospel clergymen, and leaders of voluntary reform associations who had developed more ambitious notions of reform than most prewar progressives. Some continued to hope for an early realization of their dreams as late as 1924, when La Follette went down to defeat and Massachusetts rejected the child-labor amendment, but most came earlier to a recognition that they were engaged in a long, uphill struggle. Their development of new programs and new concepts for social reform during the twenties was ignored by most Americans or looked upon as subversive.

The blurring of the lines between radicalism and reform in prewar progressivism had been matched by a blurring of religious differences. A sense of sharing a vision of Christian democ-

---

[3]Theodore Roosevelt, *Autobiography* (New York, 1913), p. 542.

[4]Quoted in Clarke A. Chambers, *Seedtime of Reform: American Social Service and Social Action, 1918–1933* (Minneapolis, 1963), p. 25. Chambers's first chapter describes the frustration in the twenties of the hopes of progressives concerned with social justice for an early realization of their aims. But his book emphasizes continuity in reform through the "small band [who] kept the faith," pioneering new methods and goals. Continuity, especially the survival of progressivism in Congress, also is the theme of Arthur Link, "What Happened to the Progressive Movement in the 1920's?" *American Historical Review*, LXIV (July, 1959). The present essay, by contrast, emphasizes the difference in national receptivity to reform efforts in the progressive era and the twenties. Recognizing continuities, it is more impressed by the dissipation in the twenties of the ethos of the prewar reform coalition and consequent loss of support from important elements of that coalition and from the wider public that responded to its appeals.

racy had obscured for reformers that growing schism between liberal and fundamentalist Protestantism that roughly paralleled divergence between urban and rural mores. In the early twenties William Jennings Bryan personally tried to keep alive a unifying emphasis on Christian ethics and brotherhood, insisting that there was no conflict between his social progressivism and his religious fundamentalism. But the loss of tolerance among progressives was all too evident in the fight at the Democratic convention of 1924 on the issue of censuring the Ku Klux Klan.

Many of the components of the old progressive coalition were present and dissatisfied during Normalcy. But, as historian Henry May observes, "What was lacking was the old idealistic cement, the thing that had made representatives of opposing interests sing hymns for Roosevelt or wipe their eyes over a Wilson peroration."[5] The idealism that did remain, especially among the minority who elaborated new programs for reform during the twenties, changed gradually in emphasis. Postwar progressives continued to combine traditional appeals to moral sentiment with a stress on fact finding and scientific analysis, but the balance changed as the latter waxed in importance and the former waned. The religious enthusiasm and rhetoric with which prewar reformers had expressed their vision of democracy to a Bible-reading generation became the exception rather than the rule.

The dissipation of support for reform coincided with an evident decline in the place and influence of religion in the lives of urban middle-class Americans. The churches continued to prosper in membership and especially in finances, but a host of signs indicated that religious affiliation had become a conventional expectation rather than a primary commitment. Religious illiteracy and secularism increased. Symptomatically, whereas Sunday School enrollment among Protestant denominations showed an average increase of nearly 40 percent between 1906 and 1916, the increase between 1916 and 1926 was only 10 percent. Customary symbols of the nation's commitment to Christianity, like faithful church attendance, grace before meals, and family devotions, were no longer usual in respectable homes. Furthermore, as Winthrop Hudson notes in his study of American Protestantism, "Religion, which had been one of the principal subjects of serious and intelligent discussion in the literary monthlies and quarterlies,

[5]Henry May, *The End of American Innocence* (New York, 1959), p. 394.

now became conspicuous by its absence, and was usually resurrected only to serve as a target for the satirical shafts of a Mencken."[6]

Protestantism lost the momentum that fed its prewar optimism about ushering in a new era of brotherhood and righteousness, of establishing the Kingdom of God on earth. In 1912 the chairman of the concluding congress of the Men and Religion Forward Movement had exulted, "There are more gifts for the cause of Christ, in money and lives, today, than ever before."[7] Never had so many American churchgoers been so actively involved in so many efforts to improve the world, from modest attempts to provide kindergartens, parks, and playgrounds for the children of urban tenements to ambitious campaigns to end child labor. Churchmen mobilized great drives to Christianize America and the world, such as the Laymen's Missionary Movement and—in the immediate aftermath of war—the Interchurch World Movement. But by 1921 it was apparent that lay support for these drives had largely evaporated.

Coincidence in the fortunes of Protestantism and reform was not an accident. Progressivism was the sensitive conscience of American Protestantism during its most expansive and optimistic era, a time when American idealism was practically synonymous with Protestant idealism and vice versa. Progressives could appeal effectively to Americans with no predisposition toward reform because the progressive vision and rhetoric derived from Protestant values pervasive among the native born. Progressives gave those values an interpretation aimed at social change, but their interpretation was made easier by fundamental changes in American religion and popular culture in the nineteenth century. The general direction was apparent in antebellum moral, humanitarian, and utopian ventures fostered by the perfectionist tendency of revivalism. The emphasis on right

[6]Winthrop Hudson, *The Great Tradition of the American Churches* (New York, 1963), p. 196. See also C. E. Olmstead, *History of Religion in the United States* (Englewood Cliffs, N.J., 1960), pp. 542–45, and Bureau of the Census, *Religious Bodies: 1926*, I (Washington, 1930), pp. 51–52.

[7]*Messages of the Men and Religion Movement*, I (New York, 1912), 9. On the relationship between evangelical Protestantism and American culture, see, in addition to Hudson, H. Richard Niebuhr, *The Kingdom of God in America* (New York, 1937). Sidney Mead, *The Lively Experiment* (New York, 1963), and W. G. McLoughlin, "Pietism and the American Character," *American Quarterly*, XVII (Summer, 1965), 163–86.

behavior rather than right belief in revivalism—and subsequently in theological liberalism—made Protestantism highly susceptible to reform impulses.

As the twenties revealed, the churches became victims of their own success in shaping American values. The intellectual framework of a distinctively Christian perspective had been eroded by the simplifying influence of revivalism and by the accommodation of new currents in secular thought since the Civil War. Instead of being the beginning of a golden age as so many Protestants had thought, the progressive years were the culminating expression of a culture that had accepted Protestant moralism but lost the piety that vivified it.

For the historian this aftermath, this loss of a sense of the distinctively Christian, poses a large temptation to discount the importance of evangelical Protestantism in shaping the progressives' perspective. Awareness of the subsequent development of American society makes it seem more plausible to emphasize the relation of progressive reforms to interest groups, the growth of academic and professional concern for planned social change, or the search for new means of social control by an urban middle class. Because a scientific emphasis was the wave of the future, it is all too easy to overlook the continuing influence of the older ethos during the progressive years even on the professional and managerial mind and to conclude, mistakenly, that modernity became fully characteristic of that mind before the war.[8]

II

Necessary as the new professionalism and the concerns of interest groups are to an explanation of reform in this period, they do not account for the peculiar slant in the progressives' way of looking at and talking about their world. The most overt expression of this perspective is found in their expectation for the immediate future, their vision of a new democracy and a new Christianity. The favorite slogan of liberal Protestantism, the Brotherhood of

[8]Samuel P. Hays, *The Response to Industrialism, 1885–1914* (Chicago, 1957), and Robert Wiebe, *Businessmen and Reform* (Cambridge, 1962), especially pp. 206–12. Wiebe's recent book, *The Search for Order, 1877–1920* (New York, 1967), is an extreme example of this tendency to push the emergence of a modern mentality backward in time and to discount the lingering influence of evangelicalism on the attitudes of urban professionals and businessmen.

Man under the Fatherhood of God, expressed a deeply felt sense of common cause and hope for men of widely different convictions. The range of meanings given to both democracy and Christianity made it possible for progressives to accommodate the methods and values of an emerging urban, bureaucratic, and relativistic society without seeming to abandon those of an older America of smaller communities and simpler, more secure faith.[9]

Progressivism began with the belief that righteousness could be restored by the exposure of wrongdoing and by appeals to conscience and civic pride. Hard experience with backsliding from the converted and the resilience of the unconverted led most progressives to put less emphasis on moral crusades and more emphasis on careful formulation and enforcement of particular measures for change. Between 1900 and 1917 the shibboleths of reform, especially among the younger generation, became scientific investigation of social problems and efficient administration of their remedies. But before 1917 few reformers abandoned the older faith that something approaching a moral perfecting of society was possible through appeals to the nation's conscience. Even those most inclined to rationalism in their approach to reform, like Herbert Croly and Louis Brandeis, pointed Americans toward the most demanding moral aspirations.

Progressives shared a sense of living in a peculiarly hopeful time when brotherhood, justice, and righteousness were about to be realized to a degree never thought possible before. The key to social progress was simple—a matter of right values—but no previous generation had had sufficient faith or understanding of society to carry out with any fullness the related ideals of Christianity and democracy. Progressives believed with Walter Rauschenbusch that organized Christianity in the past "has accepted as inevitable the general social system under which the world was living at the time, and has not undertaken any thoroughgoing social reconstruction" implementing the teachings of Jesus. Most of them also agreed with Rauschenbusch that "to undertake the gradual reconstruction of social life consciously and intelligently

---

[9]On progressivism as a mood, a perspective, and a preoccupation with realizing certain values, see May, *End of American Innocence*, Chaps. 1–3; Richard Hofstadter, *The Age of Reform* (New York, 1955), Chap. 4; George Mowry, *Era of Theodore Roosevelt* (New York, 1958), Chaps. 2, 5; Paul Glad, "Progressives and the Business Culture of the 1920's," *Journal of American History*, LIII (June, 1966), 77–78; and especially Richard M. Abrams, "The Failure of Progressivism," paper read before the Organization of American Historians, Cincinnati, Ohio, April 28, 1966.

would have required a scientific comprehension of social life which was totally lacking in the past."[10]

Looking at their immediate past, progressives shared a sense that the possibilities of human nature for joyous and wholesome living had not been fostered in the Gilded Age, with its extremes of vulgar materialism and overrefined, ascetic idealism. They saw themselves as more open to new ideas, more tolerant of differences, and freer from puritanical rejection of innocent pleasures than their mugwump predecessors in reform. They prided themselves on bringing to reform a realism and practicality that they believed the genteel reformers, Populists, and other crusaders of the late nineteenth century lacked. Their calling was to show that "practical idealism" and "applied Christianity" could remake society, that goodness need not be ineffectual.

The book *The Church and Society*, published in Macmillan's Social Progress Series in 1912, typifies the progressive coupling—without any sense of disparity or incompatibility—of an exalted vision of the future with an emphasis on immediate practicality in the means of reform. The author, R. Fulton Cutting, a founder of New York City's Bureau of Municipal Research, rejoices in the "audacious optimism" of the Laymen's Missionary Movement in looking forward to an "evangelization of the world in this generation" and himself proposes a "saturation of Society by Christianity through its public functionaries."

Cutting emphasizes throughout the book the previous "failure on the part of the Church to recognize that government is the most potent factor in social uplift and that inefficient administration can manufacture more social ill than a generation of social programs can remedy." As his concluding illustration of what can and should be done, he describes the various methods by which New York City clergymen have aided the Bureau of Municipal Research's efforts to secure an adequate city budget for schools, playgrounds, juvenile courts, and hospitals and for the prevention of crime, disease, and abuses in housing. He praised especially the ministers' "two budget Sundays to show New York congregations the religious and moral significance of scientific budget making."[11]

The juxtaposition of a practical piecemeal approach to reform

[10]Quoted in Donald B. Meyer, *The Protestant Search for Political Realism* (Berkeley, Calif., 1960), p. 17.

[11]Robert Fulton Cutting, *The Church and Society* (New York, 1912), pp. 10, 26, 28, 176–79.

with a religious or quasi-religious vision of democracy is the most satisfactory test of a progressive. Like any attempt to isolate a dominant type of reformer among the many seekers after change in early twentieth-century America, this definition leaves us with borderline cases. But it also clarifies distinctive emphases.

This definition separates progressives from businessmen concerned only with reforms favoring their own economic interests, such as the shippers who supported railroad regulation and the city bankers outside of Wall Street who supported a federal-reserve plan.[12] It also separates progressives from political leaders of the foreign born and representatives of organized labor. The latter cooperated with progressives on measures to improve the lot of the working class but did not share native-born Protestant America's preoccupation with assimilating alien elements and eliminating class divisions.[13]

This definition distinguishes the progressive outlook both from the lack of emphasis on "the art of the possible" among genteel reformers of the Gilded Age and from the explicit rejection of monism in religion and morality by younger intellectuals. The progressive did not share the genteel faith that preaching of right doctrine by the intelligent minority would of itself ultimately bring political righteousness. They regarded as pious hope the conviction—as expressed by George William Curtis—that "it is after all, 'the Remnant' that avails, even though it be the reviled Mugwumps."[14]

The older generation of reformers had not paid enough attention to realities; some of the younger generation, at the other extreme, adopted a thoroughgoing relativism that made the study of what is the precondition for a satisfactory formulation of what ought to be. In *A Preface to Politics* in 1913, the young Walter Lippmann described the idealism and moralizing of many progressive reformers as the triumph of past taboo over present need, of routine over creativity. Lippmann called for an experimental ethic that recognized that "truth is a thousand truths which grow and change."[15]

[12]Wiebe, *Businessmen and Reform.*

[13]Irwin Yellowitz, *Labor and the Progressive Movement in New York State, 1897–1916* (Ithaca, N.Y., 1965).

[14]Curtis to H. C. Potter, December 2, 1884, Henry Codman Potter MSS (Archives of the Protestant Episcopal Diocese of New York).

[15]Walter Lippmann, *A Preface to Politics* (Ann Arbor, Mich., 1962), p. 94.

In practice, progressives often moved toward relativism in their explanation of behavior, but they did not abandon the older faith in a secure and coherent moral universe. They escaped that sense of being adrift that Lippmann described for the rebels of his generation: "We are unsettled to the very roots of our being. . . . There are no precedents to guide us, no wisdom that wasn't made for a simpler age."[16] The progressives were a transition generation. The Protestant middle-class culture in which they grew up— their education, in the broadest sense—allowed them to adapt to new ideas and situations without seeing clearly how far they were departing from the world view of their childhood. This essay is intended as a brief history of that education, beginning with the influence of revivalism in shaping the culture into which they were born and then describing the kind of preparation their world provided in the years between the Civil War and the beginning of the twentieth century.

III

The chief features of the progressive vision of democracy were anticipated in the "awakened" Protestantism of the three decades after 1850, the period in which most progressive leaders were born. Revivalism in the age of Jackson had simplified piety, rendering it more susceptible to influence by popular attitudes and by secular thought. To understand this transformation is to understand how American Protestantism could become almost synonymous with American idealism, both in its more self-justifying and complacent moods and in its times of self-criticism and reforming zeal.

By the middle of the century, revivalism had become the usual means of breathing new life into the churches of most denominations.[17] Viewed simply as a technique for encouraging conversions, it was neutral theologically and could be used alike by the orthodox Calvinist, the perfectionist Methodist, and the evangelical Unitarian. In practice, revivalism after the 1830s undermined

[16]Walter Lippmann, *Drift and Mastery* (Englewood Cliffs, N.J., 1961), p. 92.

[17]On antebellum revivalism see W. G. McLoughlin, *Modern Revivalism* (New York, 1959); Timothy Smith, *Revivalism and Social Reform* (New York, 1957); Whitney Cross, *The Burned-Over District* (Ithaca, N.Y., 1950); and Charles Cole, *Social Ideas of the Northern Evangelists* (New York, 1954).

theological orthodoxies of every kind by making theology itself seem less important. It promoted a religion of the heart as against the head by insisting that the struggle for the soul of the sinner was won or lost in the heart alone.

This disjunction of emotion and intellect had not characterized the teaching of early leaders of revivalism like Lyman Beecher and Asahel Nettleton. They appealed to heart and mind simultaneously, regarding revivalism as an auxiliary to the church's normal life of instruction and prayer rather than as its central feature. The shift in emphasis in the 1830s reflected the influence of Finney and his imitators in making the churches' success in inducing conversions the test of their spiritual health. Henry Ward Beecher carried this to its logical conclusion. He recalled without any embarrassment in 1882, "I gradually formed a theology by practice, by trying it on, and the things that really did God's work in the hearts of men I set down as good theology, and the things that did not, whether they were true or not, they were not true to me."[18]

As the size of the harvests increased, optimism mounted as to the possibility of saving the entire nation. As early as 1829 one religious observer commented that "the same heavenly influence which, in revivals of religion, descends on families and villages . . . may in like manner . . . descend to refresh and beautify a whole land."[19] Such optimism, spurred especially by the nationwide revivals of 1857, gave impetus to postmillennialism in the churches. The increase in benevolent and humanitarian activities was further evidence that God was ushering in His Kingdom.

The harvests also had a leveling effect. They made social differences between men and ideological differences between denominations seem of less consequence. The vision of an entire nation saved replaced the idea of the Elect as a minority. Concerned primarily with success in inducing conversions, revivalists of various denominations banded together in prayer meetings to conduct intensive and sustained efforts on a larger scale than a single preacher could manage.

[18]Quoted in Hudson, *Great Tradition*, p. 173.

[19]Quoted in Perry Miller, *The Life of the Mind in America from the Revolution to the Civil War* (New York, 1965), p. 11; on millennialism, see the review article by David Smith, "Millennarian Scholarship in America," *American Quarterly*, XVII (Fall, 1965), 535–49.

A centrifugal tendency continued—indeed the splitting off of new sects occurred with greater frequency in an age of religious excitement—but the divisions increasingly seemed less important than a broader common identity. The latter was encouraged by the fact that so many American sects, including the numerous Methodists and Baptists, lacked a well-defined ecclesiastical tradition. With little sense of a distinctive history of their own, they tended to make Jesus and the primitive church normative. Appealing to the same models, they found it easy as theological differences became less important to stress the Brotherhood of Man under the Fatherhood of God. Christian democracy was nourished by the democracy of revivalism.[20]

Revivalism everywhere tended to make the Christian life seem simpler and more congenial to the many. Emphasis on the loving mercy of God in accepting sinners transformed the image of the Christ into an increasingly sentimentalized Jesus, friend and teacher, exemplified in Washington Gladden's hymn of 1879, "O Master, Let Me Walk With Thee." Ethics became a matter of the heart more than the head. Anxious to avoid a utilitarian line of argument that they deemed dangerous to revealed religion, the academic moral philosophers who most influenced evangelical America divorced ethics, in theory, from rational consideration of the consequences of behavior to the individual and to society. They espoused a modified Scottish realism that held that intuition or conscience was the proper guide to right action.[21]

The moral philosophers' appeal to intuition suggests their confidence that individual consciences would agree on what was virtue and what was vice. Judging from the readers and histories, Sunday School tracts and manuals on how to get ahead in life, this confidence was fully justified. Educational and other popular books endlessly enumerated and illustrated such virtues as benevolence, self-reliance, humility, sincerity, perseverance, orderli-

[20]On the way in which Protestant churchmen through "establishment and control of both public and private schools . . . stamped upon neighborhoods, states, and nation an interdenominational Protestant ideology which nurtured dreams of personal and social progress," see Timothy L. Smith, "Protestant Schooling and American Nationality, 1800–1850," *Journal of American History*, LIII (March, 1967), 679–80.

[21]Wilson Smith, *Professors and Public Ethics: Studies of Northern Moral Philosophers Before the Civil War* (Ithaca, N.Y., 1956).

ness, frugality, reverence, patience, honesty, purity, punctuality, and charity.[22]

There was nothing new in the virtues themselves, but there was in this era, as in other revivals of pietism, a tendency to take them literally. They were interpreted as demanding far more of human nature than the churches in more complacent eras would suppose. The requirement of purity was construed in favor of puritanism; benevolence became unceasing attention to the moral and spiritual improvement of other men, whether they desired it or not.[23]

The moral absolutism of the school readers was offset to some extent by an emphasis on success, an opportunistic bias that was most marked in manuals on how to get ahead in life. The difference in moral emphases between those Americans who responded most to this opportunistic bias and those who, like the progressive reformers, responded more literally to the moral idealism of their education is exemplified in an episode reported by the young Wisconsin lawyer, Robert La Follette. He had defended successfully a tramp accused of shooting with intent to kill, but the praise of his performance by local lawyers and politicians made him uneasy. "They seem to consider that I did a smart thing—that I was sharp in the management of the matter and keen in the argument—but they don't seem to think that I did it all because I thought he was innocent—that I was simply fighting a fight for the truth."[24]

The progressives grew up with a moral consensus so clear and unquestioned that they tended to assume this consensus was characteristic of human nature wherever it was permitted to develop freely. This assumption easily fostered righteous indignation

---

[22]On the moral consensus as seen in schoolbooks, see Ruth Elson, *Guardians of Tradition* (Lincoln, Nebraska, 1964); as seen in the literature of success, see Irvin Wyllie, *The Self-Made Man in America* (New Brunswick, N.J., 1954).

[23]The pietism and moralism Queen Victoria symbolized in nineteenth-century England was an outgrowth of the evangelical revival there, reminding us that the influence of revivalism was not peculiar to America. English evangelicalism influenced American abolitionism; a little later, the American Dwight L. Moody won his first great success as a revivalist on a tour of Britain. See Frank Thistlethwaite, *The Anglo-American Connection in the Early Nineteenth Century* (Philadelphia, 1959).

[24]Quoted in Belle and Fola La Follette, *Robert M. LaFollette*, I (New York, 1953), 46.

against violators of the consensus; personalities with an authoritarian warp carried this to the blind intolerance of "sinners," which frequently appears in progressive crusades against intemperance, gambling, and prostitution. But the most universal consequence of consensus was a security about fundamental values and what constituted the good life. Remembering that security with an oversimplifying nostalgia, George Creel wrote, "Life presented no soul-tearing problems necessitating a call for psychiatrists, for there were things that decent people did and things they did not do. And all knew what they were."[25] This sense of security about values makes it much easier to understand John Dewey's faith that ethics could be made an empirical science and also why Dewey's ethical pronouncements so often proved to be the same as those of liberal Christianity.

The pervasiveness of this antebellum moral code owed much to the great expansion of publishing, which reinforced preoccupation with self-improvement among the literate middle class. Conformity even on "minor morals," as manners often were termed, was encouraged by the increasing number of books devoted to them—twenty-eight in the 1830s, thirty-six in the 1840s, and thirty-eight in the 1850s. The development of a mass audience for a much broader kind of self-improvement was whetted by that spontaneous upsurge of adult education, the Lyceum movement, in which groups of citizens and whole communities organized themselves into local associations for intellectual advancement. In the 1840s a technological revolution in printing and an expanding transportation network made it easier for publishers to exploit that audience. Hot competition sprang up in cheap editions of new English and American books.[26]

The significance of this revolution for the education of the progressive generation is hard to overestimate. A nationwide popular culture emerged in the 1840s and 1850s, spurring the leveling tendency of American society by making "culture" available to the many. The best-sellers of that "culture" included the banal works of novelists like Mrs. E. D. N. Southworth as well as the more lasting contributions of Washington Irving and Feni-

[25]George Creel, *Rebel at Large* (New York, 1947), p. 24.

[26]On the emergence of mass culture, see Carl Bode, *The Anatomy of Popular Culture* (Berkeley, Calif., 1959); for the best-sellers, see F. L. Mott, *Golden Multitudes* (New York, 1947); and James Hart, *The Popular Book* (New York, 1950).

more Cooper, but even so it was a leveling upward sufficient to encourage all but the fastidious that an entire people could be elevated spiritually, morally, and intellectually.

The sentimentality of so much of the new popular culture encouraged a belief in the leveling upward of society in much the same way as revivalism's emphasis on a religion of the heart did. All men were capable of pure and exalted feelings, whatever their capacity for reasoning. Throughout the novels, the chromos, the ballads, and the melodramas, the ties of love, in weal and woe, are omnipresent. The family circle was the consummate symbol of love. In Donald Mitchell's best-seller of the forties, *Reveries of a Bachelor*, subtitled a *Book of the Heart*, the bachelor characteristically sits by his fireside entertaining visions of an ideal wife, of his own unselfish devotion to her and to his children, and of the solace she provides when his friends, relatives, and finally he himself die.[27]

The very democracy of this emphasis on feeling reinforced the evangelical tendency to hold up an ideal of human relations associated with the family and friendships as the ideal for society at large. The emotional penumbra that surrounded the ideal of the Brotherhood of Man for so many progressives makes more sense in the light of their exposure to a popular culture idealizing those relationships. This idealization was all the more potent because it came at the very time when the nuclear family in a mobile society was increasingly vulnerable to disruption of its integrity and authority and was, simultaneously, more important as a source of emotional support for the individual.

Preoccupation with the immediate family circle in popular culture reflected the situation of the family in Western society by the mid-nineteenth century. Compartmentalization of work, home life, and education replaced for increasing numbers of men the usual experience of the past where these activities occurred largely under the same roof. In middle-class homes the gradual withdrawal of the family into privacy was almost complete. Even servants within the household had separate living quarters. Whereas before the child had been educated by the larger world, which was incorporated within or moved easily in and out of the household, he now was increasingly insulated at home and at school from the workaday world of adults.[28]

---

[27]Bode, *Anatomy*, pp. 212–13.

[28]On changes in the family in the western world see Philippe Aries, *Centuries of Childhood* (London, 1962), especially the conclusion; in America, see Bernard Bai-

As the number of parental surrogates readily available decreased, the concentration of attention and affection on the immediate parent-child relationship increased. The result was a strong tendency toward indulgence. Corporal punishment in the discipline of children was replaced increasingly by appeals to their love for their parents and their shame in disobeying them, a replacement encouraged by a developing literature of child nurture. By the 1850s the new pedagogy had vanquished, in theory if not always in practice, the Puritan idea that the child's sinful will must be broken at an early age.[29]

Not all of the progressives benefited in their own childhood from the new and milder pedagogy, but they were profoundly influenced by the premium that the literature as well as the domestic arrangements of their time placed on familial intimacy and love. Woodrow Wilson was descended from a succession of Scotch Presbyterian ministers, ruling elders, or professors of theology who gloried in the logical exposition of their faith and distrusted mere emotionalism in religion. But the books that his father, also a Presbyterian clergyman, read aloud to his family—most often the novels of Dickens and Scott—did nothing to perpetuate the distinctive rational piety of his forebears.

Nor did the effusive expression of affection between parents and children encourage perpetuation of the Calvinist emphasis on the awesomeness and inscrutability of God the Father. Rather, the love of the dear Saviour Jesus for his flock—increasingly revivalism's chief appeal to the sinner—was made believable to young Wilson in the evident devotion of his parents to "our precious son" and "darling boy." It was natural for the mature Wil-

---

lyn, *Education in the Forming of American Society* (Chapel Hill, N.C., 1960), especially pp. 22–27; W. E. Bridges, "Family Patterns and Social Values in America, 1825–1875," *American Quarterly*, XVII (Spring, 1965), 3–11; Richard L. Rapson, "The American Child as Seen by British Travellers, 1845–1935," *Ibid.*, XVII (Fall, 1965), 520–34. For many Americans transiency offset this tendency to insulation. Residence in boarding houses and hotels gave children an experience of human variety and fellowship wider than that of family, social class, or locality, although it did not significantly alter the developing pattern of compartmentalization of work, education, and home life. See Daniel Boorstin, *The Americans: The National Experience* (New York, 1965), pp. 145–47. But this very rootlessness also increased yearning for secure and intimate relationships and helps explain the immense popularity of sentimentalized views of family life and friendship.

[29]On the new pedagogy and literature for children, see Bernard Wishy, *The Child and the Republic* (Philadelphia, 1968).

son to describe Christianity as a personal relationship with God, a gospel of love to which "you are drawn by the knowledge that if you come you will be received as a son. Nothing but yearning draws you."[30] Almost without exception the progressive reformers took ideal qualities associated with the home, in fact or in evangelical precept, and held them up as a standard for the wider world.

The best testimony to the success of evangelicalism in infusing American culture with a profoundly idealistic moralism is to be found among those progressives whose religion placed them outside the mainstream. Jews like Henry Morgenthau, Sr., and Louis Brandeis (before 1912) believed in the desirability of assimilation. In Morgenthau's case, his evident anxiety to become as American as possible resulted in a self-image that is almost a parody of evangelical gentility.

In his autobiography Morgenthau reports that the gift of William Penn's "No Cross, No Crown" by a Quaker doctor inspired him to compose "twenty-four rules of action, tabulating virtues that I wished to acquire and vices that I must avoid. . . . The fact is that I acquired an almost monastic habit of mind and loved the conquest of my impulses much as the athlete loves the subjection of his muscles to the demands of his will." He expresses thanks for having grown up in the era when Emerson led American thought and New England provided so many examples of moral idealism, firing his boyish imagination with "a vision of a life of unselfish devotion to the welfare of others."[31]

IV

Any generation would have found it difficult to come to terms with the new social order produced by industrialization and urbanization after the Civil War. But the problem was exaggerated for a generation raised with so refined a moral idealism and such high hopes for the future as that born in the late 1850s, 1860s, and 1870s. It escaped the chastening and sobering experiences of soldiering; more important, the war made no significant differ-

[30]Woodrow Wilson, "The Young People and the Church" (1904) in R. S. Baker and W. E. Dodd, eds., *College and State: Educational, Literary and Political Papers by Woodrow Wilson*, I (New York, 1925), 485.

[31]Henry Morgenthau, *All in a Lifetime* (New York, 1922), pp. 15, 16, 94.

ence in the popular culture in which the progressives grew up. The two antebellum decades have been called the "Sentimental Years," but as Robert Roberts has noted "the implication of sentimentalization of human relationships could with equal accuracy be applied to the Gilded Age."[32]

The direction Protestantism took in the postwar years tended to reinforce this sentimentalization rather than to call it into question. Dwight L. Moody and a number of other urban revivalists preached an otherworldly fundamentalism unsympathetic to visions of the Kingdom come on earth, but they did nothing to challenge the prewar idealization of personal relations and its projection as a standard for society. More important, the dominant tendency of urban middle-class evangelicalism was not toward fundamentalism but toward a theological liberalism optimistic about the future of American society, whether from a gospel of wealth or a social-gospel standpoint.

The response of the more sophisticated urban churches to Darwinism was the clearest indication that Protestantism had lost its intellectual rigor and any significant detachment from secular culture. With remarkable ease, clerical and lay reconcilers such as John Fiske, Henry Ward Beecher, and Lyman Abbott devised a variety of syntheses of evolutionary thought and Christocentric theism. Few of them involved serious grappling with the issues a naturalistic interpretation of human evolution posed for Christian theology. Instead they offered fairly simple ideas of animal and human progress, arguing that God was continuously working in and through natural law to bring about this progress. Irreconcilable doctrines or Biblical accounts became metaphors rather than literal truths.

This accommodation by Protestant intelligentsia to prevailing winds of secular doctrine was repeated on a much lower level by a general confusion of religion and culture. In rural and small-town America that confusion is seen most clearly in Chautauqua—which Theodore Roosevelt called the "most American thing in America." The Chautauqua movement grew out of a Methodist minister's summer program, begun in 1874, for training Sunday School teachers. A regular program of education, cultural uplift, and entertainment was soon added. By 1900 these summer sessions at Lake Chautauqua had attracted so many imitators that

[32]H. Wayne Morgan, ed., *The Gilded Age: A Reappraisal* (Syracuse, N.Y., 1963), p. 194.

promoters put Chautauqua on the road, pitching tents for a five- or six-day program in town after town across the country.

Religion degenerated into a vapid religiosity in that enthusiastically received class of inspirational speakers whom the Chautauqua managers privately labeled "mother, home, and heaven." Among the favorite items on tent programs were William Jennings Bryan's "Prince of Peace" lecture and the Rev. Russell Conwell's sanctification of the pursuit of riches, entitled "Acres of Diamonds." They shared popularity as well as the platform with such "uplifters" as the Chicago Lady Entertainers singing "My Grandfather's Clock" and "Blest Be the Tie That Binds" and chalk-talker Ash Davis with his reproduction of the "Statue of Liberty Enlightening the World."[33]

The most educated, especially in the big cities, were more restrained than Chautauqua. But both the more perfunctory and conservative kind of urban churchgoers and the social gospelers were moving in a similar direction to that of Chautauqua. They, too, identified Christ with their particular view of American culture, and those views were not so far apart as they seemed superficially. The Clarence Days who treated religion as a necessary propriety frequently could be persuaded to support institutional methods in their affluent parishes in an attempt to make them more attractive to workingmen. Among the clergy a promoter of the gospel of wealth, Russell Conwell, and a moderate social gospeler, W. S. Rainsford, were pioneers in the movement to make the individual parish a neighborhood social center as much as a place of worship. Their churches, the Baptist Temple of Philadelphia and St. George's Episcopal Church in New York City, offered a wide variety of facilities and services, including gymnasiums, employment bureaus, singing, sewing, and dramatic clubs, and agencies selling food and fuel to the poor at cost.

The same Bishop Lawrence who is forever quoted for his gospel-of-wealth dictum in 1900 that "godliness is in league with riches" also helped author the 1904 Report of the Episcopal Church's Standing Commission on the Relations of Capital and Labor, which reflected the social gospel. This report argued that,

[33]On the mentality of rural and small-town Protestantism, see Paul Glad, *The Trumpet Soundeth* (Lincoln, Nebraska, 1960); on Chautauqua, see Victoria and Robert Case, *We Called It Culture* (Garden City, N.Y., 1948); and Harry Harrison and Karl Detzer, *Culture Under Canvas* (New York, 1958).

given present commercial conditions, labor must be organized to "maintain such a standard of wages, hours and conditions as shall afford every man an opportunity to grow in mind and in heart."[34] The participation of conservatives like Lawrence in statements such as this swelled the tide of optimism during the progressive years about the possibility of meliorating social ills. It encouraged the illusion that an immensely active and prosperous Protestantism moved as one in ushering in the Kingdom.

The very vagueness and sentimentality of postwar Protestantism made it easier for reformers to claim its support for progressive causes. For the genteel middle class most influenced by it, it also heightened the shock of confronting the uglier realities of the new social order. Discovering industrial conflict and urban poverty was unsettling enough to a generation educated to a lofty idealism, but there was also the disillusionment of discovering how frequently men with the highest moral pretensions betrayed them in their behavior.

The grossest violations of traditional ideals were not the most disturbing. The financial and political misdoings of Jay Gould and Jim Fisk or the blackmail of distillers by the Whiskey Ring within the Grant administration could be chalked up to bad men. But it was not easy to explain away the discovery that some of the most respectable people profited from illegal activities like prostitution and gambling conducted on properties they owned. Yet, as Lincoln Steffens's series of articles published as *The Shame of the Cities* illustrated, that was the discovery of reformers in city after city as they tried to wipe out commercialized vice and corruption in politics.

Nor was it easy to explain away the pious John D. Rockefeller, who contributed munificently to a host of Baptist philanthropies but apparently saw no contradiction in driving independent oil refiners out of business by methods that, as set forth in Ida Tarbell's series of articles, shocked progressives everywhere. Theodore Roosevelt spoke to the experience of his generation when he said, "the longer I have lived the more strongly I have felt the harm done by the practice among so many men of keeping their consciences in separate compartments; sometimes a Sunday con-

[34]"Report of the Standing Commission on the Relations of Capital and Labor at the General Convention of the Protestant Episcopal Church held in Boston in October, 1904" (Pamphlet in H. C. Potter MSS), p. 2.

science and a weekday conscience . . . sometimes a conscience for their private affairs and a totally different conscience for their business relations."[35]

Expressing their dismay was easier for the generation that went progressive than finding a model of the idealist with which to identify. Civil-service reform tended to attract that portion of the middle class most imbued with evangelical notions of righteousness but also most vulnerable to charges of irrelevance and ineffectuality during the Gilded Age. Their ideal of the good citizen emphasized purity of motive and scrupulousness in means to a degree that men of affairs, and especially hardheaded politicians, found totally unrealistic. Senator Roscoe Conkling of New York called the reformers "the man milliners, the dilettanti and carpet knights of politics. . . . They forget that parties are not built up by deportment, or by ladies' magazines, or gush."[36]

While young progressives were learning that preaching principles was not sufficient for the political success they sought, a Harvard philosopher—also raised in the world of middle-class idealism—was criticizing the philosophies that world found most congenial. Significantly, William James used the word "refinement" to characterize rationalistic and idealistic philosophies that satisfied a desire for a simple, clean, and noble world by leaving out the contradictions of real life.

The unhappy result, said James, was that such desperately needed qualities as faith in people's capacity to shape their destiny, tender concern for others, and a sense of reverence for the wonder of the universe became identified with a philosophy that was a "monument of artificiality." In sheer reaction those who loved facts were inclined to adopt a point of view that was irreligious, materialistic, and fatalistic. What James wanted and sought to offer in his formulation of pragmatism was a philosophy that was at once grounded in experience and receptive to the

[35]Theodore Roosevelt, *Realizable Ideals* (New York, 1911), pp. 3–4; on the concern with hypocrisy in English middle-class culture, which was also profoundly influenced by evangelicalism, see Walter Houghton, *The Victorian Frame of Mind* (New Haven, Conn., 1964).

[36]Quoted in Matthew Josephson, *The Politicos* (New York, 1938), pp. 246–47; on the reputation of genteel reform see Richard Hofstadter, *Anti-Intellectualism in American Life* (New York, 1963), Chap. 7; the foundation of the reputation in fact can be seen in Geoffrey Blodgett, *The Gentle Reformers* (Cambridge, Mass., 1966).

highest human hopes.[37] What the progressives wanted was a comparable approach to social reform.

V

The initiation of the progressive generation into the problems and possibilities of their world was a peculiarly encouraging education for middle-class reformers. It was an exposure to the disturbing realities of social injustice, economic waste, and political corruption, but an exposure within the context of a substantial hopefulness that these could be changed by means consonant with middle-class values.

As a younger generation coming of age in a time of social unrest, the progressives not surprisingly showed a greater readiness than their elders to investigate that unrest, to explore the world beyond the confines of their middle-class upbringing. Some went to live in alien territory like the settlement-house workers. But many more made occasional forays into it as did the young New York assemblyman, Theodore Roosevelt, when he accepted Samuel Gompers's challenge to accompany him into the tenements to see the conditions under which cigars were made. The progressives came to pride themselves on not flinching from the most unpleasant facts. Some of them were so conscious of having been insulated in their middle-class upbringing from the harsher facts of society that they tended, if anything, to identify reality with the more sordid, corrupt, or conspiratorial behavior they discovered.

The progressives also were more open than their elders to seeing things from fresh perspectives, as Jane Addams saw the immigrant, or Fremont Older, the corrupt politician, or Ben Lindsey, the juvenile offender. Lindsey, the Kid's Judge whose Denver courtroom became a model for progressives, attributed his own interest in the influence of environment on delinquency to one case. The anguish of a toothless old woman whose boy Lindsey had just been sentenced to state reform school for stealing lumps of coal from the railroad tracks unsettled the judge and led him to look into the family's circumstances. He found that home was a cold room in a tenement where the father, a smelting worker, was dying of lead poisoning without receiving any com-

[37]William James, *Pragmatism* (New York, 1955), pp. 28, 56–57.

pensation from his employer. With this perspective, he found it impossible to think of the boy as bad or sinful by nature, still less to be treated the same as hardened criminals. Lindsey began to explore the possibilities of rehabilitation rather than punishment, of exposing the wards of his court to a new environment of better care and education.[38]

But the fresh perspective of Lindsey's generation was only in small part a matter of youthful openness to experience. The popular writers and academicians who most influenced progressives emphasized the influence of environment on behavior; by the turn of the century the earlier evangelical view that "sin" and deficiency of character explained poverty had been largely discredited. The common denominator of the progressives' mentors was an optimism about people's ability to translate their social ideals into reality.

The writers with the largest audience before 1900 made the ideal of the Brotherhood of Man under the Fatherhood of God the foundation of their discussion. The most widely read book on social policy was Henry George's *Progress and Poverty*, a best-seller in the 1880s and 1890s and the only book largely devoted to economic theory ever to win such success. Only a minority were converted to George's panacea of a single tax on land, but all carried away his message that poverty was not the result of God's will, of Nature, or of individual sin, but of society's failure to destroy monopoly and special privilege.

For the minority who did accept George's panacea as well as his vision of progress, response to the book often was akin to that experienced in revivals. Brand Whitlock said that, in reading George's books, Tom Johnson, the reform mayor of Cleveland, "had a spiritual awakening, experienced within him something that was veritably, as the Methodists would say, a 'conversion.' "[39]

Edward Bellamy's best-selling utopian novel, *Looking Backward*, took antimonopolism to a collectivist conclusion that George found abhorrent. But Bellamy's import for the middle class that read him so eagerly was much the same as George's. Christian solidarity and decency could be reinforced by proper

[38]Eric Goldman, *Rendezvous with Destiny* (New York, 1952), pp. 121–23.

[39]Brand Whitlock, *Forty Years of It* (New York, 1925), p. 155; on the quasi-religious character of American social and economic thought, conservative as well as reformist, see T. E. Cliffe Leslie, "Political Economy in the United States," *Fortnightly Review*, October 1, 1880; and Goldman, *Rendezvous With Destiny*.

social arrangements rather than being contradicted as they were under the present social system.

George and Bellamy could be dismissed as amateurs, but their optimism was backed by a growing body of academic social analysis that claimed scientific support for the idea that people can direct social change to rational purposes. Economists and sociologists like Richard T. Ely, John R. Commons, Simon Patten, Albion Small, Henry Carter Adams, and Edward A. Ross rejected the determinism that laissez-faire conservatives like William Graham Sumner read into evolution. They reinterpreted Darwin or drew upon European social analysis, especially the German historical school of political economy, to develop a justification for more centrally directed public policy making.[40]

The fact that a number of these new professional investigators identified themselves as reform-minded Christians, promoting the social gospel within Protestantism and emphasizing the importance of ethics as a dimension of their discipline, was reassuring. The most influential, Ely, insisted that "Christianity which is not practical is not Christianity at all" and altered the scope of that practicality by asserting, "God works through the State in carrying out His purposes more universally than through any other institution."[41]

This relation with the social gospel helped to obscure the shift from a religious to a scientific perspective in reform, which already was underway. Under the auspices of Christian professionals, the specific furnishings of progressive minds more often came from contemporary developments in the sciences of man, society, and nature than from religious sources. Frederick Howe, Woodrow Wilson, Walter Weyl, Albert Shaw, and others were exposed directly to the new social sciences in the universities, but many more progressives learned from them. Both La Follette and Roosevelt said that Ely affected their thinking. Roosevelt is reported as observing that Ely "first introduced me to radicalism in economics and then he made me sane in my radicalism."[42]

The new professionalization and specialization of inquiry that

[40]On the anti-Spencerian sociologists and economists, see Sidney Fine, *Laissez-Faire and the General-Welfare State* (Ann Arbor, Mich., 1964), Chaps. 7 and 8; and Jurgen Herbst, *The German Historical School in American Scholarship* (Ithaca, N.Y., 1965), especially Chaps. 6 and 7.

[41]Quoted in Fine, *Laissez-Faire*, p. 180.

[42]*Ibid.*, p. 240.

shaped progressive realism was most clearly evident in the natural sciences and in engineering. In a society that valued learning for its utility in mastering the environment, there was a natural stimulus for the newly emerging class of professional investigators to become advisors to government, private interest groups, and the nation at large on the practical implications of their subjects. In some cases, notably the four national societies representing civil, mechanical, electrical, and mining engineers, the very esprit de corps of the professionals early came to include a mission to teach society how to use its resources more efficiently. Individual scientists and engineers employed by the federal government went far beyond their assigned duties in helping to initiate policies or to create the public sentiment needed to enact legislation they desired. For example, Frederick Newell, chief hydrographer for the United States Geological Survey, agitated throughout the 1890s for a new irrigation policy.[43]

The professionals' concern for efficient use of resources produced the conservation movement, one of the greatest contributions of progressivism. As Samuel Hays has shown, the men who pushed the changes in national policy on irrigation, forest reserves, public land, mineral resources, and inland waterways did not do so out of the hatred of monopoly and special privilege that motivated many progressives. Their primary commitment was to efficiency, not to the extension of democracy. Indeed, the kind of planning and coordination they desired was hard to reconcile with the emphasis on grass-roots control, decentralization of power, and encouragement of individualism in progressivism of the New Freedom variety.

A concern with administrative efficiency and expertise, often with elitist overtones, can be found among other progressives. But it would be grossly misleading to emphasize conflict between the expansive democratic sentiments so frequently expressed and the nascent planning mentality most clearly evident among professionals in conservation, municipal reform, and the scientific-management movement. During the progressive years the conflict was more often potential than actual. Louis Brandeis, for ex-

[43]For the activities of Newell and of other federal officials who promoted conservation—such as Gifford Pinchot and Overton Price in the Bureau of Forestry, botanist Frederick Coville and engineer Elwood Mead in the Department of Agriculture, W. J. McGee in the Bureau of Ethnology, and Joseph Holmes and Marshall Leighton in the Geological Survey—see Samuel P. Hays, *Conservation and the Gospel of Efficiency* (Cambridge, Mass., 1959).

ample, was a strong believer in leadership by intelligence, but as progressivism swelled to flood tide and his own political influence increased, he became optimistic about the people's ability to choose good leaders and about the value of interaction between public and expert opinion.[44]

Wisconsin under La Follette illustrates the kind of balance usually struck in the progressive years. As governor, La Follette sought to enact a reform program grounded in a realistic appraisal of needs and so well devised that it could withstand searching opposition. His innovation, admired by progressives everywhere, was in the extent to which he drew upon the expertise available at his state university in drafting bills and in staffing state boards. The shape of particular reforms reflected the opinions of the expert, as did the civil-service reform bill La Follette asked Professor John R. Commons to draft. The broad social vision that permeated the reform movement in the state was La Follette's.[45] The progressives might be as elitist at heart as some of the experts who served them, but it was the reformers' vision of a new democracy that gave the era its distinctive quality.

VI

The old and the new coexisted in progressivism. Exposure to, even training in, the new inductive techniques of the social sciences did not immediately overcome the older evangelical propensity for moralizing issues. The habit of polarizing behavior into righteousness and iniquity was strongest among those closest to the older evangelical mentality, but it was not confined to them. An anticlerical progressive like Brand Whitlock could interpret a party platform and campaign promises as the most serious of moral obligations. He declared, "I suppose no greater moral wrong was ever committed in America" than the Democrats passing a high tariff in 1893 betraying their appeals to workingmen in 1892, which called for downward revision.[46] Protectionism as such was still an "evil" to Whitlock in 1925, echoing Woodrow

[44]Samuel Haber, *Efficiency and Uplift: Scientific Management in the Progressive Era* (Chicago, 1964), pp. 78–79.

[45]R. S. Maxwell, *LaFollette and the Rise of the Progressives in Wisconsin* (Madison, Wis., 1956), Chap. 9.

[46]Whitlock, *Forty Years*, p. 89.

Wilson's moralistic approach to the tariff question in the campaign of 1912. Describing discussion of the problem of monopoly in business, in which the tariff was so crucial a factor in his view, Wilson had said, "America began to display a broken field . . . groups contending for new ways to settle new questions; whereas there is but one way to settle questions, new or old, and that is by the old way of righteousness, of righteousness and justice."[47]

Wilson's campaign approach to the tariff problem was the moralizing of nineteenth-century free trade and antimonopolism, not the concern with efficient development of resources characteristic of scientific management. To be sure, the tendency to moralize issues exists in every generation. What makes it so conspicuous among progressives is its prominence *despite* their evident desire to escape the naiveté of genteel reform. It contrasts sharply with the remarkable modernity of intellectuals like Arthur Bentley, Charles Beard, and Thorstein Veblen in going beyond the forms of government, business, and the university to expose how these institutions actually worked.[48] The relationship of progressivism to the moral universe of nineteenth-century Protestantism is so striking precisely because progressivism also anticipated in varying degrees the attitudes of planning and scientific management.

If a moralizing tendency continued to limit the new progressive realism, so also did the incredible surge of optimism about the future of the nation and mankind that became so pronounced around 1907 and 1908. It is true that this optimism was most extravagant among the spokesmen for small-town and especially midwestern America, the world that clamored for the sunshine and sweet verities of Chautauqua. The perennial Nebraska optimist, Bryan, heralded the coming to realization of the centuries-old dream of the brotherhood of men in talks and articles after 1906. Bryan's Kansas neighbor, Republican progressive William Allen White, was just as exuberant in 1909, claiming that American institutions were becoming progressively "reflections of the spirit of Christ. . . . I think there never has been a time in the world when . . . this good will was so much a part of human

[47]Woodrow Wilson, "An Unweeded Garden," October 18, 1912, in John W. Davidson, ed., *A Crossroads of Freedom* (New Haven, Conn., 1956), p. 463.

[48]On the antiformalism and pragmatism of progressive intellectuals, see Morton White, *Social Thought in America* (New York, 1949); and Charles Forcey, *The Crossroads of Liberalism* (New York, 1961).

institutions, political and commercial and religious."⁴⁹ But even
so skeptical a product of the new learning as Walter Weyl temporarily lost his doubts about the efficacy of middle-class reformism
in describing *The New Democracy* in 1912.

Yet however much their moralizing and optimism seem limitations on their realism in retrospect, the progressive reformers found
these qualities no handicap in overcoming the Gilded Age image of
the reformer as an ineffectual wishful thinker. Quite the contrary,
these characteristics enhanced their attractiveness to contemporaries still receptive to an evangelical appeal to further the coming of
the Kingdom. Combined with the progressive emphasis on practicality, these characteristics helped make the reformer seem like a
sensible citizen who had more conscience and vision than his fellows. Theodore Roosevelt led the way, in this as in so much else, by
bringing to reform a high sense of adventure as well as respectability. No one was more conscious than Roosevelt of the importance of
identifying idealism with healthy, red-blooded, high-spirited
American manhood. Nothing upset him more than the idea that
Americans might become divided "into two camps, one camp containing nice, well-behaved, well-meaning little men, with receding
chins and small feet . . . who if they are insulted feel shocked and
want to go home; and the other camp containing robust and efficient creatures who do not mean well at all."⁵⁰

Roosevelt himself practiced as well as preached the strenuous
life, from boxing to big-game hunting. He was the young dude
from polite society who appeared in evening clothes at a district
political club meeting behind a saloon and got away with it.
Genteel reform had never been so persuasive or so much fun. And
other progressives echoed Roosevelt. Franklin K. Lane held "with
old Cicero 'that the whole glory of virtue is in activity.' " Of a
friend's career, he commented, "What a fine life—all fight interwoven with fun and friendship."⁵¹

⁴⁹White to W. E. Barton, December 20, 1909, in Walter Johnson, ed., *Selected Letters of William Allen White, 1899–1943* (New York, 1947), p. 104. If, retrospec-
tively, we are inclined to think that the progressive generation generalized a host of small and in many cases transient improvements into a bad case of wishful thinking, it is well to remember that the seeming tide of betterment was sufficiently impressive to modify even the attitudes of some skeptical intellectuals like Walter Weyl and the social gospeler, Walter Rauschenbusch.

⁵⁰Roosevelt, *Realizable Ideals*, pp. 42–43.

⁵¹A. W. Lane and L. H. Hall, eds., *The Letters of Franklin K. Lane* (Boston, 1922), pp. 6–7.

Almost universally progressives reacted against the elements of fussiness, narrowness, or preciosity in genteel reform. Just before the turn of the century Woodrow Wilson hoped out loud for "a generation of 'leading people' " who would replace the sentimentalists and busybodies in suggesting "the measures that shall be taken for the betterment of the race.... They would bring with them an age of large moralities, a spacious time, a day of vision. Knowledge has come into the world in vain if it is not to emancipate those who may have it from narrowness, censoriousness, fussiness, an intemperate zeal for petty things."[52] Progressives like Brand Whitlock wanted to avoid the "unctuous, holier-than-thou connotation" that reform had; they "wanted a healthfully gayer world, not one puritanically bleaker."[53] But even the more traditionalist among reformers tended to make much of the importance of humor, tolerance, and innocent pleasure.

The fact that Whitlock identified the word *reform* with a puritanism that he regarded as active in his own time does indicate, however, that there were important differences in interpretation of the bogey-word, *puritanical.* To Whitlock the moral reformers—those who were most concerned with prohibition and elimination of prostitution, gambling and corruption in government—were a different breed altogether. In Ohio, he noted, "the charge is freely made that an agreement or some understanding has existed between the Anti-Saloon League and the corporations by which, in return for temperance legislation, the corporations are to be let alone.... Such a feeling exists here among those who look more to economic reform than to personal reform for results."[54]

The charge had some foundation in hard experience. In retaliation for Mayor Samuel M. ("Golden Rule") Jones's failure to attack the saloons, the clergy of Toledo rallied behind the business interests in efforts to defeat him. Their idea of reform did not include efforts to bring about brotherhood by abolishing the use of billyclubs by the police or to end municipal corruption by instituting public ownership of utilities. The godly pastors went so far as to invite the Rev. Samuel P. Jones, ardent prohibitionist

[52]Woodrow Wilson, *On Being Human* (New York, 1916), pp. 41–42.

[53]Allan Nevins, ed., *The Letters and Journal of Brand Whitlock*, I (New York, 1936), p. xliv.

[54]Whitlock to Norman Hapgood, April 8, 1908, in *Ibid.*, I, 92.

and revivalist, to come to town for the purpose of exposing the unrighteousness that flourished under Mayor Jones, no relation.[55]

VII

But the evident differences between the older kind of moral reform and the unconventional humanitarianism of "Golden Rule" Jones or more conventional proponents of regulation of business can easily be exaggerated. A good many progressives did not see the sharp conflict Whitlock defined for the very good reason that during the progressive years the lines between moral and economic reformers, to use his distinction, were often blurred. Some of each kind found it possible to work together in various crusades. The Anti-Saloon League, the Women's Christian Temperance Union, and the Prohibition Party, for example, broadened their reformism shortly after the turn of the century. By 1902 the WCTU Declaration of Principles affirmed belief in a living wage, an eight-hour day, and courts of conciliation and arbitration as well as, generally, in "the coming of His Kingdom" and "the gospel of the Golden Rule."[56]

Certain reforms like the crusade against child labor attracted both those with a concern largely limited to protecting the physical, mental, and moral health of the nation's future citizens and those with an ideal of social justice seeking major changes in the condition of all laborers, their wages, working conditions, homes, and educational and recreational opportunities. Socialists like Florence Kelley and Robert Hunter were prominent in the membership of the New York Child Labor Committee in its early days; but there were also moderates like the lawyer, George Alger, who saw the committee's work as the moral obligation of a society whose "professional and business life . . . has for its essential qualities, not decadence, but rather regeneration, in which moral forces have not lost ground but are receiving a sure and constant increase of power."[57]

[55]McLoughlin, *Revivalism*, pp. 314–26.

[56]See James Timberlake, *Prohibition and the Progressive Movement* (Cambridge, Mass., 1963), especially pp. 33–38.

[57]Jeremy P. Felt, *Hostages of Fortune: Child Labor Reform in New York State* (Syracuse, N.Y., 1965), p. 217. On the pluralism of progressive reform and espe-

In other types of reform, such as improvement of municipal government, the preoccupation of business interests with improving efficiency of services they needed and with reducing taxes tended fairly early to alienate those with a broader concern for social justice. As the Chicago Civic Federation lost its first flush of enthusiasm for a wider civic renaissance after 1894, Jane Addams lost interest in the federation, maintaining only a nominal connection.

Another kind of division among reformers was even less common in the early years of progressivism. Most progressives began with assumptions of common values and of an ideal type of citizen to which Americans should conform. But among urban progressives concerned with social justice, an important and growing minority were coming to question the moral code they had inherited and the desirability of attempting to impose it upon immigrants with different values. New currents in philosophy, notably pragmatism, encouraged this tendency toward cultural pluralism as against Americanization.

Among most prewar reformers the tendency toward questioning the older morality did not go much beyond purging solemnity, overscrupulousness, and intolerance from an idea of the good life, which was native and Protestant in its sense of what was wholesome, innocent, and therefore desirable. For example, despite their rejection of the prudery of gentility in favor of the earthier fraternal democracy of Walt Whitman, "Golden Rule" Jones, Brand Whitlock, and their friends did not oppose the precepts of evangelical morality as such. Full rebellion against the older morality was not characteristic of progressivism.

It is no accident that the most popular American songs of the twentieth century celebrating an ideal of innocent romance and decent fun in a rural or small-town setting were written in the first decade. "In the Good Old Summertime" (1902), "In the Shade of the Old Apple Tree" (1905), "School Days" (1907), and "Down by the Old Mill Stream" (1910) appeared in the years when Americans were beginning to move away from the more restricting qualities of nineteenth-century evangelical and small-town culture. Yet at the same time Americans were nostalgic for

---

cially the contrast between "social justice" and "moral" or "good government" reformers, see Yellowitz, *Labor and the Progressive Movement,* Introduction; and Daniel Levine, *Varieties of Reform Thought* (Madison, Wis., 1964), pp. 109–17.

the simplicity, security, and warmth that past represented by contrast with a more complicated urban and industrial existence. The songs captured a social ideal just before the actuality and the sense of innocence associated with it vanished forever.

This ideal of democratic brotherhood, of a relaxed and good-natured neighborliness, appears in George Creel's reminiscence of the golden age before the world war. His account of how "those two blessed small towns [Independence and Odessa, Missouri] . . . helped to drive home the essential meaning of Americanism" assumes mythic proportions, embodying all the chief progressive values.

> There, throughout my formative years, I saw democracy in action—not just a word but something you could *feel*. No dividing line between the rich and poor, and no class distinctions to breed mean envies. The wealthiest merchant stood behind his counter, and the banker walked home of an evening with the round steak for supper tucked under his arm. . . . When Mother came down with a fever, the neighbors flooded in with broths and extra sheets and blankets, and in turn I ran my legs off carrying little delicacies to sick friends. ' "Miz" Jones, here's something Mamma thought you might relish.'[58]

The progressives were pre-Freudian not so much in failing to recognize the importance of sexuality as in believing that there was no necessary and warping conflict between the demands of civilization and the instincts of the human animal. They knew how sadistic and perverse in their pleasures human beings could become, but the mark of their faith was the belief that their ideal of normality and goodness was human nature itself. As William Allen White said in 1926 in an introduction to Fremont Older's poignant memoir of how he gradually lost his faith in the ability of people to change much, Older "rose up in the days following the Civil War, full of ideals, full of aspirations, full of that rampant love of man and belief in man's decency which was the motive of his time . . . that old-fashioned notion that men are good, that they want to be decent, that they would like to be honest, aspiring, neighborly and affectionately helpful."[59]

It was the vision of a new democracy realizing inherited notions of decency, of a brotherhood of man perfecting small-town notions of neighborliness, that distinguished the progressives.

[58]Creel, *Rebel at Large*, p. 24.
[59]Fremont Older, *My Own Story* (New York, 1926), pp. x–xi.

Faith in its possibility reflected a common appraisal that the vision had never really been given a full and fair trial, that even the approximations to true democracy and brotherhood in some of America's small towns never characterized the nation as a whole.

The vision did not depend upon agreement in ideas about reform, but it did involve certain consistent themes. One was the broad goal of a classless society. Progressives opposed privileges for the rich, but most of them also were uneasy about, and many were adamantly opposed to, reforms that favored a special class—even such contemporary underdogs as the factory worker or the farmer. The ideal went beyond a wish to obliterate group antagonisms and to encourage mobility according to individual merit. It verged constantly on a social ideal in which all difference of opinion on fundamentals disappeared, in which social harmony was achieved by that impulse to conformity Tocqueville feared in egalitarianism. Woodrow Wilson stated it baldly when he described the public schools as "the genuine melting pot of equality into which when children entered they came out Americans, adjusted to the conditions of our life, acquainted with each other, having a common impulse and common training, a common point of view."[60]

The second major theme of the vision directly reflects the evangelical preparation for progressivism. Christianity, at least in its primitive form, appears as a primary source of the ideal of democracy and as a continuing standard of judgment for any failures in realizing that ideal. Reminiscing about an episode of church membership as a young woman, Jane Addams offered as part of her rationale for joining a church her increasing and "almost passionate devotion to the ideals of democracy. . . . When in all history had these ideals been so thrillingly expressed as when the faith of the fisherman and the slave had been boldly opposed to the accepted moral belief that the well-being of a privileged few might justly be built upon the ignorance and sacrifice of the many?"[61]

There was nothing accidental in Herbert Bigelow's use of

[60]Woodrow Wilson, "Human Rights," September 18, 1912, in Davidson, ed., *Crossroads*, p. 194.

[61]Christopher Lasch, ed., *The Social Thought of Jane Addams* (Indianapolis, Ind., 1965), pp. 21–22.

parables, Biblical quotations, and generally a quasi-religious appeal to middle-of-the-road supporters to stay in line for the initiative and referendum at the Ohio Constitutional Convention in 1912. "Oh, my friends, we are striking down tyranny. We are forging the greatest tools democracy ever had. . . . Our task is a profoundly religious one."[62] Later in the same year the Progressive Party, as Amos Pinchot observed, deliberately went "into battle singing hymns and announcing that we will stand at Armageddon and battle for the Lord. From the very beginning, we have framed our campaign rather as a crusade than as a political fight."[63]

"Golden Rule" Jones had anticipated this fusion of religiosity and democracy when he told his employees in 1900, "We are to see in the near future a wave of revival that shall sweep over this country and, indeed, the civilized world, that shall be, in the best sense of the word, a revival of real religion; the setting up of a social and political order that will enable every man and woman to be the best kind of a man or woman that he or she is capable of being. The noble, the patriotic thing for each now is to do his best to spread the truth of Equality, of Brotherhood, that alone can bring the better days."[64]

More remarkable than this relating of democracy and the religion of Jesus was the assumption that, ultimately, most social and economic questions could be reduced to moral questions to which Christianity had a clear answer. Progressives of every type, from Bryan and the WCTU to Samuel M. Jones and Lincoln Steffens, made the Golden Rule and other precepts of Jesus the key to solving all the problems of mankind. Bryan had no hesitation, for example, about defining God's law of rewards and deducing anti-monopolism therefrom. Even those who disagreed with Bryan in politics could say, as the Springfield, Massachusetts, *Republican* did in 1908, "of lay preaching such as Mr. Bryan's we need more and not less. The message of the pulpit can gain converting power in secular lips as it is seen that the ideals of the 'sacred office' are convertible into terms of everyday good citizenship . . . and that the life and words of Jesus Christ still constitute the great solvent

[62]Quoted in H. L. Warner, *Progressivism in Ohio, 1897–1917* (Columbus, Ohio, 1964), p. 322.

[63]Pinchot to Theodore Roosevelt, December 3, 1912, in Amos Pinchot, *History of the Progressive Party*, Helene M. Hooker, ed. (New York, 1958), p. 184.

[64]Samuel M. Jones, *Letters of Love and Labor* (Toledo, Ohio, 1900), pp. 7–8.

of problems that vex the community, the nation, and the great family of nations."[65]

At the extreme of anticlericalism Lincoln Steffens came to an equal appreciation of the teachings of Jesus. Writing to Congressman William Kent in 1910, he explained that his drift toward Christianity had been slower than Kent's and directly occasioned by his search for remedies to the social questions his muckraking posed. "I studied socialism, anarchism, the single tax, and finally (from time to time), the Bible. And I was amazed at the teachings of Jesus. They seemed to me to be new . . . I think their freshness was due in part to the irreverent way in which I read the New Testament, but also to the fact that Christianity is seldom taught in the Christian churches. However that may be, I find that Jesus saw what we see; he understood, as his disciples don't, the evils, their causes; and he had a cure."[66]

The Jesus that commanded Steffens's respect was not the sweet Jesus of evangelical pietism. He was Jesus the carpenter, the first democratic reformer, fashioned from more than a half century of Biblical criticism and from the imagery of Christian Socialists and labor organizations. Steffens himself noted that the scholars "are separating the authentic from some of the bogus stuff in the book and enabling one to get a clearer, liver, more human sense of the Son of Man." This new image of Jesus was a fitting symbol for a progressivism self-consciously trying to fuse a realism of outlook and method with its Christian and democratic idealism.

So moderate a progressive as William Allen White wrote to Theodore Roosevelt in 1912, "I do not like the idea of the pale, feminine, wishy-washy, otherworldly Christ that has grown out of the monkish idea of religion. I have always thought that Paul was an old standpatter who came in and captured the Christian caucus and ran it into the organization."[67] White liked a book by the Christian Socialist Bouck White, entitled *The Call of the Carpenter*

[65]Springfield (Massachusetts) *Republican* as quoted in *The Commoner Condensed*, VII (Chicago, 1908), 132.

[66]Steffens to William Kent, April 19, 1912, in Ella Winter and Granville Hicks, eds., *The Letters of Lincoln Steffens*, I (New York, 1938), 243.

[67]White to Roosevelt, January 16, 1912, in Johnson, ed., *Letters*, pp. 130–31; for the image of Jesus as reformer, see especially Upton Sinclair, ed., *The Cry for Justice* (Philadelphia, 1915), Book VII.

(1911), which depicted Christ as the sturdy and deliberate strate-gist of "proletarian" emancipation within the Roman empire. The Kansas editor added, however, that he wished the book "had been written more in the spirit of Tolstoy."

The confusion of Christ with American culture was almost complete. In 1912 a massive evangelistic campaign by laymen from the major Protestant denominations culminated in a Con-gress that showed how far the churches themselves participated in the confusion. The Men and Religion Forward Movement had begun in 1910 under the auspices of lay brotherhoods of the Bap-tist, Methodist, Presbyterian, Episcopalian, and Congregational denominations as well as the International Sunday School Asso-ciation, the Gideons, and the International Committee of the YMCA.

The 1912 Congress reported that in a year and a half of prep-aration and six months of the campaign itself there had been an attendance of 1,491,245 at 7,062 meetings. Reports were pub-lished on Evangelism, Social Service, Christian Unity, Men's and Boys' Work, Rural Churches, and Publicity, emphasizing the im-portance to the churches of relying on experts in each of these endeavors. In his opening address the chairman said, "This won-derful age of ours, instead of pushing away from God and Christ, has by its discoveries and scientific attainment, rather brought us back to the simplicity of the gospel. . . . The harvest is white to the gathering."[68]

Two of the reports struck the major themes. That on Evan-gelism noted that "religious questions have become so closely related to ethical theories and moral issues that the line of de-marcation between the secular and religious, as such, has been erased." That on Social Service noted that in the last six months "social service had become a household phrase to laymen who before would have looked upon it with suspicion." Walter Rau-schenbusch went further, claiming that the "social gospel has now come to be one of the dogmas of the Christian faith." The churches were urged to develop councils or federations in the cities, with working committees specializing in tuberculosis, the county jail, work house, juvenile court, housing and sanitation, industrial peace and unemployment, the social evil, and substi-tutes for the saloon. These committees should work closely with

[68]*Messages of the Men and Religion Movement*, I, 9.

municipal agencies and should "combine the love of social science with the love of man."[69]

There were a few uneasy voices at the congress. One clergyman who described himself as an experimentalist and an institutionalist said nevertheless that he was worried about the tendency to submerge religion in reform: "If we are seeking for these things along so-called altruistic or humanitarian lines, then I say in the fear of God, let us be mighty cautious about this social service movement."[70] The warning went unheeded. By 1914 concern with religious experience and personal conversion had declined to such a point that Billy Sunday protested, "some people are trying to make a religion out of social service with Jesus Christ left out."[71]

Almost a century before, Charles Finney, the greatest antebellum revivalist, had prepared the way unwittingly for the fusion of Protestant Christianity and American culture, a fusion susceptible to interpretations favoring the social gospel or the gospel of wealth, reform or the status quo. His most flamboyant successor in the work of inducing religious harvests now sounded the alarm to save the gospel. But except in the most superficial sense of a reaffirmation of supernaturalism, Billy Sunday's religious fundamentalism was not a return to a gospel transcending culture. Sunday's amalgam of piety, popular prejudices, and laissez-faire conservatism simply substituted 100 percent Americanism for the crusade to make the nation and the world safe for democracy.

The very vagueness of the vision and rhetoric of a Christian democracy created a semblance of national unity of purpose, encouraging the progressive generation to minimize divisions between various kinds of reformers and conservatives within and outside the churches. In the twenties that vision and rhetoric no longer attracted many native middle-class Americans and the divisions had become all too obvious.

[69]*Ibid.*, III, 219; II, 107, 122.

[70]*Ibid.*, I, 59.

[71]Quoted in McLoughlin, *Revivalism*, p. 399.

THE CULTURE
OF THE TWENTIES

Loren Baritz / **UNIVERSITY OF MASSACHUSETTS, AMHERST**

In his elegant and searching survey of the material implications of the work done at the Paris Peace Conference, John Maynard Keynes concluded that "we are at the dead season of our fortune." He believed that the war had produced the kind of emotional exhaustion that restricted vision, feeling, and thought to the limits of the self. According to Keynes, having implicated themselves so fully in the public realm during the war, men, especially in England and America, could no longer be moved by public events of whatever magnitude or intensity. In turning to the peace, such men turned from society; the men of a wounded world demanded the time now to attend to themselves. Thus it was, as Keynes put it in the final sentence of his book, that "the true voice of the new generation has not yet spoken, and silent opinion is not yet formed."[1] If Keynes was right, that "true voice" when it became audible might tell of somewhat unaccustomed things, might find the perhaps autonomous, perhaps isolated, perhaps alienated self a continuingly satisfying subject. Even if that should occur, however, the voice of the twenties would not tell of things never before heard in ways never before imagined. It did occur, and it had a history.

Thinking of the mid-twenties, F. Scott Fitzgerald later remembered that "life . . . was largely a personal matter."[2] Fitzgerald,

[1]John Maynard Keynes, *The Economic Consequences of the Peace* (New York: Harcourt, Brace & World, Inc., 1920), pp. 297–98.

[2]F. Scott Fitzgerald, *The Crack-Up*, Edmund Wilson, ed. (New York: New Directions Publishing Corporation, 1945), p. 70. (Copyright 1945 by New Directions

along with other writers, artists, and intellectuals who flourished then, had a deep sense of the uniqueness of that decade. Fitzgerald himself claimed to have found the most descriptive and characteristic label: he had baptized those years "The Jazz Age."[3] And Gertrude Stein, following a lead given her by the manager of a garage in Paris, gave Hemingway another, and more important, characterization: "All of you young people who served in the war," she said, "you are a lost generation."[4]

The decade's writers seemed to agree with Keynes's worried prophecy. Regardless of the attribute emphasized, many of the most articulate spokesmen of the time eventually concluded that they had occupied a parenthesis in historical time, one that opened with the Armistice and closed with the crash. The feeling of having come from nowhere and of being headed toward no discoverable destination was described with sufficient power to convince later generations that at least the cultural life of the decade had in fact swung free in time. The writers of the lost generation who occupied the jazz age, in convincing themselves that they were rootless and aimless, seem also to have convinced others.

Though an important part of the brief in defense of their uniqueness is true, it is too simple. Thinking for the moment only of Keynes's description of the retreat into privacy and of Stein's intended meaning about the loss of identity that came from war, one can easily—perhaps too easily—cast up an intellectual and emotional genealogy that would presumably prove that the ideas and tonalities of the twenties had long been familiar in the American and European landscapes. The literature of disillusion has its own history, as does that of the feeling of cultural isolation. One needs only to open the American ledger to the pages devoted to Poe and Melville to see how rich and how clear that background is. The sense that the present generation has wearily climbed beyond earlier ones, that the present must suffer because of the stupidities of the past, that the son must break free from

Publishing Corporation. Reprinted by permission of New Directions Publishing Corporation.

[3] F. Scott Fitzgerald to M. Perkins, May 21, 1931, F. Scott Fitzgerald, *Letters,* Andrew Turnbull, ed. (New York: Charles Scribner's Sons, 1965), p. 225.

[4] Ernest Hemingway, *A Moveable Feast* (New York: Charles Scribner's Sons, 1964), p. 29.

the father or lose his own authenticity, has characterized perhaps every single decade of the American story from the Puritans forward. The celebration of the private self and recoil from society may be found at the very heart of what most of the New England transcendentalists had tried to say. None of this came newborn and fully developed from the forehead of Fitzgerald or anyone else.

It has been shown that a significant part of the generation immediately before World War I was itself in rebellion against many of the same aspects of middle-class American life that in the twenties were found inhibiting, stultifying, and suffocating.[5] This must mean that the war did not, as was so often assumed at the time and since, produce that pervasive wave of disillusion and, on occasion, pessimism that always seemed to rise to the surface of the twenties. If similar disillusion existed before the war, how could the war be considered its cause? The impeccable logic of that question may not turn out to be conclusive, as we will see.

I

The stage was properly set by four quite different works that were all published in 1920. To understand the mood and thrust of each is to open the larger themes of the twenties. In *Hugh Selwyn Mauberley*, Ezra Pound, with an electric condensation of rage and outrage, utterly rejected the war, repudiated the peace, and condemned that civilization whose rottenness was the cause. The corrupt complacencies of the antebellum world were replaced with new crimes. The political leaders of the world at peace were liars, and the young men who had died for their European countries had died "For an old bitch gone in the teeth."[6] The war, in Pound's view, was simply a catastrophic waste that was made

---

[5]See, for example, Henry F. May, *The End of American Innocence* (New York, 1959), passim; Christopher Lasch, *The New Radicalism in America, 1889–1963* (New York, 1965), pp. 253–54. The surge of poetry in the twenties similarly began with the prewar generation; see Conrad Aiken, "Poetry," in Harold E. Stearns, ed., *Civilization in the United States* (New York, 1922), p. 217.

[6]Ezra Pound, *Hugh Selwyn Mauberley*, reprinted in Frederick J. Hoffman, *The Twenties* (New York, 1955), p. 438. From *Personal: The Collected Poems of Ezra Pound* (New York: New Directions Publishing Corporation), copyright 1926, 1954 by Ezra Pound.

necessary because of the power held by those pretty Victorians and Edwardians on both continents who would bleed the younger generation in order to conserve the corruption of the old.

Though Pound's temperature was higher than most, he spoke for a wide circle of articulate young people. The impact of that view on America was severe. George Santayana, in *Character and Opinion in the United States*, another work published in 1920, believed that recent experience had aged America, functioning as a kind of puberty rite that symbolized the passage to adulthood, the passage from innocence to experience, from callowness to a sense of tragedy. As he saw it, America had been taught that it could no longer pretend to self-determination: "Hitherto America has been the land of universal goodwill, confidence in life, inexperience of poisons. Until yesterday it believed itself immune from the hereditary plagues of mankind."[7]

The impact of that cultural shock on an individual can be found in Fitzgerald's youthful and excited first book, *This Side of Paradise*, also published in 1920. On the last page of that novel, the narrator muses about the men at Princeton: "Here was a new generation, shouting the old cries, learning the old creeds, through a revery of long days and nights; destined finally to go out into that dirty gray turmoil to follow love and pride; a new generation dedicated more than the last to the fear of poverty and the worship of success; grown up to find all Gods dead, all wars fought, all faiths in man shaken."[8] If Santayana was right, the discovery that America was susceptible to ugliness and pain meant, for the young Fitzgerald, an instant world-weariness. American faith, when shaken once, seemed completely destroyed. Pleasure was the residual goal, along with the glamor and private power that formed the foundation of the jazz age.

Sinclair Lewis's *Main Street* completes this quartet of works published in the first year of the twenties. It was in many ways, despite its occasional cardboard characters, the most premonitory of the four. Lewis raises issues developed in each of the other works: Was the past dead? Had the war been rejected? Had America gone through its rites of passage? Were gods and faiths dead? There were places in America, he contended, where

[7]George Santayana, *Character and Opinion in the United States* (Garden City, N.Y.: Doubleday Anchor, 1956), p. 89.

[8]F. Scott Fitzgerald, *This Side of Paradise* (New York: Charles Scribner's Sons, 1920), p. 282.

the answer was no. In the American small town the terrible education suffered by an intellectual or artistic elite was simply unavailable.

The mentality of nonmetropolitan America had not had to agonize about the tragic in modern life. The pieties and faiths of a more comfortable past remained untouched or unyielding. Lewis telegraphed his attitude in the opening lines of the foreword to the novel: "Main Street is the climax of civilization. That this Ford car might stand in front of the Bon Ton Store, Hannibal invaded Rome and Erasmus wrote in Oxford cloisters."[9] The small town and small city, against which so many American intellectuals, artists, and writers revolted in the twenties, was secure enough not to appear to take particular notice of the latest noise from America's bohemia. Evidently closed to new possibilities and to alternatives, the village, as Lewis sketched it, continued to define itself as both the center and goal of the universe.

Carol Kennicott, the simultaneously rebellious and acquiescent heroine of *Main Street*, confessed that American mythology had acquainted her with only two traditions about the village. The first told that the small town was the essential repository of all virtue, the single habitat of "clean, sweet marriageable girls."[10] Ambitious boys might forsake their parental homestead in search of success or sophistication, but they would ultimately come to their senses, return to the village, rediscover the childhood sweetheart, marry, settle down, and live happily ever after. The other tradition described the town as rich in local color, picturesque, and infinitely amusing in its "whiskered rusticity." The truths that Carol discovered about Gopher Prairie reveal what most of America's creative people thought of the American village and consequently of the American past:

> It is an unimaginatively standardized background, a sluggishness of speech and manners, a rigid ruling of the spirit by the desire to appear respectable. It is contentment . . . the contentment of the quiet dead, who are scornful of the living for their restless walking. It is negation canonized as the one positive virtue. It is the prohibition of happiness. It is slavery self-sought and self-defended. It is dullness made God.
>
> A savorless people, gulping tasteless food, and sitting afterward,

[9]Sinclair Lewis, *Main Street* (New York: Harcourt, Brace & World, Inc., 1920), foreword.

[10]Ibid., p. 264.

coatless and thoughtless, in rocking-chairs prickly with inane decorations, listening to mechanical music, saying mechanical things about the excellence of Ford automobiles, and viewing themselves as the greatest race in the world.[11]

Though Carol believed that the prairie perhaps had a magnificent future, she finally concluded that she had somehow to resist its present. Urging a young man to break away, to go east, she also urged him to return in order to explain what the citizens of Gopher Prairie should do with the land they were clearing, "if," she said, "we'll listen—if we don't lynch you first!"[12]
    What Carol demanded of her husband and of Gopher Prairie was the substitution of one kind of sublimation for another. Thinking of the wives of American villagers as part of the oppressed classes of the world,[13] she thought that "we want a more conscious life." She felt unable to continue living a life of postponement as "the politicians and priests and cautious reformers (and the husbands!)" continually advised. She demanded her own utopia, and now: "All we want is—everything for all of us!"[14] She knew she would fail and explained that that was why she would never be content. She did not have secret yearnings for the heady atmosphere of bohemia; she wanted everything, to be sure, but everything that would still comport with her own sense of decorum, a sense not entirely different from her husband's.

II

To encounter provincial America only in the writings of those who had declared war on it is finally to see merely a bizarre, pathetic, and infinitely comic phenomenon. Ludwig Lewisohn, Sherwood Anderson, and, above all, H. L. Mencken could conjure up the simple yokel whose five thumbs made him a lower order of creature, but that portrayal ignores the yokel's political strength. The American province, to put it most simply, was also commit-

---

[11]Ibid., p. 265.

[12]Ibid., p. 343.

[13]Cf. F. Scott Fitzgerald to his daughter, Oct. 5, 1940, in *Letters*, p. 96: "I think the faces of most American women over thirty are relief maps of petulant and bewildered unhappiness."

[14]Lewis, *Main Street*, p. 201.

ted to war, had a vast and dangerous arsenal, and won almost every major battle it entered. It was in virtual control of America's public life during the twenties, and the dismay of the writers and artists cannot be fully understood in any other context. They could dream of a world free of the province, but the contemporary provincial hegemony made it impossible to predict what that world would be like. "Who knows," Walter Lippmann asked, "having read Mr. Mencken and Mr. Sinclair Lewis, what kind of world will be left when all the boobs and yokels have crawled back in their holes and have died in shame?"[15] And those creatures would refuse to crawl away without a bitter fight. One example will make the point; a newspaper editor and supporter of the Prohibition party designed his early tirade to catch virtually all of the vibration in America's provincial civilization:

> Besodden Europe, worse bescourged than by war, famine and pestilence, sends here her drink-makers, her drunkard-makers, and her drunkards, or her more temperate but habitual drinkers, with all their un-American and anti-American ideas of morality and government; they are absorbed into our national life, but not assimilated; with no liberty whence they came, they demand unrestricted liberty among us, even to license for things we loathe; and through the ballotbox, flung wide open to them by foolish statesmanship that covets power, their foriegn control or conquest has become largely an appalling fact; they dominate our Sabbath, over large areas of country; they have set up for us their own moral standards, which are grossly immoral; they govern our great cities, until even Reform candidates accept their authority and pledge themselves to obey it; the great cities govern the nation; and foreign control or conquest could gain little more, though secured by foreign armies and fleets.[16]

Mencken's yokel might amuse the sophisticated, but the yokel might have found the sometimes frantic parody comic, too. He must have known something about political power because, though he had to fight, he almost always won. The fight, for him, was to implement that phrase of Harding's: "not heroics but healing; not nostrums but normalcy; not revolution but restoration." As the intellectual could reject the war because the peace had not gone far enough, provincial Americans apparently grew restive

[15]Walter Lippmann, *A Preface to Morals* (New York, 1929), p. 16.

[16]Alphonso Alva Hopkins, quoted in Andrew Sinclair, *Prohibition: The Era of Excess* (Boston: Little, Brown and Company, 1962), p. 19.

because it had gone too far. The public policy the villager and burgher demanded was designed to recreate a known and presumably safer but seriously threatened earlier America. The legislation sought was intended to re-create that supposedly more congenial time when values were clearer, when religion was more secure, when intellectuals were supposedly better housebroken, when farmers were supposedly dominant in the fields cleared from God's country.

William Jennings Bryan, the spokesman of rural and sometimes of provincial America, could seem thoroughly ludicrous to some, but he too knew something. He knew that the nation had changed, that urbanization and industrialism together with enormous immigration were generating political, economic, and even moral forces that were repugnant to the idyllic, Protestant, and democratic America he envisaged. He knew that something more important than the publication of the four books mentioned above occurred in 1920: for the first time in American history, according to the census bureau, more Americans were living in cities than in the countryside and villages combined. That single fact may explain some of the urgency in the battle of the small town and small city against continued uncontrolled change.

The massive power of nonmetropolitan America may best be understood by viewing national policy and significant social phenomena as designed to arrest change rather than to recapture the alleged simplicity and morality of a past but still desired rural civilization. "Foreign" influences in national or religious terms, urban power with its pathology in crime and corruption, and the intellectual life constituted the dark trinity that the villager and the burgher were determined to destroy.

In simple economic terms, the American farmer suffered depression throughout most of the decade; in simple occupational terms, the Republican Presidents represented business, not farmers or villagers. But from a wider perspective, the provincial mentality was virtually incarnate in Harding and Coolidge, and Hoover, too, spoke with and for the village in the special circumstance of his rival's thoroughly urban, Catholic, and wet background. It is true that rural political insurgency continued to sputter through the twenties, but the dominant issues were no longer political. The collapsing alliance between old-time urban and rural reformers, the failure of national leadership, prosperity, exhaustion, boredom, and fear of change, together with Wilson's own example of defeat, all combined to wound if not destroy the earlier progressive movement.[17] The small city—Zenith, Sinclair Lewis called it—exercised its power over the nation through its values, attitudes, and ideals; though it would be beset perhaps from desperate farmers on the one side, and the urban middle classes along with intellectuals on the other, it could generally rely on enough support in all quarters to ensure victory.

In their terms, the most abstract battle fought by villagers and their allies in small cities was the place and role of the United States in world affairs. Whether they were simple isolationists is an ongoing debate.[18] We know, obviously, that the League of Nations was repudiated, though American participation, such as it was, increased throughout the decade. The Kellogg-Briand Pact was intended to outlaw war through the moral pressure of world opinion. Furthermore, American corporate interests extended to virtually every corner of the world. But public policy was not planned in the major cities; Zenith's George Babbitt, with his realtor's reflexes, could smile indulgently at the wishful thinking of the Kellogg-Briand Pact, could smile unreservedly in appreciation of the expansion and extension of American business (and therefore approve high protective tariffs), and could bristle with indignation over the League with its supposed threat of "furrin" control.

The key to provincial desires and power, one that opens the door to almost everything else, is Prohibition, the single most revealing phenomenon of the time. It too, appropriately, went into effect in the first year of the decade, and was to last almost fourteen years. That "noble experiment" was preeminently the creature of the provincial, middle-class, Protestant, white American. The alignment over the Eighteenth Amendment in the House of Representatives shows what happened. The amendment was supported by 197 representatives; 129 were from towns of less than ten thousand, and 64 came from villages of less than twenty-

---

[17]See, for example, Arthur S. Link, "What Happened to the Progressive Movement in the 1920's?" *American Historical Review*, LXIV, 4 (July, 1959), 833–51; Richard Hofstadter, *The Age of Reform* (New York, 1960), esp. pp. 272–301; Arthur M. Schlesinger, Jr., *The Crisis of the Old Order* (Boston, 1957), pp. 11–124.

[18]McGeorge Bundy, "Foreign Policy: From Innocence to Engagement," in A. M. Schlesinger, Jr., and Morton White, eds., *Paths of American Thought* (Boston, 1963), pp. 293–308; George F. Kennan, *American Diplomacy* (Chicago, 1951), pp. 55–73; William Appleman Williams, "The Legend of Isolationism in the 1920's," *Science and Society*, XVIII (Winter, 1954), 1–20.

five hundred. The amendment was opposed by 190 representatives; 109 came from cities of over twenty-five thousand. "In fact," as the movement's most acute historian put it, "national prohibition was a measure passed by village America against urban America."[19] The war brought urban allies to the villager because of the identification of beer with the kaiser, of alcohol with unpatriotic waste and selfishness during a national crisis. That alliance made the ratification of the Eighteenth Amendment possible. After the Volstead Act and the coming of peace, the urban-village coalition broke, showing the determined core of prohibitionism to be as always in the Methodist and Baptist churches, in villages and towns across the nation, among Southerners fearful of drunken Negroes, among employers wanting sober laborers and afraid of drunken agitators, and among nativists who believed that swarthy aliens would commit their worst excesses if given access to booze. A historian caught the basic strategy of the prohibitionists: "The emotion which they exploited was fear: the fear of sin and God; the fear of race against race and skin against skin; the fear of venereal diseases; the fear of idiot children; the fear of violence suppressed by conscience and loosed by liquor; and the dark sexual fears of civilization."[20] The rich and middle-class urbanite could get liquor if he wanted it, but he had to contribute to Al Capone to do it, thereby confirming the dry villagers in all of their suspicions about urban corruption, the wages of sin, and the menace of foreigners. Nothing less than the protection of God and country was involved in Prohibition, and the provincial American was militant.

Those same goals became the battle cry of the renewed Ku Klux Klan, whose membership rose to approximately four million in the twenties. Prohibition and the Klan both aimed at restoring the values of an earlier America, values that were eroding under the waves of immigrants, cities, irreligion, science, and modernity in general. A dentist from Texas, Hiram Wesley Evans, became the national leader, the Imperial Wizard and Emperor, of the Klan in 1922, and a few years later published an article claiming that his organization was the only effective defense of traditional America, a brake on noxious change, and the true locus of patriotism.

Klansmen, according to Evans, "have enlisted our racial in-

[19]Sinclair, *Prohibition*, p. 163.
[20]Ibid., p. 46.

stincts for the work of preserving and developing our American traditions and customs."²¹ He argued that the Klan had succeeded in limiting its earlier violence and internal corruption and had now thrown its full weight against the results of the melting pot, which, he said, the Klan considered "a ghastly failure" whose "very name was coined by a member of one of the races—the Jews—which most determinedly refuses to melt."²² No alien and no "alien idea" could be tolerated in the America he envisaged. In order to purge successfully, the Klan had broken with liberalism because that ideology "had provided no defense against the alien invasion, but instead had excused it—even defended it against Americanism. Liberalism," Evans said, "is today charged in the mind of most Americans with nothing less than national, racial and spiritual treason."²³ The Klan supposedly opposed the Catholic Church on political rather than religious grounds and, following the lead of Madison Grant and Lothrop Stoddard, opposed the Negro and eastern European Jews on racial grounds and western European Jews on religious grounds. All constituted a direct menace for the white, Protestant, Anglo-Saxon American villager. Knowing that he and his kind were under some kind of attack for being villagers, Evans took the offensive:

> We are a movement of the plain people, very weak in the matter of culture, intellectual support, and trained leadership. We are demanding, and we expect to win, a return of power into the hands of the everyday, not highly cultured, not overly intellectualized, but entirely unspoiled and not de-Americanized average citizen of the old stock. . . . This is undoubtedly a weakness. It lays us open to the charge of being 'hicks' and 'rubes' and 'drivers of second hand Fords.' We admit it. . . . The Klan does not believe that the fact that it is emotional and instinctive, rather than coldly intellectual, is a weakness. . . . [Emotions and instincts] are the foundations of our American civilization, even more than our great historic documents; they can be trusted where the fine-haired reasoning of the denatured intellectuals cannot.²⁴

²¹Hiram Wesley Evans, "The Klan's Fight for Americanism," *The North American Review*, CCXXIII (March–May, 1926), 35. Reprinted in Richard M. Abrams and Lawrence W. Levine, eds., *The Shaping of Twentieth-Century America* (Boston, 1965), p. 386.

²²Ibid., p. 40.

²³Ibid., p. 42.

²⁴Ibid., p. 49.

Evans was responding to all of the strains in the provincial mentality: the alleged moral superiority, evangelical and fundamentalist religion, anti-intellectualism, racism, nativism, and hypertrophy of patriotism. The imposition of quotas based on national origin (favoring those nations in which the villager's own family had probably originated) in the new immigration policies of the twenties shows that Evans was, in many ways, merely giving voice to attitudes that small-town America could and did enact into the law of the land. That the pressures for immigration restriction came from diverse interests and sections meant that, once again, the villager and small-city American could rely on outside support on specific issues. Intellectuals would protest that the idea of the great, blue-eyed blonde Nordic was a groundless "myth,"[25] but, groundless or not, it contributed to the blood knowledge of the Klan, as well as to national attitudes toward immigration.

That myth lurks also in the background of the Red Scare of 1919 and the early twenties and the subsequent Palmer raids. A. Mitchell Palmer, the attorney general, invented and initiated neither the fright nor the retribution. His action indicated vulnerability to the pressures from Zenith. Sharing the growing fear of revolution that would be caused by recent immigrants, Palmer described those aliens arrested in his raids: "Out of the sly and crafty eyes of many of them leap cupidity, cruelty, insanity, and crime; from their lopsided faces, sloping brows, and misshapen features may be recognized the unmistakable criminal type."[26] The east side of New York was the most favored lair of the Lev Bronstein, alias Leon Trotsky, type dedicated to the overthrow of Zenith, hence nation, hence God. At the very beginning of the decade, on January 2, the Palmer raids reached their height with over six thousand people taken into custody in the ensuing weeks.[27] If the alien could be deported, as legislation of May 1920 provided, or prevented from entering, as the new immigration policies provided, the old-stock American with his ideals and values would presumably be safer.

The alien threat was supposedly proved by the arrest and conviction for robbery and murder of Sacco and Vanzetti, two

[25]See, for example, C. E. Ayres, "The New Higher Criticism," *The New Republic*, XLV (Dec. 9, 1925), 85–86.

[26]Quoted in Stanley Coben, *A. Mitchell Palmer* (New York, 1963), p. 198.

[27]Ibid., p. 227.

semiliterate Italian radicals, confessed pacifists, and draft dodgers. They were convicted essentially because they were aliens. The issues dominating the trial were patriotism and radicalism. Again sophisticated men, such as Felix Frankfurter, protested: "By systematic exploitation of the defendants' alien blood, their imperfect knowledge of English, their unpopular social views, and their opposition to the war, the District Attorney invoked against them a riot of political passion and patriotic sentiment; and the trial judge connived at—one had almost written, cooperated in—the process."[28] The fears of the American provinces, whether Muncie or elsewhere, determined that Sacco and Vanzetti should be executed.

Those fears, as the Klan understood perfectly well, included the basic fear that alien gods would stalk the land, along with alien beer and ideologies, unless the Nordic American fought back. Religious fundamentalism was perhaps the most authentic expression of that native fight, and fundamentalism was a ligament that held Prohibition, the Klan, and nativism together. Billy Sunday's "Booze sermon" demanded more than abstinence; he called for the deportation of foreigners involved in bootlegging, as well as other dissenters who refused to kiss the American flag.[29] Mencken (in the *American Mercury*) and Sinclair Lewis (in *Elmer Gantry*) poured scorn on the evangelists who wrapped the cross in the flag and carried it in a Bible, who baptized by the thousands, and who attacked booze, Darwin, and anarchy in the same long breath. But fundamentalism, as an intense folk movement, could fight back, claiming, as the Klan claimed, that piety and too much education were mutually exclusive.[30]

Fundamentalism's best champion was William Jennings Bryan, and his chosen field for his final battle was Dayton, Tennessee. The Scopes trial, with Bryan and Clarence Darrow facing each other, concerned whether teaching evolution in the public schools was a punishable crime, but it also involved the continuing struggle between small and large cities. Bryan had protested the theory of evolution since the beginning of the twentieth century, but the fears that became exacerbated during the twenties con-

[28]Felix Frankfurter, "The Case of Sacco and Vanzetti," *The Atlantic Monthly*, CXXXIX, 3 (March, 1927), 421.

[29]Sinclair, *Prohibition*, p. 290.

[30]Norman F. Furniss, *The Fundamentalist Controversy* (New Haven, Conn.: Yale University Press, 1954), esp. pp. 39–41.

vinced him that direct action was then required. The silver-tongued orator shared so much of the provincial mood that he, too, adopted the usual aggressive apology for the lack of literary felicity of his adherents, and he, too, mounted an attack against cleverness and the mind, which must kill God. Early in the decade he accused that generation of "mind-worship—a worship as destructive as any other form of idolatry."[31] The head and the heart were at war, and that meant to him that America's folk religion was being subverted by most of the dark forces of the city:

> A scientific soviet is attempting to dictate what shall be taught in our schools and, in so doing, is attempting to mould the religion of the nation. It is the smallest, the most impudent, and the most tyrannical oligarchy that ever attempted to exercise arbitrary power.[32]

H. L. Mencken chortled, Darrow referred to Bryan's "fool ideas," but Bryan was more than the incredible figure that journalists and intellectuals exploited. Until he died a few days after the Scopes trial, he was the voice of nonmetropolitan America, especially with regard to fundamentalism.

The political and social power of the nonurban American means, of course, that he was something other than the silly clown that emerged from Mencken's pages. But Mencken also knew that provincial America had muscle, that he and fellow cosmopolites could not control the legislature. He betrayed this sentiment when he wrote: "Our laws are invented, in the main, by frauds and fanatics, and put upon the statute books by poltroons and scoundrels."[33] But others, too, understood the pervasive public power of the small town and wrote that it was necessary, at least secretly, to acknowledge that fact:

> The civilization of America is predominantly the civilization of the small town. The few libertarians and cosmopolites who can continue to profess to see a broader culture developing along the Atlantic seaboard resent this fact, though they scarcely deny it. They are too intelligent, too widened in vision, to deny it. They cannot watch the tremendous growth and power and influence of secret societies, of

[31]Quoted in Lawrence W. Levine, *Defender of the Faith* (New York: Oxford University Press, 1965), p. 279.

[32]Ibid., p. 289.

[33]H. L. Mencken, *Notes on Democracy* (New York: Alfred A. Knopf, Inc., 1926), p. 129.

chambers of commerce, of boosters' clubs, of the Ford car, of moving pictures, of talking-machines, of evangelists, of nerve tonics, of the *Saturday Evening Post*, of Browning societies, of circuses, of church socials, of parades and pageants of every kind and description, of family reunions, of pioneer picnics, of county fairs, of firemen's con- ventions without secretly acknowledging it. And they know, if they have obtained a true perspective of America, that there is no section of this vast political unit that does not possess—and even frequently boast—these unmistakably provincial signs and symbols.[34]

Clearly enough it was the strength, not the pathos or mere uncon- geniality, of the provinces that made the writers and artists react in the ways that they did. If it had been simply the latter, parody would have sufficed, but expatriation and high art aimed at the provinces are symptoms of the power of the enemy.

III

One result of the political power of the American small town and small city was the decision on the part of many intellectuals and writers simply to withdraw from politics. The disgust with the political process that had led to war and to Versailles also contributed to political quiescence. Whether the enemy was Bab- bitt or Woodrow Wilson or—more likely—both, the result was the same: Fitzgerald's life as a "personal matter."

Joseph Freeman, later to become an editor of a politically radical journal, remembered a canoe trip he had taken with a friend; they recited Plato and Swinburne but could not list the terms of the Treaty of Versailles.[35] A position that is much more extreme, but even more indicative of this political apathy is that of George Jean Nathan, Mencken's partner in parody:

The great problems of the world—social, political, economic and theo- logical—do not concern me in the slightest. If all the Armenians were to be killed tomorrow and if half of Russia were to starve to death the day after, it would not matter to me in the least. What concerns me alone is myself, and the interests of a few close friends. For all I care the rest of the world may go to hell at today's sunset.[36]

[34]Louis R. Reid, "The Small Town," in Stearns, *Civilization*, p. 286.

[35]Joseph Freeman, *An American Testament* (New York, 1936), p. 154.

[36]George Jean Nathan, quoted in William E. Leuchtenberg, *The Perils of Prosper- ity* (Chicago, 1958), p. 150.

The phenomenon of political retreat was sufficiently wide-spread to engage the attention of at least two important social analysts. By 1927 Walter Lippmann concluded that the combination of party splintering and affluence gave rise to bewilderment, complacency, and cynicism. It was, he argued, one thing to feel disgust with politics, but another to be able to avoid it; affluence made the difference. Social questions concerning the Klan, Prohibition, fundamentalism, immigration, evolution, and xenophobia continued to interest the electorate as phases in the war between province and city, but they were issues usually outside the formal political process. The economic boom, according to Lippmann, allowed these social issues to exist outside of politics,[37] as it allowed President Coolidge to announce that America's business was business.

John Dewey, in the same year, considered other reasons for that apathy. He also believed that the public was politically bewildered, but he concluded that the public had lost its political existence. The inability to identify with concrete issues resulted in the retreat from politics; the increasing complexity of American life made such concrete issues increasingly hard to find and, more important, created a crippling discrepancy between current political needs and the traditional political machinery. That discrepancy made the traditional actions and pronouncements of political leaders seem increasingly irrelevant to what people cared most about.[38]

> The present era of 'prosperity' may not be enduring. But the movie, radio, cheap reading matter and motor car with all they stand for have come to stay. That they did not originate in deliberate desire to divert attention from political interests does not lessen their effectiveness in that direction. The political elements in the constitution of the human being, those having to do with citizenship, are crowded to one side. In most circles it is hard work to sustain conversation on a political theme; and once initiated, it is quickly dismissed with a yawn. Let there be introduced the topic of the mechanism and accomplishment of various makes of motor cars or the respective merits of actresses, and the dialogue goes on at a lively pace.[39]

[37]Walter Lippmann, "The Causes of Political Indifference To-Day," *The Atlantic Monthly*, XXXIX, 2 (Feb., 1927), 261–68.

[38]John Dewey, *The Public and Its Problems* (New York, 1927), pp. 122–23, 134–35.

[39]Ibid., p. 139.

Furthermore, the increasing complexity of American life often made decisions too technical and specialized to create a devoted public, with the result that the public atomized. For that reason, no genuine community could be created, and that fact made a further advance in democratic efficiency impossible.[40] A genuine public, held together by political conviction and involvement, was a necessary condition for meaningful reform. As things stood, politics had degenerated into a mere reflex: "Only habit and tradition, rather than a reasoned conviction, together with a vague faith in doing one's civic duty, send to the polls a considerable percentage of the fifty percent who still vote."[41]

By now it is clear that Lippmann and Dewey had more in mind than the political withdrawal of scholars, writers, and artists. They were addressing a national problem that was manifested almost everywhere. The provincial American could retire with the conviction that he was the master of the legislature; the intellectuals and artists could thumb their noses at the public sector as they set out to explore what they believed to be more important terrain. But between the country village and Greenwich Village the rest of America lived. Relatively affluent, basically unchallenged, middle-class urban Americans constituted the middle term between the little lady in Dubuque and the literary exile in Paris. That middle term was the world of the jazz age, the flapper, the speakeasy, and the rest. Reaching both forward and backward, it knew it was not truly of either world. It was the booming new era, the Roaring Twenties. But it too was caught by the power of the village; it had to consume its booze secretly lest the village law cause embarrassment.

Middle-class urban America was not so far from its own rural or village past that the Red Scare would pass it by, that the Anti-Saloon League could find only a few urban adherents, that anti-immigration was a dead issue, that xenophobia generated no pressure. That America, as it were, would laugh with Mencken, frown with Sinclair Lewis, but do so without full certainty. It made best-sellers of both *Main Street* and *Elmer Gantry* along with Emily Post's *Etiquette* and, more revealing, Bruce Barton's *The Man Nobody Knows*. The most popular tunes, "Dinah" and "Ol' Man River," recalled the rural past, though Chaplin's popular comedies were invariably urban in spirit if not in setting.

[40]Ibid., pp. 157–58.
[41]Ibid., p. 135.

Middle-class urban America, feeling somewhat free of older sexual restraints, could tolerate the fashions of the flapper. Held's cartoon character inspired that craze and was a point-by-point repudiation of the earlier ideal of femininity, the Gibson girl. The Gibson girl had flowing hair, the flapper bobbed hers; shoulders, breasts, and the waistline were emphasized before the war, but the flapper bound her breasts flat and wore loosely fitted blouses; legs were voluminously covered by the Gibson girl, while the flapper raised her hemline above her knees and rolled her stockings below them.

The matter of sex created a vast urban market for a new publishing adventure. The sex "confession" and picture magazine made several fortunes. And yet, enough of the older morality survived to create incredible but by now familiar attitudes, as the letter an editor sent as instructions to his authors will show:

> I intend to keep—a sex magazine, but sex need not necessarily mean dirt. I want to stick to elementals, sex-elementals—the things closest to the heart of the average woman or girl, whatever her ignorance or sophistication. Above all, I mean to lift the moral tone of the magazine. I believe that to treat sex trivially is to diminish its dramatic value, while sober treatment enhances it. Characters may do anything they please but they must do it from some lofty, or apparently lofty, motive. If a girl falls, she must fall *upward*.[42]

The ostensible freedom of the flapper, her flat rejection of the modishness of the past, was countered by the village matron's firm conviction about the relevance and applicability of earlier standards and usages. Villagers had to embark on no quest for spiritual authority; morality, purity, and the home were, for them, unshaken though under criticism from the city. One civilized man struggling to keep his spirit alive while teaching at Ohio State encountered, to his obvious dismay, that provincial type: "thin-lipped, embittered by the poisons that unnatural repression breeds, with a curious flatness about the temples, with often, among the older men, a wiry, belligerent beard." He saw them with their ladies, "shallow-bosomed, ill-favored wives—stern advocates of virtue—walking on Sunday self-consciously to church."[43]

[42]Quoted in Ernest W. Mandeville, "Gutter Literature," *The New Republic*, XLV (Feb. 17, 1926), 350.

[43]Ludwig Lewisohn, *Up Stream* (New York: Liveright Publishing Corp., 1922), p. 186.

For intellectuals and artists, the brutality of the war that led only to the repugnant peace, together with the political prominence of provincial America, seemed to force them to withdraw into themselves, seemed to produce precisely what Keynes had feared. Feeling betrayed by history in war and peace and assaulted by the present in Prohibition, antievolution, and the rest, they tended to retract from society to become either exiles or unpolitical, antisocial, and alienated strangers at home. The lost generation was created by the war and nonurban America.

For the urban middle class, the brutality of the war could be forgotten in the bubbly ambience of the jazz age. Babe Ruth, Mah-Jongg, and crossword puzzles apparently could capture and hold attention. But affluence was the key; Fords and movie stars made their significant contribution to the depoliticization of the urban middle class. The sense, however, that the new era was an intense moment of personal liberation, of sexual freedom for women as well as men, evidently places the urbanite at least partly in the camp of the exiles. The past was as dead, disabling, and irrelevant to the urbanite as to the exile, as the flapper showed when she contradicted Gibson in such perfect detail. Also besieged by the village, the middle class could acquiesce more easily than the exiles. But enough feeling of futility was generated to induce the city dwellers to embark on Fitzgerald's quest for cash and success. Privacy was the result, and, though for dramatically different reasons, the flapper and the exile both turned their backs to society in their respective celebrations of the autonomous and inviolate individual. And neither could find a usable social past.

The search not for a usable past but for an alternative to the past is another of the revealing symptoms of the decade. The resulting conflict of generations gave at least one disillusioned intellectual grounds for measured optimism: "The most hopeful thing of intellectual promise in America today is the contempt of the younger people for their elders; they are restless, uneasy, disaffected." From that clash of old and new, the young would "attempt to create a way of life free from the bondage of an authority that has lost all meaning, even to those who wield it."[44] That this was an echo of a similar charge made by the prewar genera-

---

[44]Harold E. Stearns, "The Intellectual Life," in Stearns, *Civilization*, p. 149; cf., however, Lewis Mumford, "The Emergence of a Past," *The New Republic*, XLV (Nov. 25, 1925), 18–19.

tion—by Randolph Bourne in 1915, for example—should not obscure the fact that the special circumstance of the twenties gave a
new urgency and intensity to the paean to youth and the condem-
nation of age. Those circumstances similarly created the sense
that since all guideposts were down the future could be newly
charted. But those guideposts had once kept men from getting
hopelessly lost; they once had given a certain security; they once
signified that at least part of the world was known. Freedom from
the past was liberating, but also perhaps frightening.

The villager had succeeded in preventing a free experimental
method in politics, to John Dewey's dismay. Sanctifying the political institutions of the nation, the American villager was preventing significant change, maintaining control, and participating in a widespread human process: "As supernatural matters
have progressively been left high and dry upon a secluded beach,
the actuality of religious taboos has more and more gathered
about secular institutions, especially those connected with the
nationalistic state."[45] That is simply a different way of saying that
the small town had succeeded in dominating political institutions, thereby making the political process as such an anachronism for most intellectuals and artists.

Walter Lippmann's *A Preface to Morals* was a key text that tied
together the themes of the irrelevance of politics and society, the
fearfulness of an unmapped terrain, and the concomitant retreat
into self. He explained that the death of God left men without
satisfying explanations of what they were compelled to do, had
left them unable to refer to a universe teleologically organized.
When an earlier American believed that the unfolding of events
was a manifestation of the will of God, he could say:

> Thy will be done. . . . In His will is our peace. But when he believes
> that events are determined by the votes of a majority, the orders of his
> bosses, the opinions of his neighbors, the laws of supply and demand,
> and the decisions of quite selfish men, he yields because he has to
> yield. He is conquered but unconvinced.[46]

Where the small town could control events, other Americans
were conquered but unconvinced by those who preached its values. Where the small town could not control events, other Ameri-

[45]Dewey, *The Public and Its Problems*, p. 170.
[46]Lippmann, *Preface to Morals*, p. 9.

cans were freer, but that freedom brought with it complications. Lippmann believed that the twenties, for the first time in human history, made authoritative belief impossible for large masses of people. Massive and radical irreligion (always excepting provincial America) contributed to the destruction of those older guideposts that left people now free to walk new but obscure and therefore dangerous paths. Worrying that greater difficulties would only begin when people were free to do as they pleased, Lippmann got under the surface of the times:

> The evidence of these greater difficulties lies all about us: in the brave and brilliant atheists who have defied the Methodist God, and have become very nervous; in the women who have emancipated themselves from the tyranny of fathers, husbands, and homes, and with intermittent but expensive help of a psychoanalyst, are now enduring liberty as interior decorators; in the young men and women who are world-weary at twenty-two; in the multitudes who drug themselves with pleasure; in the crowds enfranchised by the blood of heroes who cannot be persuaded to take an interest in their destiny; in the millions, at last free to think without fear of priest or policeman, who have made the moving pictures and the popular newspapers what they are.[47]

By the end of the decade, Lippmann said, the problem for young urban America was no longer that of mounting an attack on the stupidities, pieties, and inhibitions of their close-kneed parents. That attack had already succeeded. The square dance was no longer audible over the bounce of the Charleston. The privacy of the back seat of their car gave the young an opportunity to be sexually freer than ever before. Their rebellion for greater moral freedom had been won, but the young, according to Lippmann, had now to deal with the sobering consequences of that success: "When he has slain the dragon and rescued the beautiful maiden, there is usually nothing left for him to do but write his memoirs and dream of a time when the world was young."[48] The distinguishing characteristic of the young generation of the twenties was therefore not merely the fact of rebellion against the ethical and moral codes of the past, but its disillusionment with its own rebellion. Such modern men, repelled by the village, bewildered by the present, were radically alone; follow-

[47]Ibid., p. 6.
[48]Ibid., p. 17.

ing Fitzgerald's sigh over a world whose past faiths and gods had died, Lippmann now probed a little deeper into the mood of the young:

> They have seen through the religion of nature to which the early romantics turned for consolation. They have heard too much about the brutality of natural selection to feel, as Wordsworth did, that pleasant landscapes are divine. They have seen through the religion of beauty because, for one thing, they are too much oppressed by the ugliness of Main Street. They cannot take refuge in an ivory tower because the modern apartment house, with a radio loudspeaker on the floor above and on the floor below and just across the courtyard, will not permit it. They cannot, like Mazzini, make a religion of patriotism, because they have just been demobilized. They cannot make a religion of science like the post-Darwinians because they do not understand modern science. They never learned enough mathematics and physics. They do not like Bernard Shaw's religion of creative evolution because they have read enough to know that Mr. Shaw's biology is literary and evangelical. As for the religion of progress, that is preempted by George F. Babbitt and the Rotary Club, and the religion of humanity is utterly unacceptable to those who have to ride in the subways during the rush hours.[49]

The meaninglessness of society, the absurdity of a purposeless nature, and the richly textured mood of combined pleasure and isolation all coalesced to encourage exploration of the increasingly fascinating world of the ego. Having just heard about Freud, the modern man learned that there were things about himself that even he did not know. The several pressures of the decade pushed him inward. His own moods and motives, preferences and aversions were hugely more interesting than the antics of villagers, and more interesting, too, than maintaining vigilance against an older generation that was too preoccupied with making money to countercharge. "His inferiority complex and mine, your sadistic impulse and Tom Jones's, Anna's father fixation, and little Willie's pyromania"[50] were, in Lippmann's view, the substitute for tradition. Personal rather than social history became relevant, and psychoanalysis was the new way to make the past usable, the past of the individual not the group. Sherwood Anderson summed this up in *Dark Laughter:* "If there is anything

[49]Ibid., p. 18.
[50]Ibid., p. 114.

you do not understand in human life consult the works of Dr. Freud."[51] Guilt replaced conscience, and Freud taught the rebels lesson after lesson and showed reason after dark reason why the rejection of the parental code was essential to health. As the parent became the metaphor of the past, the child became that of the present. Such personifications could not and were not intended to disguise what was happening: the individual and his past were replacing the world and its history.

The massive presentism that resulted was reflected in the works of some of the leading intellectuals of the decade. The presentism of the "New History" of Robinson and Beard, the institutional economics of Veblen that demanded a repudiation of classical economics, and Dewey's "reconstruction in philosophy" that rejected his empirical and classical predecessors in philosophy— all attempted to start afresh, to redesign their tools for modern tasks, and to bring serious thought to bear seriously on the pervasive present.[52]

The idea of progress was one of the casualties of the war, the peace, the village, and Freudianism. A humanistic celebration of the steady and irrevocable march of civilization to higher and higher plateaus of achievement became increasingly difficult for those who were now questioning the value of civilization itself. Emil Coué might make his incantation: "Day by day in every way I am getting better and better,"[53] but, for some, Coué's popularity merely proved that vulgarity was profitable. Edison and Ford showed that technological progress was possible, but the war showed that men were not necessarily or even probably served well as a result.[54] Cumulative disciplines would continue to make progress, but who would win in a struggle for survival between Darwin and Bryan? Social theories might grow increasingly sophisticated and ingenious, but Clemenceau, A. Mitchell Palmer, and Judge Webster Thayer (in whose court Sacco and Vanzetti were tried) seemed also to have something to say about how and by whom the world would be ruled and about the staying power

[51] Sherwood Anderson, *Dark Laughter* (New York: Liveright Publishing Corp., 1925), p. 230.

[52] Morton White, *Social Thought in America* (Boston, 1957), pp. 182, 188–89.

[53] Frederick Lewis Allen, *Only Yesterday* (New York, 1946), p. 102.

[54] Clark A. Chambers, "The Belief in Progress in Twentieth-Century America," *Journal of the History of Ideas*, XIX, 2 (April, 1958), 204–8; Sidney Kaplan, "Social Engineers as Saviors," *Journal of the History of Ideas*, XVII, 3 (June, 1956), 369.

of the past. The American economy could boom along with the proliferation of machines, but even the usually sanguine Dewey concluded that "we have harnessed this power to the dollar rather than to the liberation and enrichment of human life."[55] In the eyes of a widening circle of disaffected intellectuals and artists, modern America was a spiritual and cultural desert, committed to standardization and repression and blind to freedom and spontaneity. America was therefore a case study that showed that the older generation had used the idea of progress to camouflage its own failures.

None of this seems to have touched Herbert Hoover, the leading and most intelligent spokesman of nonmetropolitan America. His important little book *American Individualism*, published early in the decade, is a sensitive rendition of provincial values; by listing what he does not discuss, and by contradicting what he does, one may learn what the exiles, alienates, and even the flappers thought important. His optimism was unlimited because he believed that Americans were increasingly devoted to service: "Moral standards of business and commerce are improving; vicious city governments are less in number; invisible government has greatly diminished; public conscience is penetrating deeper and deeper; the rooting up of wrong grows more vigorous; the agencies for their exposure and remedy grow more numerous, and above all is the growing sense of service."[56] (The frequent reiteration of the ideal of "service" in the decade drove Mencken wild: "When a gang of real estate agents . . . , bond salesmen and automobile dealers gets together to sob for Service, it takes no Freudian to surmise that someone is about to be swindled."[57])

More than anything else, it was Hoover's idealism that connected him with the American village and separated him from serious writers and artists. Unaware of or perhaps despite the very wide rejection of idealism in both cultural and philosophical meanings, Hoover asserted that "the most potent force in society is its ideals." He was able to use both the meaning and the rhetoric that were most unacceptable to the cultural leaders: "From the instincts of kindness, pity, fealty to family and race; the love of liberty; the mystical yearnings for spiritual things; the desire

[55]John Dewey, *Individualism Old and New* (London, 1931), p. 91.

[56]Herbert Hoover, *American Individualism* (Garden City, N.Y., 1922), p. 58. Quoted by permission of the Herbert Hoover Foundation.

[57]Mencken, *Notes on Democracy*, p. 176.

for fuller expression of the creative faculties; the impulses of service to community and nation, are moulded the ideals of our people."[58]

Taking notice of the radical individualism of the period, as the intellectuals did, too, Hoover made a virtue of necessity. American individualism, he said, was not rampant and was unique, because it was founded on the "great ideals" of the nation. The supposedly classless nature of America cleared the way for individual achievement even while the "emery wheel of competition" was whirling. Progress, about which he evidently had few or no doubts, was a result of "the yearning for individual self-expression," and individualism "alone admits the universal divine inspiration of every human soul."[59] Absolutely rejecting the ideas that nature was purposeless, that historical fatality limited human choice, and that reason was an incompetent social and even personal guide, Hoover said that good ideas could replace bad ones, that reason could light the way to the implementation of eternal ideas. War was a conflict of ideas; irrationality and power were left out of his analysis.[60] For Hoover, and for those whom he represented, Wilson's wartime career and the Treaty of Versailles did not prove anything about either the emptiness or danger of idealism as such.

And yet the villagers took pride in dealing with actuality, at least on a certain level. That is what Harding meant in his diagnosis of what the American electorate wanted, and that is what Coolidge meant when he called the election of 1920 "the end of a period which has seemed to substitute words for things."[61] The "words" the villager meant included the words of intellectuals and the plans of reformers; the villager did not mean to repudiate national ideals, which seemed to serve well even in the hard and actual world of the assembly lines.

In philosophy idealism was repudiated by pragmatism and scientific realism. "New Realism" was formed on a rejection of the idealists' fusion of subject and object, on what was viewed as the obscurantism of idealist logic. John Dewey was the leading advocate of a new philosophy founded on exact science, not on

[58]Hoover, *American Individualism*, p. 16.

[59]Ibid., pp. 9, 21, 26.

[60]Ibid., p. 70.

[61]Quoted in Leuchtenberg, *Perils of Prosperity*, p. 89.

the sovereignty of the human mind. The social implications of this philosophical recoil from idealism were drawn by one critic:

> With all its incompleteness, Dewey's philosophy is undeniably that of the America of to-day. What shall we say of the future? No nation in the world has more abused its philosophies than ours. The inspirational elements of our idealisms have become the panderings of sentimentalists. The vitalizing forces of our pragmatisms threaten to congeal into the dogmata of cash-success. The war has intensified our national self-satisfaction. We tend to condemn all vision as radical, hence unsound, hence evil, hence to be put down.[62]

The peculiarly buoyant but often fretful zest of the creative people of the decade was largely a result of the feeling not that the past had somehow to be abandoned, but that the best and most authentic expression of the time actually had already freed itself from the alleged suffocation of a social past. The individual, already almost sanctified in political and economic terms by the small town and its spokesmen, already validated by Freudianism, already placed at the center of American philosophy, was to find his most elaborate and elevated position in the art and literature of the twenties.

What was being done to and for the individual was sometimes obscured by talk of freedom, adjustment, self-expression, and the war against puritanism. But under most if not all of that rhetoric was the writers' quite open assumption: if the self could be freed from the oppression of the social past and from the repression of his private past, a new private world of self-determination would become newly accessible. That new world would still find it necessary to battle the old world of custom and tradition, but though the actual world might remain unchanged, the now inviolate ego could feel for the limits of what it could do. Consigning society and history to the hell they caused and deserved, the liberated spirits of the time could themselves soar inward as they quite consciously rejected formal knowledge, economics, politics, and social service; as they quite consciously prayed at the shrine of the uncorrupted child, of the eternal present, of the equality of autonomous selves—male and female—and of freedom and paganism.[63] They were newly born into an idiot world whose power

[62]Harold Chapman Brown, "Philosophy," in Stearns, *Civilization*, pp. 176–77.
[63]Cf. Malcolm Cowley, *Exile's Return* (New York, 1951), pp. 60–61.

over them required their assent; refusing assent, they thought they discovered how to prevent that world from taking what they would not give. They thought they discovered how to nourish the self in a social madhouse, as e. e. cummings showed in *The Enormous Room*. Some chose a French or English setting out of their fear or conviction that America was stultifying or otherwise dangerous, but all sought that self whose discovery was, they believed, the basis of art.

Dada was merely the verge of freedom and privacy, the extreme and essentially unformulated assault on the morbid if not moribund civilization of the time, and the appropriate reflex of that eternal present. Moving from the avowedly destructive antirationalism of dada to the avowedly revolutionary unconscious of surrealism, the art of that moment was of a piece with the other cultural currents. Western man with his exquisite and urgent sublimatory necessities had created mind and civilization. Both led to outrageous war. By living inward one might escape those necessities, might rediscover the body and freedom known only by the uncivilized: children, Negroes, primitives, half-wits, and other heroes of the creative subculture of the twenties. Freud, after all, had already explained that mind and freedom were mutually exclusive. In their war on mind, the American writers of the period, whether in Zurich, Paris, or New York, were responding to the same impulses that dada and surrealism understood. In their war on mind, those writers were laying siege to civilization itself: society and nation, history and time. The alternative to civilization was the self, and toward that they made their sometimes unsure, sometimes nervous, often frantic, and occasionally gay way.

IV

Writers in America easily identified the hated past with the hated village. In the beginning, they suggested, all America was a village, and the contemporary village was a powerful reminder of the hold the past had on the present. Their enemy, with the double face of the philistine and the puritan, was still strong enough to rule the land, though that fact mattered less and less. Of greater moment was the enemy's continued power to create and protect an environment absolutely hostile to the necessary private nourishment of those writers. One could presumably live with both Prohibition and the Klan, but the hegemonic village seemed also to pollute that part of the American atmosphere that was essential to art. So Van Wyck Brooks could conclude that America demanded the premature death of her artists: "If America is littered with extinct talents, the halt, the maimed and the blind, it is for reasons with which we are all too familiar; and we to whom the creative life is nothing less than the principle of human movement, and its welfare the true sign of human health, look upon the wreckage of everything that is most precious to society and ask ourselves what our fathers meant when they extolled the progress of our civilization."[64] Frustration was the price the village demanded of the artist; public America might be shoved into a corner of one's mind, but it still had power to drive the artist to his death. As Fitzgerald asked from his ineffective refuge in Paris, "Can you name a single American artist except James and Whistler (who lived in England) who didn't die of drink?"[65] The profound irrelevance of public America did not mean that one could succeed, in Hemingway's language, in concluding "a separate peace." Internal secession, expatriation, withdrawal, isolation, and alienation were solutions, but evidently expensive for some, prohibitively so for others.

Fitzgerald is a special case. He was not importantly involved in the writers' sometimes loving and sometimes bitter attack on traditional language as were, for example, Gertrude Stein, James Joyce, all of the dadaists, e. e. cummings, and even Hemingway in his own way. Fitzgerald, at least at first blush, seems not to have been a man apart but rather a simple reflection of dominant America. But his playful weariness, his brooding conviction of the hollowness of the very life he desired and depicted, and the iron inevitability of collapse in his best works show him to be preeminently a writer of his time and place.[66] Thus it was that the poet laureate of the jazz age could tell his editor, "My third novel, if I ever write another, will I am sure be black as death with gloom."[67]

Fitzgerald's fascination with youth, glamor, and power was clearly real. And it is partly accurate to label him with the now

[64]Van Wyck Brooks, "The Literary Life," in Stearns, *Civilization*, p. 192.

[65]F. Scott Fitzgerald to Marya Mannes, Oct. 1925, in *Letters*, p. 489.

[66]Cf. Henry San Piper, "Fitzgerald's Cult of Disillusion," *American Quarterly*, III, 1 (Spring, 1951), 69–80.

[67]F. Scott Fitzgerald to M. Perkins, Aug. 25, 1921, in *Letters*, p. 148.

stock critical tag of the "eternal adolescent infatuated with the surfaces of material existence."[68] He made Jay Gatsby hope that hard cash could buy every desire of the insatiable heart, even the suspension of time or the eradication of the past. How is it then that, as he knew himself, his lovely, expensive, nineteen-year-old flappers came to ruin, his diamond mountains blew up, and his millionaires were damned? Fitzgerald, for all of his spiritual fraternizing with the flapper, for all of his personal needs, saw through the decade. He knew—and it was his most tense, painful, and creative knowledge—that he, and his most living characters, were inextricably involved in an unremitting search for what would turn out to be a fraud. Although he became disillusioned with the ideas of his own youth, he consistently refused to participate in American moralism about the evil of money and the corruptibility of power. Simultaneously accepting and rejecting the flapper and her friends, he could not turn away from society, as so many of the period's other writers were to do. His search for the possibilities of the self was conducted not merely in society but in Society. Fitzgerald believed that Gatsby condemned himself to loneliness, fragility, and emptiness; this author's dependence on the self even in the face of the self's willed destruction was Fitzgerald's unique and powerful way of rendering the decade. To make and throw away a life because of an ideal of self, to be drawn toward and torn between enormous power and beatific dreams[69]—that was a fact to which he owed some of his best writing. Not rejecting society in his search for the self, Fitzgerald nonetheless believed that the combat between them was mortal.

Hemingway's response to the twenties was more typical of the contemporary writers' plight, as many of them understood it. Suffering what he felt to be a hideous psychic wound by the external world, Hemingway spent both his talent and his life in that period trying to learn to endure, but with some necessary dignity, with some acceptable sense of self, with some style appropriate to the problem. As the universe seemed always to be in an active conspiracy against manhood, so, for Hemingway, art was a way to fight back. Society and tradition might be rejected, but the rejection was active and necessary to his art.

Meaning was real only for the self. War, for instance, was less

[68]Irving Howe, "American Moderns," in Schlesinger and White, *Paths of American Thought*, p. 318. The following paragraph draws heavily on this essay.

[69]Lionel Trilling, *The Liberal Imagination* (Garden City, N.Y., 1953), pp. 240, 242.

important than one's relationship to it, and one's experience of it. The world had come apart sufficiently, as the self perceived it, so that it was no longer necessary to demonstrate that fact. Starting with the assumption of meaninglessness, Hemingway, as other writers of the time, was convinced of the absurdity of attempting to supply meaning. Style and gesture became his personal substitute for meaning, and the struggle to clarify the contours of the self replaced the earlier American literary struggle to clarify the contours of the cosmos.

Hemingway was so convinced of the emptiness of large meanings, of idealism as such, that he apparently believed it unnecessary to fight that battle. His taut language is itself an evidence of his rejection of the world of idealism, of concept, of rationalism, of civilization. Unlike American writers of the nineteenth century, he showed the results of his rejections rather than attempting to prove that they were right. Only occasionally would he become explicit, as in *A Farewell to Arms:* "Abstract words such as glory, honor, courage, or hallow were obscene beside the concrete names of villages, the numbers of roads, the names of rivers, the numbers of regiments and the dates."[70]

Personal involvement and especially risk destroyed abstraction. Perhaps one could learn through a precise scrutiny of the ego in danger or crisis, through scrutiny of raw nerve endings, and through awareness of the chill in the pit of the stomach. Things had a price, as Jake Barnes in *The Sun Also Rises* knew, and one had to pay: "Either you paid by learning about them, or by experience, or by taking chances, or by money." An attempt to impose or extract large meaning would necessarily destroy the involvement and thereby necessarily obstruct learning. Endurance not progress was the point, as Barnes explained: "I did not care what it was all about. All I wanted to know was how to live in it."[71] Distance from experience would vitiate it; though life, in general terms, was not worth observing, it was worth participation if an opportunity for self-measurement could be found. So Jake Barnes explained the point of the bull fight to Brett Ashley: "the holding of ... purity of line through maximum of expo-

[70]Ernest Hemingway, *A Farewell to Arms* (New York: Charles Scribner's Sons, 1929), p. 191.

[71]Ernest Hemingway, *The Sun Also Rises* (New York: Charles Scribner's Sons, 1926), p. 153.

sure."[72] If the individual could nerve himself to will and execute maximum exposure, his personal authenticity would result in beauty, not necessarily truth. The code, the moral code, required both the risk and the gesture. The world of the other, of the nonself, was organized merely to destroy the true self, as Hemingway once explained in characteristic language:

> If people bring so much courage to this world, the world has to kill them to break them, so of course it kills them. The world breaks every one and afterward many are strong at the broken places. But those that will not break it kills. It kills the very good and the very gentle and the very brave impartially. If you are none of these you can be sure it will kill you too but there will be no special hurry.[73]

Believing that, Hemingway exalted—a word he would reject—style. One could still summon courage and dignity in a meaningless world. Importantly, the style he exalted was moral—another word he would probably have rejected. His typically wounded hero achieves selfhood by facing, not trying to overcome, his wound. The conditions of modern life had so radically annihilated any community that the individual, with whatever strength or will or sensitivity he could summon, had finally to discover in himself a psychic refuge, a way to endure. The appropriate style of endurance tended almost always to the inarticulate and the concrete. But, as Hemingway showed it, endurance was neither acquiescence nor humiliation. The *corrida*, as a substitute for society, requires endurance gracefully achieved. In the demand for such grace Hemingway's moral code of resistance to and defiance of society and social morality becomes clear. With a perfect *veronica* the individual can introduce a transitory but genuine beauty into an ugly and meaningless world.[74] But the inherent impermanence of such beauty meant that the threshold of satisfaction would be continually receding, and the sometimes aimless and comic, often frenzied, reaching out for yet a new experience that would prove that nerves were yet capable of sensation came increasingly to characterize Hemingway's work.

[72]Ibid., p. 174.

[73]Hemingway, *A Farewell to Arms*, pp. 258–59.

[74]Howe, "American Moderns," in Schlesinger and White, *Paths of American Thought*, pp. 315–17.

The decade's intellectual and literary finale came appropriately in 1929, in a humane and gentle but anguished lament by Joseph Wood Krutch. *The Modern Temper: A Study and a Confession* was, among other things, a direct summary of the difficulties of being alive and aware during the twenties; it was, and is, an intellectual's despair at the intensity and magnitude of an intellectual's peculiar problems during a decade of America's history when the material conditions of life for a vast segment of the population were daily improving, when life was sufficiently well managed so that those who were repelled by public life could afford to turn away.

Krutch feared that the scientists and industrialists who were satisfied with what they had thought and built and who, as a result, necessarily suffered a coarsening of the grain were in fact the fittest who would not merely survive but survive to rule. Others, more sensitively tuned, seized on a now superannuated humanism, trying desperately to ignore their own disbelief. The proposed retreat into self, into imagination perhaps, depended on ironic belief, an attitude Krutch thought appropriate only to proponents of a lost cause. Power seemed to ignore humanity, and humanism was out of touch with everything, even with itself. "Both our practical morality and our emotional lives are adjusted to a world which no longer exists. In so far as we adhere to a code of conduct," Krutch explained, "we do so largely because certain habits still persist, not because we can give any logical reason for preferring them, and in so far as we indulge ourselves in the primitive emotional satisfaction—romantic love, patriotism, zeal for justice, and so forth—our satisfaction is the result merely of the temporary suspension of our disbelief in the mythology upon which they are founded."[75] Deracination was the major characteristic of modernity, and that was so in emotional as well as in other terms.

Modernity was, in a sense, unconnected with the past, and, as Krutch saw it, history was discontinuous. A more total adjustment was demanded by his decade than ever before. Extinction was the price of failure to understand—as the artists and writers of the period understood—and the failure to find a way to live with unprecedented uncertainties and necessities. Science, so far from providing answers, was itself part of the prob-

[75]Joseph Wood Krutch, *The Modern Temper: A Study and a Confession* (New York: Harcourt, Brace & World, Inc., 1929), pp. 22–23.

lem. With growing and spreading freedom, the objects—men, women, love—once summoned as the goals for which freedom was demanded had lost their significance, desirability, or meaning altogether.

Displaying something of the vogue of primitivism, new experience, and delicately wrought anti-intellectualism, Krutch thought that the future would fall to those who were then too deeply involved in living and loving to have time to think about how to live and love. Such people will come, he announced, "as the barbarians have always come, absorbed in the processes of life for their own sake, eating without asking if it is worth while to eat, begetting children without asking why they should beget them, and conquering without asking for what purpose they conquer."[76]

The modern mood, as it came through the filter of Krutch's critical intelligence, was desperate, rootless, aimless, disillusioned with everything including disillusion, and evidently secure in the knowledge that knowledge would not help. In often wonderful prose Krutch told of the meaninglessness of language and mind, of the need somehow to act for goals no longer desired or believed real. The age apparently longed to find a faith that could fire the imagination and had lost faith in the possibility of faith. Above all (and it is strange to say of so simple a thing that it was above all), modern humanity was exhausted—not from a particular exertion but chronically so. The burden of needing to ask not why to endure, but how, was murderously heavy. When people added this burden to their other labors, they staggered into modernity.

One aspect of the grotesque humor of the Great Depression is that, in establishing a concrete task to perform, it did not solve but at least temporarily obscured the peculiarly modern anguish. That is probably why many of the most articulate American writers and scholars then seemed to have found new energy, new zest, and even a new joy in their work. It is too much to say that as the stock market declined, intellectual spirits rose. But for some at least the Depression was a relief, a chance to engage a world larger than one's own skin, a time to deal with problems that were simpler because capable of some measure of solution. It was a time when village and city could combine in common cause, when material privation seemed almost able to re-create an American community, almost coterminous with the nation.

[76]Ibid., p. 237.

And World War II continued the happy chance to ignore the increasingly relevant legacy of the twenties. With peace and returning affluence, with skirts rising again and traditional morality declining again, those now old questions reasserted themselves. This time a much larger group of Americans could think of the discontinuity of history and of "a separate peace."

THE
THIRTIES

Warren I. Susman / RUTGERS UNIVERSITY

So far as I am concerned, what had been the twenties ended that night. We would try to penetrate the fogs to come, to listen to the buoys, to read the charts. It would be three years before we took down a volume of *Kunstgeschichte* from our shelves to be replaced by a thin narrow book in red entitled *What Is To Be Done?*, by V. I. Lenin. Then in a few years it would be taken down to be replaced by another. And so on.[1]

The time was August 23, 1927; Sacco and Vanzetti had been executed. But for Josephine Herbst this political event, significant as it was, did not in itself mark the end of an era. For it was also on that day that she and John Herrmann were forced to abandon their twenty-three-foot ketch after a difficult passage through thick fog.[2] In her brilliant memoir of the year 1927—"A Year of Disgrace"—Herbst demonstrates the extraordinary complexity that results from the mixture of private misfortune and public joys, public disasters and private triumphs, personal seekings and social developments. In April, for example, there were the discovery of John Herrmann's illness and the happy preparations for the boating venture in Maine; the scandal and excitement of Antheil's *Ballet-Mécanique* at Carnegie Hall and Herbst's unfulfilled

---

[1]Josephine Herbst, "A Year of Disgrace," in S. Bellow and K. Botsford, eds., *The Noble Savage 3* (Cleveland, Ohio: The World Publishing Company, 1961), p. 160. Copyright 1961 by The World Publishing Company. Miss Herbst's memoirs (of which two sections have thus far appeared) promise to be one of the classic accounts of the intellectual life of the 1920s and the 1930s.

[2]Herbst in *The Noble Savage 3*, p. 160.

longing to be moved by the music as her friends had been; and the death sentence irrevocably passed on Sacco and Vanzetti, crushing to those who had come to believe so fervently in their innocence.

This very mixture of events of different kinds and qualities provides a lesson. The past is not preserved for the historian as his private domain. Myth, memory, history—these are three alternative ways to capture and account for an allusive past, each with its own persuasive claim. The very complexities of the record raise questions about the task of reconstruction in any form. Herbst, for example, is wise enough to ask:

> But is there such a thing as the twenties? The decade simply falls apart upon examination into crumbs and pieces which completely contradict each other in their essences. The twenties were not at all the museum piece it has since become where our literary curators have posed on elevated pedestals a few busts of the eminent. Even individual characters cannot be studied in a state of static immobility. It was all flux and change with artistic movements evolving into political crises, and where ideas of social service, justice, and religious reaction had their special spokesman.[3]

So complex, so varied are events and motives that Erich Auerbach shrewdly suggests, "To write history is so difficult that most historians are forced to make concessions to the technique of the legend."[4] For no matter how great the difficulties, each of us—in a private capacity or as propagandist or as historian—demands some order, some form, from the past. (In spite of her own questions about the nature of the twenties, Herbst's personal reconstruction dates the "end" of the period with precision.) Yet for the maker of myths, the propagandist for a cause, the memoirist, and the historian, there are frequently different, compelling psychological and social needs dictating different forms and different ways of reconstruction.

Memory is often the historian's most potent ally. But hovering as it does in that strange psychological zone between nostalgia and regret, it can often strike out on its own, producing not so much the ordered vision of the past the historian aims to develop as a picture of The Past (even a lurid Past) in the Victo-

---

[3]Herbst in *The Noble Savage* 3, p. 145.

[4]Erich Auerbach, *Mimesis: The Representation of Reality in Western Literature*, trans. by W. R. Trask (Princeton University Press, 1953), p. 20.

rian sense. What had seemed so right at the moment it happened becomes in retrospect not only wrong but criminal.[5] The personal needs of the present demand of the memoir writer a strangely skewed version of what happened.[6] In the time of Hiss trials and McCarthy accusations, the thirties appeared to be a period dominated by ideological commitment to Stalinism. Even for those who opposed witch-hunting, there was a lesson to be learned from the "tragic innocence" of the 1930s: avoid any ideology at all cost.[7] Yet sober historical evaluation, confirming the fact of an obvious movement toward the political left by many American intellectuals, raises serious questions about how deep and how significantly ideological such political interest was.[8] An examination of the literature of the period reveals an enormous number of tracts, polemics, and political, social, and economic analyses, but when one looks for major contributions to the literature of ideology—if such a phrase can be used—the only work that seems to stand out as read by "everyone" and regarded as a "powerful instrument" is *The Coming Struggle for Power* by England's John Strachey.[9] Today it is hard to regard that work as a

---

[5]Alistair Cook, in *Generation on Trial* (New York: Alfred A. Knopf, Inc., 1952), his study of the Hiss trial, makes this point vividly, especially in his first chapter, "The Remembrance of Things Past," one of the very best essays on the 1930s.

[6]Daniel Aaron presents an excellent account of this problem based on his own research difficulties in writing his study of communism and American writers in the 1930s in an important article, "The Treachery of Recollection: The Inner and the Outer History," in Robert H. Bremmer, ed., *Essays on History and Literature* (Columbus: Ohio State University Press, 1966), pp. 3–27.

[7]See especially the collection of articles by Daniel Bell, *The End of Ideology* (New York: The Free Press, 1960). Most relevant are "The Mood of Three Generations," pp. 286–99, and "The End of Ideology in the West," pp. 369–76. See also Leslie Fiedler, *The End to Innocence* (Boston: Beacon Press, 1955).

[8]See Daniel Aaron, *Writers on the Left* (New York: Harcourt, Brace & World, Inc., 1961); also his previously cited article (fn. 6), as well as "The Thirties—Now and Then," *American Scholar*, 35 (Summer, 1961), 490–94. Frank A. Warren III, *Liberals and Communism: The "Red Decade" Revisited* (Bloomington: Indiana University Press, 1966), throws further light on this question.

[9]Josephine Herbst, "Moralist's Progress," *Kenyon Review*, 28 (Autumn, 1965), 773. George K. Anderson and Eda Lou Walton, eds., have an interesting discussion of the importance of this work in their anthology *This Generation*, rev. ed. (Chicago: Scott, Foresman and Company, 1949), pp. 545–46. Obviously, I do not mean to suggest that there were no ideologies or ideologists in the 1930s. I mean rather that there were several; that ideological thinking was not as striking an aspect of intellectual life as has been supposed or indeed as can be discovered in earlier periods (like the progressive era, for example).

serious ideological contribution and the historian must be a little puzzled that a period regarded as so heavily ideological failed to produce a Lenin or a Gramsci, or indeed even a moderately significant contribution to the literature of ideology. Ideology may indeed have been important in the thirties, but many of the most brilliant and long-lasting contributions to political analysis written in the period were distinctly anti-ideological.[10]

Certainly there was a movement to the left; certainly there was a change in the intellectual and literary climate. As George Orwell put it when discussing the English-speaking literary community:

> Suddenly we got out of the twilight of the gods into a sort of Boy Scout atmosphere of bare knees and community singing. The typical literary man ceases to be a cultured expatriate with a leaning towards the Church, and becomes an eager-minded schoolboy with a leaning towards communism. If the keynote of the writers of the twenties is "tragic sense of life," the keynote of the new writers is "serious purpose."[11]

But it is all too easy to see a political thirties contrasting dramatically with an apolitical twenties. And while memory seems to demand of the figures of the 1930s a *mea culpa* for having joined the Communist party or having been a "fellow traveller" (as that period itself demanded of the writers of the 1920s a *mea culpa* for having been duped into expatriation or into some art-for-art's-sake movement), history demands an examination of the deeper issues that underlay such cries of regret.

The 1960s forced memory to look again at the 1930s, and this time with considerable nostalgia. Fashions in clothes and furniture returned to the decade for inspiration.[12] Some of what Susan Sontag has characterized under the rubric of "camp" represented an effort to recapture the mood of the thirties, its films, its radio programs, its heroes. The literary marketplace suddenly redis-

[10]See footnotes 42, 43, and 44 below.

[11]George Orwell, "Inside the Whale," reprinted in *A Collection of Essays* (New York: Doubleday & Company, Inc., 1954), p. 236 in the Anchor paperback edition; quoted by permission of Harcourt, Brace & World, Inc. and Miss Sonia Brownell and Secker & Warburg, Ltd. This brilliant essay written in 1940 provides a stimulating view of the whole period.

[12]See, for example, "Making the 1930's Pay Off—At Last," *Business Week* (August 20, 1966), pp. 128–32.

covered novels virtually unread and critically ignored in the period but now hailed as significant: Nelson Algren's *Somebody in
Boots*, the works of Nathanael West, Daniel Fuchs's trilogy, Henry
Roth's novel of immigrant life, and even Horace McCoy's "existen-
tialist" treatment of the dance-marathon craze, *They Shoot Horses,
Don't They?*[13] Several anthologies of the writings of the period appeared, each discovering a verve and importance in the literary
output of the period previously denied or overlooked.[14] And some
of the collected memories of the period reinforced significant new
scholarship that revealed not only a fascination with the "proletar-
iat" and a literature and reportage concerned with industrial
workers, strikes, and coming revolution, but also, in the North as
well as in the South, a widespread agrarian utopianism, a deep
interest in communitarian ventures smacking more of the America
of Brook Farm than of the U.S.S.R. of Five-Year Plans.[15]

The past summoned up before us by the forces of memory is
important; it is part of the record that cannot be ignored. But
because it serves the special functions that memory demands, be-

[13]The original sales of the Fuchs's novels are as follows: *Summer in Williamsburg*
(1934), 400 copies; *Homage to Blenholt* (1936), 400 copies; *Low Company* (1937),
1200 copies. So Fuchs reports in a new preface to the paperback edition (New
York: Berkley Publishing Corporation, 1965), p. 7. These novels were also reprinted in hard covers in 1961. West's *Miss Lonelyhearts* (1933) sold only 800
copies in its original edition, according to Robert M. Coates in his afterword to the
Avon paperback reprint of the McCoy novel (New York: Avon Books, 1966), p. 134.
McCoy's novel of 1935 may be almost regarded as a best-seller in this company: it
sold 3000 copies. It was reprinted in paperback in 1948, 1955, and for the third
time in 1966 (which text I am using).

[14]Harvey Swados, ed., *The American Writer and the Great Depression* (The American Heritage Series) (Indianapolis, Ind.: The Bobbs-Merrill Co., Inc., 1966), has a
fine introductory essay and a good bibliography; Jack Salzman, ed., *Years of
Protest* (New York: Pegasus, 1967), covers many issues and has especially useful
headnotes. Louis Filler, ed., *The Anxious Years* (New York: G. P. Putnam's Sons,
1963), is wide ranging, and the introduction provides useful information but also
some strange opinions.

[15]See Henry Dan Piper's valuable collection of Malcolm Cowley's important
pieces of reportage, controversy, and criticism from the 1930s, *Think Back on Us*
(Carbondale: Southern Illinois University Press, 1967). On this point see especially
pp. 51–55. Caroline Bird, *The Invisible Scar* (New York: Simon & Schuster, Inc.,
1966), is in many ways a good social history. On this question see pp. 89–90. In
addition to Paul Conkin's solid work *Toward a New World* (Ithaca, N.Y.: Cornell
University Press, 1959), see the valuable essay (the third chapter) in Warren
French's *The Social Novel at the End of an Era* (Carbondale: Southern Illinois
University Press, 1966) for important data on this point.

cause it is often colored by nostalgia or regret, the historian must be on guard. He or she is obligated to seek some more solid foundation that will hold in spite of the psychological and social demands of the moment. In building this vision of the thirties, the historian does not seek to debunk what the memoir writers recall or what has been written previously about the period, but rather to understand it all in a way that at least helps to account for the complexities and contradictions, the confusions of flux and change.

In sketching this structure no fact is more significant than the general and even popular "discovery" of the concept of culture. Obviously the idea of culture was anything but new in the 1930s, but there is a special sense in which the idea became widespread in the period.[16] What had been discovered was "the inescapable interrelatedness of . . . things" so that culture could no longer be considered what Matthew Arnold and the intellectuals of previous generations had often meant—the knowledge of the highest achievements of men of intellect and art through history—but rather a reference to "all the things that a group of people inhabiting a common geographical area do, the ways they do things and the ways they think and feel about things, their material tools and their values and symbols."[17] The remarkable popularity

[16]A. L. Kroeber and Clyde Kluckhohn, *Culture: A Critical Review of Concepts and Definitions*, originally published as Volume XLVII, No. 1, of the Papers of the Peabody Museum of American Archaeology and Ethnology, Harvard University, in 1952 and reprinted in paperback (New York: Random House, Inc., 1963), is the crucial work in the whole area of definition and use and a starting point for any study. It deals largely with professional social scientists, however, and does not deal with what I would call the acculturation of the concept. Charles and Mary Beard wrote an important book as part of their series *The Rise of American Civilization* a final volume called *The American Spirit* (New York: The Macmillan Company, 1942). This volume, too often overlooked and much more significant than scholars have acknowledged, was the study of the idea of civilization in the United States, which the authors felt was the key American idea and a molding force in the development of American civilization itself. In my own work I have argued that the idea of culture always existed somehow opposed to and in tension with the idea of civilization, but the Beards' book is significant. Kroeber and Kluckhohn also discuss the distinction between culture and civilization. In a different context, using very different material, the anthropologist Clifford Geertz has provided a very stimulating essay, "The Impact of the Concept of Culture on the Concept of Man," in John R. Platt, ed., *New Views of the Nature of Man* (Chicago: The University of Chicago Press, 1965), pp. 93–118.

[17]Robert S. Lynd, *Knowledge for What? The Place of the Social Sciences in American Culture* (Princeton, N.J.: Princeton University Press, copyright 1939, 1967 by Princeton University Press), pp. 16, 19.

of Ruth Benedict's *Patterns of Culture* (1934)—surely one of the most widely read works of professional anthropology ever published in the United States—provides us with a symbolic landmark. Its impact was significant; but more importantly, her analysis of the possibility of different cultural patterns and the way such patterns shape and account for individual behavior itself was part of a more general discovery of the idea itself, the sense of awareness of what it means to *be* a culture, or the search to *become* a kind of culture. "The quest for culture," one student of the problem suggests, "is the search for meaning and value."[18] It is not too extreme to propose that during the thirties the idea of culture was domesticated, with important consequences. Americans then began thinking in terms of patterns of behavior and belief, values and life styles, symbols and meanings. It was during this period that we find, for the first time, frequent reference to "an American Way of Life." The phrase "The American Dream" came into common use; it meant something shared collectively by all Americans, yet something different from the vision of an American mission, the function of the organized nation itself.[19] It is not surprising that H. L. Mencken believed (erroneously, it appears) that the expression "grass roots" was coined in the 1930s, for during the decade it became a characteristic phrase.[20]

[18]F. R. Cowell, *Culture in Private and Public Life* (New York: Frederick A. Praeger, Inc., 1959), p. 5.

[19]Mitford M. Matthews in his *Dictionary of Americanisms* (Chicago: University of Chicago Press, 1951) does list a use of "the American Way" as early as 1885, but his other references reinforce the opinion that it came especially into vogue in the 1930s and 1940s. There were at least four books in the period that used the phrase in a title (including a collection of essays edited by Newton D. Baker in 1936 and Earle Looker's 1933 study of FDR in action). Kaufman and Hart used it as a title of a play in 1939. The play traces the history of an immigrant family in America and ends with patriotic flourishes. Certainly there were more books and articles using the phrase in the 1930s than ever before. Merle Curti has some extremely interesting things to say about the idea of an American dream in his article "The American Exploration of Dreams and Dreamers," *Journal of the History of Ideas*, 27 (July–September, 1966), 391. He believes that James Truslow Adams invented or at least publicized the phrase in 1931. George O'Neils's play of that name was produced in 1933 and showed the progressive deterioration of the ideals and character of a New England family through American history. The word *culture* itself begins to appear commonly. Many titles are cited in this essay. Others include Jerome Davis, *Capitalism and Its Culture* (New York: Holt, Rinehart & Winston, Inc., 1935).

[20]On this issue see Matthews, *Dictionary of Americanisms*, as well as Raven I. McDavid, Jr.'s revised one-volume abridgement of Mencken's *The American Lan-

The "promises" that MacLeish insisted were America contrast dramatically in image, rhetoric, and kind with *The Promise of American Life* Herbert Croly discussed in the progressive era. For Croly that promise depended on a definition of democracy and the creation of new institutional patterns divorced from history; it involved political, social, and economic readjustments. But for MacLeish the promises could be best found within history, a special kind of folk-history:

> Jefferson knew:
> Declared it before God and before history:
> Declares it still in the remembering tomb.
> The promises were Man's; the land was his—
> Man endowed by his Creator:
> Earnest in love; perfectible by reason:
> Just and perceiving justice: his natural nature
> Clear and sweet at the source as springs in trees are.
>   . . .
> It was Man who had been promised: who should have.
> Man was to ride from the Tidewater: over the Gap:
> West and South with the water: taking the book with him:
> Taking the wheat seed: corn seed: pip of apple:
> Building liberty a farmyard wide:
> Breeding for useful labor: for good looks:
> For husbandry: humanity: for pride—
> Practicing self-respect and common decency.[21]

Clearly the two works differ in form and purpose. Further, it is obvious that we can discover common values and beliefs in the writings of the progressive and the poet. But it is still proper to suggest that in the work of the thirties MacLeish actually proposes a redefinition of the promise of American life, placing great emphasis on what we might call the cultural visions: questions of

---

guage (New York: Alfred A. Knopf, Inc., 1963), p. 183. An important book of the 1930s published as the result of a symposium organized by the Department of Agriculture, with a preface by Charles Beard that stressed the key role of agriculture as a base for any democracy in America, was M. L. Wilson, *Democracy Has Roots* (New York: Carrick & Evans, Inc., 1939). We need further studies of the rhetoric of American history.

[21]From "America Was Promises," *Collected Poems 1917–1952*. Copyright 1952 by Archibald MacLeish. Reprinted by permission of the publisher, Houghton Mifflin Company. Reprinted in Filler, *The Anxious Years*, pp. 225–26.

life style, patterns of belief and conduct, special values and attitudes that constitute the characteristics of a special people.

It is undeniable that certain extremely popular works of fiction obtained their popular hold because they provided a means
of escape from contemporary problems. But from the point of
view of an increased interest in a particular life style, in patterns
of belief and their consequences, as well as in the consequences of
the destruction of such cultures, it becomes possible to read in a
different light the enthusiastic reception given to Oliver La-
Farge's *Laughing Boy* (1929), with its touching and even sentimental plea for cultural pluralism (only one of many works in the
period carrying on a rich American tradition of works dating
back at least to Cooper in which the Indian's admired "culture" is
threatened by the white man's "civilization"), or to Margaret
Mitchell's *Gone With the Wind* (1936), with its historical reconstruction of the destruction of a way of life (again, only one of
many historical romances in the 1930s recounting in extraordinary detail life styles and values different from those of the
1930s).[22]

In 1931 Stuart Chase produced a best-seller: *Mexico, A Study
of Two Americas.* The book was to play an important role in the
whole discussion of the nature of culture, especially "popular
culture."[23] But even more importantly, it made explicit for a large
audience the very kind of distinction that became increasingly
characteristic of the period. Drawing specifically not only on his
own experiences but on the works of American social scientists
(the Lynds' study of *Middletown* and Robert Redfield's analysis of
a Mexican community), Chase sharply contrasted the urban-
industrial culture of the United States with the folk culture of a
more primitivist and traditional Mexico. While the United States
might well have the advantages that come with civilization, the
author of *Mexico* clearly found special benefits in the simple folk-
ways of Tepoztlan. It was a community free of the business cycle
and of mechanical civilization, an "organic, breathing entity."
While it had no machines, it was "impossible for Mexicans to

[22]Leo Gurko, *The Angry Decade* (New York: Dodd, Mead & Co., 1947), has some
useful information, especially on the context of American reading in the period,
although its analysis is not very penetrating. James D. Hart, *The Popular Book*
(New York: Oxford University Press, 1950), is invaluable.

[23]See the perceptive essay by Reuel Denney, "The Discovery of Popular Culture," in Robert E. Spiller and Eric Larrabee, eds., *American Perspectives* (Cambridge, Mass.: Harvard University Press, 1961), p. 170.

produce the humblest thing without form and design." Time was measured by sun and climate, not by clocks. The clock was "perhaps the most tyrannical engine ever invented. To live beyond its lash is an experience in liberty which comes to few citizens of the machine age." The villages are self-sustaining. The men want neither money nor the things money can buy. And perhaps most importantly, Chase frequently sees in Tepoztlan echoes of what American life itself once was before machine-age Middletown developed "a culture which has found neither dignity nor unity": "While each family harvests its own fields, community spirit is strong—as in old New England barn raisings. For machineless men generally, it is both necessity and pleasure to assist, and be assisted by, one's neighbor" or "When all is said and done, [the government, a kind of village communism] is 'a form of play.' Thus the working of the sublime principles of Jeffersonian democracy in Tepoztlan."[24]

As early as 1922 William Fielding Ogburn had defined the concept of "cultural lag."[25] But again, it was in the 1930s that the phrase and its implications became part of common discourse. "The depression has made us acutely aware of the fact that our brilliant technological skills are shackled to the shambling gait of an institutional Caliban," one of our most brilliant and widely read sociologists declared; his was an urgent appeal for a social science devoted to the study of the whole culture in the endeavor to develop the consequences of such knowledge for man.[26] And the distinguished historian Carl Becker mournfully announced that "mankind has entered a new phase of human progress—a time in which the acquisition of new implements of power too swiftly outruns the necessary adjustment of habits and ideas to novel conditions created by their use."[27] This is a far cry from the glorious hopes of a progressive era when *progress*, *power*, and indeed

[24]Stuart Chase, *Mexico, A Study of Two Americas* (New York: The Macmillan Company, 1931). This book, written in collaboration with Marian Tyler, begs for more extensive treatment, especially since Hart, *The Popular Book*, indicates it was a best-seller in the period. I have quoted almost at random: pp. 170, 130, 154, 171, 128.

[25]William Fielding Ogburn, *Social Change with Respect to Culture and Original Nature* (New York: Viking Press, 1922).

[26]Lynd, *Knowledge for What?*, pp. 3–4. He also speaks, in the passage immediately preceding, about what has spoiled "the American Dream."

[27]Carl Becker, *Progress and Power* (Palo Alto, Calif.: Stanford University Press, 1936), p. 91.

efficiency or *organization* were magic words, when it was felt that the application of the very techniques of the communications revolution might create a more desirable community and society.

It is in fact possible to define as a key structural element in a historical reconstruction of the 1930s the effort to find, character-ize, and adapt to an American way of life as distinguished from the material achievements (and the failures) of an American in-dustrial civilization. Civilization meant technology, scientific achievement, institutions and organizations, power, and material (financial) success. The battle between "culture" and "civiliza-tion," between the quality of living and the material, organized advancement of life was anything but new as an intellectual issue.[28] But the theme becomes central in the 1930s and even those older followers of the progressive tradition who valued the march of civilization and progress sought to emulate Thorstein Veblen and make from an industrial civilization a meaningful culture or way of life.[29]

However, civilization itself—in its urban-industrial form—seemed increasingly the enemy. It stood for the electricity that was used to destroy Sacco and Vanzetti;[30] or, as the hero of Al-gren's novel muses, " 'Civilization' must mean a thing much like that mob that had threatened his father."[31] Writers as different in other ways as Reinhold Niebuhr and Lewis Mumford wondered whether the civilization that had triumphed was in fact worthy of the highest aspirations of man. The increased interest in the so-cial sciences in the period and the tendency to point to the failure of the natural sciences to solve human problems are additional evidence for a newfound cultural awareness; we may add the

[28]See footnote 16. I have developed this argument at length in my paper "The Nature of American Conservatism," which I delivered at the First Socialist Schol-ars' Conference, September, 1965.

[29]I have not dwelled in this essay on what happened to progressive ideas in the period. Obviously, there was considerable continuity at least in some aspects of the culture of the period. Otis L. Graham, Jr., *An Encore for Reform* (New York: Oxford University Press, 1967), is enlightening on differences as well as similari-ties, but Rexford G. Tugwell has written a most brilliant essay "The New Deal—The Progressive Tradition," *Western Political Quarterly*, 3 (September, 1950), 390–427, which can be missed by the cultural and intellectual historian only at great peril.

[30]Herbst in *The Noble Savage 3*, p. 159.

[31]Nelson Algren, *Somebody in Boots* (New York: Berkley Publishing Corporation, 1965), pp. 82–83. Originally published in 1935.

growth of serious study of popular culture, of cultures other than
our own, or of the remains of folk or other subcultures within our
own.[32]

Again, the effort to define precisely the nature of American
culture itself—as it had been historically and as it was now—characteristic of so much of the writing of the 1930s is no new effort,
but it appears more widespread and central than in any previous
time. (This effort is also distinctly different from that which seeks
to show the development of the achievements of civilization in the
United States.) Constance Rourke's *American Humor* (significantly
subtitled *A Study in National Character*) (1931) and her essay on
"The Roots of American Culture" provide special landmarks.
Rourke did not devote herself to an analysis of the great contributors to culture; she sought rather to find the significant cultural
patterns to which she might relate such figures and from which
they could and must draw their material. And when Van Wyck
Brooks emerged from long silence in 1936 with *The Flowering of
New England* to begin his monumental multivolume cultural history, he had not so much changed his way of thinking—he still
sought a usable past, some meeting ground between highbrow and
lowbrow—as his method of analysis. Following in some sense the
lead of Rourke, he attempted in his own way to discover the basic
cultural patterns, values, and attitudes, using minor and forgotten
figures as well as the major writers to show the underlying structure of the culture from which they came.[33]

The issue then is not that the 1930s simply produced a new
era of nationalism.[34] Certainly few, if any, decades in our history

[32]In addition to works already cited, Alfred Kazin, *On Native Grounds* (New
York: Harcourt, Brace & World, Inc., 1942), has an extraordinary analysis, considering the date of its appearance, in the section on the 1930s, especially the
chapter "America, America." We need an extended study of the newly awakened
popular interest in anthropological and archaeological studies in the 1920s and
1930s, which produced not only an outpouring of scholarly discoveries and works
but also a considerable popular literature as well.

[33]Brooks edited a collection of Rourke's essays and provided a most significant
preface in *The Roots of American Culture and Other Essays* (New York: Harcourt,
Brace & World, Inc., 1942). Vico and Herder play an important role in the new
concern for culture. Brooks quotes Herder to the effect that "folk-forms were
essential to any communal group, they were the texture of the communal experience and expression." All of the key words were, as we shall see, especially important in the 1930s.

[34]See the essay of Harvey Swados with which he introduces his anthology, *The
American Writer and the Great Depression*.

could claim the production of such a vast literature—to say nothing of a vast body of films, recordings, and paintings—which described and defined every aspect of American life. It was not, then, simply that many writers, artists, and critics began to sing glowingly of American life and its past. It was, rather, the more complex effort to seek and to define America as a culture and to create the patterns of a way of life worth understanding. The movement had begun in the 1920s; by the 1930s it was a crusade. *America in Search of Culture* William Aylott Orton had called his not always friendly analysis of the phenomenon of 1933. The search was to continue throughout the decade in the most overwhelming effort ever attempted to document in art, reportage, social science, and history the life and values of the American people.[35]

If there was an increased awareness of the concept of culture and its implications as well as a growing self-consciousness of an American way or a native culture of value, there were also forces operating to shape that culture into a heightened sensitivity of itself as a culture. The development of systematic and supposedly scientific methods of measuring the way "the people" thought and believed is certainly one important example. The idea of public opinion was an old one (it can be traced back at least to Tocqueville), and the political, social, and even economic consequences of such opinion had been studied by a number of serious students: Lowell, Lippmann, and Bernays, to point to the most obvious examples. The Creel Committee of World War I days had already paid careful attention to the advantages and special techniques of manipulating such opinion. But it was not until 1935, when George Gallup established the American Institute of Public Opinion, that polling became commonplace in American life. Now Americans had empirical evidence of how they felt and

---

[35]In 1928 Niebuhr published *Does Civilization Need Religion?*, the first of many important works on this theme; in 1954 Mumford began his series of four volumes pleading for a harnessing of science and technology in the interest of a better life for man with his *Technics and Civilization*. The series as a whole is called *The Renewal of Life*. The decade saw the publication of the *Dictionary of American Biography* as well as the *Encyclopedia of the Social Sciences*, *Recent Social Trends*, and *Recent Economic Trends*. Many of these works had been begun, of course, during the 1920s. But the 1920s and the 1930s produced an enormous body of literature on the nature of history, culture, and the social sciences as well as the gathering of significant data about our history and society. See Merle Curti, ed., *American Scholarship in the Twentieth Century* (Cambridge, Mass.: Harvard University Press, 1953).

thought regarding the major issues of the day and generally shared attitudes and beliefs. It was easier now to find the core of values and opinions that united Americans, the symbols that tied them together and helped define the American way. It was not just the discovery of techniques that might be manipulated by experts to produce desired results, although this was a part of what happened; the polls themselves became a force, an instrument of significance, not only for the discovery and molding of dominant cultural patterns, but also for their reinforcement.[36]

Other technological developments played an even more vital role. The decade of the thirties was a dramatic era of sound and sight. It is impossible to recall the period without recourse to special sounds: the talkies, the machine-gun precision of the dancing feet in Busby Berkeley's musical extravaganzas, the Big Bands, the voices of Amos and Andy, to say nothing of the magic of Franklin Roosevelt's Fireside Addresses. For our immediate purposes, examples of the consequences of a new age of sound can best be found by looking briefly at some of the effects of national radio networks. Through their radio sets a unique view of the world and a way of interpreting it came to the American people. Nothing more dramatically illustrates the power of this newfound sound medium than the response to the Orson Welles Mercury Theater dramatization of H. G. Wells's story of a supposed Martian invasion. Expertly using the recently developed news-broadcasting techniques, Welles's company made thousands of people accept (as they were used to accepting) the rhetoric of a radio show as a description of reality; the resulting panic is famous.[37] Sound helped mold uniform national responses; it helped create or reinforce uniform national values and beliefs in a way that no previous medium ever had before. Roosevelt was able to create a new kind of Presidency and a new kind of political and social power partly through his brilliant use of the medium.

The photograph and the film, too, changed the nature of cultural communication in America. Unlike the printed word in newspapers and books, the photograph affected even those who could

[36]For a brief introduction to this whole subject treated historically, see Stow Persons, *American Minds* (New York: Holt, Rinehart & Winston, Inc., 1958), chapter 21.

[37]Hadley Cantril has provided us with a social-psychological study of this affair in *The Invasion from Mars* (Princeton, N.J.: Princeton University Press, 1940).

not or would not read. The thirties brought home the impact of the image created by the photograph in a more universal way. *Life*, founded in 1936, can perhaps be credited with the invention of the picture-essay; however, it is but one example of the novel way Americans could experience the world. Luce's extraordinary empire also produced "The March of Time," the most brilliant of the newly developed newsreels, which provided a fresh way of understanding events. The whole idea of the documentary—not with words alone but with sight and sound—makes it possible to see, know, and feel the details of life and its styles in different places and to feel oneself part of other's experience.[38]

We are not yet in a position to evaluate the full consequences of these events. But the newly developed media and their special kinds of appeal may have helped reinforce a social order rapidly disintegrating under economic and social pressures that were too great to endure. They may also have helped create an environment in which the sharing of common experiences—of hunger, dust bowls, or war—made the uniform demand for action and reform more striking and urgent. The resultant unity deserves some special role in the story of the 1930s. Whatever else might be said about the New Deal, its successes and its failures, it was obviously a sociological and psychological triumph. From the very outset of his Presidential campaign in 1932, Franklin Roosevelt showed himself fully aware of the importance of symbols. "Let it be symbolic," he told the Democratic Convention after an unprecedented flight to Chicago to accept its nomination in person, "that I broke the tradition. Let it be from now on the task of our Party to break foolish traditions."[39] The history of the ill-fated National Recovery Administration offers a series of examples of a brilliant sense for the symbolic in the administration itself: the Blue Eagle, the display of flags, the parades. Roosevelt on radio was to reach out to Americans in their living rooms and make them feel that the administration was thinking specifically of them, that they had a place in society. The film and the picture-essay brought the figures of power, in every aspect of their activity, personal as well as public, into the immediate experience of most Americans.

[38]Beaumont Newhall provides a good starting point for further analysis in *The History of Photography*, rev. and enl. ed. (New York: Doubleday & Company, Inc., 1964), Chapter 10.

[39]Quoted in T. V. Smith, "The New Deal as a Cultural Phenomenon," in F. S. C. Northrop, ed., *Ideological Differences and World Order* (New Haven, Conn.: Yale University Press, 1949), p. 212.

Even the lowly soap opera, the most frequently mocked of radio's innovations, played a role in reinforcing fundamental values and in providing the intimate experience of other people's lives so that millions of housewives knew they were neither alone nor unique in their problems. Timeless and consistent in portraying patterns of crisis and recovery, they provided a sense of continuity, assuring the triumph of generally shared values and beliefs, no matter what reality in the form of social and economic conditions might suggest.[40]

It is possible to see in the notorious soaps the operation of what might be called the force and power of myth. In his famous American Writer's Congress address in 1935, Kenneth Burke analyzed the function of myth in society. He argued that a myth was "the social tool for welding a sense of interrelationship by which the carpenter and the mechanic, though differently occupied, can work together for a common social end."[41] He was concerned, it is true, in this paper with the role of revolutionary myths and symbols. But an analysis of the 1930s reveals how significant a role the new media played in providing a huge public with a body of symbols and myths. In this sense it might not be unfair to consider the extraordinary mythic role the absurd soap opera played. The form may appear ridiculous to some today, but then so do many myths once socially operative and nonetheless later discarded.

The photograph, the radio, the moving picture—these were not new, but the sophisticated uses to which they were put created a special community of all Americans (possibly an international community) unthinkable previously. The shift to a culture of sight and sound was of profound importance: it increased our self-awareness as a culture; it helped create a unity of response and action not previously possible; it made us more susceptible than ever to those who would mold culture and thought. In this connection it is possible to see how these developments also heightened a growing interest among social and political thinkers in the role of symbol, myth, and rhetoric. Kenneth

[40]The best analysis of the soaps is still the delightful series James Thurber did for the *New Yorker*, reprinted in his *The Beast in Me* (New York: Harcourt, Brace & World, Inc., 1948) as "Soapland."

[41]Kenneth Burke, "Revolutionary Symbolism in America," in Frederick J. Hoffman, ed., *Perspectives on Modern Literature* (New York: Harper & Row, Publishers, 1962), p. 181.

Burke's study of the significance of Hitler's rhetoric and of the importance of the careful development of revolutionary symbolism in the United States showed how important such factors were in shaping cultures, the vast power (and therefore dangers) involved in language and symbol.[42] The major works of Thurmond Arnold, one of the more original thinkers of the period, deal with political life not in terms of ideology or the rational implementation of philosophies but in terms of the role of "folklore" and symbols.[43] And perhaps the leading academic student of political life, Harold Lasswell, developed a whole school of political analysis dealing with psychological and sociological factors barely touched on in previous periods.[44] While a progressive generation was much interested in problems of communications and even made small but significant use of the photograph, the painting, and the cartoon, it is not possible to compare this with the developments in the 1930s when an unusual sense of sight and sound along with a peculiar interest in symbol, myth, and language created a novel kind of community, breaking down barriers, creating often new common experiences for millions. For no matter how great their interest in communication, how deep their concern for the social role of the arts, the progressives relied primarily and most profoundly on the written word, the rational argument on the printed page. They were a generation of writers who produced an enormous political literature; but they did not and could not make their appeal to the ear and eye with a sense of symbol and rhetoric that compared to the stunning techniques and effects developed during the 1930s. One significant difference between the two eras is this: the progressives were people of the book; the children of the 1930s were people of the picture and the radio.

[42]Kenneth Burke, "The Rhetoric of Hitler's 'Battle,' " reprinted in his *The Philosophy of Literary Form* (Baton Rouge: Louisiana State University Press, 1941). This is an important collection of pieces for purposes of this essay.

[43]Thurmond Arnold, *The Folklore of Capitalism* (New Haven, Conn.: Yale University Press, 1937). I have a reprint edition that indicates that at least ten printings of the work occurred between 1937 and 1941. There is an extended analysis of the work in Richard Hofstadter, *The Age of Reform* (New York: Random House, Inc., 1959), pp. 317–22. Previously, Arnold had published *The Symbols of Government* (New Haven, Conn.: Yale University Press, 1935).

[44]Lasswell's career began with a study of *Propaganda Technique in the World War* (New York: Alfred A. Knopf, Inc., 1927). In 1930 he published *Psychopathology and Politics* and in 1936 *Politics: Who Gets What, When, How.*

In a stimulating essay "The New Deal as a Cultural Phenomenon," T. V. Smith suggests that "sportsmanship is the key to contemporary American Life." Speaking of the American way of life itself, Smith argues:

> The *game* is a fitting symbol. Long before baseball came to furnish the chief metaphor of American life there was (and there remains) another game—a game of cards: 'poker' it is called—in which 'to deal' was but to initiate a cooperative activity that could be its own exciting reward, even to those who 'lost their shirts' in its honor. Politics is in common American parlance a game, and in expert parlance it is 'the great American game.' Moreover, the symbolism carried over into business: a deal is a trade, any transaction for gain from which both sides are presumed to profit. Thus the very name of the Rooseveltian movement in question raises connotative echoes in the culture organic to America, in its full multi-dimensionality.[45]

In this passage Smith has done more than to suggest additional evidence about the cultural responsiveness of the New Deal in its selection of symbols. For culture is reflected in and shaped by its games, something analysts writing in the 1930s themselves understood.[46] Most social historians take great pains to point out the significant increase in popular participation in sports, the development of new games and fads, and the enormous increase in various forms of gambling in the period.[47] Too often, once again, these facts are explained as the search for escape—a truism to be sure—when they demand more fundamental analysis in terms of the *kind* of escape they propose. The dramatic increase was in special types of gaming, games of competition and chance, games frequently involving cooperation and carefully arranged regulations and limits. The "democratization" of golf and tennis in the 1930s provided a special outlet for the competitive spirit the traditional values of the culture de-

---

[45]Smith in *Ideological Differences and World Order*, p. 209.

[46]It was in 1938 that the distinguished Dutch cultural historian J. Huizinga published his landmark study of play and civilization, *Homo Ludens*.

[47]In addition to the Bird volume already cited (fn. 15), see the excellent social history of Frederick L. Allen, *Since Yesterday; The Nineteen-Thirties in America* (New York: Harper & Row, Publishers, 1940), chapter 6. There are some illuminating suggestions in Robert M. Coates's "Afterword" to the Horace McCoy novel previously cited (fn. 13). See also Foster Rhea Dulles, *A History of Recreation* (New York: Meredith Press, 1965), a revised edition of his *America Learns to Play*.

manded and that cannot easily be satisfied in the "real" world
of economic and social life. The Parker Brothers' fantastically
successful board game Monopoly enables would-be entrepreneurs to "make a killing" of the kind the economic conditions of
the times all but prohibited. Dance marathons, roller derbies,
six-day bicycle races, flagpole-sitting contests, goldfish-swallowing competitions—these are not just foolish ways out of the rat
race, but rather alternative (if socially marginal) patterns duplicating in structure what institutionalized society demanded and
normally assumed it could provide. Thus the bank nights and
the bingo games, the extraordinary interest in the Irish Sweepstakes, the whole range of patterns of luck and success offered
on the fringes of social respectability but certainly within the
range of social acceptance all provided a way to maintain and
reinforce essential values, to keep alive a sense of hope. Roger
Caillois, in his brilliant book *Man, Play and Games*, suggests that
there are "corruptions" of games as well as cultural forms found
at the margins of the social order: resort to violence, superstition, alienation and even mental illness, alcoholism, and the taking of drugs.[48] Certainly there is evidence that among some elements in the population such corruptions could be found in the
1930s. Yet the striking fact remains that the particular kind of
games that did dominate in the 1930s tended to provide significant social reinforcement. Even the dances of the period marked
a return to an almost folk-style pattern of large-scale participation and close cooperation. The holding of block parties, which
took place even in slum areas of large cities, indicates special
qualities of life in the 1930s, a fact not overlooked by those
whose memories of the period are colored by nostalgia.

As Caillois tells us:

> Any corruption of the principle of play means the abandonment of
> those precarious and doubtful conventions that it is always permissible, if not profitable, to deny, but arduous adoption of which is a
> milestone in the development of civilization. If principles of play in
> effect correspond to power instincts . . . , it is readily understood that
> they can be positively and creatively gratified under ideal and circumscribed conditions, which in every case prevail in the rules of play.
> Left to themselves, destructive and frantic as are all instincts, these
> basic impulses can hardly lead to any but disastrous consequences.

[48]Roger Caillois, *Man, Play and Games* (New York: The Free Press, 1961), especially Chapters 3 and 4.

Games discipline instincts and institutionalize them. For the time that they afford formal and limited satisfaction, they educate, enrich, and immunize the mind against their virulence. At the same time, they are made fit to contribute usefully to the enrichment and the establishment of various patterns of culture.[49]

Commentators are right then to indicate the importance of the kind of games played in the 1930s.

Furthermore there is the widespread and continuous use of the game metaphor, not only in the business and politics of the period but also by writers indicating the meaning or the meaninglessness of life. When Robert Sherwood sought an appropriate image for the fatuous and yet vicious forces of nationalism and international business, he too selected a game of cards. In his pacifist assault on those forces, which were insensitive to the human condition and hell-bent on destruction, he allows his heroine to speak of God:

Yes. . . . We don't do half enough justice to Him. Poor, lonely old soul. Sitting up there in heaven, with nothing to do, but play solitaire. Poor, dear God. Playing Idiot's Delight. The game that never means anything, and never ends.[50]

And from an entirely different perspective, William Saroyan built his sentimental tribute to the gentle, innocent, and good American people out of a whole series of games and toys. Most memorable, perhaps, is the pinball machine that the bartender assures Willie he cannot beat. Willie undertakes to try; he

stands straight and pious before the contest. Himself vs. the machine. Willie vs. Destiny. His skill and daring vs. the cunning and trickery of the novelty industry of America, and the whole challenging world. He is the last of the American pioneers, with nothing more to fight but the machine, with no other reward than lights going on and off, and six nickels for one. Before him is the last champion, the machine. He is the last challenger.

[49]Caillois, *Man, Play and Games*, p. 55.

[50]Robert Sherwood's *Idiot's Delight* (1936) is conveniently reprinted in Harold Clurman, ed., *Famous American Plays of the 1930's* (New York: Dell Publishing Co., Inc., 1959). This passage appears on p. 253. Quoted by permission of Charles Scribner's Sons.

In the last act of *The Time of Your Life* Willie finally beats the machine. Saroyan tells us "the machine groans." And then

> the machine begins to make a special kind of noise. Lights go on and off. Some red, some green. A bell rings loudly six times. . . . An American flag jumps up. Willie comes to attention. Salutes. 'Oh boy (he says) what a beautiful country.' A loud music-box version of the song 'America.' (Everyone in the barroom rises, singing). 'My country, 'tis of thee, sweet land of liberty, of thee I sing.' Everything quiets down. . . . Willie is thrilled, amazed, delighted. Everybody has watched the performance of the defeated machine.[51]

The analysis of the structure that underlies a historical picture of the 1930s suggests some tentative conclusions at this point. First, there was in the discovery of the idea of culture and its wide-scale application a critical tool that could shape a critical ideal, especially as it was directed repeatedly against the failures and meaninglessness of an urban-industrial civilization. Yet often it was developed in such ways as to provide significant devices for conserving much of the existing structure. A search for the "real" America could become a new kind of nationalism; the idea of an American way could reinforce conformity. The reliance on basic cultural patterns, stressed by further development of public opinion, studies of myth, symbol, and folklore, the new techniques of the mass media, and even the games of the period could and did have results far more conservative than radical, no matter what the intentions of those who originally championed some of the ideas and efforts.

Other studies bear out this conservative trend—no matter what memory may tell us about disorganization and a Red menace. The Lynds' return to Middletown in the 1930s led to the discovery that the schools of that community, for example, had had their heyday of freedom in education in the 1920s; by 1935 "the culture was tightening its grip on the schools to insure that 'only the right things' were being taught."[52] And perhaps the most

[51]William Saroyan's *The Time of Your Life* (1939) is also reprinted in Clurman, ed., *Famous American Plays of the 1930's*. The passages quoted appear on pp. 388 and 463. Quoted by permission of William Saroyan.

[52]Robert S. and Helen Lynd, *Middletown in Transition* (New York: Harcourt, Brace & World, Inc., 1937), pp. 233–34, and Lynd, *Knowledge for What?*, pp. 236–37.

significant experiment in higher education in the decade under Robert M. Hutchins at the University of Chicago can be considered an effort to reassert traditional values and standards in a retreat from the educational philosophy of the supposed followers of John Dewey. An important study of white acceptance of jazz documents the fact that when such music left the confines of the smaller Negro subculture and achieved wide-scale circulation and popularity in the larger national community through radio, records, and the Big Bands of the period, the lyrics of older jazz and blues as well as new works created tended to lack the bite and social criticism found in the jazz of the 1920s and earlier. In fact, lyrics tended to be bland, mouthing even more forcefully the commonplace and accepted values and beliefs, personal and social.[53]

In no field, however, was the consequence of the new approach stressing the role of existing patterns of culture to be as significant and striking as in the realm of popular psychology or in that strange combination of religion and psychology that frequently ruled in the 1930s as a substitute for liberal Protestantism, as Donald Meyer has brilliantly shown.[54] Any student of the 1930s must be impressed with the enormous body of literature designed to instruct and inform concerning ways to succeed.[55] It was the great age of the how-to book. But what is most unusual about all such literature, in view of the enormous critical assault on capitalism and even the widely held assumption among many, right, left, and center, that capitalism was doomed, is its initial principle: failure is personal, not social, and success can be achieved by some adjustment, not in the social order but in the individual personality. Dale Carnegie's *How to Win Friends and Influence People* was the best-seller of the period, and its publication in 1936 is a landmark for the study of American popular

[53]Neil Leonard, *Jazz and the White Americans* (Chicago: University of Chicago Press, 1962), chapter 6.

[54]A good deal that follows is based on Meyer's superb analysis in *The Positive Thinkers* (New York: Doubleday & Company, Inc., 1965), certainly one of the most important recent studies in the field of American civilization. See especially Chapters 14, 18, and 19.

[55]Hart, *The Popular Book*, pp. 255–56, is excellent here. Carnegie's book sold 750,000 copies its first year. By 1948 it had sold over 3,250,000 copies in all editions. Also popular were Pitkin's *Life Begins at Forty* and Dorothea Brande's *Wake Up and Live*, among the hundreds of best-selling self-help books.

culture. In simplest terms, Carnegie called for adjustment to the existing order. Everyone wanted to feel important; the way to get ahead was to *make* other people feel important. Smile! In the same year Henry C. Link published his best-selling *The Return to Religion.* In it religion joined hands with psychology "to promote not ego strength but surrender." Urging people to "behave themselves" rather than to "know themselves," Link reemphasized the importance of work and of just keeping busy (even by dancing, playing cards, or joining clubs). Most important of all was the development of personality. Link's work in psychological testing led him to invent a method of "testing" personality, a way of measuring "Personality Quotient." PQ was clearly more important than IQ. Make people like you; fit in; develop habits and skills "which interest and serve other people." Here again the radio soap operas played their reinforcement role. They repeated the line of Carnegie and Link: "Just Plain Bill" kept smiling and "Ma Perkins" kept busy. Everyone tried to fit in and be well liked. The wisdom of the sages of the soaps—and few were without their wise man or woman—follows closely the patterns of advice suggested by the Carnegies and the Links and the Norman Vincent Peales who offered similar proposals during the decade. The stress on personal reasons for success and failure is also typical. New business ventures, relying heavily on the new methods of advertising made possible by the new media, proposed a host of products to help individuals guard against failure and perhaps even achieve success. New "diseases" could be countered with new remedies: bad breath, body odor, stained teeth, dish-pan hands. Advertising also assured us that a host of new mail-order courses might help us achieve success by home study; all we needed to do was improve our spelling or our vocabulary, learn how to develop our personalities, or develop our talent for drawing or writing.[56]

All this stress on conforming to what was demanded by society had its more sophisticated counterpart in the emerging field of human-relations management. In his important work in the 1930s, Elton Mayo urged adjustment to the patterns of industrial organization from the perspective not of the worker, aiming to "get ahead," but from that of the manager anxious to provide an

[56]All of the social historians comment on this point. Bird, *The Invisible Scar*, p. 277, has some especially interesting material.

effective and happy work force.[57] Mayo, speaking from a post at Harvard Business School, was certainly a more learned and sophisticated student of human affairs than Dale Carnegie or Henry C. Link, and yet his work strangely seems of a piece with theirs insofar as it seeks adjustment to the existing and ongoing patterns of cultural development. Other intellectuals not influenced by development in popular culture might find, interestingly enough, something at least analogous happening in other areas of professional psychology in the period. For the intellectual community the emergence of what has been called American neo-Freudianism is undoubtedly the most important development. In the thirties no representative work of the group may have been more widely read and more influential than Karen Horney's *The Neurotic Personality of Our Time* (1937). In analyzing the problem of anxiety, she argues that the contradictions within a culture itself bring about specific neurotic patterns in individuals. The attitudes that prevail within the culture to which we relate provide us with the basic conflicts that create our neuroses, and our culture itself is patterned by the very nature of our anxieties, providing institutionalized paths of attempted escape from anxiety. The neurotic personality reflects the conflicts within the culture; the culture provides the mechanisms to escape from anxieties. It is understandable that neo-Freudians have often been accused of advocating an adjustment to the patterns of culture as a way of curing more serious problems of anxiety, and it is fair to read neo-Freudianism in this aspect as a highbrow translation of what we have already suggested marked the mainstream of popular psychology in the 1930s.[58]

If the idea of culture and the self-awareness of cultural involvement play crucial roles in a structuring of the history of the 1930s, another related idea also cannot be overlooked: the idea

[57]Mayo deserves serious treatment. He influenced Harold Lasswell's studies, for example, and his books *The Human Problems of an Industrial Civilization* (Cambridge, Mass.: Harvard University Press, 1933) and *The Social Problems of an Industrial Civilization* (Cambridge, Mass.: Harvard University Press, 1945) are important works. Meyer discusses Mayo briefly in his book, cited above (fn. 54), and Loren Baritz has an important analysis in *The Servants of Power* (Middletown, Conn.: Wesleyan University Press, 1960).

[58]Clara Thompson has a brief analysis of the Neo-Freudians in the last chapter of her *Psychoanalysis: Evolution and Development* (New York: Hermitage House, 1950), and there is a stimulating critique of the movement in the epilogue to Herbert Marcuse's *Eros and Civilization* (Boston: Beacon Press, 1955).

of commitment. A commonplace of contemporary language, the idea and its current forms came to significant fruition in the 1930s.[59] Hemingway's heroes of the 1920s had a sense of obedience to a code, to be sure, but perhaps nowhere in our fiction is the basic idea brought so much to the center of consciousness as in the mystery writing of the 1930s. This genre was extraordinarily important in the period; more significant (in quality and in number of volumes published) detective fiction was produced in the decade than in any previous period.[60] Unfortunately, too few historians have followed up Professor William Aydelotte's superbly suggestive article on "The Detective Story as a Historical Source."[61] Here we cannot detail all the consequences of the popularity of the form in the 1930s. But we can look at an early and archetypical detective hero of the period and see the form the idea of commitment begins to take. Sam Spade first appeared in Dashiell Hammett's masterpiece of 1930, *The Maltese Falcon*, and was immortalized in Humphrey Bogart's portrayal in John Huston's film version of the novel. Few people who have read the book or seen the film can forget Sam's great last speech to Brigid O'Shaughnessy, the woman he loves, the woman who offers him love and money (both of which the culture values highly). Yet Brigid is a murderess, and Sam vows to surrender her to the police. His argument forms a whole new cultural stance for several generations:

> Listen. This isn't a damned bit of good. You'll never understand me, but I'll try once more.... When a man's partner is killed he's supposed to do something about it. It doesn't make any difference what you thought of him. He was your partner and you're supposed to do something about it. Then it happens we were in the detective business. Well, when one of your organization gets killed it's bad for busi-

[59]The word was perhaps not widely used in the decade, certainly not as widely used as it was to become in the 1940s and 1950s. It did not quite gain the currency that the word *culture* did. But the idea was a concept important to the period. On the whole question of the word, its origins, and its meanings in contemporary discussion, see Edmund Wilson, "Words of Ill-Omen," in his *The Bit Between My Teeth* (New York: Farrar, Straus & Giroux, Inc., 1965), pp. 415–16.

[60]Hart, *The Popular Book*, p. 259, points out that nearly a quarter of all new novels published in the decade were detective-mystery stories. Only 12 books of this type appeared in 1914; only 97 in 1925. By 1939 the production of new titles (to say nothing of reprints) had reached 217.

[61]*Yale Review*, 39 (September, 1949), 76–95.

ness to let the killer get away with it. . . . Third, I'm a detective and expecting me to run criminals down and let them go free is like asking a dog to catch a rabbit and let it go. It can be done, all right, and sometimes it is done, but it's not the natural thing. . . . Fourth, no matter what I wanted to do now it would be absolutely impossible for me to let you go without having myself dragged to the gallows with the others. Next, I've no reason in God's world to think I can trust you and if I did this and got away with it you'd have something on me that you could use whenever you happened to want to. . . . Sixth, . . . since I've got something on you, I couldn't be sure you wouldn't decide to shoot a hole in *me* some day. . . . It's easy to be nuts about you. . . . But I don't know what that amounts to. Does anybody ever? But suppose I do? What of it? Maybe next month I won't. . . . Well, if I send you over I'll be sorry as hell—I'll have some rotten nights—but that'll pass. . . . If that doesn't mean anything to you forget it and we'll make it this: I won't because all of me wants to—wants to say to hell with the consequences and do it—and because—God damn you—you've counted on that with me the same as you counted on that with the others. . . . I won't play the sap for you.[62]

This is a remarkable passage, and it is in its way especially a passage that could only have come out of the 1930s: hard, yet romantic (Spade will wait for Brigid until she is released from prison); pragmatic, yet with rigid adherence to a code of belief and values; commonplace, yet strangely elevated in mood. Most remarkable of all, Sam expects Brigid to understand and accept, and Hammett expects his audience to understand and accept. It represents a remarkable effacement of the desires of the ego, and yet its adherence to a particular scheme of values (meaning at the same time the rejection of still other things of value) allows for survival itself.

The very nature of the period and of the new dominant approach in the idea of culture created special problems for the individual. To be sure, the problem suggested by "individualism" as early as the 1830s, when Tocqueville coined the expression, was whether or not the individual could survive in an age of mass civilization and industrialization. But the effort could be made nonetheless: witness the frequently wild antinomian spirit that infected so many of the young intellectuals of the 1920s with their hopes of asserting the supremacy and persistence of their unique

---

[62] I am using the Dell paperback reprint (New York: Dell Publishing Co., Inc., 1966), pp. 188–89. Copyright by, and quoted by permission of, Alfred A. Knopf, Inc.

personalities and the survival of their own egos. But the "cultural" approach of the 1930s seemed (even as it resisted the claims of "civilization") to pose still further problems rather than easy solutions. As John Dewey explained,

> The function of culture in determining what elements of human nature are dominant and their pattern or arrangement in connection with one another goes beyond any special point to which attention is called. It affects the very idea of individuality. The idea that human nature is inherently and exclusively individual is itself a product of a cultural individualistic movement. The idea that the mind and consciousness are intrinsically individual did not even occur to any one for much the greater part of human history.[63]

Thus individualism can exist only if the culture permits it, that is, if it can have a necessary function within the structure of the culture itself.

There was a deep current of pessimism in the thirties about the possible survival of individualism. In 1935 Robert Sherwood gave Broadway audiences *The Petrified Forest,* a play in which the rootless, wandering poet-intellectual and the fiercely independent gangster both represent types doomed to extinction by society, types as dead as the trees of the petrified forest itself. The drive for unity and conformity (ideals often reinforced by the concept of culture itself) that appears such a striking fact in the history of the period—no matter how noble and desirable the end—threatens the survival of individualism. Karen Horney's discussion of solutions to the problem of anxiety nowhere suggests a rebuilding of the ego so it can stand alone.[64] Yet the hunger for such survival of "I" remains; the search for immortality persists as an acute source of anxiety.

Observe Edward G. Robinson's memorable characterization of the title role in *Little Caesar,* the film of 1931. In an early scene he explains to his friend why he must have a major career in crime. He is not fighting back against social injustices done him; he is not trying to escape from the ghetto and the slum. The women

[63]John Dewey, *Freedom and Culture* (New York: G. P. Putnam's Sons, 1939), p. 21.

[64]Karen Horney, *The Neurotic Personality of Our Time* (New York: W. W. Norton & Company, Inc., 1937), pp. 47 ff. It is interesting, in passing, to note how much Professor Lynd makes use of Horney's analysis in his own book *Knowledge for What?* previously cited.

and the money fail to attract him, and he expresses no interest in the excitement of a contest between law and outlaw. He is Ricco, he announces proudly, and "I want to *be* someone." In the film's final scene, lying shot and dying under a billboard, he exclaims almost without belief, "Mother of Mercy, is this the end of Ricco?"

Thus, too, the movements and ideologies of a period—and certainly of the 1930s—helped people to "be" somebody. Malcolm Cowley comments on the special advantages Communist party membership afforded:

> There was an enormous prestige at that time for people who belonged to the party. They were listened to as if they had received advice straight from God; as if they weren't quite inspired prophets, but had been at meetings where the word was passed down from Mount Sinai. . . . So they had a sort of mana that surrounded them.[65]

One of the few novels written in the period that could be called political, Tess Slesinger's *The Unpossessed* (1934), treats with considerable satiric effect the social and psychological uses to which middle-class intellectuals and writers put their involvement in the political Left.

Yet status and prestige represent only one part of the story of the survival of the ego. The period was one in which social anxieties heightened personal anxieties. Cowley, commenting on the large number of breakdowns among intellectuals, expresses his own belief that party membership provided a way of helping "these people with psychological problems [who] were looking for some cure outside themselves."[66] Certainly the method could easily fit into one or more of the "dodges" Karen Horney tells us we build into our culture in our effort to escape our anxieties. Katherine Anne Porter, writing in 1939, saw the political tendency since 1930 as

> to the last degree a confused, struggling, drowning-man-and-straw sort of thing, stampede of panicked crowd, each man trying to save himself—one at a time trying to work out his horrible confusions. . . .
> I suffer from it, and I try to work my way out to some firm ground of personal belief, as others do. I have times of terror and doubt and

---

[65]In "Symposium: The First American Writers' Congress," *American Scholar*, 35 (Summer 1966), 505.

[66]Cowley in *American Scholar*, 35, 500.

indecision, I am confused in all the uproar of shouting maddened voices. . . . I should like to save myself, but I have no assurance that I can.[67]

"I suspect that it was the question of my own fate that took me to Spain as much as it was any actual convulsion going on in that country," Josephine Herbst shrewdly comments.[68]

There is, of course, a significant difference between becoming a gangster and joining the battle against fascism, no matter what a crusader against the Red Decade might think. But the act of commitment itself had a psychological and sociological significance often unrelated to the specific nature of the profession or movement. For some the act itself could be defined in ways that made it sufficient in itself. For Ernest Hemingway, the Spanish War presented an easy and positive answer for the individual. Herbst tells us that Hemingway was "at home" in Spain and that she was not. For him the war offered

> a part in something which you could believe in wholly and completely and in which you felt an absolute brotherhood with others who were engaged in it. . . . Your own death seemed of complete unimportance; only a thing to be avoided because it would interfere with the performance of your duty. But the best thing was that here was something you could do about this feeling and this necessity, too, you could fight.[69]

The simplicity of such an act of commitment almost overwhelms, especially in Hemingway's rhetorical flight. This act Hemingway describes is simple, clear, direct; it is obvious and essential.

Yet not everyone could find such immediate satisfaction in an act of commitment. The act might be necessary, but there still remained in fact new dilemmas developed as a consequence of the act itself. Compare Herbst's response with Hemingway's:

---

[67]In her reply to the *Partisan Review* questionnaire "The Situation in American Writing," first published in 1939 and reprinted in William Phillips and Philip Rahv, eds., *The Partisan Reader* (New York: Dial Press, Inc., 1946), p. 617.

[68]Josephine Herbst, "The Starched Blue Sky of Spain," *The Noble Savage 1* (Cleveland: The World Publishing Company, 1960), p. 78.

[69]From *For Whom the Bell Tolls* (1940), quoted in Norman Holmes Pearson, "The Nazi-Soviet Pact and the End of a Dream," in Daniel Aaron, ed., *America in Crisis* (New York: Alfred A. Knopf, Inc., 1952), p. 337. *For Whom the Bell Tolls* was originally published by Charles Scribner's Sons.

I was probably trying to find some answers to the confusions in my own mind. The thirties had come in like a hurricane. An entire young generation had been swept up in a violent protest against the realities of events. But the answers were numbing. The slogans were pieces of twine throttling something that was struggling. Phrases like 'the toiling masses' did not answer terrible questions. There were always people, real people, each was an individual spirit with its own peculiar past. The Spanish War was doubtless the last war in which individuals were to enter fully with their individual might. But what a welter of conflicting views this implies! The soldier is not only fighting *against* an enemy but also *for* some beyond.[70]

The special dilemma for the intellectual that this passage reveals is central to any serious study of the 1930s, but Hemingway's contemporary response was perhaps more characteristic of writers of the times.

How important the ability was to make some commitment, to associate with some idea of culture, may best be seen if we look briefly at those who lacked it. Frederick J. Hoffman tells us

The age of the Great Depression . . . was of course the time of the marginal man *malgre lui*. Time and again, he moves by necessity from place to place, vainly seeking employment, dreadfully aware of his lack of status, his emotional reaction varying from extreme despair to extreme anger.[71]

The 1930s had its forced wanderers, its vagabonds, its tramps. Indeed, such "marginal men" became the subjects of a literature that has emerged as a special legacy from the period. Such marginality is not desired or accepted voluntarily; life on the road is not romanticized, nor is it a source of any genuine pleasure or special wisdom. It is not a journey that ends in discovery or explanation. There is little to suggest the appeal of any particular ideology. (Even anarchism, so popular in the literature of marginal men in previous periods, is almost strikingly absent.) Seldom can the wanderer find alleviation of distress and anxiety by adherence to a group or a community of any lasting kind. Mar-

[70]Herbst in *The Noble Savage 1*, pp. 79–80.

[71]Frederick J. Hoffman, *Marginal Manners* (Evanston, Ill.: Harper & Row, Publishers, 1962), p. 7. This excellent anthology has an important section on the 1930s: "The Expense of Poverty: Bottom Dogs," pp. 92–126, with material reprinted from Dos Passos, Steinbeck, Dahlberg, and Maltz and very intelligent headnotes by Hoffman.

ginal men do not participate in any culture, real or imagined. They do not listen to the radio, go to the movies, or read *Life* magazine. They do not participate in sports or play traditional games. Here, rather, among the marginal men we find those corruptions of games of which Caillois speaks; here is the violence (sometimes personal, sometimes social, but generally in the end without meaning), the alienation, the drunkenness, the unacceptable and antisocial forms of "play." Even the strike takes on this aspect; it seems almost a perversion of sport without purpose or meaning, since it is generally lost or blunted. It can provide, for the moment, common purpose and brotherhood, the suggested beginnings of a pattern of belief or a way of life—as other events or acts also can do on occasion—but such common action is too easily dissolved and the individual marginal man is on the road again, the road to nowhere. He has no commitments and no culture (in the sense these words are used here). The phenomenon produced a strong body of literature: Edward Dahlberg's *Bottom Dogs* (1930), Jack Conroy's *The Disinherited* (1933), and Nelson Algren's *Somebody in Boots* (1935) are among the very best. These works, however, have become more admired and treated with fuller critical seriousness in our time than they were in the thirties.

Only one novel that might be said to be of the same genre was greeted with considerable enthusiasm when it appeared, John Steinbeck's *The Grapes of Wrath* (1939). Yet it is a novel of the enforced wanderings of marginal men with a difference, in fact with several crucial differences. Marginal man here was not alone; the strength and power of the family as a unit went with him. Frequently on the road he shared with other travelers a strong sense of common purpose and destiny, even the incipient form of a culture. There was an end in view: sometimes a romantic agrarian utopia, sometimes at least a sense of revolutionary enthusiasm and optimism. And the Joad family most especially, therefore, had what can be defined as a sense of commitment.

Thus it was characteristic in the 1930s for the idea of commitment itself to merge with some idea of culture and to produce, at least for a time, participation in some group, community, or movement. The 1930s was *the* decade of participation and belonging. This is obvious on almost every level of cultural development. The 1920s saw a growth of spectator sports; the 1930s mark a new era in sports participation. The 1920s found the intellectuals in revolt *against* the village; the 1930s witnessed the intellectuals in flight *to* the village. Such generalizations are obviously extreme, but they do suggest a basic truth about the decade: the need to feel oneself a part of some larger body, some larger sense of purpose. Harold Clurman's excellent memoir of the Group Theater and the thirties, *The Fervent Years* (1945), makes clear that it was not only the excitement of new plays and new theater ideas or even a new sense of social purpose that made the venture memorable. It was the sense of working together, sharing ideas and beliefs, the sense in fact of being a group.

It is not possible to come away from wide reading in the literature of the period without some sense of the excitement—even the enthusiasm and optimism shared by many. They *were* "fervent years." A participant in the intellectual life of the decade comments that there was an "almost universal liveliness that countervailed universal suffering."[72] The historian must wonder whether the "facts" warranted such enthusiasm. Depression problems were not solved during the period, although they were considerably alleviated. Yet even while political events at home suggested some grounds for hope (although surely no grounds to anticipate any "revolutionary" triumph of the workers), abroad the international order was rapidly collapsing and the menace of fascism constantly growing. One explanation for this mood may very well be found in the additional "fact" of increased participation: in groups, in movements, in what appeared to be the major action of the time.

Political participation has most consistently attracted the attention of scholars and citizens who revisit the 1930s. The growth of the Communist party and its position as a rallying point, at least for a time, of considerable numbers of outstanding American intellectual and artistic figures, helped create the image of the decade as heavily political. Such political participation has received excellent scholarly treatment recently; we are now able to understand such activity more fully than ever before. Yet, the historian analyzing the culture of the thirties must attempt to appraise this activity in terms of the total record. There were political tracts; there were petitions and manifestos. The Communist party did receive considerable political support, especially in 1932, from leading intellectuals. But somehow there also seems to have been a paucity of political ideas and, more significantly, an inability to maintain effective political stances except

[72]Herbst in *Kenyon Review*, 28, 776.

on negative issues: against Franco, against the menace of fascism, against the dehumanization of Depression America. When it came to vital issues of political involvement as distinct from commitment to ideas and often vaguer ideals, that is, issues of power, strategy, and organization that are the lifeblood of actual political movements, the party soon found itself divided; each issue of genuine political importance brought not only division into factions but actual withdrawal of increasing numbers of intellectuals from the party itself.[73] It was easy, as Herbst suggested, to be against; it was harder by far to look beyond for something.

The genius of the Communist movement of the 1930s was its ability to use the obvious social and psychological needs of the period. It effectively recruited individuals who had no other place to go and who sought to belong and to do, those who had a commitment to ideals shared by those in the party if not complete knowledge or understanding of its ideology. There were sentiments and values that united members; there were in those remarkably confused and complicated times little political knowledge and intelligence among intellectuals whose training and preparation usually left them ill-suited to face the political realities of a collapsing capitalist order. And the party offered more than political participation: there were its camps, its discussion groups, its magazines, even its dances and social affairs, its lecturers, its writers' congresses. For the first time in the twentieth century the party had attempted to organize writers and intellectuals and to bring them together to exchange views, political and aesthetic, to feel themselves an important part of the American scene. This was an important development—and a major contribution of the party—for writers who had grown up in the 1920s with the view that America offered no place for the artist and the intellectual. (The New Deal, of course, in this area offered considerable competition with its own projects in the arts, in the theater, and in the Federal Writers' Project.) There was, furthermore, great satisfaction for many in

the idea of uniting themselves with the mass or the group, and being not leader, but just one in the ranks of the great army that was marching toward a new dawn. If they could forget themselves, they could

---

[73]The article by Norman Holmes Pearson, "The Nazi-Soviet Pact," is excellent on this whole question. It is an important piece on the intellectuals and the Left in the 1930s. The works of Daniel Aaron previously cited (fnn. 6 and 8) are basic.

solve their psychological problems. So there was a great deal of almost religious feeling going on at the same time among people you
would never suspect of having it, and who tried to hide their religious
feeling in talk of Marxian dialectic. . . . The feeling was there.[74]

It is all too facile to describe the commitment to the Left as a
religious surrogate, and yet it is a fact of some importance that
American Protestantism was itself suffering in the 1930s. Liberal
Protestantism had tended to disintegrate into a strange breed of
mind-cure and positive thinking; the social gospel found itself
usurped by the political magic and action of the New Deal; and
the mighty search for "political realism" among intellectual
leaders of Protestantism was just itself in process.[75] The rise of
Neo-Thomism at the University of Chicago and the efforts of the
Southern Agrarians in the period offer additional evidence of an
effort to make religion and religious values relevant to society. It
is therefore not farfetched to see for some in the movement to the
political left quasi-religious motives.

In a sense, Granville Hicks came to communism through
youth groups of the Universalist Church, theological school, and
the teaching of the Bible at Smith College. But there was perhaps
something even more important, as a reviewer of his memoir of
the period has observed: "His native feeling for the decentralized,
for the communion of the small group, for collective action coming from individuals drawn together for a common purpose, acting out their parts of a common aim, is thoroughly consistent
with his life pattern as it is revealed to us in *Part of the Truth*."[76]
Thus Hicks's participation in the Communist movement of the
1930s seems somehow related to his later enthusiastic efforts to
make the *Small Town*[77] an operative factor in American culture.

Mary McCarthy selected a most apt image when she called her
novel about the 1930s *The Group*. In addition to the Communist
party itself, the various groups within it, and the leagues of authors, there were the Southern Agrarians who issued a group

[74]Cowley in *American Scholar*, 35, 500.

[75]On this whole subject Donald B. Meyer has produced a key book in our understanding of the 1930s with his *The Protestant Search for Political Realism* (Los
Angeles: University of California Press, 1960).

[76]Herbst in *Kenyon Review*, 28, 777.

[77]Granville Hicks, *Small Town* (New York: The Macmillan Company, 1946). This
is the autobiographical account Hicks has given us of his involvement in his New
York community after his break with the Communists.

manifesto, *I'll Take My Stand,* in 1930 and joined in yet another, *Who Owns America?,* in 1936. Allen Tate indicated his desire to participate in more genuine and meaningful group life than that offered by industrial capitalism: a producers' capitalism, the peasant community, the religious community, or a sense of regional community.[78] Ralph Borsodi was not only a widely read critic of modern urban living who urged a *Flight from the City* (1933), but he also organized Homestead Units, one of many communitarian ventures in the period. Arthur Morgan of Antioch College and the TVA founded in 1939 an organization designed "to promote the interests of the community as a basic social institution . . . concerned with the economic, recreational, educational, cultural and spiritual development of its members."[79]

In part this was a continuation of a tradition well established during the progressive era and perhaps traceable to the mid-nineteenth-century movements, but there is little question that the 1930s saw a general revival of communitarian concern. Stuart Chase's description of the Mexican village has already been cited. Lewis Mumford looked forward to the creation of a new, human city while he looked back with considerable enthusiasm to the achievements of the medieval city.[80] Black Mountain College, which opened in September of 1934, advanced a special communitarian ideal of college living. There was an unusual equality between students and faculty; they built the institution together, literally sharing even tasks of physical construction. The students developed a strong tradition of native arts and craft work as a part of their college experience.

Thornton Wilder's sentimental hit of 1938, *Our Town,* provided a far different picture of village life than, for example, Sherwood Anderson's *Winesburg, Ohio,* his "book of grotesques" published in 1919. Clifford Odets treated the idea of the strike almost as ritual; *Waiting for Lefty* (1935), his vision of labor solidarity and common action, also created a sense of audience participation in a special community with the workers in the play. The

[78]Allen Tate, in his answer to the 1939 *Partisan Review* questionnaire, reprinted in *The Partisan Reader,* p. 622.

[79]Morgan is quoted here from a pamphlet published by the organization, About Community Service Incorporated, n.d.

[80]Lewis Mumford, *The Culture of Cities* (New York: Harcourt, Brace & World, Inc., 1938), the second volume in the already cited *The Renewal of Life* series (fn. 35). Mumford had begun his career in the 1920s with a study of various utopias people had devised through the ages.

unions themselves were or tried to be more than economic institutions: union membership meant group consciousness, and the
union supplied important social functions, sometimes even cultural ones—for example, *Pins and Needles* (1937), the International Ladies Garment Workers' marvelous theatrical review that
delighted audiences in the 1930s and once again in the 1960s. The
MacDowell Colony, a long-time center affording artists the opportunity to work and live away from the demands of jobs and other
kinds of social pressures, seemed to some almost a communitarian dream come true in this period. And Mary McCarthy was to
satirize in *The Oasis* (1949) the kind of communitarian venture
attempted by some intellectuals in the 1930s. There was a whole
new interest in "the folk society," which led to a whole reappre-
ciation of Indian life and especially pre-Columbian Indian life
despoiled by the coming of European civilization.[81]

Individual acts of commitment led to particular visions of culture, often through participation in specific groups or movements
or hoped-for participation in ideal ones. This search often involved
a new emphasis on tradition. Mention has already been made of
the special search for an American tradition. But the movement
went beyond this. Robert Penn Warren has said, "The past is always a rebuke to the present,"[82] and the 1930s indeed demonstrated this special use of history, so different from the uses to
which history had been put in the progressive period or in the
debunking 1920s. Not only did the Agrarians attempt to create a
picture of the pre–Civil War South as an aid to the development of
their twentieth-century Agrarian stand, even those of left-wing
persuasion found much in the past—miniature class wars, slave
revolts, revolutionary heroes—as V. F. Calverton shows in his *The
Awakening of America* (1939). Gilbert Seldes's *Mainland* (1936)
found much to praise in our past; as a work it stands in sharp
contrast to his depressing and negative report on Depression
America, *The Year of the Locust* (1932). The professional historians'
more favorable assessment of previously despised Puritanism led

---

[81]See Edward Dahlberg's interesting piece on the communitarian tradition reprinted in *Alms for Oblivion* (Minneapolis: University of Minnesota Press, 1964),
"Our Vanishing Cooperative Colonies," pp. 91–103. Dahlberg, as well as Hart Crane
and Archibald MacLeish, became interested in pre-Columbian Indian life and its
extinction by the conquest. William Carlos Williams may have led the way in his *In
The American Grain* as early as 1925. At the end of the Dahlberg essay cited, the
author asks, "Is the solitary American superior to the communal Indian?"

[82]Quoted in Louis Rubin, Jr.'s, introduction to the Harper Torchbook reprint of
I'll Take My Stand (New York: Harper & Row, Publishers, 1958), p. xiii.

to a reassessment of our whole intellectual past. And the work of Mumford, once again, sees much in early history destroyed by the coming of modern technology and urban civilization.

The idea of tradition itself—and most especially the supposed tradition of civilization in the west before the industrial revolution and the French Revolution—becomes increasingly important in the period. Not only was there an appeal to the Southern Agrarian tradition and various versions of an American tradition, but the humanists Irving Babbitt and Paul Elmer More offered a lively source of debate in the early 1930s and were widely read in intellectual circles.[83] T. S. Eliot, long interested in "The Tradition and the Individual Talent," placed considerably more of his attention on the tradition in the thirties, especially in *After Strange Gods* (1934) and *The Idea of a Christian Society* (1939). At the University of Chicago, Robert M. Hutchins not only reorganized the institution but also produced a significant defense of his version of *The Higher Learning in America* (1936). His work was a direct confrontation to the previous work of Thorstein Veblen and a specific challenge to the pragmatists. He would use the tradition to help shape and reinforce the culture.

> In general education we are interested in drawing out elements of our common human nature; we are interested in the attributes of the race, not the accidents of individuals.... We propose permanent studies because these studies ... connect man with man, because they connect us with the best that man has thought, because they are basic to any further study and to any understanding of the world.... Real unity can be achieved only by a hierarchy of truths which show us which are fundamental and which subsidiary, which significant and which not.[84]

The pragmatists, already under attack in the 1920s, found themselves fighting for their intellectual lives under the heavy assault of the traditionalists and the antinaturalists.[85]

---

[83]See Malcolm Cowley's critique, "Angry Professors," written in 1930 and reprinted in *Think Back on Us*, pp. 3–13.

[84]Robert M. Hutchins, *The Higher Learning in America* (Chicago: University of Chicago Press, 1936), pp. 73, 77, and 95.

[85]Gail Kennedy, ed., *Pragmatism and American Culture* (Boston: D. C. Heath & Company, 1952) is an excellent anthology with a good bibliography to help the reader trace this development. One of Dewey's own best answers appeared in 1943 in the *Partisan Review:* "Anti-Naturalism in Extremis." It is reprinted in *The Partisan Reader*, pp. 514–29.

Even the writing of the period, diverse and different as it was in form and content, shared a common commitment, no matter what the individual participation, to various movements. The Marxist critics may have tried to mold a special kind of proletarian writing, but they did not succeed, even among party members; the movement was surprisingly brief in spite of all the attention paid to it. However, Joseph Freeman's interesting introduction to the anthology *Proletarian Literature in the United States* (1935) is worth examination:

> Art, then, is not the same as action; it is not identical with science; it is distinct from party program. It has its own special function, the grasp and transmission of experience. The catch lies in the word "experience."[86]

That is indeed where the catch did lie. Even John Dewey had defined art as experience, and the word "experience" had been a crucial one for the progressive generation. Freeman himself argued for the virtues of the *avant-garde* in America from the poetic renaissance of 1912 to the economic crisis of 1929. In this period American writers had repudiated "eternal values" of traditional writers and had emphasized immediate American experience.

> The movement has its prophet in Walt Whitman, who broke with the "eternal values" of feudal literature and proclaimed the here and now. Poetry abandoned the pose of moving freely in space and time; it now focused its attention on New York, Chicago, San Francisco, Iowa, Alabama in the twentieth century.[87]

The next stage was to be a rendering of the experience of the class struggle itself as it emerged to consciousness with the depression of 1929, and finally, it was hoped, there would come a literature of the party.

But literature in general—no matter what the political allegiance of individual writers might be—did not generally respond to the demands of political leadership. There was a new sense of a widening range of experience dramatically brought home because of the events of the era and their widespread transmission by the media. Jack Conroy was associated with party activities, but *The*

---

[86]*Proletarian Literature in the United States*, ed. by Granville Hicks et al. with a critical introduction by Joseph Freeman (New York: International Publishers Co., Inc., 1935), p. 10.

[87]Freeman, *Proletarian Literature*, p. 19.

Disinherited is not an ideological novel. As Conroy himself remarked, "I, for one, considered myself a witness to the times rather than a novelist. Mine was an effort to obey Whitman's injunction to 'vivify the contemporary fact.'"[88] Allen Tate was a Southern Agrarian, but as he has suggested, "The success or failure of a political idea is none of my business; my business is to render in words the experience of people, whatever movement of ideas they may be caught up in."[89] And Alfred Kazin, recalling his own *Starting Out in the Thirties*, declared, "What young writers of the Thirties wanted was to prove the literary value of our experience, to recognize the possibilities of art in our own lives, to feel we had moved the streets, the stockyards, the hiring halls into literature—to show our radical strength could carry on the experimental impulse of modern literature."[90]

This search for experience and ways to record it produced some interesting new forms, especially the "documentary" techniques characteristic of the period, not only in Dos Passos's *U.S.A.*, but in various Federal Theater productions and works like Agee and Walker's *Let Us Now Praise Famous Men*. But in many cases this aim was related to the discovery of significant myths, symbols, and images from the culture itself that might also serve as a basis of reinforcement or indeed the re-creation or remaking of culture itself. The efforts of William Faulkner in the South and of Hart Crane to build his *The Bridge* (1930) stand out, with their self-conscious striving to use our history and even our technology mythically and symbolically. The most persistent symbol to emerge from the bulk of the literature of the period, however, was "the people." It was the theme of Burke's lecture on "Revolutionary Symbolism in America." In 1936 Carl Sandburg insisted, at extraordinary length and with much sentimentalism, *The People, Yes*. Others pointed to the "workers"—Burke's preference for "people" rather than "workers" created something of a literary battle at the First American Writers' Congress[91]—to brotherhood or even to Man (always capitalized).

[88] Jack Conroy, in his contribution to "The 1930s, a Symposium," *The Carleton Miscellany*, 6 (Winter, 1965), 39.

[89] In his answer to the 1939 *Partisan Review* questionnaire, reprinted in *The Partisan Reader*, p. 622.

[90] From *Starting Out in the Thirties* by Alfred Kazin, by permission of Atlantic–Little, Brown and Co. Page 15. Copyright © 1962, 1965 by Alfred Kazin.

[91] The story is told by Burke in his comments in the "Symposium" in *American Scholar*, 35, 506–8.

This self-conscious interest in myth, symbol, and image (to become in succeeding decades a special branch of criticism and philosophy, if not a cult among writers and scholars) was in the 1930s a way in which literature could once again relate experience to culture, not necessarily to political action. Herbert Agar, in his introduction to *Who Owns America* (1936), declared that the social and economic system in America was on the rocks. There was a need to "build a better world" and to provide some picture "in human terms" of what this would be like. Reformation was necessary, but social and economic theories were not enough: "if a reformation is even to begin, it must be based on an ideal that can stir the human heart."[92]

In an age demanding an image—or a myth or symbol—did the social and political movements provide one effective enough? Josephine Herbst has asked whether a phrase like "toiling masses" is enough, and Edward Dahlberg, a former "proletarian novelist" himself at one time associated with left-wing politics, was to write devastatingly in 1941 of the failure of the Left to provide meaningful symbols and myths. The mystery of the mythic strike, for example, was not enough. "The strike fails as tragic purification, as psychic ablution; the strike is barter, a pragmatic expedient, not a way of seeing." Thus he demanded of ideology more than it can provide, indicating in his extraordinary and special rhetoric a dissatisfaction with communism and fascism that may have led others out of the kinds of political involvement they sought earlier in the 1930s. "The drama of Bread can never be a substitute for the Wine and the Wafer, because man must not only have his loaf of bread, but he must also have an image to eat. Communism and fascism fail as awe and wonder. They are weak as image-making sources."[93] Dahlberg demands what others in this decade so interested in myth, symbol, and image tried to find in a variety of ways. Perhaps in the long run, too, the New Deal succeeded even in its limited way because it, rather than the artist or the intellectual, the Communist party or other political and social movements like Technocracy, commanded the set of images, symbols, and myths with most meaning for the bulk of the American people.

[92]Herbert Agar, *Who Owns America* (Boston: Houghton, Mifflin Company, 1936), p. vii.

[93]Edward Dahlberg, "The Proletarian Eucharist," in *Can These Bones Live* (New York: Harcourt, Brace & World, Inc., 1941), pp. 73–74.

At least two recent critics of the 1930s have argued that one of the great failures of the period, especially on the left, was the effort to associate itself with the "folk" rather than the "intellectual" tradition in America, that is, with "mass culture."[94]

> The most important effect of the intellectual life of the 30's and the culture that grew out of it has been to distort and eventually to destroy the emotional and moral content of experience, putting in its place a system of conventionalized 'responses.' In fact, the chief function of mass culture is to relieve one of the necessity of experiencing one's life directly.[95]

William Phillips has suggested that the writers of the Concord school mark the first appearance of an American intelligentsia. In their revolt against commercialism and the Puritan heritage, he suggests, "they set out consciously to form, as Emerson put it, 'a learned class,' and to assimilate the culture of Europe into a native tradition."[96] In the 1930s, it might be argued, the self-conscious American intelligentsia set out to become an unlearned class, to assimilate the culture of the "people" into the inherited European tradition, perhaps especially those ideas and forms brought back from long stays abroad in the 1920s.

Whether the criticisms voiced above constitute a valid perspective on the period or not, the fact remains that there is in much of the literature and thought of the period a kind of sentimentalism, a quality of intellectual softness all too often apparent: Saroyan's "gentle people," the extraordinary messages of hope with which Odets so frequently ended his plays, and for which the content of the plays themselves provided no warrant, Carl Sandburg's positive nod to "the people," MacLeish's hymn to Man. The idea of commitment frequently led, when combined with the idea of culture, not to revolution but to acquiescence.

Significantly, there emerged in the decade of the thirties two other voices from two other rooms, but they achieved full cultural voice and power primarily in the post-Depression period. One may be called the commitment to irresponsibility as a cultural

---

[94]William Phillips, "What Happened in the '30s," *Commentary*, 34 (September, 1962), 204–12; Robert Warshow, "The Legacy of the '30s," reprinted in his *The Immediate Experience* (New York: Doubleday & Company, Inc., 1962).

[95]Warshow, *The Immediate Experience*, p. 7.

[96]William Phillips, "The Intellectuals' Tradition," reprinted in *The Partisan Reader*, p. 489. This essay originally appeared in 1941.

stance; extreme antinomianism, glorying in the experiences of the self and saying to hell with everything else. At first in a kind of underground of the literary world, Henry Miller emerged in 1934 with *Tropic of Cancer*. George Orwell, home from the Spanish war, was to hail Miller in 1940 as "the only imaginative prose-writer of the slightest value who has appeared among the English-speaking races for some years past."[97] Miller was neither a defeatist nor a yea-sayer. "Where Miller's work is symptomatically important," Orwell explains,

> is in its avoidance of any of these attitudes. He is neither pushing the world-process forward nor trying to drag it back, but on the other hand he is by no means ignoring it. I should say he believes in the impending ruin of Western Civilization much more firmly than the majority of 'revolutionary' writers; only he does not feel called upon to do anything about it. He is fiddling while Rome is burning, and, unlike most of the people who do this, fiddling with his face toward the flames. . . . He feels no impulse to alter or control the process that he is undergoing. He has performed the essential Jonah act of allowing himself to be swallowed, remaining passive, *accepting*.[98]

Miller's is an act of commitment in which the act itself is the most important thing. There is no need for "participation," no sense of "belonging" as a part of a group or a culture, real or imagined. If he is part of a tradition, it is personal tradition picked up among fragments left behind in history. In Miller there is little sense of history; there is a religious sense, but again antinomian and highly personal. His work attempts a direct expression of his own experience, unstructured by philosophy, ideology, or society, by traditional myths or symbols. There is no glorying in the "folk" or special interest in the culture of the "people." American history means no more to him than European, and the America that interests him is only the America of his own experience. Miller's special stance belongs to the cultural history of the thirties: it represents an important modification of the idea of commitment, and one that was to become increasingly important in later decades. For Orwell, Miller's writing is symptomatic: "it

[97]George Orwell, *A Collection of Essays*, p. 256 in the Anchor paperback edition. Quoted by permission of Harcourt, Brace & World, Inc., and Miss Sonia Brownell and Secker & Warburg, Ltd.

[98]Orwell, *A Collection of Essays*, pp. 248 and 249.

is a demonstration of the *impossibility* of any major literature until the world has shaken itself into its new shape."[99]

The other room might be called "Kierkegaardian" in its decor (and it is important to note that this Danish philosopher was translated for the first time into English in the 1930s, although it is not proper to say that the movement under discussion depended upon his thinking). In 1932 Reinhold Niebuhr "loosed his bombshell on individualistic and utopian social thinking, *Moral Man and Immoral Society.*"[100] From this time on Niebuhr and other like-minded theologians (generally called neo-Orthodox) developed a position that was eventually to rule advanced Protestant thinking and ultimately to supply many intellectuals in America with an important world view.

Any generalized picture of the basic structure of the neo-Orthodox position necessarily risks becoming a parody. But it is fair to suggest that it demanded of people difficult commitment. People must live in the world but not be of the world; they are both creature and creator; they are involved in history and yet transcend it. Restoring the doctrine of original sin to a central position once again, Niebuhr asked humanity to continue to participate in the job of political reform knowing full well that human limitations would make it impossible to succeed fully. He dramatized the distinction and the tension that must exist between the Biblical view of history and the "modern" or "progressive" view. Life was a paradox that must be taken with due seriousness. Sydney Ahlstrom offers this summary of the major features of the movement that emerged while the Protestant neo-Orthodoxy sought some alternative to the types of cultural surrender implicit in both liberal Protestantism and social-gospel Protestantism:

> its critique of group, class and personal complacency; its demand for personal appropriation of Christian truth; its insistence that man's moral obligation under the Gospel cannot be stated in terms of legalistic precepts; its warning against the dangers of rationalizing the great Biblical paradoxes; its emphasis upon a radically personalistic

---

[99]Orwell, *A Collection of Essays*, p. 256.

[100]Sydney E. Ahlstrom, "Theology in America," in James Ward Smith and A. Leland Jamison, eds., *The Shaping of American Religion*, Vol. I (Princeton, N.J.: Princeton University Press, 1961), p. 312. Copyright © 1961 by Princeton University Press.

understanding of the self, and of God: above all, the reality, the objectivity, and the sovereignty of God and His judgments.[101]

The fundamental role of Christ was, in effect, to stand in opposition to culture. Humanity was somehow caught in between. Christ was to offer a constant criticism of life in the world, of culture; yet people must continue to operate within the culture with a more realistic sense of the situation. There was no essential morality in any group, party, or class. Ultimately, human beings were alone in their struggle within culture and had to rely on their commitment, their belief in Christ to sustain them.

Thus by the end of the decade two new general positions emerged from the confusions of the period and from the idea of culture and the idea of commitment itself, two positions implying significant criticism of the other views of culture and commitment that had characterized the period. With the growing acceptance of these positions by American intellectuals during the Second World War and after, the thirties came to an end.

Yet, in our effort to achieve an honest understanding of what the decade did achieve, a postscript is called for. In 1941 James Agee and Walker Evans finally published their extraordinary book (begun in 1936) *Let Us Now Praise Famous Men*. It may be the decade's classic, for the book represents much of what was characteristic of the thirties' finest contributions. It is, of course, a documentary; it deals in intimate detail, not with "the people," but with specific members of three families of sharecroppers in the American South. Brilliantly combining photographs and texts, it responds especially to the demands of an era of sight and sound. Significantly, Agee tells us the text was written "with reading aloud in mind. . . . It is suggested that the reader attend with his ear to what he takes off the page: for variations of tone, pace, shape, and dynamics are here particularly unavailable to the eye alone, and with their loss, a good deal of meaning escapes."[102] The text was intended to be read continuously "as music is listened to or a film watched." He wishes that he did not have to use words at all but could put together pieces of cloth,

[101]Ahlstrom in *The Shaping of American Religion*, pp. 315–16. Meyer's *Protestant Search* is again a crucial study here.

[102]James Agee and Walker Evans, *Let Us Now Praise Famous Men* (Boston: Houghton Mifflin Company, 1941), p. xv.

lumps of earth, bits of wood and iron, phials of odors, plates of food and of excrement.

"Above all else; in God's name don't think of it as Art." For Agee struggles to achieve a direct confrontation, by his audience, with the experience of these people themselves, their style of life, their very being. The true meaning, he argues, of a character in his work is that he *exists* "as you do and as I do and as no character of the imagination can possibly exist. His great weight, mystery, and dignity are in this fact."[103] Thus the concentration on the direct experience and the recreation of the total cultural environment in rich detail marks the work. It is a work of passion, a work that involves a fundamental act of commitment by its authors, a belief in the meaningfulness of the lives of such people, a belief in human dignity. There is a moral intensity, albeit without a particular social or political lesson to teach or doctrine to preach. There may be, as Lionel Trilling suggests, a refusal to see any evil in the universe and thus a moral flaw in the work, but the passion and the innocence are also ways of seeing, perhaps characteristic ways of seeing in the best of the work of the 1930s, ways of seeing that we may forget are part of a genuine and valuable legacy of the decade.[104] Later critics were to hail the end of innocence—that lack of a sense of personalism, the sentimentalism, the failure to see complexity and inherent evil in the world, the optimistic faith in simple solutions to all human problems. These same critics greeted a newer "realism" with considerable enthusiasm. The innocence of the period can be documented; that it was all weakness, perhaps not so easily. The decade was also to be criticized for its commitment to ideologies, but also we cannot comment on this charge because there is so little evidence that such a commitment existed. Rather, what appears to have been the stunning weakness of the decade was that innocence *replaced* all ideological sense, when *both* may in fact be essential.

The thirties this essay has attempted to portray and under-

[103]Agee and Evans, *Let Us Now Praise Famous Men*, p. 12.

[104]The Trilling criticism comes in his excellent review of the work that appears in *The Mid-Century*, Number 16 (September, 1960), 3–11, on the occasion of the appearance of the newly revised edition. On the subject of the various attacks on American "innocence" in recent American scholarship and criticism, see the interesting article by Robert A. Skotheim, " 'Innocence' and 'Beyond Innocence' in Recent American Scholarship," *American Quarterly*, 13 (Spring 1961), 93–99.

stand may not correspond to the decade as it exists in myth and memory. It had more than its share of grave weaknesses. But the fact remains that the era made a significant contribution to our development in the acculturation of the idea of culture and of the idea of commitment. Later decades would determine whether better use could be made of these discoveries.

THE MOVEMENT OF THE 1960s AND ITS CULTURAL AND POLITICAL LEGACY

Peter Clecak / UNIVERSITY OF CALIFORNIA, IRVINE

The fifties was a dry season for the American Left. The disappointing showing of the Progressive Party in the presidential campaign of 1948 revealed the inner exhaustion and political feebleness of what later became known as the old Left. Rather than representing the nucleus of a fresh political opening, as some had hoped, this congeries of independent radicals and Stalinists constituted a divided remnant committed to tarnished ideals and lost causes. It was weakened further by steady and largely gratuitous external pressure: governmental interrogations of suspected radicals; infiltration of the Communist party and other radical groups by agents of the Federal Bureau of Investigation; the trial and imprisonment of Communist leaders; systematic exclusion of leftists from positions in government, education, and the media. The old Left, then, died of multiple wounds: some self-inflicted and others externally imposed.

By the middle fifties the ideas of socialism, communism, and anarchism had been virtually expunged from American public life. Popular opposition to communism, which had been absorbed into American civil religion, was apparently secure. Opposition

261

among the intelligentsia, though more modulated, seemed similarly secure. Of course, thoughtful intellectuals discriminated among left theories, ranging from democratic to authoritarian; and they distinguished these theories from the historical experiences of Soviet, Eastern European, and Chinese "socialisms," which, for both valid and bogus reasons, had failed to achieve tolerable democratic norms. But these were only qualified defenses of the Left issued by a fringe of the intelligentsia. The more vibrant main body emphasized American achievement and promise. As Arthur Schlesinger, Jr., observed in *The Vital Center* (1949), his early postwar attempt to stake out the left boundary of respectable social-democratic opinion in America: "What the democratic parties of the developed nations have done . . . has been to use the state to force capitalism to do what both the classical capitalists and the classical Marxists declared was impossible: to control the business cycle and to reapportion income in favor of those whom Jackson called 'the humble members of society.' "[1]

Echoing Schlesinger in 1960, C. Wright Mills sarcastically summarized the main coordinates of American political and social vision in the fifties: "The mixed economy plus the welfare state plus prosperity—that is the formula."[2] America, it was widely supposed, possessed the productive genius to assure rising affluence and eventual abundance for every citizen. By appropriating major radical ends, the reformist system of welfare-state capitalism had eliminated both the possibility and the desirability of revolutionary shortcuts to social justice. Some disagreement within the consensus might persist, but sustained, deeply disruptive protest was supposed to be at an end in America and the developed nations of the West. Hence it was no longer plausible—if it ever had been—for serious political people even to contemplate a risky sacrifice of democracy and stability in a revolutionary pursuit of socialism, communism, or anarchism.

Not everyone managed Schlesinger's early postwar optimism. Not everyone needed to, for such optimism was optional: the American consensus accommodated a range of moods, from buoyancy to pessimism. It was fashionable among certain intellectuals

[1]Arthur M. Schlesinger, Jr., *The Vital Center* (Boston: Houghton Mifflin, 1962), p. xii (first published in 1949).

[2]C. Wright Mills, "The New Left," in Irving Louis Horowitz, ed., *Power, Politics and People* (New York: Ballantine Books, 1963), p. 248.

to accept the consensus skeptically. Such people as David Ries-
man, Richard Hofstadter, and Daniel Bell rejected radical alternatives and fronted the present and future cautiously, stressing
the irony, complexity, and ambiguity of public action in highly
developed, technological societies. At the level of mood, then, the
American consensus excluded only radical despair. This attitude
was reserved as an option for scattered radical voices, for those
who in the middle fifties rejected both the rigidities of the old
Left and the prevailing terms of the liberal-conservative consensus without being able to imagine a way beyond their isolation
and powerlessness. Established radical critics and activists might
participate importantly in a renewal of American radicalism (especially at the level of critique), but they lacked the will to initiate a revival. A new left-wing movement, if there was to be one,
had to be created by a new generation under somewhat different
social circumstances.

Although most of the theoretical and organizational links to
the old Left had been severed by the end of the fifties, a few
important transitional figures such as A. J. Muste, David Del-
linger, William A. Williams, Irving Howe, Michael Harrington,
and C. Wright Mills witnessed the emergence of the new radicalism of the sixties and even assisted in crucial ways. Mills's letter
to the new Left, written in 1960, provides a fascinating account of
the continuities and disjunctures between the old Left and the
new. Steeped in the dilemmas of the old Left, conscious of the
potency of the American consensus, Mills is at once wary and
hopeful about the new stirrings of radicalism.[3] He begins with an
outsider's characterization of the "weary" postwar discourse carried on by "smug conservatives, tired liberals and disillusioned
radicals."[4] Although the ideology of the American consensus included a left liberal edge, it faithfully mirrored existing structures of power. All other discourse on the Left was dismissed as
neurotic dissent or utopian reverie.

Nor could politically isolated American leftists any longer find
confirmation of their vision abroad. Historical events had made a

[3]Mills, "The New Left," in *Power, Politics and People*. It is important to note that
Mills's letter, first published in *New Left Review*, was not directed primarily to an
American audience. Mills considered the new Left an international phenomenon.
His hopes for a revival of American radicalism were especially guarded, and they
grew increasingly somber between 1960 and his death two years later. See Saul
Landau, "C. Wright Mills: The Last Six Months," *Ramparts*, 4 (August 1965), 50.

[4]Mills, "The New Left," in *Power, Politics and People*, p. 247.

shambles of old Left theory: the revolution had been betrayed in the USSR and aborted in the West. Having rejected the American consensus and the old Left, Mills concentrates his hopes on "the young intelligentsia" as the new opening for radical thought and activity. By spring of 1960, he notes, young people had become the main ferment of opposition in Turkey, South Korea, Cuba, Britain, Japan, and even the American "Southland."[5] Though weak, scattered, inexperienced, theoretically primitive, morally vague, and politically naive, the young intelligentsia was a vital, international source of radical hope. "Let the old men ask sourly, 'Out of Apathy—into what?' Let the old women complain wisely about 'the end of ideology.' We are beginning to move again."[6] Mills foresaw both the emergence and growth of the Movement and its main dilemmas.

By the end of the sixties, the old men's question, which Mills brushed aside, had to be posed once again. For the hopes of a generation of radicals had grown sour; their early social visions had taken on disturbing shapes; and their politics had turned into revolutionary fantasies. Another decade has passed and the Movement's organizations, theories, and ethos seem a memory clouded by the resurgence of a vague conservative mood in American culture and politics. The questions of what went wrong with the Movement and what lasting impact it had on society continue to be debated, and I will address them here.

I

The task of discovering why—and in what senses—the Movement disintegrated is compounded by problems of definition. Just what *was* this elusive Movement, which, by most accounts, began fitfully in the middle fifties with scattered cultural and political protests and ended, say, by 1973, when members of the Symbionese Liberation Army murdered Marcus Foster, the first black superintendent of schools in Oakland, California. No single definition fits the entire Movement. It did not display a consistent set of attitudes toward self, others, society, and the future. Political activists and social dropouts of all sorts identified themselves in varying degrees with the Movement: liberals,

[5]Ibid., pp. 257–258.
[6]Ibid., pp. 259.

Marxists, Maoists, libertarians, populists, anarchists, existential-
ists. The long-term aims of the Movement were diverse, vague,
and frequently incompatible: a reformed, more just democratic
capitalism; democratic socialism; communism; anarchism; and a
spate of semiarticulated, largely anti-ideological visions of self-
fulfillment and community. The scope of dissent, which matched
the ambitious social visions, ranged from a concern with such
particular injustices as racism and poverty to inclusive condem-
nations of Western civilization.

There was no organizational unity and little organizational
continuity to this sprawling Movement. At its peak, the Movement
was far larger than the organizations that attempted to give it full
articulation and political direction. The principal *new* American
organizations—the Student Non-Violent Coordinating Committee
(SNCC) and Students for a Democratic Society (SDS)—were not
large even at the height of their influence.[7] They were in disarray
by 1970. The most common modes of organization were *ad hoc*
committees, which sprang up by the hundreds and often dissolved
as quickly as they appeared. Although coalitions of unstable
groupings were attempted in the middle sixties, none succeeded
for long, as the divided 1967 National Conference for a New Politics revealed. If the political sectors of the Movement were wary
about organization, the more amorphous counterculture resisted
all impulses to organize: indeed, Yippies reveled in parodies of the
idea of organizations, whether of the larger society or of the new
Left. As Paul Krassner put it, "The Crazies have a rule that in order
to become a member one must first destroy his membership card."

The Movement, then, eludes precise definition. But its diver-

---

[7]Estimates of the size of the principal new Left organizations are vague at best.
From the outset, SDS was a decentralized collection of local groups. Since many
people identified themselves with SDS without ever joining, the notion of membership is informal. According to official membership statistics, SDS grew from
250 members in eight chapters in 1960 to between 30,000 and 100,000 members in
three hundred and fifty to four hundred chapters in 1968 through 1969. Kirkpatrick Sale, *SDS* (New York: Random House, 1973), pp. 663–664. SNCC was a
smaller, more tightly structured organization than SDS. It mobilized large numbers of people for voter-registration drives in the South and exerted an influence
on SDS—and the nation—far in excess of its numbers. SNCC grew from an organization with fifteen full-time field workers in 1961 to about two hundred full-time
organizers in 1964. After 1965, members began to drift away, and SNCC went into
permanent decline. Figures on SNCC are from Edward J. Bacciocco, Jr., *The New
Left in America: Reform to Revolution* (Stanford, Calif.: Hoover Institution Press,
1974), pp. 45, 56, 60.

sity testifies to its vitality as a social and a cultural presence in the sixties, as well as to its continuing influence in the seventies. A complete definition would require a complete history. In his massive documentary history *The New Left,* Massimo Teodori underlines the frustration of characterizing this phenomenon by proposing a catchall definition: "the complex of positions, actions and attitudes which have developed over the last ten years [1958 through 1968], including not only political and social aspects, but psychological and cultural ones as well."[8] The Movement, then, was an umbrella covering particular sectors, "which . . . developed around a specific theme or a particular period," for example, the civil-rights movement, the student movement, the new Left, the counterculture, and the antiwar movement.[9] This fluid and various social world was selectively apprehended and is selectively remembered by observers and participants. What is chosen as fundamental determines largely the diagnosis of what went wrong and colors estimates of the lasting impact of radical protest on American politics and culture.

The relationships between the parts of the Movement and the idea of the Movement are, as I have indicated, obscure. Although the organizational entities may be identified with some precision, there is disagreement over which ones ought to be included in the idea of the Movement, and hence disagreement over what this amorphous idea stands for. Kirkpatrick Sale, for example, locates the main energy of the Movement on the left, but he tends to equate the Movement with its expressly political dimensions: "SDS was of course only a part of the larger process of cultural upheaval of the time, but it was the organized expression of that Movement, its intellectual mentor and the source of much of its energy, the largest, best known, and most influential element within it for a decade."[10]

My own inclination is to define the Movement broadly to include aspects of the counterculture as well as the more obviously political sectors. In its broadest thematic terms, the Movement was a multifaceted critical response of elements of a new postwar generation and radicalized or reradicalized elders to emerging shapes and imagined trends: the persistence of social injustice in

[8]Massimo Teodori, ed., *The New Left: A Documentary History* (Indianapolis and New York: The Bobbs-Merrill Company, 1969), p. 4.

[9]Ibid.

[10]Sale, *SDS,* p. 7.

American society; the growth of a relatively affluent consumer culture in America and throughout the West; the quasi-imperialist stances of both superpowers, especially the United States; the rigid, sclerotic, authoritarian "socialisms" of nations in the Soviet sphere; and the deep unrest and revolutionary ferment in the third world.

The Movement responded to these conditions piecemeal and haphazardly. Shaped in part by the pressures of its own ideological and organizational history, the Movement was challenged increasingly by the generally negative and often repressive responses of the larger society: government, the media, and public opinion. It was influenced dramatically by major international events such as the Cuban Revolution, the Cultural Revolution in China, the Paris uprising of May 1968, and, above all, the long war in Vietnam. Under these pressures, the Movement grew rapidly toward an awareness of connections between what Mills termed private troubles and public issues, though it never achieved a common understanding of their intricate interplay. It groped toward the future largely through trial and error, through a commitment to direct action considered variously as an ideal, a means of self-discovery, and a mode of inducing social change.

While bearing in mind its breadth, I will concentrate here mainly on the radical elements—the political and cultural left—because much of the creative energy and most of the destructive energy of the Movement was located in these regions of ideology, sensibility, and activity. The early new Left was largely the creation of college students from relatively affluent, well-educated middle-class families who came of age in the late fifties and early sixties. In the incipient stages of the new Left, many were moved by their sense of a wide disparity between liberal and old Left ideals of social justice and their perception of the realities of American life: racial discrimination in the South and in northern ghettos and the needless persistence of poverty in the midst of affluence.[11] Of equal, and perhaps ultimately greater, importance was a vague but insistent spiritual malaise, a profound anxiety and alienation from the technological, affluent culture young

---

[11] A sensitive discussion of the class origins of early new Left activists may be found in Richard Flacks, "Revolt of the Young Intelligentsia: Revolutionary Class-Consciousness in a Post-Scarcity America," in Roderick Aya and Norman Miller, eds., *The New American Revolution* (New York: The Free Press, 1971), pp. 223–263.

white people were expected to inherit and manage. American society offered occupational success, leisure, and high consumption
to many of its young rebels. Higher education had evolved from a
privilege of elites to a right of masses: in the 1960s enrollments
grew from 3.5 million to nearly 7.5 million. And the new media of
communication proliferated, establishing an exciting and bewildering world of sight and sound. Yet despite this embarrassment of riches—and partly because of it—anxiety, confusion, and
anger haunted many sensitive young people.

A sense of injustice and a sense of meaninglessness were the
two principal sources of dissent that moved young people, black
and white, to radical action throughout the sixties: to nonviolent
protest, reformist political activity, and confrontation politics.
These sources of dissent also disposed people to withdraw, in
varying degrees, from the dominant culture to form urban and
rural communes; to explore the frontiers of consciousness
through rock music and drugs; and eventually to engage in scattered acts of violence. Critiques of society, which sprang from
visceral feelings and encounters with power, centered on the
persistent exploitation of so-called "left-outs"—the poor, blacks,
and such other marginals as dropouts, draft resisters, and even
criminals. Critiques of culture, which also sprang from personal
sources, centered on the persistence and growth of alienation in
its several facets.[12] Throughout the sixties, elements of these two
sorts of critique mixed, merged, and separated in the consciousness of people associated with the Movement. Politics became
cultural; culture and personal life became political. By the late
sixties, "the personal is political" became a popular slogan in
some Movement circles. Early on, many student rebels and disaffected intellectuals applied the elastic category of left-outs re-
flexively, imagining *themselves* as politically powerless and culturally alienated. Jerry Farber's crude essay, "The Student as
Nigger" (1969), whose title tells the story, was admired widely
on campuses. By the end of the sixties, in fact, everyone could
locate himself or herself at the bottom of one social-cultural
heap or another.

[12]On the distinction between *exploitation* and *alienation*, see Peter Clecak, *Radical Paradoxes: Dilemmas of the American Left, 1945–1970* (New York: Harper &
Row, 1973), chapter 2, pp. 15–30. On the distinction between political activism
and cultural alienation, which Kenneth Keniston proposes as two ideal, and
largely opposed, varieties of dissent, see Keniston, *Young Radicals: Notes on Committed Youth* (New York: Harcourt, Brace & World, 1968), pp. 297–325.

The distinctive characteristics of the Movement emerge from a central concern with personal authenticity and the corollary conviction that the structures of social power, the liberal ideological consensus, and the cultural apparatus formed multiple obstacles to self-fulfillment and community. The search for fulfillment stressed varieties of dissent and protest—silent and vocal, public and private, nonviolent and violent, personal and cultural, reformist and revolutionary. Such acts, whether primarily political or cultural in intent or consequence, were regarded widely as means of creating authentic selves and liberated zones where such selves could mingle: social spaces, media spaces, and imaginative spaces.

The main goal was to become free from the obstacles to self-fulfillment through various combinations of personal and public action aimed at changing the offending structures, traditions, and customs and to set the self apart from what could not be changed immediately. People associated with the Movement wished to expand the frontiers of liberty—for example, by working for civil rights (their own and others') or by attacking culturally introjected values allegedly responsible for feelings of guilt, anxiety, and inauthenticity. They wished to reduce or eliminate all manifestations of inequality—economic, political, intellectual, emotional, personal, even perceptual—so as to transcend the impulse to compete that divides individuals from communion and stratifies society. And they wished to achieve fraternity, a community of unalienated individuals "doing their own thing."

The impulses toward personal liberation and community through protest against the larger society and culture ran through the Movement, from its beginnings to the nightmarish ending staged by the most "radical" minorities (with the generous assistance of the Nixon administration). These personal impulses are evident in the pained cries of such Beat writers as Allen Ginsberg and Jack Kerouac; in the struggles for freedom of blacks in the middle fifties; in the student movements in the early sixties; in the antipoverty community-action programs; in the antiwar movement and the resistance; in the black-power movement; in the emergence of Hispanic, Asian American, and Native American civil-rights movements in the middle and late sixties; in the rhetoric of third-world liberation fronts; in the inchoate counterculture; and in the appearance of women's liberation, gay liberation, and Gray Panther groups toward the end of the sixties.

Despite their genuine differences, which critics and participants have stressed, perhaps too energetically, these foci of dissent and protest all considered personal fulfillment and authenticity within the context of community to be the underlying issue. As one Free Speech Movement slogan put it: "The issue is not the issue." Much of this activity, as critics within and outside the Movement have shown, was inauthentic and destructive: cheap posturing; selfish manipulation of others; delusion; self-indulgent, unearned anguish; and simpleminded rhetoric. But there also were authentic expressions of utopian sentiment, action taken against real pain, telling critiques of the American consensus, and moments of genuine heroism. In retrospect, the Movement exhibits a more intricate balance of salutary and destructive characteristics than its contemporary critics and supporters allowed.

II

What went wrong in the sixties? How did significant elements of the Movement acquire the characteristics of marginal revolutionary sects in less than a decade? Why did nonviolence give way to nihilistic violence, hope to frustration and despair, anti-ideology to rigid ideology, and reformist politics to revolutionary antipolitics? Why did the most visible political and cultural thrusts of the Movement seemingly lose their vitality and virtually disappear by 1973? Christopher Lasch anticipated part of the answer in his analysis of the new Left, published in 1969: "Both the strengths and weaknesses of the New Left derive from the fact that it is largely a student movement based on 'alienation.' From the beginning, the New Left defined political issues as personal issues. How does one achieve personal integrity—'authenticity'—in a mechanized, bureaucratized, dehumanized society?" Lasch suggests that because the new Left acted "out of an ideal of personal heroism rather than from an analysis of the sources of tension in American society and the possibilities for change," it "vacillates between existential despair and absurdly inflated estimates of its own potential."[13]

[13]Christopher Lasch, *The Agony of the American Left* (New York: Alfred A. Knopf, 1969), pp. 180, 182. The passages on the *Port Huron Statement* and the Weathermen are adapted from Clecak, *Radical Paradoxes*, pp. 232–258.

The literature on the Movement is large, and I shall not attempt even a summary here. A recent interpretive study worth looking at is Nigel Young, *An Infantile Disorder? The Crisis and Decline of the New Left* (London and Henley: Routledge & Kegan Paul, 1977).

Lasch's general estimate makes some sense. The new Left *was* essentially a student movement based on the experience of alienation and a quest for personal authenticity. It therefore was subject to unavoidable structural faults that weakened its political potential: high rates of turnover, youth, and isolation from other age and class constituencies. But Lasch underestimates the political intentions and savvy of the founders of SDS and their sensitivity to exploitation and social injustice in American society. More crucially, he overestimates the potential political efficacy of radical social theory by implying that a more sophisticated analysis of the sources of tension and possibilities for change could have enabled more effective short-term results, including the beginnings of a mass socialist movement in America. The energy of the Movement in the early years did not depend upon theoretical clarity or historical insight, but upon an almost studied confusion of theoretical antinomies, an emotional fusion of short-term reformist political aims and communitarian visions. Theoretical clarity of the sort recommended by Marxists was precisely what the Movement had to avoid, and many participants sensed this.

The Movement exhibits a four-part, overlapping cycle. First, as long as the logics of communitarian vision and political reform remained in rough equilibrium, the Movement created new energy, providing a succession of jolts to the political system whose effects persisted through the late seventies. The vision of liberated selves in a loose community of equals moved people to imagine cultural forms and political strategies that appeared unfeasible to others, even to those who shared their basic hopes and values. This culture vision, which was *experienced* momentarily within foci of the Movement, especially the civil-rights movement of the early sixties, also gave participants the will to act politically in the larger society.

But there was no way to sustain the equilibrium of communitarian vision and reformist politics. Sooner or later the pressure of social forces and the disposition of a minority of radicals to push communitarian perspectives to their extremes had to discredit a politics of reform. Simultaneously, visions of community—detached from political contexts—took on stark, frequently perverted, antipolitical forms. In this second phase, beginning in the middle sixties, the "Beloved Community" that early SNCC—and SDS—members envisioned turned into a series of parodies: ingrown countercultural communes, solipsistic reveries of symbolic communities, and apocalyptic intimations of bloody collectivities (the "Beloved Community" imagined in revolutionary metaphors of socioeconomic power).

Third, when the polarization of political reform and communitarian vision occurs in a stable, affluent, modern social order, the far left, revolutionary side of the momentarily fruitful tension quickly collapses as a visible public form, the victim of its own excesses, negative public opinion, and state repression. Early in this disintegrative phase, however, fundamental assumptions concerning personality, culture, and politics were questioned most radically (if not always thoughtfully). And defeated radical ideas were resurrected and circulated widely. All of the ideas, values, strategies, and tactics that the Movement's various political and cultural elements employed had ample historical precedents.[14] In this last spasm of energy, the Movement administered a jolt to the cultural order whose effects persisted through the seventies. The cultural fallout of this final explosion of Movement energy persists, as fragmented ideas undergo dilution and diffusion, creating the potential for long-term shifts in cultural perception that ultimately may affect the political process. In the short run, however, polarization of reformist and communitarian impulses fatally sapped the energy for dramatic, sustained political change, though not before substantial changes had been registered. And the *idea* of the Movement, which always was mystical, dimmed, depending as it did on a fusion of incompatible impulses.

Finally, other forces of opposition and repression in American culture were aroused, further slowing the rate and altering the direction of subsequent "progress" as measured from radical and left liberal vantage points.

The major early public documents of SDS, the *Port Huron Statement* (1962) and *America and the New Era* (1963), illustrate the first phase of this cycle. Both displayed an informed sense of radical political options and a growing awareness of structural connections among various foci of power. The *Port Huron Statement* reveals the incipient tension between radical, communitarian sentiments and the reformist conceptualization of American political possibilities. Young activists experienced American life through a dialectic of alienation and community. At the same

---

[14]For twentieth-century analogues of the Movement, see Henry F. May, *The End of American Innocence: A Study of the First Years of Our Own Time, 1912–1917* (New York: Oxford University Press, 1959).

time, many of them wished to act democratically for reformist ends, using a politics of pressure within and against the Democratic party.

Although largely repudiated by later leaders of SDS factions, the *Port Huron Statement* is in many respects a remarkable record of the dominant moods of an articulate minority of the young in the early sixties. Fresh perceptions of American dilemmas—perceptions unmediated by a deeply informed sense of the past—shaped the mood of urgency among the young radicals at Port Huron. "Our work," they declared, "is guided by the sense that we may be the last generation in the experiment with living."[15] Still, they believed that most of their fellow citizens had learned not to care about the drift toward apocalypse. To reestablish radical vision after its virtual disappearance in the 1950s, activists formulated an optimistic though tentative statement of their values. They asserted that "man is infinitely precious and possessed of unfulfilled capacities for reason, freedom, and love." But in America the myth of unlimited consumption had diminished everyone—the affluent who had too much, the poor who had too little, and those in between whose expectations outran their rewards. The expression of the dormant capacities of Americans required a new social setting, "a democracy of individual participation, governed by two central aims: that the individual share in those social decisions determining the quality and direction of his life; that society be organized to encourage independence in men and provide the media for their common participation."

After portraying the defensive ennui and the flight into private life by the vast student majority, the *Port Huron Statement* provisionally traced individual frustrations to structural causes, noting that "apathy is not simply an attitude" but rather "a product of social institutions and of the structure and organization of higher education itself." Though sketchy, the radicals' analysis of the larger political scene identified the primary problems that would haunt the nation throughout the sixties and seventies and outlined the intricate social, psychological, and political dimensions of a fresh departure from the pace and direction of American life. Drawing heavily on the work of Mills and their own civil-rights and campus experiences, they identified the dominant trend toward increasing private power under a public facade of democracy.

[15]References to the *Port Huron Statement* are from Paul Jacobs and Saul Landau, eds., *The New Radicals* (New York: Vintage Books, 1966), pp. 150–162.

To rescue the essential values of American liberalism from the complacency of intellectuals and the deformations of philistines, the founders charted a vague politics of radical reform that included protest and confrontation as well as electoral activity. In general, the early SDS advocated a left-liberal coalition of students, civil-rights and peace groups, labor, the poor, and the conscience constituency of affluent professionals. Since the wide range of available tactics was supposed to serve the larger ends of their vision, they ruled out violence, which "requires generally the transformation of the target, be it a human being or a community of people, into a depersonalized object of hate." Insofar as possible, the community of authentic, liberated selves was to be foreshadowed in the loose, participatory, virtually leaderless "organizations" of SDS, SNCC, and a host of *ad hoc* groups. And the community was to be extended to the wider society initially through a radical politics of reform. Such a utopian project obviously required an experimental attitude since it appeared impossible when articulated in received political and cultural categories.

It soon became evident that the bold project of the new radicals would fall short of its aims. In *Rebellion and Repression* (1969), Tom Hayden, a principal author of the *Port Huron Statement*, cast the brief history of the Movement in the context of what had become its most representative new Left theme: frustration, anger, and a loss of innocence. At the outset of the decade, he recalls, the hopes of the young were raised by the election of John Kennedy and the establishment of the Peace Corps, which "represented an alternative symbolically, a way out of the Cold War; and at the same time, an alternative to the ratrace careers that most young people faced unhappily." But the Peace Corps turned out to be little more than a facade that concealed the "more brutal and exploitative patterns of American foreign policy."[16]

The principal encounters that initially turned the new Left away from postwar liberal politics and ideology were domestic— the civil-rights and black-power movements. Much of the history of the young radicals must be understood as a series of reactions to shifting currents in the black movement. As Carl Oglesby put it, somewhat hyperbolically, in 1965: "I see SNCC as the Nile Valley of the New Left and I honor SDS to call it part of the delta

[16]Tom Hayden, *Rebellion and Repression* (New York and Cleveland: World Publishing Company, 1969), p. 23.

that SNCC created."[17] Students went South "with a confidence that the conscience of the United States" was on their side, only to discover that racism permeated the institutional structures and consciousness of the entire nation. The South, they learned at first hand, was organically connected to the rest of the country by tissues of economic, social, and political power. Disappointing early efforts at community organizing and a series of black rebellions in northern cities after 1964 dramatized and extended the lessons of the South. Local structures of power everywhere seemed resistant to change. The poor—black and white—were locked into ghettos, oppressed by city governments, and for the most part unrepresented.

Beginning in 1965, the same rhythm of defeated expectations unfolded on a global scale as the war in Vietnam echoed the "violence and racism . . . we were already seeing at home."[18] Many young leftists and millions of others felt betrayed as the war dragged on. Moreover, the variety of protest tactics—marches, sit-ins, teach-ins, acts of personal resistance to the draft—had little immediate impact on the direction of American foreign policy. Throughout the decade, then, the experiences of activists seemed to fit the same basic pattern of disillusionment: despite relatively rapid growth of the Movement, especially after the escalation of the war in 1965 and the subsequent extension of the draft to include college students, the experience of failure and impotence quickly destroyed the fragile balance of communitarian vision, theory, and reformist politics that the founders of SDS had intended to maintain.

The hypothesis I have been pushing toward is this: the increasingly radical sensibilities of young activists, which constituted the driving force of the early Movement, also figured prominently in its undoing. Although the Movement emerged in an ideological wedge between old Left revolutionary perspectives and the left side of the American consensus, it did not have primarily ideological or theoretical origins. Rather, it took root primarily at the level of sensibility in a largely personal revolt against postwar American society and culture. Activists confronted the American performance with American values of per-

[17]Carl Oglesby, "Democracy Is Nothing If It Is Not Dangerous," in *Peacemaker* (SDS reprint, 1965–1966). Quoted from Bacciocco, *The New Left in America*, p. 228.

[18]Hayden, *Rebellion and Repression*, p. 25.

sonal fulfillment, democracy, community, equality, and social justice. The momentary break in the spell of ideology, as I have suggested, enabled the Movement to launch itself, to act its way into existence on the basis of moral idealism, native pragmatism, and a studied innocence of past and present limits of power. Through encounters with larger social forces that produced both limited successes and large defeats, activists experienced a radicalization of their earlier sentiments.

This radicalization of sentiment and the pragmatic imperatives of organization and public action prompted a hasty and reluctant search for theory and ideology in the middle sixties. Most people in the Movement were uninterested in theory and had little time for theorizing in the rush of antiwar activity beginning in 1965. Nevertheless, leaders and intellectual members did seek analytic equivalents of their feelings of growing opposition of American society and culture and their total commitment to a half-articulated vision of a community beyond alienation. Liberal and conservative perspectives proved incapable of matching the feelings of the most vocal and newsworthy members of the Movement. These perspectives failed to provide satisfactory explanations of persistent domestic injustices—especially of poverty and racism—or apparent imperialism and racism in American policies toward the third world. Many found Leninist theories of imperialism plausible once again.

These considerations prompted a recovery, more or less by default, of several varieties of Marxism: old Left variants; the works of Antonio Gramsci, and of Herbert Marcuse and other representatives of the Frankfurt school; the more orthodox analyses of Leo Huberman and Paul Sweezy, editors of *Monthly Review;* and the activities of revolutionaries from the third world (Fidel Castro, Che Guevara, Mao Zedong). Marxism was the only surviving grand theory that fused faith and science, personal troubles and public issues, communitarian vision and political activity. It supplied ideological and, in many instances, romantic personal models for the most extreme expressions of personal disaffection and political radicalism.[19]

---

[19]The subject of the reading habits of the Movement is a touchy—and hopelessly difficult—one. It is probably safe, though not very illuminating, to say that tastes in reading varied widely and further that certain writers—like Marcuse—attained a measure of celebrity in spite of their inaccessible texts. Largely unread, I suspect, they nevertheless became mythic figures, quotable in fragments and hyped by the media. Non-Marxists such as Camus and Gandhi probably were even more important as inspiring figures in the Movement, especially during its early phases.

The recovery of Marxism clarified and reinforced the main radical drift of Movement sensibility, further polarizing growing tensions between communitarian vision and reformist, coalition politics. It also rationalized a growing fragmentation of groups within the Movement by stressing a politically irrelevant though intellectually powerful class analysis of the American social order.

Through the categories of Marxism, theorists of the Movement confronted, but could not solve, the perennial and central problem of the American Left, which Mills and others anticipated. Despite the emergence of many foci of protest in the sixties, there was no historical agency of dramatic change that the Movement could mobilize. The student movement was self-consciously isolated from the start, confined mainly to campuses. Attempts to transcend the campus constituency were largely abortive. The traditional working class of Marxian theory had refused its appointed revolutionary mission. And the reformist coalition of labor, students, and left-outs was fragile, tentative, and, from the point of view of many activists, sluggish and nearsighted.

The initial strategy of direct action, which was based on a politics of reform energized by communitarian vision, produced both success and failure and set the direction for subsequent theoretical debate within Movement circles. As the Movement grew rapidly in the middle sixties, the composition of these circles changed. To the original core of activists, drawn mainly from professional families, were added representatives of other social and ethnic groups. This enlarged base contributed to the growing militancy and inflated radical rhetoric of the most publicized elements of the Movement after 1965. The third-world connection was forged in these years, as militant minority groups identified with their counterparts in Asia, Africa, and Latin America. In the early phases, however, reformist strategies of coalition within the Movement and beyond competed with strategies of building autonomous bases of power: community control, parallel instiutions, and liberated zones. But by 1965, after Berkeley, the election of Lyndon Johnson, and the expansion of the war, those within SDS and SNCC who favored coalition and nonviolence lost ground.[20]

[20]By 1966, with the election of Stokely Carmichael as president, SNCC dropped its commitment to nonviolence. See "The Basis of Black Power," the position paper prepared by SNCC in spring 1966 and published in the *New York Times*, August 5, 1966. Reprinted in Teodori, *The New Left*, pp. 271–275.

The principle of autonomous growth of the various foci of dissent gained ascendancy. After the Mississippi summer of 1964, militant blacks told whites to work among their own people. One segment of SDS, headed by Carl Davidson and Greg Calvert, expressed the growing mood of separatism, arguing that "no individual, no group, no class is genuinely engaged in a revolutionary movement unless their struggle is a struggle for their own liberation."[21] And by 1967, following the divisive National Conference for a New Politics, a group of women disillusioned with the attitudes of male radicals launched what was to become an influential current in the women's movement. In their paper addressed "To the Women of the Left," this group declared that "women must not make the same mistakes the blacks did at first of allowing others (whites in their case, men in ours) to define our issues, methods and goals. Only we can and must define the terms of our struggle."[22]

Radicalized by the anarchist-communitarian dynamic of their own sensibilities, overwhelmed by the rapid growth of sympathizers after 1965, pushed into autonomous strategies of resistance by the perceived failures of coalition, elements of the Movement began to make a theoretical point of their separation before they had come together. As separation along the lines of class, occupation, race, age, status, sex, and ethnicity grew, theoretically inclined activists sought old and new theories, visions, and agencies of change, some involving armed struggle, that ultimately would unite disparate groups in a revolutionary movement. These strategies buttressed vain hopes for an even larger victory over majority social forces in the long run.

Such theorizing also provided a specious rhetorical cover for the new burst of political and cultural energy released in the course of autonomous struggle. While justifying neglect of left-liberal coalition politics in theory, the *ex post facto* notion of autonomous struggle implicitly confirmed the *categories* on which coalitions in America are formed. Under the principle of autonomous activity, radicals opposed to coalition found themselves working increasingly among their own kind: students, women,

[21]Gregory Calvert, "In White America: Radical Consciousness and Social Change," *The National Guardian*, March 25, 1967. Reprinted in Teodori, *The New Left*, p. 414.

[22]Sara Evans, *Personal Politics: The Roots of Women's Liberation in the Civil Rights Movement and the New Left* (New York: Knopf, 1979), p. 200.

blacks, and gays. Thus the larger society's categorization of disadvantaged people by age, race, gender, and economic status was tacitly endorsed. Single-issue and single-group politics flourished, and the Marxian notion of class struggle was undercut.

At the same time, however, the idea of autonomous struggle facilitated growth of cultural radicalism and intensified the search for personal authenticity and fulfillment. Within each fragmented nodule of dissent, individuals could seek a community of equals among their own kind. The strategy of autonomous struggle supposedly ruled out arrangements that brought diverse people into systematically unequal and "inauthentic" relationships. Of course, tensions among social unequals marked all phases of the Movement. Even in the early phases, when communities within the Movement were small and relatively homogeneous, fragments of the social gospel persisted as privileged people set out to help their less fortunate brethren. The idea of autonomous struggle fit the later, enlarged, more diverse, and more radical phase of the Movement. Acknowledging new realities, this notion sanctioned the issue beneath the issues—namely, the quest for personal fulfillment within a more narrowly defined community of equals. As Cathy Cade described her joining the new women's liberation movement: "In the black movement I had been fighting . . . someone else's oppression and now there was a way that I could fight for my own freedom and I was going to be much stronger than I ever was."[23]

Meanwhile, radical theorists tried to apprehend the new, scattered energies unleashed by autonomous struggle within class analyses of American society. They submitted several nominees for the role of agency of revolutionary change: the new working class (of students and members of the helping professions), blacks, women, the poor, the lumpenproletariat, the cultural rebels, and the traditional working class of Marxian theory. Not one was interested in pursuing, or able to pursue, the task. Hence by the end of the sixties, the frustrations of action and the confusions of theory were reflected in the bizarre pronouncements of splintered factions of SDS and the Black Panthers.

Accepting the dilemma of powerlessness and obliterating the moral ambiguities of radical activity, the Weathermen, an SDS splinter, concluded that white revolutionaries in America could act only as a support group to the blacks (the chief internal col-

[23]*Ibid.*, p. 205.

ony) and to revolutionaries in underdeveloped parts of the world. To define socialism in "national terms within so extreme and historical an oppressor nation" was, according to the Weathermen, an instance of "imperialist national chauvinism." The implications drawn from this analysis were frightening to most Americans and to a majority of Movement sympathizers. The Weathermen dissolved economic, political, social, moral, and cultural ties with nearly everyone in America. All groups except the lumpenproletariat and the "colonized" blacks whom they supported from a distance were guilty of national chauvinism, imperialism, and "white skin privilege."[24] They were so guilty, in fact, that the overwhelming majority could not participate in their own salvation. White America, the Weathermen concluded, must resign itself to being ruled by a collection of blacks and third-world revolutionaries. Solving the perplexing question of the revolutionary agency of change by denying the existence of one in the United States, the Weathermen renounced all serious political pretensions. Freed from social, political, and moral obligations, they could operate freely and irresponsibly at the edges of American society, acting out personal fantasies of guilt and rage against an undifferentiated and dehumanized enemy.

The path toward disillusionment and disintegration was carved, then, in large part by the emotional dynamic of the far-Left sectors of the Movement: the rapid ascendance of anarchistic and communitarian sentiments made a politics of coalition and reform seem both impossible and pointless. A growing commitment to myths of community and revolution in the late sixties led activists to emphasize the values of an extreme egalitarianism, personal liberty, and community (dealienation) without sufficient regard for the tensions and trade-offs among them that must characterize any civilized modern social order. This emotional dynamic made varieties of utopian Marxism and communitarian visions ever more attractive to influential opinion leaders in the Movement. It lent theoretical coherence to the anarchistic and communitarian sentiments of the burgeoning counterculture. And it enabled young people to make sudden and total personal commitments to the most extreme visions of personal and social change—commitments that, as the seventies revealed, turned out also to be rooted in mercurial sentiments.

[24]Quoted in Jack Weinberg and Jack Gerson, "The Split in SDS" (New York: International Socialist Pamphlet, 1969), p. 5.

This emotional dynamic, which celebrated subjectivity and will, also made attractive a variety of intellectual and organizational superstructures. Although most people sympathetic to some facet of the Movement remained unorganized and largely unorganizable, rigid, talmudic Marxist sects such as the Maoist Progressive Labor Party (PLP) flourished briefly in the late sixties, along with terrorist cells and rural communes composed of cultural dropouts.

The common intellectual thread running through these various positions and organizations was a growing disaffection with democratic politics and the liberal values of tolerance, pluralism, moderation, cultural excellence, and gradual social and cultural change.[25] These values were psychologically constricting, for they aimed for a more just society rather than a community of fully and freely participating equals. At most, they promised a reordering of roles rather than an annihilation of them in favor of "authentic" selves. The radical elements of the Movement exchanged the broken promises of democratic capitalism and socialism for the false promises of anarchism and communism, a mythical community where people are free, equal, and fraternal, able to act out their own desires within the fluid context of a benevolent general will. In the process, these ultraradical elements blurred their vision of the present and the future. They lost touch with political realities and possibilities and the utopian character of communitarian ends.

The freewheeling radical individualism adopted in hopes of achieving a voluntary communist community of abundance through political action brought multiple political disasters. It yielded impotence in relation to the larger society, accompanied by the withdrawal of disaffected minorities into small, antidemocratic sects ruled by charisma and the authority of sacred texts, such as the PLP. It also hastened dissolution of temporary charismatic communities into anarchy, as seen with the Yippies. Because a voluntary community of fully realized equals is politically impossible to bring off on a national, not to mention a global, scale, it turns out to be a cruel illusion. Yet without this social matrix of community, the ambitious personal dimensions of communitarian vision turn sour.

[25]See Carl Oglesby's address at the November 1965 antiwar March on Washington, "Liberalism and the Corporate State," reprinted in *Monthly Review*, 17 (January 1966), 21–30.

Insofar as it ignores the importance of *some* calculus of moral costs, the idea of romantic communism produces personality disorientation, loneliness, and spiritual hunger rather than full disclosure, or satisfaction, of individual desires. It leads individuals to overstress submissive, remissive, authoritarian, and narcissistic dimensions of personality. As a perspective on culture, romantic vision may inspire an occasional brilliant text, but to the extent that it infects audiences it yields less sanguine results. The audience upon which a rich culture depends loses its bearings as standards of excellence sag, disciplined learning falls into disfavor, and the delicate webs of meaning, spun out of reason, history, and tradition, unravel. Genuine experiment degenerates into mere novelty, and cultural life turns into spectacle. Such an attempt to escape the competitive, status-conscious, and anxious character of bourgeois individualism ends in a radical individualism without community or a moral center.

Here is the central irony of the Movement. The initial deemphasis of history and theory enabled action, which in turn nurtured an extremist dynamic of radical sensibility. Emotional radicalism prompted a receptivity in some activists to sustained exercises in theory. In order to articulate strong feelings of opposition and utopian hopes for community, those activists who paid attention to theory sought out the most radical perspectives. Sympathetic critics like Christopher Lasch, James Weinstein, and Eugene Genovese pressed for cultivation of an undogmatic Marxism and a socialist organization to give coherence and direction to the Movement's growing strength in the middle sixties. Weinstein declares,

> The first step is for new leftists to examine the content of their radicalism and determine if they are committed to a transformation of American capitalism into that higher form of society envisaged by Marx. If they are, then all of their activities should be consciously determined by an intention to build a revolutionary movement and then a party that has the perspective of gaining power in the United States.[26]

Others, such as Howard Zinn, celebrated the freewheeling, existential ethos of the Movement and advocated only tentative ap-

---

[26]See Martin J. Sklar and James Weinstein, "Socialism and the New Left," *Studies on the Left*, 6 (March-April 1966), 70.

proaches to theory.[27] By the late sixties, however, militant elements of the Movement had succumbed to the worst possibilities of both: flirtation with the thoughtless, sclerotic Marxism of the sects and romantic self-indulgence that ended in personal withdrawal into cultural radicalism or deliquescence into terror (for example, the "days of rage" conducted by the Weathermen in 1969).

The recurrent faith of intellectuals in radical theorizing as a crucial step in the formation of a mass American socialist movement, then, is illusory, a projection of their own desires and disappointments. I suspect that there never is sufficient social space and time for communist and anarchist visions to unfold. In any case, it seems safe to say that the idea of a mass American socialist movement turned out to be an idle hope harbored by certain Left social critics and activists during the sixties and seventies. It was an illusion based on an amalgam of hubristic ideological desires of Marxist intellectuals and faulty rationalistic speculations concerning structural trends and possibilities in America. This amalgam created false hopes because it failed to take full account of the main trajectory of the sensibilities of the people who energized the Movement and, in the end, contributed significantly to its destruction.

Thus, between 1965 and 1970, when Left dissent and protest peaked, the Movement drifted into the old options that its founders and its sympathetic critic-participants had intended to avoid.

First, as I have indicated, those who pushed (or followed) their radical sentiments toward revolutionary ideological and political articulations ended up in possession of the principal organizations of the new Left, SDS and SNCC. Rigid ideologues—"new fogies," according to one critic—gravitated toward the PLP, which remained old Left in spirit.[28] Others, driven by total radicalization of feeling, drifted into underground terrorist cells. In the course of achieving control of the new Left

[27]Howard Zinn, "Marxism and the New Left," in Priscilla Long, ed., *The New Left* (Boston: Porter Sargent Publisher, 1969), p. 58, states, "I am not arguing here against theoretical discussion, or against long-range principles, or the analysis of sub-surface realities, but I am asserting that theory must be informed by observation and expressed in action."

[28]See Kirkpatrick Sale's account of the PLP "takeover" of SDS in 1969 in *SDS*, pp. 453–657. For a tour of the far left in the seventies, see Jim O'Brien, *American Leninism in the 1970's, Radical America* (Nov. 1977–Feb. 1978), 1–36.

organizations, however, "revolutionaries" soon destroyed them, driving the majority away and leaving hollow, short-lived organizational shells.

Second, those who followed their radical sentiments away from political metaphors and action into personal and cultural domains participated to some degree in the counterculture. So did a far larger number of people who short-circuited this process of choice by never acquiring a taste for political liberalism or radicalism. Here, unmediated by the discipline of politics, the expressive potentialities of the Movement displayed themselves most fully. The theatrical and therapeutic dimensions of politics, which infected "political" sectors of the Movement, completely overwhelmed the counterculture, most of whose various constituencies never seriously concerned themselves with mundane questions of raw power or the changing shapes and possibilities of the welfare state.

Third, as the extremist dynamic of the Movement made its way toward the dead ends of political revolution and personal-cultural solipsism (Weatherman bombers and Timothy Leary at the end of his mantra), a significant minority of individuals affected by the Movement continued in politics. They sought conventional—and new—single-issue causes, worked in and around the Democratic party, and organized in local communities. Their activity helped to change the Democratic party in the early seventies, pushing its left-liberal constituencies several degrees to the left. But in the middle and late seventies much of the energy supplied by communitarian vision was lost. As the visible energy of the Movement dwindled, most people ceased active participation in radical politics, in left-liberal politics, and in the counterculture, though they have carried some of their acquired values, beliefs, and styles of behavior into the seventies.

Of course, the main options were not mutually exclusive. The increasingly syncretic culture produced revolutionary counterculture types, pot-smoking members of SDS, culturally straight Maoists, lesbian Marxist feminists, and politically schizophrenic activists who alternated between local radical activity and some semblance of coalition politics within the Democratic party. Nevertheless, the three main options of postwar American radicalism reasserted themselves in new forms during the sixties and early seventies.

By the end of the sixties, all three options had run into difficulties. Revolution seemed impossible and reform undesirable.[29] Insofar as the Movement had cast itself in terms of the dilemmas of American radicalism, it was all but dead. The organizational centers were virtually destroyed by 1969, though opposition on campuses survived, making one last surge after the invasion of Cambodia in 1970. The increasingly militant Movement of the sixties had aroused the opposition of large sectors of the working and middle classes and had triggered the paranoia of the Nixon administration, whose operatives often failed to distinguish guerrilla theater from guerrilla warfare. Of course, the Nixon administration did not pioneer government harassment of the Movement: it began in the early sixties and occurred at every level, from federal to local. But state repression became increasingly violent by the late sixties. In the wake of antiwar protests, for example, four Kent State University students were killed and nine were wounded by National Guardsmen on May 4, 1970. On May 14, police and state patrolmen killed two students from Jackson State College and wounded twelve.[30]

By the early seventies, conditions that facilitated growth of the student sectors of the Movement had changed. The wave of postwar youth crested as the large generation born in the early fifties passed beyond college. The war in Vietnam was winding down; the pressures of the draft were easing; and opposition to the war had become respectable. The novelty of the Movement began to wear thin after 1968, and media coverage of protest, so brilliantly used by radicals, worked to their disadvantage during the ultraradical phase. After 1970, national media coverage waned. Some of the political gains—in civil and voting rights, relaxed campus rules, and enlarged services of the welfare state— had reduced the commitment of Movement constituencies to pursue increasingly radical action. Much of the counterculture also had been assimilated in diluted forms by the larger culture. Failure, opposition, repression, assimilation, boredom, and exhaustion all took their toll. The cycle of dramatic radical activity was coming to an end.

[29]In the late sixties, as revolutionary rhetoric intensified, there appeared a number of serious essays arguing against the possibility of such fantasies. See, for example, Barrington Moore, Jr., "Revolution in America?" *The New York Review of Books*, 12 (January 30, 1969), 6–12. See also the essays in Aya and Miller, *The New American Revolution*.

[30]For a statistical overview of Movement and state violence in the bloody month of May 1970, see Sale, *SDS*, pp. 635ff.

III

It is tempting to dwell on the failures of the Movement, to compare the grandiose pronouncements of its leading voices and apologists with its brief historical cycle, which ended in the early seventies. The Movement did register massive failures, although they should not be allowed to obscure the Movement's lasting impact on American life. No major focus of Left dissent and protest in the sixties—the black movement, the student movement, the new Left, the women's movement, the counterculture—fulfilled the impossible intentions of its most radical voices. None managed to trigger a full-scale redistribution of opportunity and reward in the political economy or to direct the values of most Americans away from possessive individualism toward a radical communitarianism. But then no relatively small social movement composed of fragments of minorities could have been expected to carry out such far-reaching alterations in people and institutions over a mere decade.

Assessed against these large ambitions and large failures, even the immediate political successes of the Movement may appear unduly modest, problematic, and fragile. Sympathetic observers of the Movement recall a string of political and cultural triumphs in the sixties: the antiwar protest, the unseating of Lyndon Johnson, a relaxation of rules (and, alas, of standards) in higher education, a revolt against racism and sexism, and a loosening of cultural conventions. Eighteen-year-olds were enfranchised in 1972. But particular issues, even large ones, are cloudy after such a brief interval. In every area touched by the Movement—poverty, civil rights, civil liberties, education, foreign policy—the same difficulties of assessing its immediate impact arise: the nature of registered changes and their value and durability are in dispute.

Although they claim much of the attention of critics and veterans of the sixties, major short-term failures and less dramatic medium-range successes easily can obscure the large and long-term impact of the Movement on American politics and culture. Failures appear most thorough when contrasted either with conservative norms of authority, order, and hierarchy or with the most grandiose radical intentions of certain sectors of the Movement. Radicals who grow skeptical about their long-range hopes for community often retain their stern criteria of criticism: in retrospect, then, *their* historical moment (or some past moment) seems brighter than it was, and subsequent moments seem bleaker than they are. Hence in the aftermath of the Movement, radical nostalgia, pessimism, and cynicism filled the cultural air in the seventies, which was characterized variously as a decade of selfishness, narcissism, survival, conservative reaction, or inaction by such critics as Tom Wolfe, Jim Hougan, and Christopher Lasch.[31] This range of vision is not confined to radicals (and conservatives), however, for the Movement also disappointed left-liberals like Arthur Schlesinger, Jr., and democratic socialists like Michael Harrington who hoped its energies could be harnessed to their separate visions of a decent America.[32] Although many exactivists have pursued careers in public life during the seventies, penetrating lower regions of established power and returning to the reformist political vision of the early SDS, only a portion of the continuing impact of the Movement can be discerned in the fallout of chastened radical attitudes along the more moderate left-liberal band of the American ideological spectrum. For during the seventies American opinion shifted toward a vague neoconservatism stressing the need for limits on governmental attempts to redistribute wealth and power.[33]

An estimate of the enduring contribution of the Movement should be sought primarily in the regions of personality and culture rather than in Left or left-liberal ideology and politics, in civil society rather than in the state. It should be sought in beginnings (or in historical revivals and continuations) rather than in endings; in diffuse cultural influences rather than in direct lineages; in unintended and ambiguous consequences rather than in predicted or anticipated effects. Considered in these ways, the impact of the Movement of the sixties on American life appears

[31]See Tom Wolfe, "The Me Decade and the Third Great Awakening," *New West* (August 30, 1976), 27–48; Jim Hougan, *Decadence: Radical Nostalgia, Narcissism, and Decline in the Seventies* (New York: William Morrow, 1975); Christopher Lasch, *The Culture of Narcissism: American Life in an Age of Diminishing Expectations* (New York: W. W. Norton, 1978). See also Howard Junker, "Who Erased the Seventies?" *Esquire*, 88 (December 1977), 152–155ff.

[32]A good example of left-liberal nostalgia may be found in Arthur M. Schlesinger, Jr., *Robert Kennedy and His Times* (Boston: Houghton Mifflin, 1978). Examples of democratic-socialist disappointment may be found in issues of *Dissent* in the middle and late seventies; for example, Michael Harrington, "A Collective Sadness," *Dissent*, 21 (Fall 1974), 486–491.

[33]In a 1979 *Los Angeles Times* poll, about 67 percent of American voters said they favored cuts in services if these were translated into a tax cut. Nearly two-thirds said they favored a Constitutional amendment to limit government spending. See the *Los Angeles Times*, January 15, 1979, p. 1, but see note 44.

significant, ubiquitous, and likely to extend at least through the eighties.

The Movement brought certain buried sequences of ideas, attitudes, sentiments, and strategies of behavior into public focus once again, popularized them, and made them immediately available parts of the American cultural repertoire. The main lines of influence included characteristic attitudes toward the self, toward dissent, and toward action that have survived the sixties. These are the central components of a bare logic of essential concerns running in various patterns through the diverse political and cultural strands of the Movement. The Movement, I have argued, was fundamentally a multifaceted, expressive quest for an authentic, esteemable self and an experience of community. Although.it was animated largely by a desire to relieve the symptoms of alienation, this quest had important political dimensions and consequences as well. In the process of seeking self-fulfillment, elements of the Movement encountered the obstacles of stubborn cultural values and entrenched structures of power. The quest, then, entailed dissent—an interrogation and rejection of much of the prevailing American society and culture and a pursuit of alternatives. The quest came to include direct action—expressive behavior as a means of securing the space (liberty) for fulfillment and expressive behavior as a constituent of fulfillment.

Emphasis on self-fulfillment, dissent, and direct action were by no means novel in the American experience.[34] But this essential logic of concerns was explored most powerfully by the Movement in the sixties. These three dispositions comprised the driving energy that helped the Movement achieve its articulated shapes, to self-destruct, and to exert its less obvious though equally important influences in the seventies. Emphasis on self-fulfillment, dissent, and direct action persists, despite a decline (perhaps temporary) in political interest and activity that fits older left and left-liberal values, norms, and styles. Indeed, the thrust of the essential logic of concerns of the Movement led early on to alienation from this traditional range of political perception and activity. Hence, as the Movement pushed toward extremes and disintegrated, its expressly left political dimensions began to wither away. But the cultural quest for personal fulfillment and

[34]In various combinations, these themes were evident in the bohemian revolt of the early twentieth century against high culture as well as against middle- and working-class styles of life. See May, *The End of American Innocence*, pp. 217–329.

community, which assumed various shapes, persisted and spread beyond the Movement across the entire spectrum of American political ideology and contributed, often indirectly, to a reshaping of opinion. In the seventies, the quest became more visibly apolitical and antipolitical, though it continued to influence American politics and to broaden subsequent political debate. Let me elaborate and qualify my hypothesis by examining this map of central concerns, concentrating on dissent and action.

Dissent. The beginnings triggered by dissent may represent the most important and far-reaching legacy of the Movement. Indeed, dissent was the common denominator. Dissent moved Americans to think and feel in different ways, and it moved significant numbers of them to act. The following groups provided individuals with symbolic, visible shapes for their social and spiritual discontents and hopes, partly through public dissent and political action: (1) the civil-rights movement, beginning with blacks but gradually encompassing American Indians, Chicanos, Asian-Americans, and Puerto Ricans; (2) the young, especially college students and disaffected intellectuals; (3) the peace movement; (4) the poor; (5) women; (6) the human-potential movement; (7) prisoners and other "outcasts"; (8) gays; (9) consumers; (10) environmentalists; (11) the old; and (12) the physically different (the disabled, the very fat, the very tall, the very short).[35]

Organizations within each of these categories created their own inner histories with distinctive stages of development, intramural conflicts, and ideological schisms. Within each focus, tensions between radical and left-liberal perspectives developed. Each group exerted influence in complicated ways, providing structures of feeling, styles of dissent, and patterns of protest that others adopted. Antiwar activists borrowed from the civil-rights movement. The radical wing of the women's movement, which appeared in 1967, was inspired largely by the insensitive behavior of leading "revolutionary" males. The gay-rights movement of the late sixties and seventies adopted styles of radical dissent. Through such synergistic processes of imitation, repetition, and variation, dissent and protest became dominant forms of cultural

[35]The new Left cut across these foci of dissent and protest: a range of left opinion could be found in each. So did left-liberal perspectives, which often overlapped left views at the level of ideology if not as frequently at the level of sensibility.

behavior during the sixties and, in less dramatic, more personalized ways, during the seventies.

The overall impact was a rapid growth of dissent, which took visible forms: marches, sit-ins, strikes, be-ins, boycotts, local political campaigns, and class-action suits. Beginning with the civil-rights movement, the patterns of dissent and public protest grew steadily wider, touching nearly every group in society. They grew deeper, creating what H. L. Nieburg termed a "culture storm" in the late sixties.[36] By the early seventies, the "culture storm" had passed: the idea of a Movement paled and its left political dimensions faded away—or faded into the left wing of the Democratic party. But the visible and well publicized facets of the Movement represent only the surface of dissent in the sixties and seventies. Seen with the perspective of two decades, dissent persisted and spread. By the late sixties, the Movement had activated other groups outside its amorphous perimeters: (1) working- and middle-class taxpayers (middle Americans); (2) ethnic groups (Poles, Italians, Greeks, Slavs, and Jews); (3) disaffected Catholics; (4) evangelical and charismatic Protestants; and (5) neoconservative intellectuals. These forces were stirred into dissent and protest that has survived the seventies.

Radical challenge and successful conservative response represent the most evident ideological pattern of the sixties and seventies. Yet this schema is too simple, for the radical challenge survives and the vague conservative response has not triumphed, despite important electoral victories in 1980. Rather, the explosion of dissent in the sixties set in largely irreversible motion an interactive pattern of political and cultural shifts that establish fresh opportunities—and fresh perils—for self-definition and self-fulfillment. In sketching the background and tracing the outlines of this pattern, let me concentrate mainly on the opportunities.

Movement dissent was aimed at two inclusive and interrelated targets within postwar liberalism. There was considerable disaffection with industrial civilization, including science, technology, and the institutions of capitalist political economy: the dominant multinational corporations, big unions, the huge apparatus of the state, and unresponsive political institutions. And by the middle sixties, there was diffuse opposition to the dominant culture, especially to the thinned-out and confused version

[36]H. L. Nieburg, *Culture Storm: Politics and the Ritual Order* (New York: St. Martin's Press, 1973).

of white, Anglo-Saxon, Protestant standards of beauty, taste, morality, success, work, sex, and spirituality. Both targets were broad. Both evoked a range of opposition and a bewildering variety of response, within the Movement and beyond. Postwar liberal ideology and vision were challenged from the Left, from within, and from the right.

In the early sixties, as the Movement began to assume its loose shape, a decisive majority of Americans lived outside—and under—contemporary representatives of the faltering WASP cultural ideal and the roughly congruent structures of power that located this ideal in cultural space. Acting through various foci of protest, as well as on their own, millions of Americans came to reject the authority of this ideal, though not all its facets. They grew increasingly suspicious of the character of its official representatives.[37] By the seventies the perspective of dissent had gone far beyond an ephemeral conflict of generations or an opposition between Left and Right, important as these were. The patterns of dissent appeared so confused if only because individuals, starting at different places, pursued different mixes of the aims of self-fulfillment.

Despite the confusion generated by the proliferation of dissent, the social and cultural status quo of the sixties did introduce certain priorities that members of disadvantaged groups respected. Individuals in certain groups—racial and, to a less evident and less significant degree, ethnic minorities; women; gays; old people; young people—were most obviously handicapped in their personal search for fulfillment by virtue of their group characteristics: the color of their skin, their age, their sex, their religious affiliation, the shape of their nose, the accent of their speech. Because they did not meet certain specifications of the changing WASP cultural ideal, they were, to one degree or another, systematically denied elementary forms of social justice and the full measure of liberty, opportunity, and responsibility. There may have been other, more fundamental causes of systematic disadvantage such as social class, but the connections between prejudice and disadvantage were visible parts of American social perception.

The pragmatic logic of first things first—political and legal equality and a measure of economic opportunity—was influential

[37]See Peter Schrag, *The Decline of the WASP* (New York: Simon and Schuster, 1973).

in shaping the aims of political and quasi-political dissent in the sixties. Most of the protests, after all, involved a pursuit of civil rights and civil liberties. But this pragmatic logic was by no means decisive, for the issue of civil rights was tangled with the issue of cultural rights, which go beyond civil liberties. Cultural rights encompass the right to a degree of social tolerance, even acceptance, of differences in attitude, style, and behavior. Many members of these disadvantaged groups sought full integration into the American enterprise by demanding that the abstract promises and the risks of liberty and opportunity be extended to them. In exchange, they hoped to take on the cultural characteristics—the speech, manner, dress, even the cool sensibility—of the WASP. Others representing varieties of cultural nationalism sought fulfillment of the political and economic promises while they rejected the specific cultural forms of the WASP ideal. It appears in retrospect that most hoped to loosen the hold of the WASP ideal further while claiming its political promises and perhaps contributing something of their own to dominant fashions.

This explosion of dissent and social anger spread beyond the vague borders of the Movement and survived its formal demise. It is evident in the largely irreversible gains in civil rights and in the more precarious gains in economic, political, and social opportunities among minorities and women. Its long-range potential is perhaps even more evident in the beginnings of a vast redefinition of the culture and politics of everyday life. As the idea of human rights was enlarged greatly and particularized by the Movement of the sixties, no area of American life remained immune from criticism, redefinition, and experiment: the work place, marriage and the family, the community, the military, the church. In every sphere of activity, individuals began to conceive of themselves as possessing equal rights to self-fulfillment and to control over their outer and inner lives. This surge of the egalitarian and libertarian spirit required gradual redefinition and democratization of social conceptions of people and roles to match proliferating individual and group preferences. It signaled the eventual end of WASP male cultural and social domination in public spheres and in the minds of citizens.

Although the pace and ultimate outcome of this shift in perception of people and in valuation of cultural hierarchies defies sensible prediction, a recurrent pattern seems to have surfaced. Beginning with the black movement, dissent against social injustices has given way to dissent against cultural injustices. The pattern quickly becomes interactive as cultural and political categories interpenetrate in consciousness. The cultural dimensions of the pattern, which permit a broader exercise of imagination, provide a basis for continuing critiques of political gains. Frequently blinding radical practitioners to short-term achievements, these critiques nevertheless set the terms of subsequent political debate. In the fifties and early sixties, for example, gays were in the closet; in the late sixties and seventies they took to the streets, protesting legal and cultural discrimination. Even though a majority of Americans still resist the idea of gay life as an acceptable equivalent to straight culture (and probably will continue to do so) and even though a sizable minority express reactionary sentiments, gay *civil* rights are on the political agenda. Moreover, altered perceptions of the value of gay styles of life are on the cultural agenda.

Of course, there is no reason to suppose that the center of gravity of cultural perception will or should shift to the extremes of the dissenting imagination. A Robin Morgan may lend a furious eloquence to the extreme option of revolutionary lesbianism.

> Women are the real Left. We are rising, powerful in our unclean bodies; bright glowing mad in our inferior brains; wild voices keening; undaunted by blood we who hemorrhage every twenty-eight days; laughing at our own beauty we who have lost our sense of humor; mourning for all each precious one of us might have been in this one living time-place had she not been born a woman; stuffing fingers into our mouths to stop the screams of fear and hate and pity for men we have loved and love still; tears in our eyes and bitterness in our mouths for children we couldn't have, or couldn't *not* have, or didn't want, or didn't want *yet*, or wanted and had in this place and this time of horror.... [Women] are rising with a fury older and potentially greater than any force in history, and this time we will be free or no one will survive.[38]

Although lesbianism does not threaten to become the American norm, its presence as an articulated possibility gradually loosens the hold of older, narrower visions of sex roles. It creates a number of frequently competing suboptions, from apolitical lesbianism to Marxist and cultural lesbianism. Making life at the

---

[38]Robin Morgan, "Goodbye to All That," in *Rat*, February 6, 1970. Reprinted in David Horowitz, Michael P. Lerner, and Craig Pyes, eds., *Counterculture and Revolution* (New York: Random House, 1972), p. 95.

widening edges of cultural respectability possible if confusing, the dissent of gay women and radical women also has enriched the possibilities for self-definition around the more moderate and displaced cultural center.

Throughout the sixties and seventies, Betty Friedan's "problem with no name" was addressed by millions of American women. "Each suburban wife," she wrote in *The Feminine Mystique*, "struggled with it alone. As she made the beds, shopped for groceries, matched slipcovers, ate peanut butter sandwiches with her children, chauffeured Cub Scouts and Brownies, lay beside her husband at night—she was afraid to ask even of herself the silent question—'Is this *all?*' "[39] The question of fulfillment was articulated and answered in various ways, some new, some used. Whereas the most politically and culturally radical feminists sought a conception of culture, sexuality, and self totally separate from a male-centered civilization, a far larger percentage of American women sought entry into the industrial civilization on equal terms with men, along with renegotiation of the conditions of family and personal life. In response to the feminist protest movement of the late sixties and early seventies, a significant minority of women attempted to redefine the role of housewife, to reinvest the expanded role of "home manager" with dignity through an uneasy blend of traditional and contemporary values and strategies. Most of the answers posed by women—even the incompatible and extreme ones—are sensible: they at least are plausible ways to chart very different lives.

Once set in motion, the modulation from civil to cultural rights is hard to sustain but even harder to reverse. Its momentum may be uneven; its extreme visions may be ridiculed even as they set the outer boundaries of subsequent public debate. But the *status quo ante* seems unlikely to be restored. True, the uneven and partially overlapping currents of fiscal, moral, and social conservatism of the seventies seem to have blunted the force of radical dissent of the sixties. Unless the entire structure of economic *and* psychic opportunity shrinks dramatically in the eighties and nineties, however, these conservative currents cannot destroy the largely positive legacy of dissent bequeathed by the Movement. Indeed, it may be that malfunctions of late capitalist economy will be the catalyst for a fresh radical probe by the end of the century. In any case, the radicalized sensibilities that

[39]Betty Friedan, *The Feminine Mystique* (New York: Dell, 1963), p. 11.

dominated media versions of the ultraradical phases of the Movement figured importantly in evoking the conservative responses of the late sixties and seventies. This unintended legacy of conservative response, which was rather mild in the seventies compared to previous historical moments of reaction, is salutary to a point. It provides a way of tempering and absorbing into the American cultural repertoire some of the best insights of radicals.[40]

In the sixties and seventies, then, dissent from all ideological perspectives and social directions challenged the hegemony of postwar liberal ideological and cultural norms. Thus far, however, neither extreme radical nor extreme conservative challenges have been able to destroy the framework of liberal vision that permeates the responsible Left and the responsible Right. The values of individualism, political democracy, equality of opportunity, social concern for others, and cultural excellence survived, though tattered and embellished.[41] Public-opinion polls covering the sixties and seventies, Ben Wattenberg observes,

> show that Americans accepted racial equality, but not reverse discrimination; they accepted environmental clean-up, but not the no-growth economy; they accepted women's demands for equal pay for equal work, but not the notion that roles for wife, mother, or homemaker are demeaning; they accepted the notion that we ought to get out of Vietnam, but did not accept the idea that America was an imperialist, immoral warmonger; they accepted the consumerist notion that big business might well be ripping us off, but did not accept the idea that the basic economic system was corrupt.[42]

Thus, the radical challenge quickly discovered the left ideological edges of popular social vision in America. And it encountered structural limits as well, although, as a result of Movement dissent and protest, positions within the fluid American class structure are—and probably will continue to be—more evenly distributed with less regard to those group characteristics that previously barred certain groups of individuals from full participation. Despite these changes, the essential features of the Ameri-

[40]On neoconservatives, see Peter Steinfels, *The Neoconservatives: The Men Who Are Changing America's Politics* (New York: Simon and Schuster, 1979).

[41]See Everett C. Ladd, Jr., "Traditional Rights Regnant," *Public Opinion* 1 (March-April 1978), 45–49.

[42]Ben Wattenberg, "The Second Shoe Falls—and Maybe a Third," *Public Opinion*, 3.

can political economy seem secure, having withstood dramatic outbursts of dissent and radical proposals for massive redistributions of wealth and opportunity.[43] Moreover, the conservative challenge of the seventies, though it seems to have exerted a considerably wider appeal, probably will be contained, too. Not only does the dynamic of dissent survive, but Americans of all ideological persuasions remain fiscally bound to a large welfare-warfare state.[44]

Although the long-term impact of dissent remains speculative, the short-term impact seems clear: greater attention to civil rights for all citizens; a slight lessening of inequality in the political economy; minimal material support for all citizens; partial disintegration of traditional cultural stereotypes. These things, together with a lively exploration of various radical patterns of personal and cultural definition, should widen the context of subsequent political debate. These changes, which are in part fruits of dissent and Movement activity, seem likely to exert a continuing and largely positive impact on American life.

So, too, do the general idea and habit of dissent that began to emerge in the late fifties, interrupting what C. Wright Mills termed the "great American celebration." The continuing impact of dissent that the Movement evoked is evident in the proliferation of social criticism, in the spread of the general idea of dissent, and in the legitimation of social anger. These survivals constitute additional reasons for supposing that the interactive

[43]Few serious observers deny the formal existence of a highly influential, though fluid, class structure in America. See Richard P. Coleman and Lee Rainwater, *Social Standing in America: New Dimensions of Class* (New York: Basic Books, 1978). On the growing importance of class resulting from recent political and economic gains of blacks based mainly on considerations of race, see William J. Wilson's controversial study, *The Declining Significance of Race* (Chicago and London: The University of Chicago Press, 1978).

[44]See Roger A. Freeman, *The Growth of American Government: A Morphology of the Welfare State* (Stanford, Calif.: Hoover Institution Press, 1975). Although the statistical evidence is both fragmentary and mixed, it does suggest a growing, moderate-conservative mood in the seventies. There was a widespread belief that taxes were too high, that government spent too much, and that government spending was inefficient. At the end of the seventies, public sentiment in favor of tax cuts, more efficient spending, and limitations on the overall future size and growth of the welfare state ran high. But there was no significant public desire to dismantle the welfare state. Indeed, if opinion polls are to be believed, many people held inconsistent ideas in balance, believing at once that government spent (and wasted) too much in general and that a range of specific existing services ought not be cut. Thus, support for continuing past programs, especially those

pattern of political and cultural dissent will persist, increasing the chances of Americans to pursue self-fulfillment.

First, consider the growth of social criticism. Since the aims of self-fulfillment were limitless, the obstacles seemed ubiquitous, and elements of the Movement pursued them one by one, initiating a national burst of social criticism and personal introspection perhaps as intense as that of any period in American history. Elements of the Movement identified all facets of industrial civilization and WASP culture as the main targets of dissent. They questioned the distribution of wealth, the distribution of political power, the purposes of American foreign policy, the impersonality of large bureaucracies, and the values of consumer culture. They investigated the social and psychological functions of education. They challenged the scope and authority of scientific method. They examined the structure of work roles, family roles, and community roles. And they called public attention to systematic prejudice against individuals by categories of race, sex, age, class, religion, education, sexual preference, marital status, and physical condition.

Other major critical revivals survive the explosion of dissent: doubts about the wisdom and feasibility of the industrial drive toward unlimited growth, about the prevailing ethics of competition, consumption, and success, about a preoccupation with work to the exclusion of other facets of life; and about exaggerated contrasts between masculine and feminine "traits." All of the issues raised and resurrected by the Movement remain live,

---

that benefited large sectors of society, remained high. Clear majorities did not favor substantial cuts in spending on health, education, urban problems, and aid to blacks. In 1978 only 7 percent of those polled considered government spending on health excessive, and only 11 percent found expenditures on education to be too high. Only 25 percent believed the government spent too much to help blacks, though the percentage rose slightly between 1973 and 1978. Only 19 percent believed government allocated too much to urban problems, though this figure climbed by 7 percent between 1973 and 1978. In 1978, however, nearly 70 percent believed too much was devoted to "foreign aid," and 58 percent regarded "welfare" spending as excessive (up 7 percent between 1973 and 1978). Between 1973 and 1978 the percentage of those polled who believed military and defense spending was too high *declined* from 38 percent to 22 percent. Clearly in the eighties, the neoconservative rhetoric will be tested: Americans will need to adjust the rhetoric of limits to the realities of life. The source for this information is "Surveys by National Opinion Research Center, General Social Surveys," in *Public Opinion*, 1 (July-August 1978), 32–33.

though they have become subject to a broader range of ideological interpretation. In the seventies, the emphasis of criticism shifted somewhat from social to psychological concerns, and from left and left-liberal to conservative perspectives. Still, the left edge of criticism survives, especially in the helping professions and in the academy. By the middle seventies, left-wing veterans of the Movement found a permanent base in departments of literature, philosophy, history, economics, sociology, and anthropology from which to pursue a long-term, multifaceted critical inquiry into all the targets of dissent brought into preliminary focus by the Movement.[45]

Second, the general *idea* of dissent survives the explosion of Movement social criticism and protest. As dissent generated further dissent, the general idea of dissent was popularized. The Movement helped to popularize two related strategies of dissenting criticism, which, though ideologically diffuse, nevertheless are radical in spirit. It pursued connections between personal troubles and public issues, stressing the interrelatedness of political, economic, social, and cultural-psychological dimensions of the quest for self-fulfillment and social justice. And the Movement lent authority to a powerful populist vein of sentiment and a style of dissent characterized by an expressive psychology and rhetoric of exposure. Generally less sophisticated than its Marxian and Freudian prototypes, this strategy of unmasking turned on disparities between surface appearances and hidden structures, between manifest meanings and latent implications. It exposed disparities between pretense and performance, between the professed intentions and the "real" (usually the darkest imaginable) motives of elites in society. Rooted also in the American tradition of muckraking and facilitated by the media explosion of the sixties, this mode intensified public awareness of social injustice and personal powerlessness. And it generated insights into the workings of the American social order, especially its patterns of privilege.[46]

[45]The most impressive radical-Marxist academic base is in departments of economics. The Union of Radical Political Economists (URPE) has more than two thousand members.

[46]The idea of connections, of a pseudo-Hegelianism beyond rationality, which spread in the sixties and seventies, was brilliantly—and poignantly—prefigured in Saul Bellow's satire, *Herzog* (New York: Viking Press, 1960). A rich collection of the literature of muckraking may be found in Harvey Swados, ed., *Years of Conscience: The Muckrakers* (Cleveland and New York: The World Publishing Company, 1962).

Dissent became habitual, even addictive; as a consequence, authority in every sphere—political, cultural, social, religious, and parental—became subject to automatic challenge and deep skepticism. Even the authority of history withered. The antiauthoritarian, egalitarian spirit of contemporary dissent was projected onto the past, and history came to be viewed, as Jesse Lemisch put it, from the "bottom up"—or from any angle of entry an observer chose.[47] History's winners—the ideas, values, attitudes, heroes, and classes that prevailed—were subjected to intense scrutiny. And the losers—the defeated people and movements, the discarded ideas, traditions, and values—became the subjects of largely admiring inquiry. In the course of this reviewing of the past, a range of fresh possibilities presented itself: the entire past became potentially available. The late sixties and seventies witnessed a profusion of nostalgia for the American past and its customs, styles of dress, regional peculiarities, "antique" trinkets, neglected characters, and overlooked ideas. In the burst of cultural energy released during the later phases of the Movement, each focus of dissent—from blacks to women and gays—searched out its neglected and frequently misinterpreted past. And, by analogy, as dissent became more customized and tailored to personal wishes, individuals searched out their family roots. As a consequence of this democratization of the past, almost no one had reason to be ashamed of his or her roots by the end of the seventies.

Third, the stress on dissent characteristic of the Movement helped to sanction public expression of social anger. By the early seventies Americans of all persuasions could feel freer to say in anticipation of Peter Finch's plea for a general expression of dissent in the motion picture *Network* (1976): "I'm as mad as hell." The willingness of citizens to speak out and to act out personal frustrations has cut across class and ideological lines. In the seventies, left protest continued, though on a less dramatic scale. Protests against the construction of nuclear-power plants and later against excesses of the arms race were staged around the country, and the women's movement pressed for adoption of the Equal

[47]See Jesse Lemisch, "The American Revolution Seen from the Bottom Up," in Barton J. Bernstein, ed., *Towards a New Past: Dissenting Essays in American History* (New York: Vintage Books, 1969), pp. 3–45. This shift in perceptions of history enabled Marxist perspectives to enjoy a modest revival in the academy, but not in the larger society, during the late sixties and seventies. Social history became the dominant fashion among historians.

Rights Amendment. At the same time, however, lively opposition to the ERA took shape. Groups of parents actively opposed mandatory busing of school children designed to promote racial integration, using techniques popularized by the integrationist civil-rights movement of the early sixties. Following the lead of tax protesters of the sixties who opposed large military appropriations, middle- and working-class taxpayers protested against what they considered excessive and inefficient state spending (especially in the area of welfare).[48] In January 1979 an estimated sixty thousand advocates of laws against abortion marched on Washington, bearing signs reminiscent of the antiwar movement of the sixties; "Give Peace a Chance" had become "Give Life a Chance." Demanding changes in government policy, about three thousand representatives of the American Agriculture Movement marched on Washington in February 1979 using tractors and other farm machinery to bring traffic on the main arteries to a standstill. The protest was followed by a series of intensive lobbying sessions on Capitol Hill. The idea of vigorous dissent thus survived the vagaries of Movement ideology, having become available to constituencies outside the Movement.

Direct Action. Various segments of the Movement typically apprehended self-fulfillment and dissent in the context of action. It is here, in this culminating facet of the logic of concerns, that the principal political and cultural legacies of the Movement come together. A virtual obsession with action ran through the Movement; it was an ideal, a means of self-creation, and a mode of inducing external change. Terms such as "struggle," "protest," "resistance," and "do your own thing" dominated the consciousness and rhetoric of Movement people. The past was dead, the present was characterized by public apathy, and the immediate future belonged to those daring enough to act. As Mills announced in 1960, "We are beginning to move again." The civil-rights movement stressed immediate, direct, personal action: sit-ins, marches, boycotts, and demonstrations. The new Left stressed participatory democracy, community organization, laying one's body on the line, and resisting the draft. Political radicals who dreamed of an impossible action tirelessly quoted Marx's eleventh thesis on Feuerbach: "Philosophers have only interpreted the world; the point is to change it." They talked incessantly about *praxis* while looking in

---

[48]See the poll in the *Los Angeles Times*, January 15, 1979, p. 1.

vain for levers of massive historical change they might push. *Do It!*, the title of one of Jerry Rubin's books, summarizes the commitment to action espoused by many representatives of the counterculture.

Action enabled the Movement to begin, and desperate action, which formed a central part of the extremist dynamic, contributed to its collapse. Yet the entire array of strategies and styles of protest that the Movement revived has become part of the American repertoire of political action once again, available to relatively powerless individuals and groups in the ideological center and on the right. Moreover, certain forms of dissent and protest contributed to apparently lasting political successes. Partly as a consequence of protest in the sixties and seventies, there is a new body of law and convention dealing with civil rights of minorities and women, with protection of the environment and protection of consumers, with assistance to the very young and the very old, and with the advancement of the health, education, and welfare of all citizens.[49] Largely the result of more than a century of political efforts, these changes have facilitated far-reaching experiments in personality, culture, sensibility, and styles of life, which will influence the terms of subsequent political debate in America.

The Movement's commitment to personal, direct action as the culminating facet of its central logic of concerns significantly shaped two major and complexly related trends of the late sixties and seventies. First, the commitment to action ironically contributed to a growing public acceptability of apolitical and antipolitical attitudes throughout American society, as well as to a deepening skepticism concerning left-liberal ideology and politics. Second, the commitment to action lent high visibility and respectability to the belief that individuals can be fulfilled, on all levels, through the most direct forms of action—personal efforts to alter the shapes of the self that short-circuit political involvement and deemphasize extensive state assistance.

In large measure, the concern with action in the sixties was a response to personal and political powerlessness. Passivity, helplessness, and powerlessness were symptoms of alienation—from

[49]For a sober estimate of the impact of the Great Society programs, see Eli Ginzberg and Robert M. Solow, eds., *The Great Society: Lessons for the Future* (New York: Basic Books, 1974). A more positive assessment may be found in Sar A. Levitan and Benjamin H. Johnston, *The Job Corps: A Social Experiment That Works* (Baltimore: Johns Hopkins Press, 1975).

existing constellations of power and from a growing cultural apparatus, which disseminated images and information about a far larger and more intricate world than Americans had ever known. But the aims of fulfillment were so large and the targets of dissent so formidable that action—especially drastic, purgative action—came to seem both necessary and impossible. Since nothing promised to do well for long, anything would do; from expressed personal dissent to large marches, from social criticism to political campaigning, from guerrilla theater to guerrilla warfare.

By the middle sixties, the main energy of the Movement was focused on power and liberation: student power, black power, chicano power. The task of liberation no longer was defined in the essentially liberal terms of altruism and justice that appear in the *Port Huron Statement* or in the early documents of SNCC, but rather in terms of the interests of the exfoliating self. Action at this level was possible. Power was to be discovered and cultivated in the liberated, authentic self. In this context, the stress on liberty became libertarian; all people, it was supposed, ought to have the right to "do their own thing." The stress on equality, which included demands for equal access to the resources of society, became increasingly egalitarian. No one is superior in any way to anyone else (especially to me). And the accent on community became local, despite the survival and proliferation of grandiose global visions.

As one consequence of the conceptions of action in the Movement, the idea of politics—especially a gradual politics of reform—lost considerable appeal. A politics of radical pressure, as early Movement activists reminded us, has important but limited uses. Dependent upon a complex interplay of moral appeals to third parties and upon implicit political threats to dispensers of material favors, a politics of protest was able to accelerate partial inclusion of left-outs on the system's own basic terms. It promoted a reordering of priorities, and it led to the creation of new forms of cultural status, without entailing destruction of the essential features of the political economy.[50] Beyond this, however, protest politics lacks staying power. It calls for a return to ordinary politics. But protest accustomed Movement people to heady kinds of freewheeling action not easily converted to a routine politics of the long haul. In the Movement, the aims of therapeu-

---

[50] On the factors of protest, see Michael Lipsky, "Protest as a Political Resource," *American Political Science Review*, 62 (December 1968), 1144–1158.

tic relief conflicted increasingly with the demands of ordinary politics and, in the end, overwhelmed them.

By the middle sixties, then, a decline of Movement confidence in the styles of left-liberal politics was matched by disillusionment with its leading ideological assumptions. Radicals who controlled or sought to control the direction of the Movement's most publicized sectors lost faith in the willingness and capacity of the federal government to respond favorably to a politics of pressure. The fleeting images of revolution only diverted attention momentarily from the main issue: a gathering crisis of liberal faith in the capacity of politics and government to carry out the long process of achieving social justice. Revolution was rejected, but reform, far from being vindicated, went on an extended trial—this time by liberals and conservatives.

Antiliberal, antipolitical, and apolitical themes, which fermented partly within the Movement, spread throughout American society in the late sixties and seventies. Distrust of politics, politicians, bureaucrats, and big government became what Wattenberg terms a "wipeout" issue, affecting the entire ideological spectrum. In the years following Watergate, even politicians adopted a rhetoric of distrust of their own kind, frequently presenting themselves to voters as amateurs untainted by political experience. Active engagement in politics lessened, and voters, especially newly enfranchised young voters, stayed away from the polls in larger numbers.[51] Yet concern with a primarily defensive politics persisted at high levels. American politics in the seventies centered largely on protection and advancement of group interests in an atmosphere of vague public dissatisfaction with government.

As confidence in large institutions declined, a second, related trend intensified: a desire for faith in the capacity of individuals acting on their own and in small groups. The locus of desirable action shifted from impersonal institutions to smaller units. The idea of a perpetually growing welfare state, which liberals had conceived and for the most part had managed since the thirties, lost public favor, a trend solidified by the election of Ronald Reagan in 1980. Ideas and ideals traditionally employed by American conservatives, libertarians, and defeated sectors of the historic American Left found their way into the Movement and

[51]See Daniel Yankelovich, "A Crisis of Moral Legitimacy?" *Dissent*, 21 (Fall 1974), 526–533. See also Everett Carll Ladd, Jr., *Where Have All the Voters Gone? The Fracturing of America's Political Parties* (New York: W. W. Norton, 1978).

into the larger society once again: the supreme value of the individual, self-reliance, self-help, local initiative, and the importance of family, neighborhood, church, and voluntary organizations, which mediate between individuals and government.[52]

As the Movement reached *its* limits in the late sixties, the idea of limits in culture and politics became a key word in America, perhaps *the* key word.[53] The rediscovery of limits on fiscal resources, social systems, governments, politics, even people was partly a response to the disposition of the Movement's most radical elements to search out the far boundaries of experience, behavior, morality, and action. But the rediscovery of limits was mainly a response to a series of social changes that few anticipated in the middle sixties: reallocations of global power, stagflation, high taxes, energy shortages, impending resource limitations, burgeoning governmental costs, public corruption, and a demographic shift toward middle age. When gains in real productivity fell from the 2.5 percent annual average maintained from 1950 through 1965 toward .8 percent in the late seventies, the American political economy began to undergo what may become a long-term structural shift toward persistent high inflation and relative scarcity.[54] Under pressures exerted by actual, perceived,

---

[52]See Peter L. Berger and Richard John Neuhaus, *To Empower People: The Role of Mediating Structures in Public Policy* (Washington, D.C.: American Enterprise Institute for Public Policy Research, 1976).

[53]See Mancur Olson, ed., "The No Growth Society," *Daedalus*, 102 (Fall 1973). For an interesting philosophical discussion of the idea of limits, see William Leiss, *The Limits to Satisfaction: An Essay of the Problem of Needs and Commodities* (Toronto and Buffalo: University of Toronto Press, 1976). Fred Hirsch's *Social Limits to Growth* (Cambridge, Mass.: Harvard University Press, 1976) is a perceptive study of the interrelated dimensions of limits. Instead of following the usual argument stressing imagined physical limits, Hirsch emphasizes what he considers narrower social limits to growth. Of course, Marxists have long predicted that advanced capitalism would reach its breaking point—economic, political, cultural and even psychological—as in the apocalyptic vision in Baran and Sweezy [see *Monopoly Capital* (New York: Monthly Review Press, 1967)]. In the postwar period, when general abundance still seemed a possibility under capitalism, critics such as Herbert Marcuse speculated that the managers of the system would use increased wealth to pacify the population and blunt revolutionary initiatives [see *One-Dimensional Man* (Boston: Beacon Press, 1964)]. In the seventies, younger Marxists forecast fiscal limits to the capitalist state's ability to maintain domestic tranquility. See, for example, James O'Connor, *The Fiscal Crisis of the State* (New York: St. Martin's Press, 1973). But the idea of abundance under an alternative political economy seems, at least for the moment, utopian.

[54]Economic Report of the President, 1978.

and contrived limits, the left-liberal dream of social justice through endlessly rising affluence administered by a growing welfare state lost much of its imaginative force.

Although the vague goal of transforming society into community through a Marxist revolution, a countercultural revolution, or the politics of reform lost plausibility among Movement people by the end of the sixties, the cultural dimensions of the quest for self-fulfillment through direct personal action endured and spread. So did the idea of pursuing communities within a largely impersonal society. The ideologies of self-fulfillment and community changed, and the arenas of enactment shifted. But active cultivation of the self within smaller communities—friends, family, neighborhood, churches, small groups, even cults—survived a decline of political ambitions among members of the Movement.

The main course of cultural and political dissent after about 1965 underlined the commitment to self-liberation within one's own special group: students, blacks, chicanos, women, gays. Political activity of various sorts was formally consistent with, and sometimes required, a quest for fulfillment and actualization. But politics was not a sustained part of the quest. If there appeared no way to universalize liberty and equality, it remained possible for individuals who had gained or been bequeathed a degree of each to "do their own thing," to insist that nobody was superior to them, and to cultivate some community of essentially remissive or submissive personalities in which their fantasies could be nurtured. The search for fulfillment spread as Movement politics—indeed, all politics—came to seem either futile or merely unsatisfying to millions of Americans in the seventies.

Throughout American society, faith in political solutions to the cultural crisis of alienation was on the wane in the late sixties and seventies. Freed from the discipline of political imagination, visions of fulfillment as grandiose as the utopian Marxism of the late new Left spread: visions of divine light, of cosmic awareness, of inner enlightenment. Though usually connected imaginatively to images of personal power, these visions were self-consciously detached from questions of public power. Having dropped even the pretense of interest in politics, some prominent revolutionaries of the sixties sought new modes of ending alienation in the seventies. To escape a charge of drug dealing, Abbie Hoffman went underground for a time, though he still managed regularly to call attention to himself. Rennie Davis became a disciple of Maharaj Ji, the young Perfect Master (subsequently labeled a self-indulgent playboy by his mother). Jerry Rubin, once ostensibly committed to social revolution, sought to revolutionize his own consciousness through a smorgasbord of ancient and modern therapies from Tai Chi to Fischer-Hoffman Psychic Training—and then reappeared as a businessman in a three-piece suit. Eldridge Cleaver, the former Black Panther leader, returned to America from exile to declare his conversion to evangelical Christianity and his admiration for the Reverend Sun Myung Moon, the South Korean businessman who considers himself the reincarnation of Christ.

Attempts within extreme sectors of the Movement to obliterate tensions between society and community, between politics and culture, and between private and public spheres succeeded in the minds of those who abandoned or never seriously took up politics or rational inquiry. Failing to transform social reality into community, they did not abandon their vision of utopia; rather, they extended and deepened it. In addition to desiring public power, they came to regard liberation of self and the transformation of culture as simultaneous tasks. Throughout the seventies, democratic and charismatic longings remained in tense opposition in the larger society. At the extremes, millions were still willing to give up their personalities in the quest for fulfillment. "Mind blowing," that sport of the sixties, stayed in fashion, though perhaps not in high fashion. In 1979, an estimated eight million Americans belonged to some three thousand cults. The Jonestown, Guyana, murder-suicide of more than nine hundred People's Temple members in 1978 brought into public focus the terrors of unrestrained commitment to community: the dehumanization of followers and the emergence of an insane, destructive, omnipotent charismatic leader, a Kurtz for the seventies.

In between, the dramatic rise in numbers, visibility, and respectability of evangelical, charismatic Christianity also underlined the burdens of freedom, the attractions of submission to authority figures, and the fears of apocalypse. The Movement itself provided numerous analogues for this trend, which began in the middle sixties and gained momentum in the seventies.[55] Most

---

[55]The Jesus movement, which began in Berkeley in the late sixties, represents the most direct analogue. See Donald Heinz, "The Christian World Liberation Front," in Charles Y. Glock and Robert N. Bellah, eds., *The New Religious Consciousness* (Berkeley and Los Angeles: University of California Press, 1976), pp. 143–161. See also Richard Quebedeaux, *The Worldly Evangelicals* (New York: Harper & Row, 1978).

Americans, however, refused highly publicized extremes, choosing instead to live in and around the changed political and cultural centers. Here the quest to overcome alienation and to discover the values of community turned on more moderate actions—efforts to find significant personal relationships, to restore family ties, to achieve the consolations of religion, and to rescue the self from the stresses of an impersonal society.

IV

Although I have stressed positive legacies of the Movement in the seventies, the preliminary results of the search for self-fulfillment through dissent and action obviously have been mixed. Over the past two decades, each facet of this quest contributed to an indiscriminate weakening of authority—legitimate and illegitimate—in American society and to the growth of submissive and remissive themes in culture and personality.[56] The dominant style of radical social criticism, with its emphasis on unmasking and its promise of connections, generated both insight and confusion, action (some of it misguided) and paralysis. In addition to clearing cultural space for fresh probes in the quest for self-fulfillment and exposing one sham after another—from racism to imperialism, from political graft to spiritual corruption—an addiction to a rhetoric of unmasking helped to enlarge populist cynicism and paranoia about public and personal life that have survived the decline of left-wing ideology in the seventies. The connections between private troubles and public issues that elements of the Movement proposed often were unsubstantiated and remote. The *idea* of connections, which was easy enough to grasp, established a popularized Hegelian ethos in which theoretically everything was linked somehow to everything else. Political and cultural categories blurred in individual consciousness. Patterns of public action also blurred. A spate of pseudo-sciences—from astrology to metaphysics—exerted a renewed appeal to individuals trying to get a fix on themselves as characters in contemporary life. In such an atmosphere, the personal dimensions of social criticism easily overshadow the social

[56]Within any complex modern society, of course, patterns of authority are constantly in the process of being built up and torn down. Generalizations about the whole structure of authority therefore are hazardous. See also Robert Nisbet, *Twilight of Authority* (New York: Oxford University Press, 1975).

dimensions. The dense web of connections around the self assumes central—often blinding—importance. Selfishness was not new to the seventies. Its celebration in the media and among sectors of newly educated middle- and upper-middle classes, however, represented an extension of certain remissive themes of the consumer culture and the counterculture, as well as a departure from the early spirit of the Movement. Moreover, in the seventies the range of selves displayed by the media changed. The cast of Michael Harrington's *The Other America*, so briefly remembered in the sixties, was all but forgotten, as poverty ceased to be an object of sustained, sympathetic media attention.

A profusion of schemes to facilitate fulfillment of the self made no pretense of locating the self within any community. Other connoisseurs of the remissive and submissive self, however, imagined improbable connections between self-improvement and social issues. Those who engaged in transcendental meditation, for example, supposed that if a tiny percentage of the inhabitants of a city concentrated hard enough, peace and prosperity would reign. Many born-again Christians in large numbers supposed that Jesus would come soon to judge a doomed world and sweep them away in the rapture. All they had to do was find personal salvation and warn others of the consequences of their unregenerate ways. Health-food faddists told one another that if leaders would adopt their dietary prescriptions conflict in the world would cease.

As one center of authority after another was weakened, in part by the impact of dissenting criticism, authority increasingly came to be vested in the subjective self and the small group, grandiose idea, or fleeting experience that it chose to follow for the moment. In these circumstances the easy expression of social anger exerts mixed effects. Triggering dissent and protest against real injustices, it also accelerates a noticeable decline of civility. It disposes individuals merely to express their frustration in immediately satisfying ways rather than to control, organize, and expend it in a politics of the long haul. The idea of the liberated self, then, often promises more than it delivers. Democratization and widening of the possibilities for self-fulfillment may be offset in large part by a trivialization of the self. Freed from the restraints of the past, the liberated self gains a vague sense of connections at the cost of losing the capacity to make genuine social or serious intellectual connections. No longer weighed down by past forms of oppression and repression, the therapeutic personality, which

Philip Rieff so brilliantly delineated in the middle sixties, becomes insubstantial and weightless—unable to draw strength or gain solidity from the bonds of tradition and community.[57] What appears as a path toward overcoming alienation becomes a blind alley, reinforcing basic symptoms of anxiety, isolation, boredom, and powerlessness. When this occurs, the liberated self becomes a prisoner of its own illusions, able to choose widely among life styles but unable to build a solid life.

It is too early to tell whether the therapeutic, remissive personality will merely win a prominent place in American culture or, far less likely, whether it will triumph, establishing a society of selves perhaps incapable of managing their increasingly difficult collective affairs. Many postwar radical and conservative critics, such as Lionel Trilling, Philip Rieff, Herbert Marcuse, Andrew Hacker, Daniel Bell, Robert Heilbroner, and Christopher Lasch have lamented the decline of orthodoxy: Judeo-Christian, Marxist, Freudian, and bourgeois-democratic.[58] Apprehending the present through past realities and, more often than not, through the prisms of past *ideas*, the more reckless of these critics project the bleakest possible cultural futures. Such speculative visions of the worst possible outcomes of present dilemmas—Marcuse's one-dimensional man or Lasch's culture of narcissism—supply more reliable evidence of the shape of present fears and disappointments of certain intellectuals than of future probabilities. Despite the conspicuous—and probably growing—presence of remissive and submissive personalities in America, these types have not yet triumphed. Nor should we believe that they represent the main images of the American future. Such speculations form aspects of a long-term crisis in Western culture that predates the Movement by more than a century. In such contexts, the Movement appears more as a local symptom than as an active historical force.

These are the main changes of the sixties and seventies, changes wrought largely, though not exclusively, through dissent

[57]Philip Rieff, *The Triumph of the Therapeutic: Uses of Faith after Freud* (New York: Harper & Row, 1966).

[58]See Lionel Trilling's *Sincerity and Authenticity* (Cambridge, Mass.: Harvard University Press, 1972); Philip Rieff, *Triumph of the Therapeutic;* Herbert Marcuse, *Eros and Civilization* (Boston: Beacon Press, 1955); Andrew Hacker, *The End of the American Era* (New York: Atheneum, 1970); Daniel Bell, *The Cultural Contradictions of Capitalism* (New York: Basic Books, 1976); Robert L. Heilbroner, *An Inquiry into the Human Prospect* (New York: W. W. Norton, 1974); and Christopher Lasch, *The Culture of Narcissism.*

and protest animated by the Movement: feeling in search of form; individuals in search of power (broadly defined) and a secure, more ample sense of self. Over the past two decades, rising expectations pursued relatively scarce opportunities in the existing material order and in the WASP cultural order with some success. Egalitarian and libertarian sentiments ground down and leveled old forms of authority. A widespread disaffection with ideology and politics accelerated a search for charismatic metaphors and leaders. The growth and partial eclipse of left-liberal ideology and politics accompanied the emergence of a vague conservative mood. There were slight modifications in the structure of industrial civilization, more significant modifications in the old cultural order, and a further syncretization of American culture that enabled the creation of new dimensions of status and new areas of individual expression.

Rather than approaching the sixties as a drama that ended between about 1968 and 1972 and then characterizing the remaining years of the seventies as either a decade that "didn't happen" or a decade of selfishness and reaction, I believe that the biases of nostalgic radicals and disappointed left-liberals should be tempered. More of both decades can be understood by taking the view that the sixties constituted a dramatic period of outward thrust, a throwing out of all possibilities and the realization of a few—some good, some bad—whereas the seventies were principally a time of consolidation, much of it fruitful, some not. The period in American civilization after the late fifties can be imagined most fruitfully as a two-part, uncompleted chapter featuring a number of intertwined themes, rather than as two separate eras, one characterized by hopeful direction, the other by reactionary drift.

Attempts to strike a working balance between radical, communitarian impulses and conservative, individualist impulses will not be completed in the eighties to everyone's satisfaction. In this time of consolidation, political and cultural boundaries are being redrawn, largely in a conservative atmosphere. But the conservative mood itself unfolds within a culture that has drifted several degrees to the left over the past two decades. Some of the aspirations and visions of the Movement have been shaped into important and solid political advances within industrial civilization. Attempts to enlarge the boundaries of cultural space have yielded more impressive, if frequently disturbing, results whose long-range political implications remain largely opaque. In the seventies, the vision of community was displaced into expressly psychological and religious contexts not typically associated with left-wing ideology. So were the concepts of ideology and politics, which yielded somewhat to the apolitical personal pursuit of charismatic authority and therapeutic independence.

Although these disturbing trends may lower the odds of synthesizing and containing radical and conservative impulses democratically within a framework of liberal values and procedures, the options of individuals seeking fulfillment nevertheless have widened. And this represents progress, however ambiguous and tenuous. During the sixties and seventies, the chances of millions of people—women, minorities, children, old people, Southerners, evangelicals, working people, young people, even white males—making the effort to advance social justice over the long haul while increasing personal fulfillment improved considerably. The legacy of the Movement, then, is powerful, complex, salutary, and probably enduring.

MAINSTREAM AMERICA AND THE IMMIGRANT EXPERIENCE

John D. Buenker / **UNIVERSITY OF WISCONSIN, PARKSIDE**

In the past century and a half some 35 million immigrants have entered the United States and begun a complex process of inter- action with the existing society and culture.[1] For at least that long, scholars have struggled to comprehend the precise nature of that process with its interwoven components of assimilation and acculturation. Although often used interchangeably and distin- guished with difficulty in dynamic situations, assimilation and

[1] This paper was presented originally, in a much earlier draft, at the annual meeting of the Wisconsin Association of Teachers of College History held in Mil- waukee on October 16, 1976. The insights presented are primarily those gained by the author in examining with Nicholas C. Burckel over fifteen hundred books, articles, and documents relating to the subject during the preparation of our volume *Immigration and Ethnicity: A Guide to the Information Sources* (Detroit: Gale Research Company, 1977). On a microcosmic scale, they are the result of several years' research into patterns of assimilation and acculturation in Racine and Kenosha, Wisconsin, which have thus far culminated in two publications: "Immigration and Ethnic Groups," in John A. Neuenschwander, ed., *Kenosha County in the Twentieth Century: A Topical History* (Kenosha, Wisc.: Kenosha County Bicentennial Commission, 1976), pp. 1–50, and "Immigration and Ethni- city," in Nicholas C. Burckel, ed., *Racine: Growth and Change in a Wisconsin County* (Racine, Wisc.: Racine County Bicentennial Commission, 1977), pp. 1–67.

acculturation are conceptually different and often occur at significantly different rates. Assimilation is the process by which immigrants are structurally absorbed into the larger society so that ethnically derived patterns of association in work, residence, friendship, worship, recreation, politics, and marriage eventually disappear. Acculturation is the procedure by which newcomers eventually shed their distinctive heritage of values, styles, accumulated patterns, solutions, and practices and adopt those of the mainstream culture. Together assimilation and acculturation constitute what Thomas C. Wheeler has dubbed "the immigrant experience," a dynamic process that unfolds over several generations and is a major key to understanding the nature of modern American society and culture. In a very real sense, as Wheeler sensitively observes, the immigrant experience stands for the American experience in both its tensions and its vitality. Only by confronting the reality that America remains, despite the passage of generations and the supposedly irresistible forces of modernization, a "nation of immigrants," can both individuals and society acquire the wisdom necessary to deal constructively with the complexities of urban, industrial life.[2]

Most explanations of immigrant adjustment have essentially been variations on one of three basic models, none of which by itself provides an adequate understanding of the variegated process. The oldest and most popular of these—the melting pot—is based upon the belief, as Oscar Handlin put it, "that all could be absorbed and that all could contribute." Its advocates posit the constant reforming of national identity and culture out of the raw materials provided by the diverse groups that have entered the American cauldron. But even its most enthusiastic proponents never seriously included all population sources in their schema and usually settled for minor modifications of a fundamentally British-American Protestant core. "As the foreign elements, a little at a time, were added to the pot," George R. Stewart has argued, "they were not merely melted but were largely transmuted, and so did not affect the original material as strikingly as might be expected." In recent years, the notion of the melting pot has been increasingly rejected by scholars and ethnic spokesmen alike as a misleading explanation and an undesirable goal, leav-

[2]Thomas C. Wheeler, *The Immigrant Experience, The Anguish of Becoming American* (New York: The Dial Press, 1971).

ing its defenders to argue only for its retention as a symbol rather than as a description of reality.[3]

According to the second model—that of Anglo-conformity or core culture—the host society has demanded and received almost total acculturation of its ethnic minorities, either because of the presumed dominance of its institutions and culture, periodic "Americanization" crusades, or the irresistible logic of modern, technological life. Once acculturated, most white ethnics could safely be assimilated into the host society. But most core-culture advocates never seriously anticipated or desired the amalgamation of most ethnic minorities, even if they became totally acculturated; they wanted "them" to be more like "us," but to keep their distance. Moreover, even its proponents could never agree upon the precise nature of "American" identity and culture and were frequently forced to resort to legislated coercion to effect what they purported to be inevitable. Ironically, the evidence suggests that such efforts actually retarded assimilation and acculturation, strengthening ethnic resolves for distinctiveness.[4]

Critics of the melting-pot and core-culture models developed a third formulation based upon the notion of pluralism, but they have experienced great difficulty in agreeing upon its specifics. The older view, first delineated by the German-born Jewish philosopher Horace Kallen, stressed "cultural pluralism," viewing the United States as a single political and economic unit with a variety of subcultures, each with "its own peculiar dialect or speech, its own aesthetic and intellectual forms." More recent observers have discounted the importance of cultural diversity in favor of social or structural pluralism, asserting with Milton Gordon that "the most salient fact . . . is the maintenance of the structurally separate subsocieties of the three major religious and

---

[3]The most thorough discussion of three models is in Milton Gordon, *Assimilation in American Life: The Role of Race, Religion, and National Origins* (New York: Oxford University Press, 1964), pp. 84–159. See also Oscar Handlin, ed., *Immigration As a Factor in American History* (Englewood Cliffs, N.J.: Prentice-Hall, 1959), p. 146; George R. Stewart, *American Ways of Life* (New York: Doubleday and Company, 1954), p. 23; and Philip Gleason, "The Melting Pot: Symbol of Fusion or Confusion," *American Quarterly*, 16 (1964), 20–26.

[4]Gordon, *Assimilation in American Life*, pp. 84–114; Edward George Hartmann, *The Movement to Americanize the Immigrant* (New York: Columbia University Press, 1948); Henry Pratt Fairchild, *The Melting Pot Mistake* (Boston: Little, Brown, 1926); and Roy L. Garis, *Immigration Restriction* (New York: The Macmillan Company, 1927).

the racial and quasi-racial groups, and even vestiges of the nationality groupings, along with a massive trend toward acculturation of all groups . . . particularly their native-born . . . to American cultural patterns."[5] Pluralists of both types have sometimes overemphasized the degree and persistence of diversity, just as the advocates of the first two models have overemphasized integration. Often the latter have seemed to mistake the ideal for the real and to substitute nostalgia for analysis. Pluralists likewise have often failed to account adequately for the wide variations in the saliency of ethnicity among individual members of an ethnic community or for the mutations that inevitably occur over time, distance, and generations. Carried to its apparent logical extreme, the pluralist position almost posits a kind of "ethnic determinism" that threatens to shackle individuals with ineradicable identity and heritage even if they would prefer to reject them.

A few theorists have tried to avoid the confines of this three-sided conundrum by concentrating upon stages or degrees of assimilation and acculturation. Arthur Mann has contended that most individuals fall into one of five major ethnic categories: (1) total identifiers, (2) partial identifiers, (3) disaffiliates, (4) hybrids, and (5) the "loneliest crowd."[6] Andrew Greeley has focused on groups rather than individuals, concluding that there is a six-step process of "ethnogenesis" over two or three generations ultimately leading to some type of pluralist situation.[7] Rejecting assimilation because it does not allow for differences and pluralism because it fails to answer the need for universals, John Higham has proposed "pluralistic integration," in which ethnic groups can be preserved as nuclei for social action from which their members can interact with a common culture, allowing for alternate phases of ethnic mobilization and assimilation with no final solution.[8] Gordon has introduced the concept of "ethclass," which places the individual at "the intersection of the vertical stratifications of ethnicity with the horizontal stratifications of social class," while Daniel Patrick

[5]Horace M. Kallen, *Culture and Democracy in the United States* (New York: Arno Press, 1970), p. 116; Gordon, *Assimilation in American Life*, p. 159.

[6]Arthur Mann, *Immigrants in American Life* (Boston: Houghton Mifflin, 1974), p. 274.

[7]Andrew Greeley, *Why Can't They Be Like Us?* (New York: E. P. Dutton and Company, 1969), pp. 31–33.

[8]John Higham, *Send These to Me: Jews and Other Immigrants in Urban America* (New York: Atheneum, 1975), pp. 230–350.

Moynihan and Nathan Glazer have developed a "northern model" in which everyone shares in the benefits of the wider society and culture, but individuals choose their degree of participation in ethnic-group life.[9] These and similar models of adjustment have enhanced our appreciation of the complexity of the process, made us aware that individuals and groups proceed at different paces, and underlined the fact that ethnic identity fluctuates over time in response to outside stimuli. For all that, though, it is still clear that we are a long way from developing a truly comprehensive model of ethnocultural interaction.

The inability of so many dedicated and intelligent observers to conceptualize the nature of the immigrant experience is due to a wide variety of factors. Ethnicity is such a complex phenomenon that it has engaged the attention of sociologists, anthropologists, political scientists, philosophers, psychologists, historians, demographers, linguists, musicologists, artists, and humanists. These disparate groups have difficulty communicating their insights to one another, and few scholars would be so bold as to try to synthesize their various findings. Studies also have usually focused on specific groups in particular locales within a certain time period, making results difficult to compare. Ethnicity has also usually been investigated in a purely American context, neglecting the opportunity to test the American experience against a wider spectrum of options. Despite the rhetoric of the core-culture and melting-pot models, few American spokesmen have ever really proposed the total amalgamation of ethnic minorities through intermarriage. At the other end of the scale, few pluralists have ever gone to the lengths of asking for geographical separateness, as in the Soviet Union. When a group of Irish-American societies petitioned Congress to set aside a territory for indigent members of their nationality, they were refused on the grounds that such action could set a precedent for ultimate fragmentation. It was, in the view of Marcus Lee Hansen, an affirmation that "the immigrant was to enjoy no special privileges to encourage his coming; also he was to suffer no special restrictions. His opportunities were those of the native, nothing more, nothing less." The same fate has generally befallen efforts directed at the perpetuation of a bilingual or bicultural system such as prevails in

[9]Gordon, *Assimilation in American Life,* p. 51; Nathan Glazer and Daniel Patrick Moynihan, *Beyond the Melting Pot: The Negroes, Puerto Ricans, Jews, Italians, and Irish of New York City* (Cambridge, Mass.: M.I.T. Press, 1970), pp. vii–lxxxii.

French Canada. The United States has never recognized, as have many other nations, the legitimacy of group adjustment or group rights, reserving such privileges to individuals.[10]

Ethnic institutions, such as churches, parochial schools, and fraternal and benevolent societies, have been permitted only so long as membership was voluntary and financing private. Efforts to cross those lines through proposals for aid to parochial schools, for instance, have usually been considered "un-American." Nor has anyone ever really advocated the physical extermination of an ethnic minority, an all too frequent solution in other parts of the world. Debates over ethnic relations in the United States, for all their passion, have been conducted within fairly clearly defined limits. All this has fully justified Nathan Glazer's observation that "whatever was happening to ethnic groups in the United States, we didn't have a language, a rhetoric, and ideology that explained it." Moreover, until recently, our understanding of ethnicity has been hampered by an "assimilationist bias"—a conviction that ethnic differences would and should disappear over time. Such a view has been held not only by Anglo-conformists but also by those who were at great pains to assert the fundamental equality of all men. Many saw ethnic appeals as essentially irrational "opiates" served by conservatives to prevent the formation of political alliances upon "rational," that is, socioeconomic, goals. The usefulness of most adjustment models has also been limited because, as Edgar Litt has observed, they often "claim not only to describe what actually is the case, but what ethically and ideally ought to be."[11]

More than that, we have understandably been so concerned about studying the impact of adjustment upon ethnic groups that we have taken the nature of the host society and the core culture for granted. We have too often proceeded as if both were

[10]Marcus Lee Hansen, *The Immigrant in American History* (New York: Harper and Row, 1964), p. 132. For a worldwide focus on ethnicity, see Nathan Glazer and Daniel Patrick Moynihan, eds., *Ethnicity: Theory and Experience* (Cambridge, Mass.: Harvard University Press, 1975); Cynthia H. Enloe, *Ethnic Conflict and Political Development* (Boston: Little, Brown, 1973); and Wendell Bell and Walter E. Freeman, *Ethnicity and National Building: Comparative, International, and Historical Perspectives* (Beverly Hills, Cal.: Sage Publications, 1974).

[11]Nathan Glazer, "The Issue of Cultural Pluralism in America Today," in Joseph A. Ryan, ed., *White Ethnics: Life in Working Class America* (Englewood Cliffs, N.J.: Prentice-Hall, 1973), pp. 170–171; Edgar Litt, *Beyond Pluralism: Ethnic Politics in America* (Chicago: Scott, Foresman, 1970), p. 11.

static and all of one piece and as if minorities either were assimilated and acculturated to the totality or they remained somehow
separate. Both Americanizers and pluralists have usually carried
on their debate in either-or terms. They have rarely asked the
questions, "Assimilation into what?" and "Acculturation to
what?" Yet a closer examination of both the polemics and the
scholarly studies often reveals that they are talking about significantly different aspects of society and culture, ranging from political affiliation to intermarriage to deviant behavior to occupational mobility to residential patterns to family structure to religious practice. The terms *host society* and *core culture* embrace a
wide range of human organization and behavior that engage different aspects of the personality.

Actually, the American host society consists of at least three
major layers or tiers, each of which has its own core culture. The
first tier consists of the political-legal-governmental system. Its
essentials are too well known to require any detailed elaboration.
It is clearly British-American in origin, the product of several
hundred years of struggle for parliamentary-constitutional government in England, as modified by the American colonial experience. It has been altered in the past two hundred years in important ways, but the essentials of the Constitution, the Bill of
Rights, and the Declaration of Independence have survived. Despite its many acknowledged weaknesses and inequities, the political-legal-governmental complex provides a framework and a
value system that a wide range of socioeconomic, geographical,
and ethnoreligious groups rely upon to compromise their differences without recourse to violence. The membership of political
parties, lobby groups, and activist organizations cut across many
socioeconomic, ethnoreligious, and geographical lines to form an
important facet of associational life for millions of Americans.[12]

The second tier of the host society is the urban-industrial system. It is generally within the confines of its corporations, bureaucracies, professional associations, universities, schools, trade
unions, factories, shops, farms, and cooperatives that an American earns a livelihood and defines an important part of his or her
identity and status. In their youth, people prepare to take their
places in it; in their old age they seek to exist on what they have

[12]Robert Dahl, *Pluralist Democracy in the United States: Conflict and Consensus*
(Chicago: Rand McNally, 1967), is the best treatment of the dimensions of the
American political consensus.

been able to take from it. A good part of everyone's life is spent consuming its goods and services; its mass media provide universal role models and popular culture. According to prevalent social theory, the urban-industrial system is "modernizing" American society by "a reordering of human relations by rational procedures designed to maximize efficiency based upon occupational function rather than ideological faith or primordial relationships." The industrial system aims to eliminate ethnocultural differences so that everyone can play the role assigned by the "functional necessities of technological industrialism." The values of the culture of technology are efficiency, economy, systematization, rationalization, productivity, accountability, profitability, stability, predictability, impersonality, homogeneity, and hedonism. In return for acceptance of these tenets, modernization promises unparalleled prosperity, increased life expectancy, spatial mobility, leisure time, and liberation from parochialism.[13]

The third tier of the host society is much more personal and deep-seated. The first two tiers are concerned with secondary relationships, largely political and socioeconomic. Relationships in these secondary groups are often depersonalized, superficial, and compartmentalized. Membership in them is acquired largely through training, education, and experience; they are most commonly referred to as "interest groups." For the great majority of Americans, however, these secondary relationships engage only parts of their lives, and often not the parts they value highly. They are also members of a variety of primary groups—families, churches, ethnic groups, neighborhoods, and friendship networks. They are born into many of these groups and inculcated with their values and behavioral patterns during the most formative periods of their lives. No matter how far they may be removed from their primary groups physically, emotionally, or intellectually, individuals never completely escape their influence. Among those who try, probably intellectuals, artists, and professionals are most able to establish communities that provide some of the satisfactions of primary groups among those of diverse origins. Both Gordon and Greeley have even argued, half seriously, that

[13]Robert H. Wiebe, *The Search for Order, 1877–1920* (New York: Hill and Wang, 1967), pp. 11–163; Oscar Handlin and John Burchard, eds., *The Historian and the City* (Cambridge, Mass.: M.I.T. Press, 1963), pp. 1–26; Herbert J. Gans, "Urbanism and Suburbanism as Ways of Life: A Re-evaluation of Definitions," in Arnold Rose, ed., *Human Behavior and Social Processes* (Boston: Houghton Mifflin, 1962), pp. 625–648.

intellectuals are ethnic groups in almost every important sense—save a common gene pool. Relationships in primary groups are personal, even intimate, and engage a person's total personality. They come first in the socialization process and are vital in personality formation. It is through these relationships that the individual first forms attitudes and behavior patterns toward marriage, sex, childrearing, anger, happiness, sorrow, death, work, leisure, success, religion, food, drink, and the whole range of personal behavior.[14]

The third tier of the host society in the United States originally consisted almost exclusively of primary groups of white Protestants, predominantly English with a smattering of French, Dutch, Scots, Scotch-Irish, and Welsh. Assimilation into the primary tier of American society has largely meant acceptance into the families, neighborhoods, churches, friendship circles, schools, and recreation and social centers of the descendants of these original settlers and their progeny. These were heirs of the Renaissance, the Reformation, the Enlightenment, the English and American Revolutions, and the colonial experience. Their culture stressed the work ethic, material success as a proof of salvation, rationality, individuality, social and geographical mobility, freedom, the suppression of emotional extremes, man's ability to master nature, the perfectibility of man and society, and civic-mindedness. They were suspicious of pleasures of the flesh and recommended their official suppression, whatever the norm of private behavior. Many of these cultural values, such as the work ethic, material proof of salvation, and mastery over nature were clearly compatible with the culture of technology, making British-American Protestants highly capable of adjustment to urban, industrial life. But the two cultural systems are far from identical; the British-American antedated the culture of modernization and has had to adapt to the latter in many important ways. The former stresses asceticism and the latter, hedonism. The former is heavily laden with moral values while the latter professes to be value free. The former celebrates the free individual and the latter, the organization. To the early Puritan, *progress* meant moral perfectibility; to the modernist it means economic growth.[15]

[14]Gordon, *Assimilation in American Life*, pp. 19–59, 160–232; Greeley, *Why Can't They Be Like Us?*, pp. 23–31.

[15]Charles H. Anderson, *White Protestant Americans: From National Origins to Religious Group* (Englewood Cliffs, N.J.: Prentice-Hall, 1970); E. Digby Baltzell,

Integration into this three-tiered system has been accomplished largely through the mechanism of voluntary, self-help institutions. These, paradoxically, increased an ethnic group's sense of solidarity and uniqueness even while providing its members with the organizational bases necessary to operate in the political and socioeconomic order. The pattern was exemplified first by the Irish, over three million of whom arrived between 1846 and 1891 to become "pioneers on the urban frontier." Lacking economic resources, fleeing from famine, disease, and persecution, and beset by hostility and discrimination in the United States, the Irish largely subsisted on the most menial, dangerous, and low-paying jobs. They inherited the most decrepit, overcrowded, and unsanitary housing and suffered staggering incidences of infant and child mortality, criminality, pauperism, alcoholism, insanity, delinquency, and all forms of social disorganization. Moreover, they served as the primary target of the virulent nativism of the 1850s.

Forced largely upon their own devices, the Irish responded by establishing or capturing a wide range of institutions that defined their emergence as Irish-Americans. The Catholic Church ministered to spiritual, psychological, and even material needs and provided a career ladder for tens of thousands of young men, while becoming a medium for a peculiarly Irish-American species of Catholicism. Parochial schools served as a bridge between two cultures and provided the intellectual skills necessary for the emergence of a second-generation middle class. Fraternal and benevolent societies, such as the Ancient Order of Hibernians and the Friendly Sons of St. Patrick, functioned as the Irish equivalents of native lodges, dispensing material benefits, defending their members against discrimination, and providing familiar food, drink, and fellowship. Building and loan associations, banks, burial societies, and employment services served other needs in a privatist society, while saloons, restaurants, and a variety of small businesses catered largely to fellow nationals, while creating a stake in the economy. Labor unions, especially in the building trades, mining, and transportation, served as vehicles for Irish-American mobility, as did sports and a variety of other occupations not

The Protestant Establishment (New York: Random House, 1964); August B. Hollingshead and Fredrick C. Redlich, *Social Class and Mental Illness* (New York: John Wiley, 1958), pp. 68–79.

coveted by the native born. Newspapers, theaters, and literary and musical societies increasingly offered a mixture of Irish and American fare. Entirely Irish units fought in American wars, while all-Irish teams played such American sports as baseball, football, and basketball.

More than any other nationality, the Irish excelled at blending elements of their Old and New World struggles into a combination that served as a model of ethnic politics. Consolidation behind their own candidates and the capture of party posts on the local level paid off in jobs and other material gains, self-esteem, "recognition" by the wider community, and protection against discrimination. By the late nineteenth century, according to one observer, the roster of many urban political parties "read like the Limerick telephone directory"; the Irish-American political boss became a literary staple. In the highly mobile world of nineteenth-century America, the descendants of earlier settlers advanced into the professions and the upper echelons of business, while the continuous influx of cheap labor at the bottom of the socioeconomic scale pushed the Irish upward. Lacking access to higher education and capital, possessing a flair for and a devotion to hierarchy, and making the most of their political skills and connections, the Irish almost instinctively gravitated to managerial positions in government, labor unions, the church, and business. In terms of their time of arrival, their facility with English, their religious affiliation, their settlement patterns, and their occupational skills, the Irish formed the ideal "intermediate group" between native Americans and newer immigrants. By 1900, Irish-Americans had become society's premier middlemen, ubiquitously standing between newer arrivals and the establishment as policemen, firemen, civil servants, teachers, priests, and foremen, to the point where many southern and eastern European immigrants actually regarded them as the quintessential "Americans." Yet, for all their "Americanization," Irish-Americans remained an "identifiable subgroup with boundaries of social interaction and individual perception based on ethnic identity," which was manifested primarily in politics and religion.[16]

[16]For a discussion of the Irish as an "intermediate group," see Carey McWilliams, *Brothers Under the Skin* (Boston: Little, Brown and Company, 1964), pp. 333–336, and Milton L. Barron, "Intermediacy: Conceptualization of Irish Status in America," *Social Forces*, 27 (1949), 256–263. The literature on Irish-Americans is voluminous. See, for example, Andrew Greeley, *That Most Distressful Nation: The Taming of the American Irish* (Chicago: Quadrangle, 1972); Oscar Handlin,

The Irish-American experience was emulated in its general outlines by all immigrant groups, with similar results. Even though its own resources and proclivities and the changing nature of the American society, economy, polity, and culture caused each immigrant group to rely upon its own unique mix of institutions and occupations, the dynamics of group integration and the evolution of a hyphenated identity and culture were much the same. "Community institutions of all new immigrant groups in the United States," as Humbert Nelli has observed, "more closely resembled each other and native-American counterparts than they did homeland organizations." Over a generation or two, such efforts generally resulted in a significant degree of occupational and residential mobility and acceptance for what remained of their cultural and associational distinctiveness. "The fundamental nature of an ethnic group's common culture and its associational expression," as Cynthia Enloe has noted in a much wider context, "permit a surprising degree of adaptation without surrender to complete assimilation."[17]

Until recently, it was fairly widely assumed that the great migration of blacks into northern cities was merely a new wave of immigrants who would be caught up in the same process of social and cultural integration. Typical was Oscar Handlin's 1957 assertion that "what has been true of the ethnic groups set off by immigration is also true of those distinguishable by their color."[18] The experience of the past two decades, however, has raised serious doubts about the accuracy of such predictions and has revealed many dissimilarities between the immigrant experience and that of blacks. For one thing, race has proven to be a much more immutable and emotionally charged source of differentiation than have national origin, religion, or culture. Immigrants,

---

Boston's Immigrants, 1790–1800 (Cambridge, Mass.: Harvard University Press, 1959); Joseph P. O'Grady, *How the Irish Became Americans* (New York: Twayne, 1973); and Edward M. Levine, *The Irish and Irish Politicians* (Notre Dame, Ind.: University of Notre Dame Press, 1966). The final quotation is from Michael Parenti, "Assimilation and Counter-Assimilation," in *Dissenting Essays In Political Science* (New York: Vintage, 1970), pp. 174–175.

[17]Humbert Nelli, "Italians in Urban America: A Study in Ethnic Adjustment," *International Migration Review*, 11 (1967), 38–55; Enloe, *Ethnic Conflict and Political Development*, pp. 15–33.

[18]Oscar Handlin, *Race and Nationality in American Life* (Garden City, N.Y.: Doubleday, Anchor, 1957), p. 164.

both as individuals and groups, at least had the option of retaining, altering, or dropping many elements of their identities, a choice that is clearly not open to those distinguished by color. Being black in America has amounted to a castelike status, carrying with it a seemingly inherited condition of restricted access to public facilities and unequal treatment in most areas of life.

Although scholars still debate the extent to which enslavement deprived blacks of their African heritage, it is certain that white America did not value whatever they retained to the degree it did European culture and that Afro-Americans received no support or reinforcement from their "old country." Bereft of outside aid and lacking even the minimal resources of the Irish, the black migrant has been, in the view of civil rights advocate Louis Lomax, "the only American who . . . must reach beyond his own group for absolute identification."[19] Although Herbert Gutman has demonstrated that the family played a much more positive and stabilizing role in the adaptation of blacks to slavery, emancipation, and migration than previous scholars have alleged, it is still clear that modern-day conditions have prevented that basic institution from providing the same benefits to its members that the extended immigrant families of yesterday provided to theirs. The phenomenal growth of the black middle class in the last thirty years has been offset by the high rate of unemployment among lower-class black youth and thus has failed to generate group social mobility. Upwardly mobile blacks have found, unlike most similar whites, that class gains have not resulted in a diminution of prejudice.[20]

Finally, modernization and centralization, in both the private and public sectors, have eliminated many of the traditional vehicles of upward mobility and integration. The constricting need

[19]Louis Lomax, *The Negro Revolt* (New York: Harper and Row, 1962), pp. 7–8.

[20]Herbert Gutman, *The Black Family in Slavery and Freedom, 1750–1925* (New York: Pantheon Books, 1976). Compare Gutman to E. Franklin Frazier, *The Negro Family in the United States* (Chicago: University of Chicago Press, 1966). For comparisons of the black and immigrant experiences, see John J. Appel, "American Negro and Immigrant Experience: Similarities and Differences," *American Quarterly*, 18 (1966), 95–103; Richard Wade, "Historical Analogies and Public Policy: The Black and Immigrant Experience in Urban America," in Margaret F. Morris et al., *Essays in Urban America* (Austin: University of Texas Press, 1975), pp. 127–147; Robert Blauner, "Internal Colonialism and Ghetto Revolt," *Social Problems*, 16 (1968–1969), 393–408; and Pierre Van der Berghe, *Race and Racism: A Comparative Perspective* (New York: John Wiley, 1967).

for unskilled labor, the virtual elimination of small business, structural unemployment, and the inability of self-help institutions to provide even the minimal security that they provided for immigrants in a localized economy have combined to generate a hereditary black welfare class in some cities. These conditions, along with discrimination in jobs, housing, and education, have made the black ghetto more of a permanent enclosure than a staging area for residential and social mobility. Within a generation or two, most immigrant groups could at least expect to own the residences and businesses in their neighborhood and to control its public institutions; older residents were generally willing to relinquish control in their own quest for mobility. Absentee ownership and management in the private sector remains the norm in the ghetto, however, as does the manning of vital public agencies by a disproportionate number of whites, many of whom even reside in suburban communities. Political power exists in city hall or in Washington, not in the clubhouse of the local alderman or precinct captain. These conditions have prompted blacks to characterize themselves as victims of "colonialism," while many white ethnics, unaware of or unimpressed by these differences, testily turn back black demands with an admonition to "make it on your own like we did." Contrary to the view of the 1950s, the majority of observers now hold with John J. Appel that the black and immigrant experiences contain "few significant analogies and many significant differences."[21]

For most ethnic minorities, integration into the political system has proved to be the least traumatic, precisely because it has allowed effective participation without the surrender of any deeply held practices or values. For all its faults, the American political system was so superior to what most immigrants left behind that they were only too eager to reject any allegiance to their former governments. Many southern and eastern Europeans delayed naturalization because of plans to return to the old country, but they were a tiny minority in the overall picture of immigration. Nearly all immigrants agreed with Vilhelm Lundstrom that "we do not want to form a state within a state, but we want the Swedes to be a salt in America that has a savor."[22] Native-born

---

[21]Appel, "American Negro and Immigrant Experience," p. 96.

[22]Quoted in Victor Greene, "Becoming American: The Role of Ethnic Leaders—Swedes, Poles, Italians, and Jews," in Melvin G. Holli and Peter d'A. Jones, eds., *The Ethnic Frontier: Group Survival in Chicago and the Midwest* (Grand Rapids, Mich.: William B. Erdmans Publishing Company, 1977), p. 143.

Americans, for the most part, favored speedy naturalization and enfranchisement as incentives to new arrivals. The Wisconsin constitution permitted a male immigrant to vote if he resided there one year and declared his intention to become naturalized; Tammany Hall and its counterparts rarely required that much red tape. Periodic efforts to disfranchise immigrants or extend the period for naturalization marred the nation's record but were rarely successful for any long period of time. Despite waves of anti-Catholicism and anti-Semitism, the anti-German hysteria of World War I, the Japanese "relocation" of World War II, the Red Scare, and the National Origins Quota Act, most native-born Americans eventually accepted the loyalty of hyphenated Americans. Millions of ethnic Americans demonstrated their loyalty by fighting under the American flag against their former homelands. "We take this fact for granted," as Nathan Glazer has noted, "but it is one of the most remarkable in American history." Even racial minorities have had an easier time acquiring political and civil rights than they have had making social or economic progress.[23]

Ethnic minorities have been integrated into the political system so readily because, unlike modernization and Americanization, politics accepts the existence of diversity and provides mechanisms for interest groups to compromise their differences without surrendering much of their uniqueness. The Constitution specifically recognized sectional, economic, and religious diversity and the Founding Fathers rejected as "impracticable" the notion that national unity could be accomplished by "giving to every citizen the same opinions, the same passions, and the same interests."[24] Within that context, ethnic groups, once they had attained sufficient numbers, skill, and clout, have been regarded as interest groups with legitimate aims to pursue, provided that they accept the results of elections and roll calls, abide by laws and judicial decisions, and work through established constitutional processes. Historically these aims have included material benefits, political office, recognition, and the defense of cultural heritage. Appeals to come to the aid of homelands have been considered legitimate, provided that they also further American interests. Political parties have consistently kept ethnic and religious sensibilities

[23]Nathan Glazer, "The Integration of America's Immigrants," *Law and Contemporary Problems*, 21 (1956), 264.

[24]Edward Mead Earle, comp., *The Federalist: A Commentary on the Constitution of the United States* (New York: Modern Library, 1937), pp. 53–62.

in mind when constructing tickets and platforms. Especially in cities, ethnic groups have openly vied for control of party and government, with positions in each being roughly apportioned on the basis of a group's clout, as determined by its leadership, resources, religious and class unity, and experience.[25]

In most cities, Yankees eventually withdrew from the rough and tumble of popular politics, preferring to exercise power through corporations, churches, foundations, universities, and civic clubs. Given the chance, ethnic groups used "their numerical base and nationalistic pride to force recognition and legitimate a piece of the action," Irving Levine has insisted, adding that "this is as much the American way as is the road chosen by more universalist civic reformers." Influence in state and national politics has naturally been harder to achieve, but even a casual glance at the makeup of party tickets and hierarchies demonstrates that many ethnic groups have enjoyed substantial success. As has regional outlook, ethnicity has enriched American political culture but only within the context of a wider national consensus. Ethnic politics has too often led to bitter clashes over spoils and recognition, blatant appeals to group interest, slurs and epithets, and even international crises. In short, it has been politics in a democratic context.[26]

The acceptance by the American people of the legitimacy of ethnic politics is best demonstrated by the indisputable evidence of its survival. Despite continual predictions of its imminent demise, the persistence of ethnic politics is constantly being documented by historians, sociologists, political scientists, and practicing politicians. Significant ethnic differences still exist in party affiliation, policy preferences, level of participation, and "public

[25]The literature on ethnic politics is large and growing. See especially Litt, *Beyond Pluralism;* Harry Bailey and Ellis Katz, eds., *Ethnic Group Politics* (Columbus: Ohio State University Press, 1969); Brett W. Hawkins and Robert A. Lorinskas, eds., *The Ethnic Factor in American Politics* (Columbus, Ohio: Merrill Publishing Company, 1970); Dahl, *Pluralist Democracy;* Michael S. Kramer and Mark R. Levy, *The Ethnic Factor: How America's Minorities Decide Elections* (New York: Simon and Schuster, 1973); Lawrence Fuchs, ed., *American Ethnic Politics* (New York: Harper and Row, 1973); Perry J. Weed, *The White Ethnic Movement and Ethnic Politics* (New York: Praeger, 1973); and Robert P. Swierenga, "Ethnocultural Political Analysis: A New Approach to American Ethnic Studies," *Journal of American Studies,* 5 (1971), 59–79.

[26]Irving M. Levine, "New Institutional Responses to Group Differences," in the American Jewish Committee, *Pluralism Beyond the Frontier* (San Francisco: The American Jewish Committee, 1971), p. 11.

regardingness" or "civic-mindedness." Ethnic outlook also profoundly influences attitudes on a wide variety of issues, most notably those that specifically deal with cultural values, such as liquor, gambling, birth control, pornography, and abortion. In the view of two recent observers, the evidence suggests that "there is ethnic-native American conflict over what policies the system will adopt, and also over the very character of the urban political system." The National Opinion Research Center has documented statistically significant differences among nine major ethnic groups on a whole range of issues, as well as on the indices of political participation and civic, as opposed to neighborhood and family, orientation, even with class and education controlled. For many, according to Edgar Litt, "ethnicity is a marginal device imposing rationality, congruity, and consistency on political choice made by ordinary citizens who have relatively low investments in normal political activity."[27] Studies in a wide variety of locales have effectively documented the contention that ethnocultural differences were the most significant determinant of party preference in the late nineteenth century and have remained so down to the present day. Generally speaking, the core of Republican strength has remained white British-Americans of Protestant leanings; their ranks were augmented largely by accretions of other northern European Protestant groups, such as Germans and Scandinavians. The Democrats, outside the Solid South, relied heavily upon the Irish and other Catholic immigrant groups in the nineteenth century and eventually achieved majority status by the effective courting of southern and eastern Europeans of Catholic, Jewish, and Eastern Orthodox faiths. Local conditions and specific issues have frequently skewed these alignments, but they have proven to be remarkably resilient over

[27]Hawkins and Lovinskas, *The Ethnic Factor*, p. 138; Litt, *Beyond Pluralism*, pp. 36–37. See also Andrew Greeley, *Ethnicity in the United States: A Preliminary Reconnaissance* (New York: John Wiley, 1974), pp. 186–216; Gerald Pomper, "Ethnicity and Group Voting in Nonpartisan Municipal Elections," *Public Opinion Quarterly*, 30 (1966), 79–97; John H. Kessel, "Governmental Structure and Political Environment: A Statistical Note About American Cities," *American Political Science Review*, 56 (1962), 615–620; Robert L. Lineberry and Edmund P. Fowler, "Reformism and Public Policies in American Cities," *American Political Science Review*, 61 (1967), 701–716; Daniel N. Gordon, "Immigrants and Urban Governmental Form in American Cities, 1933–1960," *The American Journal of Sociology*, 74 (1968), 158–171; Richard E. Dawson and James A. Robinson, "Ethnicity and State Welfare Policies," in Herbert Jacob and Kenneth E. Vines, eds., *Politics in the American States: A Comparative Analysis* (Boston: Little, Brown, 1965).

the long haul. A survey based upon Presidential elections from 1952 to 1968 has demonstrated that the ethnic and religious affiliation of one's parents is a better predictor of political affiliation than is socioeconomic status. According to two recent students of American politics, ethnic groups "may have become political groupings with a life of their own. Once formed, such political groupings may persist despite changes in the class, cultural, and residential characteristic of ethnics."[28]

One could argue that the very existence of ethnic politics proves that minorities have not been integrated into the political process. To do so, however, one would have to accept the absolute identification of "American" and "white, Anglo-Saxon Protestant." It need hardly be said that even British-American Protestants practice ethnic politics. They often favor their own kind and have frequently sought to impose their world view by legal and political devices. British-Americans generally demonstrated intense loyalty to their motherland during both world wars, causing Randolph Bourne to call them "foolish Anglophiles . . . whose reversion to cultural type sees uncritically in England's cause the cause of Civilization, and, under the guise of ethical independence of thought, carried along European traditions which are no more 'American' than the German categories themselves."[29] Ethnicity is only one of several identifications that shape political behavior, but it is as legitimate as any of the rest. To some degree, it influences the political outlook of all Americans, no matter what brand or degree of ethnic they are. It is this commonality that resolves any apparent conflict between ethnic politics and integration into the American political system. In the words of the President's Commission on the Causes and Prevention of Violence, "Americans have historically identified with their national citizenship through their myriad sub-national affiliations."[30]

[28]Paul Kleppner, *The Cross of Culture: A Social Analysis of Midwestern Politics, 1850–1900* (New York: Free Press, 1970); Richard Jensen, *The Winning of the Midwest: Social and Political Conflict, 1888–1896* (Chicago: University of Chicago Press, 1971); David Knoke and Richard B. Felson, "Ethnic Stratification and Political Cleavage in the United States, 1952–1968," *The American Journal of Sociology*, 80 (1974), 630–642; Hawkins and Lorinskas, *The Ethnic Factor*, p. 196.

[29]Randolph Bourne, *A History of a Literary Radical and Other Essays* (New York: S. A. Russell, 1956), p. 273; Anderson, *White Protestant Americans*, pp. 154–172.

[30]Quoted in Irving M. Levine, "Government's Role in Meeting the Needs of White Ethnic Citizens," in Otto Feinstein, ed., *Ethnic Groups in the City* (Lexington, Mass.: D. C. Heath, 1971), pp. 359–366.

Integration into the structure and culture of urban-industrial society presents a somewhat different pattern. The host society has always exhibited an ambivalent and fluctuating attitude toward the place of minorities in the economy. Land companies, railroads, steamship agencies, and state immigration bureaus competed with one another to attract settlers from overseas. Later industries and mines did the same. But when there was an economic downturn, these same agencies often led the fight for restriction; immigration largely responded to the fluctuations of the American business cycle. Because of the abundance and opportunity present in the economy, those immigrants who came in the pre–Civil War era were generally the most fortunate, often being able to purchase cheap land, open a small business, or practice a craft. Even then, however, destitute Irishmen were forced to accept the most menial, dangerous, and low-paying jobs, while living in substandard housing. Later arrivals generally found their opportunities progressively limited because of the increasing amount of capital required, the continuous centralization of business, industry, and finance, and the advantages in education and inheritance enjoyed by the descendants of earlier settlers. Most southern and eastern Europeans were forced to seek a livelihood in mining and heavy industry, in the sweatshops of the garment trades, or as strikebreakers. "My people do not live in America," a prominent Ruthenian priest once charged, "they live underneath America. America goes on over their heads."[31]

The only alternatives, for the first generation at least, lay in the small businesses serving predominantly ethnic clienteles—grocery stores, bakeries, taverns, restaurants, and boarding houses. Although most immigrants and their descendants eventually experienced measurable upward mobility, there were always significant ethnic differences. In his widely acclaimed study of occupational mobility in Boston between 1890 and 1940, Stephan Thernstrom concluded that "there were dramatic differences in

[31]Maxine Seller, *To Seek America: A History of Ethnic Life in the United States* (New York: Jerome S. Ozer, 1977), pp. 58–81, 104–123; Maldwyn Allen Jones, *American Immigration* (Chicago: University of Chicago, 1960), pp. 117–146, 207–246; Simon Kuznets and Ernest Rubin, *Immigration and the Foreign Born* (New York: National Bureau of Economic Research, 1954); Lowell E. Gallaway et al., "The Distribution of the Immigrant Population in the United States. An Economic Analysis," *Explorations in Economic History*, 11 (1974), 213–226. The Ruthenian priest is quoted in Emily Greene Balch, *Our Slavic Fellow Citizens* (New York: Arno Press, 1969), pp. 419–420.

the occupational opportunity open to immigrants, the children of immigrants, and Americans of native stock, with the second generation in a particularly critical and uncertain position *vis-à-vis* both their parents and their more established WASP rivals." Although the descendants of European immigrants have been able to close the income gap between themselves and the progeny of British Protestant Americans, there still remain impressive differences in occupational status among the various nationality groups. By all odds, the most spectacular success has been enjoyed by the children of eastern European Jews, who have made their leap out of the sweatshops and into the professions in one generation, but even they are heavily concentrated in education, medicine, communications, and the arts. Northern European immigrants, including the Irish, have made the same journey to middle- or upper-middle-class status over three or four generations, usually choosing different avenues of social mobility. Few of the descendants of Jews or old immigrants sit on the boards of directors of the nation's corporations, however, or head its foundations, universities, or financial institutions.[32]

Americans of southern or eastern European, French-Canadian, or Spanish ancestry still remain heavily blue-collar, even though they have made undeniable gains in income. Among Italian-Americans, nearly 60 percent were still operators, craftsmen, laborers, or service workers in 1970, causing Richard Gambino to conclude that "the economic mobility of second generation Italian-Americans up from their parents was simply a question of doing better economically in the same categories of skilled, semi-skilled, and unskilled labor. It did not involve much rising out of these to executive (managerial) or professional categories." Ironically, affirmative action and similar programs designed to aid currently designated minorities seem likely to further retard the progress of white ethnics into the professions, government, and the universities, since they are usually the most marginal in terms of prestige education, family ties, and professional connections. They are not found in large numbers in the informal "old boy" networks of the established. Despite increasing signs of upward mobility, the majority of Italian, Slavic, and other eastern

[32]Stephan Thernstrom, "Immigrants and WASPs: Ethnic Differences in Occupational Mobility in Boston, 1890–1940," in Stephan Thernstrom and Richard Sennett, eds., *Nineteenth Century Cities: Essays in the New Urban History* (New Haven, Conn.: Yale University Press, 1969), pp. 125–164; Greeley, *Ethnicity in the United States*, pp. 63–89.

European Americans remain outside the confines of what has been called the "diploma elite."[33]

To progress even that far into urban-industrial society, ethnic Americans have embraced many of the tenets of the culture of technology. Recent scholarship has modified substantially the picture of peasant immigrants being overwhelmed by the cultural experiences of urban, industrial life. By no means all immigrants came from preindustrial societies, and even those who did proved amazingly resourceful and resilient at constructing organizational networks to preserve their Old World traditions, while ameliorating the transition to the New. Even so, adjustment to the new environment required substantial and rapid alterations. English quickly replaced the mother tongue, not because anyone believed in its cultural superiority, but because it was necessary to survive and prosper. The time clock and the stopwatch, rather than the gradual rhythm of the seasons, demarked time. Large families, an economic asset in agricultural societies, often became a liability; extended families were more difficult to hold together. Energies that traditionally had gone into the family went into the competitive market. Yankee values such as ambition, hard work, thrift, and the desire to acquire property were easily cultivated; in that sense they were Americans before they landed. The need for speed and mobility made it difficult to maintain a sense of place or tradition. The public schools and the mass media presented children with role models and values that were often more attractive and exciting than those of relatives and neighbors. Individual achievement, primarily measured in economic terms, became the standard for judging a person's worth, rather than masculinity or femininity, soul, charity, piety, or allotted role in family or community. The acquisition and consumption of material goods became a major function for many whose traditional culture regarded such activity as sinful, foolish, or vicious. It is to this culture of modernization, much more than to the culture of America's original settlers, that ethnic minorities had to adjust.[34]

[33]Andrew Greeley, "The Ethnic Miracle," *The Public Interest*, 45 (1976), 20–36; Andrew Greeley, "Making It in America: Ethnic Groups and Social Status," *Social Policy*, 4 (1973), 21–29; Richard Gambino, *Blood of My Blood: The Dilemma of the Italian-Americans* (Garden City, N.Y.: Anchor Press/Doubleday, 1975), pp. 77–127; Anderson, *White Protestant Americans*, pp. 140–158.

[34]Handlin and Burchard, *Historian and the City*, pp. 1–26; Oscar Handlin, *The Uprooted* (New York: Grosset and Dunlap, 1951), pp. 63–285; Rudolph Vecoli, "The Contadini in Chicago: A Critique of *The Uprooted*," *Journal of American History*, 51 (1964), 404–417.

Yet, there is increasing evidence that, for many white ethnics, modernization has not gained the same hold that it has on mainstream Americans. Much of the revival of interest in ethnicity has sprung from a profound questioning of the values of urban, industrial life, manifesting itself in a search for alternatives in ethnic identity and culture. The movement to use selected elements of ethnicity as a means of differentiating oneself from mass society is seemingly on the increase, with one of its most articulate spokesmen proclaiming that "resistance to social engineering and their stubborn hold on supposedly outmoded beliefs . . . will save us from the goal of technology to homogenize in the name of efficiency." Many ethnic cultures still stress the superiority of small institutions over large, of local control over centralization, of continuity over innovation, of loyalty to family and friends over impersonal regulations, of spontaneity over predictability, of variety over standardization, of responsibility over gratification, and of acceptance over success. While many of these values are potentially parochial and regressive if carried to extremes, they could also prove to be healthy correctives to the contrary tendencies of technological culture, if properly appreciated. Environmentalists and advocates of the youth culture and the counterculture have sometimes been surprised to find sympathetic allies for their battles against growth and consumerism among people they considered hopelessly reactionary. Many Americans who earn their living in mainstream America retreat to old neighborhoods in free time to gain a sense of identity and continuity, becoming in the words of Michael Novak, "Saturday Ethnics." For some the motto "work like an American but live like a European" has become an acceptable compromise.[35]

By far the least assimilation and acculturation has taken place at the primary level of society and culture. It seems fair to concur with Gordon that "there is no good reason to believe that white Protestant Americans ever extended a firm and candid invitation to its minorities. . . . Whatever the implications of its public pronouncements, it had no intention of opening up primary group

[35]Richard Gambino, "Twenty Million Italian-Americans," *New York Times Magazine* (April 30, 1972); Joseph Fitzgerald, "Agencies and Individual Services in Integration," in William S. Bernard, ed., *Immigration and Ethnicity: Ten Years of Changing Thought* (New York: American Jewish Committee, 1973), pp. 33–38; Michael Novak, *The Rise of the Unmeltable Ethnics* (New York: Harper and Row, 1972), pp. 267–292; see also several of the essays in Michael Wenk et al., *Pieces of a Dream: The Ethnic Worker's Crisis With America* (New York: Center for Migration Studies, 1972).

334 *Mainstream America and the Immigrant Experience*

life to entrance by these hordes of alien newcomers." Even ethnic Americans who fully embraced the political system and enjoyed some measure of success in the socioeconomic order experienced significant resistance when they sought to join the "right" fraternity or country club, buy a home in an exclusive neighborhood, or marry into a WASP family. In New Haven Raymond Wolfinger found that Italians, Irish, and Jews constituted 82 percent of the city's elected officials, 28 percent of its economic leadership, and but 4 percent of its social elite, a representative index of the dynamics of the nation's three-tiered social structure. Even those who have become totally acculturated to the mainstream in appearance and behavior are still often denied primary-group membership because of the stereotypes harbored about their ethnic origins. The realities of primary-group life in America still bear out the wisdom of the observation made over a half century ago by Horace Kallen that "men may change their clothes, their politics, their religion, their philosophy, to a greater or lesser extent: they cannot change their grandfathers."[36]

For their part, ethnic Americans have usually demonstrated very little enthusiasm for amalgamation into Yankee primary groups, preferring to create parallel and competing networks of organizations. While readily participating in the political and socioeconomic life of the mainstream, most immigrants and many of their descendants have preferred to live much of their personal private lives among "their own kind" in families, neighborhoods, churches, parochial schools, and fraternal, benevolent, and cultural societies. Though loyal, modern Americans, they have "reserved the right to remain distinct, unassimilated entities in certain limited cultural, social and identificational respects." Social and residential mobility, higher education, intermarriage, the mass media, social security, the loss of the mother tongue, and other forces of modern life have altered the form and purpose of these institutions, but they have not eliminated them. There are still somewhere between fifteen and eighteen hundred ethnic organizations in the United States and over two thousand schools teaching Old World languages, history, and culture. Catholic, Lutheran, Jewish, and Eastern Orthodox churches provide primary

---

[36]Gordon, *Assimilation in American Life*, pp. 111–113; Raymond Wolfinger, "Ethnic Political Behavior," in Ryan, *White Ethnics*, pp. 133–143; Frank J. Cavaioli and Salvatore La Gumina, *The Ethnic Dimension in American Society* (Boston: Holbrook Press, 1974); Kallen, *Culture and Democracy*, p. 122.

associational contact for more than half the population. Neighborhood and foreign-language newspapers in most large cities continue to advertise ethnic dances and socials, while many groups continue to hold their own debutante balls and coming-out parties as rites of passage into adult group life. Even many professionals locate in the old neighborhoods or continue to serve primarily ethnic clienteles. Despite the generalized mobility and transience of modern life, many ethnic Americans continue to regard their neighborhoods as "social turf," as extensions of themselves to be protected against invasion by outsiders or against the efforts of bureaucrats to reorganize them. The neighborhood peer group provides for millions both the cohesion and the continuity necessary to start dealing with the larger society. The family, the church, and the neighborhood are placed where the ethnic American "gets back his face and his name, where he has a say, where he experiences participation and community." Nor are American ethnic subsocieties even necessarily limited to any specific locale; they exist essentially in the minds and emotions of the community.[37]

Intermarriage, the ultimate in integration, has proceeded only along limited lines. In his study of exogamous marriage among Catholics in 1973, Harold Abramson concluded that 55 percent of the people in his sample married others from their own ethnic groups and that Catholics were two and one-half times as likely to marry people from their own ethnic groups than they would have been if ethnicity had not been a factor. In challenging Abramson's data, Richard Alba developed estimates of exogamous marriage that averaged between 5 and 12 percent higher per ethnic group but still found such unions the exception among Spanish, French, and Italian Catholics and only slightly more likely among Poles and eastern Europeans. His data, he concluded, "modify but do not completely overturn Abramson's con-

[37]Michael Parenti, "Ethnic Politics and the Persistence of Ethnic Identification," *American Political Science Review*, 61 (1967), pp. 717–726; Gabriel Fackre, *Life in Middle America* (Philadelphia: Pilgrim Press, 1971), p. 42; see also Lubomyr Wynar, *An Encyclopedic Directory of Ethnic Organizations in the United States* (Littleton, Col.: Libraries Unlimited, 1975); Greeley, *Why Can't They Be Like Us?*, p. 3; Richard J. Krickus, *Pursuing the American Dream: White Ethnics and the New Populism* (Bloomington: Indiana University Press, 1976), pp. 262–272; Herbert Gans, *The Urban Villagers* (Glencoe, Ill.: Free Press, 1962), pp. 74–119; Paul Wrobel, "Becoming A Polish American: A Personal Point of View," in Ryan, *White Ethnics*, pp. 52–58.

clusions" and indicate that "ethnic differentiation may continue at the primary level." Intermarriage across religious lines is even less frequent, and there is little evidence of an increase in such unions outside the confines of a general Protestant-Catholic-Jewish division. For many, especially in blue-collar America, the ethnic group still provides a "pool of preferred associates for the intimate areas of life." These ethnic associations, both formal and informal, put their members on a sliding scale somewhere between the world of their progenitors and mainstream America. They take on dual tasks of preserving ethnic identity while meeting the needs of life in urban, industrial, pluralistic America.[38]

Nor has there been anything like complete acculturation to the tenets of British Protestantism, despite Prohibition, Sunday blue laws, Americanization drives, enforced public-school attendance, compulsory use of English, and religious missionary activity. There is little indication that ethnic minorities have generally adopted British Protestant attitudes toward child rearing, family structure, sex roles, sex outside marriage, the use of food and alcoholic beverages, death, the mode of expression of joy, sorrow, anger or affection, celebrations, education, religion, sin, and guilt. The confusing plethora of laws respecting alcoholic beverages and Sunday observances are largely traceable to the ethnoreligious makeup of various jurisdictions. Calvinism's view of the individual directly communicating with God has had little impact on Catholic, Lutheran, and Orthodox Christian views of religion as a community experience. Moral fervor in political appeals, so exhilarating to Yankee Protestants, bothers many ethnic voters who regard politics and morality as separate spheres. Statistically significant ethnic differences in trustfulness, fatalism, authoritarianism, anxiety, conformity, moralism, the use of liquor, sexual attitudes, happiness, and reaction to pain still exist. Ethnicity has also been shown to affect career choice and job expectations as well as intellectuality, orientation toward people or security, and religious participation. On the basis of the findings of the National Opinion Research Center, Andrew Greeley has concluded that "the stereotypes of the tight Italian family,

[38]Harold J. Abramson, *Ethnic Diversity in Catholic America* (New York: John Wiley, 1973), pp. 49–100; Richard D. Alba, "Social Assimilation Among American Catholic National-Origin Groups," *American Sociological Review*, 41 (1976), 1030–1046; Milton L. Barron, *The Blending American: Patterns of Intermarriage* (Chicago: Quadrangle Books, 1972); Anderson, *White Protestant Americans*, pp. 127–139; Greeley, *Why Can't They Be Like Us?*, p. 18.

the dominating Jewish parent, and the clannish Irish sib group are, at least to some extent, backed up by hard statistics." Surviving elements of *gemutlichkeit, carnalidad, la vida, la via vecchia, joie d'vivre, yiddishkeit,* and similar world views still partially differentiate millions of ethnic Americans from the descendants of the Puritans. As opposed to the extrinsic behavior and values of the polling booth and the marketplace, these are intrinsic, passionate, and so internalized as to make accurate measurement difficult.[39]

Ethnic institutions refract mainstream cultural patterns through the prism of Old World heritage and create a new strain of ethnicity more self-conscious and tenuous than the old but better adapted to the realities of a multicultural, metropolitan, technological society. Perhaps the most suggestive finding of some of the new research into the persistence of ethnic subcultures is the notion that they can survive independently of objective and material factors, so that even those with a low level of ethnic consciousness often score high in the retention of ethnic traits. Greeley has suggested that America is really divided into "communities of consciousness," defined largely by "expectations about close relations," while Nathan Glazer had defined ethnic subculture as "the customs, the language, or if the language goes, the accent, the food, the stores, the weddings, the street life, the comfortable expectation that you know what will happen next in your own group, that you know how to approach a person on the street or how to address someone."[40]

These communities and their cultures are clearly hyphenated American, at once different from the national mainstream and from the Old World left behind by their residents' ancestors. The degree to which individuals partake of their comforts varies immensely with education, place of residence, social class, occupation, generation, and the vagaries of personal preference. Ethnic survivals are probably most observable among blue-collar Americans who often have lived all their lives within an ethnic enclave

[39]Greeley, *Why Can't They Be Like Us?*, p. 52. See also Joshua Fishman, *Language Loyalty in the United States* (Stanford, Cal.: Stanford University Press, 1972), pp. 390–411; Greeley, *Ethnicity in the United States*, pp. 34–216; Novak, *Unmeltable Ethnics*, pp. 3–50, 167–195; Gambino, *Blood of My Blood*, pp. 128–182, 352–376; see also several of the essays in Wenk et al., *Pieces of a Dream.*

[40]Greeley, *Ethnicity in the United States*, pp. 320–322; Glazer, "The Issue of Cultural Pluralism in America Today," in Ryan, *White Ethnics*, pp. 170–171.

and maintained close ties with family, peer group, church, and national society. Three scholars have recently posited the notion of "situational ethnicity," concluding that ethnic identification and life style are reinforced by common occupational patterns, residential concentration and stability, and dependence upon common institutions and services, conditions that most commonly characterize working-class life. At the other end of the scale, ethnic ties and heritage are probably the least important among intellectuals and professionals who constitute a sui generis subsociety drawn from diverse ethnic sources and sharing a universalist, cosmopolitan *haute culture*. Somewhere between these two extremes are millions of middle-class Americans who occupy uniquely personal positions between the mainstream and their ethnic origins. Every individual, as Lydio Tomasi has sensitively observed, "has to find the supporting measure of self-acceptance and pride-in-self from somewhere to live a tolerable existence. Some people passing into majority society can derive sufficient self-esteem out of the stuff of their individual personalities above, beyond, or despite the character and situation of their group. Others have to depend heavily upon group identities to supply what their own individual lives may too often deny them. And most people need all they can get from both sources."[41]

Being Jewish in metropolitan New York is clearly different from being Jewish in Houston or Minneapolis. To be Polish in south Chicago or south Milwaukee is far different from being Polish in rural Connecticut. The inhabitants of Boston's "Southie" or Chicago's Bridgeport are clearly Irish in a much different way than are Eugene McCarthy, Daniel Patrick Moynihan, or Edward Kennedy. Second-generation Americans of any ethnic background relate to their origins and heritage in a far different manner than do their parents or their children. Qualified scholars still debate the validity of "Hansen's Law" about third generations searching for lost ethnic roots. Americans of mixed ethnic ancestry consciously or unconsciously select that part of both traditions that best fills their needs, while their own children inherit yet another mixture. Ethnicity is clearly not the sole or even necessarily the most im-

[41]Lydio F. Tomasi, *The Ethnic Factor in the Future of Inequality* (New York: Center for Migration Studies, 1972), p. 33; William L. Yancey, Eugene P. Ericksen, and Richard N. Juliani, "Emergent Ethnicity. A Review and Reformulation," *American Sociological Review*, 41 (1976), 391–403.

portant determinant in forming a person's cultural identity, but it remains for most people a substantially important ingredient.[42]

Recognition of the existence and legitimacy of these three tiers of American society and culture explains much about the different pace of assimilation and acculturation on the part of both individuals and groups. It also suggests the need for public policies promoting integration of American life to concentrate upon the first two tiers—the political and the socioeconomic—while allowing a great deal of diversity to persist in the primary, personal tier. Such policies should focus upon the exercise of equal political, civil, and legal rights and upon the fostering of prosperity and security in such areas as taxation, housing, jobs, education, health care, and retirement. In developing the specific operations of those programs, however, governmental agencies and private institutions need to become more sensitive to the legitimate desires of ethnic groups by allowing for greater decentralization and community involvement in planning and decision making, while respecting cultural sensibilities in such sensitive areas as child rearing, mental health, and education and while building upon the strengths that already exist in families, churches, neighborhoods, and societies. Above all, ethnic and mainstream Americans alike must come to recognize subsocieties and subcultures as "sanctuaries in which individuals can find cultural comfort, but which also encourage them to use their abilities in the wider society."[43] For all of them, and for America's racial minorities as well, national survival and progress depend upon constructive cooperation in the po-

[42]Eugene I. Bender and George Kagiwada, "Hansen's Law of 'Third Generation Return' and the Study of American Religio-Ethnic Groups," *Phylon*, 29 (1968), 360–370; Vladimir Nahirny and Joshua A. Fishman, "American Immigrant Groups: Ethnic Identification and the Problem of Generation," *Sociological Review*, 13 (1965), 311–326; Raymond Breton, "Institutional Completeness of Ethnic Communities and the Personal Relations of Immigrants," *American Journal of Sociology*, 70 (1964), 193–205; Andrew M. Greeley and William C. McCready, "The Transmission of Cultural Heritages: The Case of the Irish and Italians," in Glazer and Moynihan, eds., *Ethnicity*, pp. 209–235; John M. Goering, "The Emergence of Ethnic Interests," *Social Forces*, 49 (1971), 379–384.

[43]Victor Greene, "Becoming American: The Role of Ethnic Leaders—Swedes, Poles, Italians, and Jews," in Holli and Jones, *Ethnic Frontier*, p. 175. Levine, "Governments' Role," in Feinstein, *Ethnic Groups in the City*, pp. 359–366; Novak, *Unmeltable Ethnics*, pp. 237–292; Gambino, *Blood of My Blood*, pp. 313–376; Peter Riga, "The Plight of the Ethnics," *Catholic World* (1971), pp. 289–291. See also several of the essays in Wenk, et al., *Pieces of a Dream*.

litical and economic arena and acceptance and tolerance in the cultural sphere. The passage of time will reveal the ultimate wisdom of the observation of Ralph Ellison in *Invisible Man:* "America is woven of many strands. I would recognize them and let it so remain. Our fate is to become one, and yet many . . . this is not prophesy but description."[44]

[44]Ralph Ellison, *Invisible Man* (New York: Random House, 1952), pp. 435–436.

AMERICAN FAMILIES IN TRANSITION: HISTORICAL PERSPECTIVES ON CHANGE

Tamara K. Hareven / CLARK UNIVERSITY

The American family has recently been the subject of much concern. Anxiety over its future has escalated since the youth movement and subsequently the women's movement have brought it
under scrutiny. Policy debates over governmental programs have
directed attention to it. The isolation of the elderly has highlighted its inadequacies. In addition, divorce rates are increasing,
birth rates are declining, and the proportion of single-parent
families is growing. All these problems have given rise to fears
that the family might be breaking down or going out of existence.

Through much of American history the family has been seen as
the linchpin of the social order and the basis for stable governance.
Even though the family changes more gradually than other institutions, educators, moralists, and social planners have often feared
family disintegration under the pressures of social changes. Indeed, every generation has thought itself to be witnessing the
breakdown of the "traditional" family. In the era of the American
Revolution, the possible disappearance of the American family
was a source of much anxiety, and during the Civil War the nation's crisis was projected onto the fate of the family itself. More

than any other developments, however, industrialization and urbanization have been viewed over the past decade and a half as the major threats to traditional family life. This very intense concern over the family in both the past and the present points to the crucial place that the family holds in American culture. Still, important questions need to be asked: Is the family in crisis? Or is it simply undergoing some important changes? What can we learn from the past about the transitions that family life is undergoing and about the direction in which it is heading?

In order to come to grips with the problems of the present, it is essential to assess the actual changes in family life over the past two centuries. Commonly held myths about American family life in the past maintain that there once was a golden age of family relations when three generations lived together happily in the same household. Nostalgia for this mythical past has resulted in the idealization of the Waltons and their world and has led people to depict the present as a period of decline. Even adaptations of the family to social change have been interpreted as manifestations of breakdown. Thus family disorganization has been identified as a major characteristic of modern industrial society and has been associated with the loss of a utopian preindustrial past.

Besides countering such myths, historical consideration of the family puts changes in their proper context, enables us better to assess the uniqueness of present conditions, and helps us to tell the difference between long-term and temporary developments. Most importantly, a historical perspective enables us to distinguish between passing fads and critical changes, and it can even offer some precedents from the past that could be revived and applied to present conditions. The current seemingly "dramatic" changes in the American family relate to major historical changes that have altered the organization of the family and kin, family functions and values, and the timing of life transitions.

I

Recent research on the family in preindustrial American society has dispelled the myths about the existence in any era of ideal three-generational families.[1] In the American past, the "great ex-

[1]John Demos, *A Little Commonwealth: Family Life in Plymouth Colony* (New York: Oxford University Press, 1970); Phillip Greven, *Four Generations: Popula-*

tended families" that are part of the folklore of modern industrial society rarely existed. In fact, households and families were simple in structure and not drastically different in organization from contemporary families. Nuclear households, consisting of parents and their children, were characteristic residential units. Three generations rarely lived together in the same household. (Based simply on the high mortality rate in preindustrial societies, most parents could not have expected to live with their grandchildren.[2]) Contrary to popular assumption, preindustrial households were not filled by large numbers of extended kin, and thus arguments that industrialization destroyed the great extended family of the past are invalid since such a family type rarely existed. Indeed, as will be shown later, the process of industrialization in many ways strengthened family ties and increased the chances of family members staying together in the same place for longer time periods.

In one respect, however, the composition of the household in the preindustrial and early industrial period was significantly

---

tion, Land and Family in Colonial Andover, Massachusetts (Ithaca, N.Y.: Cornell University Press, 1970); Peter Laslett, *The World We Have Lost* (New York: Scribner, 1966); Peter Laslett and Richard Wall, eds., *Household and Family in Past Time* (Cambridge, England: Cambridge University Press, 1972); William J. Goode, "World Revolution and Family Patterns," in Arlene S. Skolnick and Jerome H. Skolnick, eds., *Family in Transition: Rethinking Marriage, Sexuality, Child Rearing, and Family Organization*, (Boston: Little, Brown and Co., 1971), pp. 111–122. Historians have frequently confused *family* with *household*. This distinction must be clear, however, if we are to put changes in the family in proper perspective. The *household* is the residential unit, which has also been recorded in the population censuses. The *family* can contain kin living inside the household, as well as relatives outside the household. It is now clear that preindustrial households were not extended. But this does not mean that the family was nuclear and isolated. Although several relatives did not reside in the same household, they were still interactive. See Tamara K. Hareven, "The History of the Family as an Interdisciplinary Field," *Journal of Interdisciplinary History*, 2 (October 1971), 399–414; Tamara K. Hareven, "The Family as Process: The Historical Study of the Family Cycle," '*Journal of Social History*, 7 (1974), 322–29.

[2]Kingsley Davis, "The American Family in Relation to Demographic Change," in Charles F. Westoff and Robert Park, Jr., eds., *Demographic and Social Aspects of Population Growth* (Washington, D.C.: United States Government Printing Office, 1972); Paul C. Glick, *American Families* (New York: Glick-Russell, 1957), and "The Family Cycle," *American Sociological Review*, 12 (April 1947), 164–74. On the changing life cycles of American women, see Peter R. Uhlenberg, "A Study of Cohort Life Cycles: Cohorts of Native-Born Massachusetts Women, 1830–1920," *Population Studies*, 23 (November 1969), 407–20.

different from that in contemporary society. The household then was not the exclusive abode of the nuclear family. Although the household did not include relatives other than nuclear-family members, it did include strangers who lived in the home as boarders, lodgers, apprentices, or servants. The presence of strangers in the household continued in different forms throughout the nineteenth and into the early twentieth century. Although apprentices virtually disappeared from households by the middle of the nineteenth century and dependent, delinquent, and sick people were being placed in institutions, the practice of taking strangers into the household persisted—primarily through the boarding and lodging. Throughout the nineteenth and early twentieth century about one-fourth to one-third of the population either had lived in another household as a boarder or had at some point taken in boarders or lodgers.[3]

The tendency of families to include strangers in the household was connected with an entirely different concept of family life. In contrast to the current emphasis on the family as a private retreat, the household of the past was the site of a broad array of functions and activities that transcended the more restricted circle of the nuclear family. This fact had especially important implications for the role of women. It meant that women were responsible for tasks of domestic management far beyond the care of their immediate family members. They took care of apprentices, boarders, and possibly other strangers who were placed with the family because they were delinquent youth, orphaned children, or abandoned old men or women.

Boarding and lodging fulfilled the function of what Irene Taeuber referred to as "the social equalization of the family."[4] Young men and women in their late teens and twenties who had left their own parents' households and who had migrated from other communities lived as boarders in the households of older people whose own children had left home. This practice thus enabled young people to stay with surrogate families while it allowed old people to continue heading their own households without being

[3]John Modell and Tamara K. Hareven, "Urbanization and the Malleable Household: An Examination of Boarding and Lodging in American Families," *Journal of Marriage and the Family*, 35 (August 1973), 467–78.

[4]Irene B. Taeuber, "Change and Transition in Family Structures," The Family in Transition (Fogarty International Center Proceedings), Washington: U.S.G.P.O., 1969.

isolated. Furthermore, it provided valuable continuity in urban life and allowed new migrants and immigrants to adapt to urban living. Its existence suggests the great flexibility in families and households that has been lost over the past half century.

The practice of boarding and lodging has been replaced since the 1920s by solitary living. Increasing availability of housing and the spread of the value of privacy in family life have led to its phasing out. The practice has survived to some extent among black families but has virtually disappeared from the larger society. On the other hand, the increase continues in the rates of "primary individual" households, as the Census Bureau refers to individuals residing alone. While solitary residence was almost unheard of in the nineteenth century, now a major portion of the population resides alone. The disquieting aspect of this pattern is the high percentage of aging widows living alone. For a major portion of the population, solitary residence is not a free choice, but an unavoidable, and often unbearable, arrangement. What has been lost is not the great extended family of the past, but rather the flexibility that enabled households to expand when necessary and to take people in to live with surrogate families rather than in isolation.[5]

II

Another pervasive myth about family life in the past is that industrialization broke up traditional kinship ties and destroyed organic interdependence between the family and the community. Once again, historical research has shown that industrialization led to the redefinition of the family's roles and functions, but by no means broke up traditional family patterns. Because preindustrial family patterns and values carried over into the industrial system, they provided important continuities between rural and urban life.[6] Thus migration to industrial communities did not

[5]Frances Kobrin, "The Fall in Household Size and the Rise in the Primary Individual in the United States," *Demography*, 13 (1976), 127–38.

[6]Tamara K. Hareven, "The Dynamics of Kin in an Industrial Community," in John Demos and Sarane Boocock, eds., *Turning Points*. Chicago: A Supplement to the *American Journal of Sociology*, 84 (1978), 151–82, and her *Family Time and Industrial Time*, forthcoming. Michael Anderson, *Family Structure in Nineteenth-Century Lancashire* (Cambridge, England: Cambridge University Press, 1971).

break up traditional kinship ties; instead, families used these ties to facilitate their transitions into industrial life.

Despite changes wrought under the impact of industrialization, reliance on kin as the very basic resource for assistance persisted. Throughout the nineteenth and twentieth centuries, kin in rural and urban areas continued to provide mutual assistance and reciprocal services. Kin performed a crucial role in initiating and organizing migration from rural areas to local factory towns and from rural communities abroad to American cities. Families migrated in groups to industrial centers, recruiting workers into the factory system, and often several family members continued to work in the same place. Once in industrial communities, the family continued to function as a work unit. Relatives acted as recruitment, migration, and housing agents, helping each other to shift from rural to industrial work. While urban or overseas migration temporarily depleted the original kinship groups, networks were gradually reconstructed in the new location through chain migration. Thus, although people did not share the same household with relatives outside the nuclear family, they were still enmeshed in close ties with their kin.

In nineteenth-century American cities, chain migration facilitated transition and settlement, assured a continuity in kin contacts, and made possible mutual assistance in personal and family crises, an important factor in the adjustment of immigrants to the urban environment. Even during the later part of the last century and the early part of this one, in most industrializing communities workers who migrated from rural areas to cities carried major parts of their kinship ties and family traditions into new settings. Young unmarried sons and daughters of working age, or young married couples without their children, tended to migrate first. After they found jobs and housing they would send for their relations. Chain migration thus reinforced ties between family members in their new communities of settlement.

In factories or other places of employment, the good offices of relatives who were already working in the establishment facilitated the hiring of their newly arrived kin. Hiring and placement through kin often continued even in large-scale modern factories. Kinship networks were able to permeate and infiltrate formal, bureaucratized industrial cooperatives and to cluster within them. Even when they worked in different locales, kin made collective decisions about the work careers of their members. Thus immigrants successfully adapted their traditional kinship patterns to modern modes of production and the industrial organization of work, which required familiarity with bureaucratic structures, adherence to modern work schedules, responsiveness to the rhythms of industrial employment, and specialization in technological skills.[7]

III

Despite the adaptation of traditional patterns of kin assistance to the requirements of modern work, industrialization did effect major changes in family functions. Through a process of differentiation, the family gradually surrendered functions previously concentrated within it to other social institutions. During the preindustrial period, the family not only reared children but also served as a workshop, a school, a church, and an asylum. Preindustrial families closely meshed with the community and carried a variety of public responsibilities within the larger society. "Family and community," writes John Demos, "private and public life, formed part of the same moral equation. The one supported the other and they became in a sense indistinguishable."[8]

In preindustrial society, most of the work took place in the household. Reproductive roles were therefore congruent with social and economic roles. Children were considered members of the work force and were seen as economic assets. Childhood was a brief preparatory period terminated by apprenticeship and the commencement of work, generally before puberty. Adolescence was virtually unknown as a distinct stage of life. Such a social system encouraged the integration of family members into common economic activities. The segregation along sex and age lines that characterizes middle-class family life in modern society had not yet appeared.

As long as the household functioned as a workshop as well as a family home, there was no clear separation between family life and work life. Even though preindustrial families contained large numbers of children, women invested relatively less time in motherhood than their successors in the nineteenth century and in our time. Despite nuclear households, family members were

[7]same as above

[8]John Demos, *A Little Commonwealth: Family Life in Plymouth Colony* (New York, 1970).

not totally isolated from kin who resided in the neighborhood. Consequently, the tasks of child rearing did not fall exclusively on mothers—other relatives living nearby participated in this function. As long as the family was a production unit, housework was inseparable from domestic industries or agricultural work and was valued, therefore, for its economic contribution. Since children constituted a viable part of the labor force, motherhood, too, was valued for its economic contribution and not only for nurturing. This integration of family and work allowed for an intensive labor sharing between husbands and wives and between parents and children that would not exist in industrial society.

Under the impact of industrialization, many family functions were transferred to outside agencies and institutions. The work place was separated from the home, and functions of social welfare were transferred from the family to asylums and reformatories. "The family has become a *more specialized agency* than before," wrote Talcott Parsons, "probably more specialized than in any previous known society . . . but not in any general sense less important, because the society is dependent *more* exclusively on it for the performance of *certain* of its vital functions." These vital functions include childbearing, child rearing, and the socialization. Thus, the family has ceased to be a work unit and has limited its economic activities primarily to consumption and child care.[9]

The transformation of the household from a busy work place and social center to a private family abode involved the withdrawal from the household of strangers, such as business associates, partners, journeymen, apprentices, boarders, and lodgers, as well as a more rigorous segregation in the tasks and the work responsibilities of different family members. New systematized work schedules led to the segregation of husbands from wives and fathers from children in the course of their workday. In middle-class families, housework lost its economic and productive value.[10] Since it was not paid for and was no longer related to the production of visible goods, it had no place in the occupational hierarchy. Differentiation and specialization in work schedules significantly altered the daily lives of men and women who worked outside the home. Housework, on the other hand, continued to be governed by traditional time schedules, remaining throughout the nineteenth cen-

[9]Talcott Parsons and R. F. Bales, *Family Socialization and Interaction Process* (Glencoe, Ill.: Free Press, 1955), pp. 3–9.

[10]same as above

tury a nonindustrial occupation. In addition to economic explanations, this is another reason why housework has been devalued in modern society where achievement is measured not only by product but also by systematic time and production schedules. This may also explain why, since the nineteenth century, the home-economics movement has been so intent on introducing efficient management and industrial time schedules into the home. For several decades reformers maintained the illusion that if housework were more systematically engineered, it would become more respectable.

Of course these changes in family life due to industrialization were gradual, and they varied significantly from class to class as well as among different cultural groups. While historians have sometimes generalized for an entire society on the basis of middle-class experience, it is now becoming clear that preindustrial family patterns persisted longer in urban working-class and in rural families. During the process of industrialization, domestic industries and a variety of small family enterprises carried over into the industrial system. In New England, for example, during the first half of the nineteenth century, rural families sent their daughters to work in factories while the farm continued to be the family's economic base.[11]

In most working-class families, work continued to be considered a family enterprise even if it did not take place in the home. In such families, the work of wives, sons, and daughters was carefully regulated by the collective strategies of the family. Working women were bound by family obligations and contributed most of their earnings to their parents. A woman's work was considered part of the family's work, not an independent career. Even during periods of large-scale industrial development, families continued to function as collective economic units, where husbands, wives, and children were all responsible for the well-being of the family unit. This continuity in the function of the family economy is significant for understanding the limited changes in gender roles under the impact of the industrial revolution. Industrialization changed the nature and the pace of the work, but families survived as collective economic units for a long time to come.[12]

[11]Thomas Dublin, *Women at Work: The Transformation of Work and Community in Lowell, Massachusetts 1826–1860* (New York: Columbia University Press, 1979).

[12]Tamara K. Hareven, *Family Time and Industrial Time*, forthcoming.

IV

Industrialization more dramatically affected the middle class. With the separation of the home and the work place came the new ideology of domesticity, which relegated women to the home and glorified their domestic role.[13] These changes were closely connected with a decline in the number of children a woman had and with new attitudes towards childhood. The discovery of childhood as a distinct stage of life was intimately tied to the emergence of the middle-class family in Europe and in the United States in the early nineteenth century. Stripped of the multiple functions that previously had been concentrated in the household, these families developed into private, domestic, child-centered retreats. Children were no longer expected to join the work force until their late teens, a major indication of the growing recognition of childhood as a distinct stage of development. Instead of considering children as potential working members of the family, parents perceived them as dependent subjects of tender nurture and protection. This was the emergence of the domestic middle-class family as we know it today.[14]

The glorification of motherhood as a full-time career both enshrined the family as a domestic retreat from the world of work and made families child-centered. The gradual separation of the home from the work place that had started with industrialization reached its peak in the designation of the home as a therapeutic refuge from the outside world. As custodians of this

[13]On the cult of domesticity, see Barbara Welter, "The Cult of True Womanhood, 1820–1860," *American Quarterly, 18* (Summer 1966), 151–74, Richard Sennett, "Families Against the City: Middle-Class Homes of Industrial Chicago, 1872–1890" (Cambridge, Mass.: Harvard University Press, 1971); Michael D. Young and Peter Wilmott, *The Symmetrical Family: A Study of Work and Leisure in the London Region* (London: Routledge & K. Paul, 1973); Kirk Jeffrey, "The Family as Utopian Retreat from the City, The Nineteenth-Century Contribution," in Sallie Te Selle, ed., *The Family, Communes and Utopian Societies* (New York: Harper and Row, 1972), pp. 21–41.

[14]Philippe Aries, *Centuries of Childhood,* translated by R. Baldick (New York: Knopf, 1962); John Demos, *A Little Commonwealth;* Phillip Greven, *Four Generations;* Robert H. Bremner et al., *Children and Youth in America,* vols. 1–3 (Cambridge, Mass.: Harvard University Press, 1970–74); Joseph H. Kett, "Growing Up in Rural New England, 1800–1840," in Tamara K. Hareven, ed., *Anonymous Americans: Explorations in 19th-Century Social History* (Englewood Cliffs, N.J.: Prentice-Hall, 1971), pp. 1–16.

retreat, women were expected to have attributes distinctly different from those of the working wives who had been economic partners in the family. Tenderness, gentleness, affection, sweetness, and a comforting demeanor were all considered ideal characteristics for the domestic wife. Sentiment began to replace reciprocal relationships.

The ideology of domesticity and the new view of childhood combined to revise expectations of parenthood. The roles of husbands and wives became gradually segregated; a clear division of labor replaced the old economic partnership, with the husband now responsible for economic support and the wife for homemaking and child rearing. With men leaving the home to work elsewhere, time invested in fatherhood occurred primarily during leisure hours. Hence there was a separation of husbands from wives and parents from children for major parts of the day.

This cult of domesticity emerged as a central part of the ideology of family life in American society. One of its main assumptions, the role of women as custodians of the domestic retreat and as full-time mothers, has dominated perceptions of women's roles in American society until very recently. One of its major consequences has been the insistence that women confine their main activities to the domestic sphere and that women's work in the labor market would harm the family and society.[15]

Ironically, this ideology was adopted by middle-class families just when rural and immigrant women were recruited into the newly established giant textile centers. Even though the ideology of domesticity originated in urban middle-class families, it emerged as part of the ideology of American family life in the larger society and subsequently handicapped women as workers outside the home as well. In the late nineteenth century, despite the convergence of many demographic and technological factors that could have facilitated women's work outside the home, very few women actually entered the labor force. At this time the birth rate declined, particularly among native-born families, and women also benefited from new laborsaving appliances, which

[15]Barbara Welter, "The Cult of True Womanhood"; Gerda Lerner, "The Lady and the Mill Girl," *Mid-Continent American Studies Journal*, 10 (1969); Anne Firor Scott, *The Southern Lady: From Pedestal to Politics 1830–1930* (Chicago: University of Chicago Press, 1970). On family sentiment, see Philippe Aries, *Centuries of Childhood*, and "Wills and Tombs: The Rise of Modern Family Feeling," *New Society*, 25 (September 1962), 469–71.

should have considerably freed up their time. Expanded industrial and commercial facilities, made easily accessible by new
transportation systems, provided increased employment opportunities for women. But despite all this, 97 percent of all married
women did not assume gainful employment because ideological
barriers placed women's domestic and work roles in conflict.[16]

The ideology of domesticity also began to influence working-
class and immigrant families during the early part of the twentieth century. As immigrants became Americanized, particularly in
the second generation, they internalized the values of domesticity
and began to view women's work outside the home as demeaning,
as having low status, or as compromising for the husband and
dangerous for the children. Consequently, married women entered the labor force only when driven by economic necessity.
Despite these ideological pressures, many working-class and ethnic families continued to adhere to earlier ways of life. Most importantly, they maintained a collective view of the family and its
economy that contrasts with the values of individualism governing much of family life today.

With the growth of industrial child labor in the nineteenth
century, working-class families continued to recognize the economic value of motherhood, as they had in rural society. Segregation by age groups within working-class families was almost non-
existent. Children were socialized for industrial work from an
early age and began to contribute to the family's work effort at a
lower age than that specified by law. They were considered an
asset, both for the contribution to the family's economy during
their youth and for the prospect of their support during their
parents' old age. Parents viewed their efforts expended on child
rearing as investments in future social security.

Such relationships between husbands and wives, parents
and children, and other kin were based upon reciprocal services, support, and assistance. These exchanges, often called *instrumental relationships*, were based on the assumption that
family members all had mutual obligations and reciprocal re-

[16]Ellen and Kenneth Kenniston, "An American Anachronism: The Image of
Women and Work," *American Scholar*, 33 (Summer 1964), 353–75; Louise Tilly
and Jean Scott, *Women, Work, and Family* (New York: Holt, Rinehart & Winston,
1978); Robert W. Smuts, *Women and Work in America* (New York: Columbia University Press, 1959); James Sweet, *Women in the Labor Force* (New York: Academic
Press, 1973).

sponsibilities. Although such obligations were not specified by contract, they rested on the accepted social norms of what family members owed each other. Before the welfare state and public assistance, these instrumental relationships provided important supports to individuals and families, particularly during critical situations.[17]

Based on this collective view of familial obligations, marriage and parenthood were not merely love relationships but partnerships governed by family economic and social needs. In this respect, the experience of nineteenth-century working-class families and of ethnic families in the more recent past was drastically different from that of middle-class ones, where sentimentality emerged as the dominant base of family relationships. This is not to argue that husbands and wives in the past did not love each other or that parents harbored no sentiment for their children. Rather, sentiment was secondary to family needs and survival strategies. Under such conditions, childbearing and work were not governed by individual decisions. Mate selection and the timing of marriage were guided not by individual whim but by collective family considerations, which included matters such as the transfer of property and work partnerships. At times such collective family plans took priority over individual preferences. For example, parents tried to delay the marriage of the last child in the household, particularly a daughter, in order to secure continued economic support, especially in later life when they were withdrawing from the labor force.

The major historical change in family values has been from this collective view of the family to individualism and sentiment. The latter have led to an increasing emphasis on individual priorities and preferences over collective family needs. They have also led to an exaggerated emphasis on emotional nurture, intimacy, and privacy as the major justifications for family relations. This shift in values has considerably liberated individuals, but it has also eroded the resilience of the family and its ability to handle crises. Moreover, it has contributed to a greater separation among family members and especially to the isolation of older people.

[17]Michael Anderson, *Family Structure in Nineteenth-Century Lancashire* (Cambridge, 1971); Tamara K. Hareven, "The Dynamics of Kin in an Industrial Community," in Demos and Boocock, *Turning Points.*

V

The full impact today of changes in family values and functions can be clarified by demographic data about the timing of life transitions, such as marriage, parenthood, the empty nest, and widowhood.[18] The decline in the American birth rate from 7.04 children in 1800 to 3.56 children in 1900, as well as the subsequent decline since, has profoundly affected the cycle of family life, especially the timing of marriage and of the births of children. In traditional society, little time elapsed between marriage and parenthood, since procreation was the major goal of marriage. In modern society, contraception has permitted a gap between these two stages of the family cycle. Thus marriage has become important in its own right, rather than being merely a transition to parenthood.[19]

One widely held myth about the past is that the timing of these life transitions was once more orderly and stable than it is today. Life in the placid past is contrasted to family life today with its variations in family roles and in transitions into them. The historical record, however, frequently reveals precisely the opposite condition. Patterns of family timing in the past were often more complex, more diverse, and less orderly than they are today. Despite greater societal complexity, voluntary and involuntary demographic changes since the late nineteenth century paradoxically have resulted in greater uniformity in the timing of transitions along the life course. This growing uniformity has been accompanied by an increase in the voluntary factors affecting the timing of family events. The increase in life expectancy, the decline in fertility, and the earlier marriage age, for example, have greatly increased the chances for temporal overlap in the lives of family members. In contrast to past times, most families see their children through to adulthood with both parents still alive. Thus families now are able to go through the life course

---

[18]Tamara K. Hareven, "Family Time and Historical Time," *Daedalus* (Spring 1977), pp. 57–70.

[19]Daniel Scott Smith, "Family Limitation, Sexual Control, and Domestic Feminism in Victorian America," in Hartman and Banner, eds., *Clio's Consciousness Raised* (New York: Harper and Row, 1974), pp. 119–37. See also Yasukichi Yasuba, *Birth Rates of the White Population in the United States 1800–1860* (Baltimore: Johns Hopkins University Press, 1961); Robert V. Wells, "Demographic Change and the Life Cycle of American Families," *Journal of Interdisciplinary History*, 2 (Autumn 1971), 273–282.

much less subject to sudden change than were most families in the nineteenth century.

The typical modern American family cycle includes early marriage and early commencement of childbearing, but few children. Families following this cycle experience a compact period of parenthood in the middle years of life, then an extended period (one-third of the adult life) without children, and finally a period of solitary living following the death of a spouse, most frequently the husband.[20] This cycle has important implications for the composition of the family and for relationships within it: husbands and wives are spending a relatively longer lifetime together, they invest a shorter segment of their lives in child rearing, and they more commonly survive to be grandparents.

This sequence has been uniform for the majority of the population since the beginning of the twentieth century. As Peter Uhlenberg points out:

> The normal family cycle for women, a sequence of leaving home, marriage, family formation, child-rearing, launching and survival at age 50 with the first marriage still intact, unless broken by divorce, has not been the dominant pattern of family timing before the early twentieth century.[21]

Prior to 1900, only about 40 percent of the female population in the United States experienced this ideal family cycle. The remainder either never married, never reached marriageable age, died before childbirth, or were widowed while their offspring were still young children.

In the nineteenth century, the combination of later marriage, higher fertility, and more widely spaced childbearing resulted in a different timing of family transitions. Individuals became parents later but carried child-rearing responsibilities almost until the ends of their lives. As a result of higher fertility, children were spread over a wider age range; frequently the youngest child was

---

[20]Paul C. Glick, "The Life Cycle of the Family," *Marriage and Family Living*, 18 (1955), 3–9; "Updating the Life Cycle of the Family," *Journal of Marriage and the Family*, 39 (February 1977), 5–13; Paul C. Glick and Robert Parke, Jr., "New Approaches in Studying the Life Cycle of the Family," *Demography*, 2 (1965), 187–212.

[21]Peter Uhlenberg, "Cohort Variations in Family Life Cycle Experiences of United States Females," *Journal of Marriage and the Family*, 36 (May 1974), 284–92.

just entering school as the oldest was preparing for marriage. Consequently the lives of parents overlapped with those of their children for shorter periods than they do in current society, and few families experienced an empty-nest stage. Prior to the decline in mortality among the young at the beginning of the twentieth century, marriage was frequently broken by the death of a spouse before the end of the child-rearing period. Even when fathers survived the child-rearing years, they rarely lived beyond the marriage of the second child. Certainly a meaningful overlap in the lives of grandparents and grandchildren—a twentieth-century phenomenon—was uncommon, counter to the popular myth of the three-generational family of the past.

Under these demographic conditions of the nineteenth century, functions within the family were less specifically tied to age, and members of different age groups were consequently not so completely segregated by the tasks they were required to fulfill. The spread of children over a longer period of time had important implications for family relationships as well as for children's preparations for adult roles. Children grew up with more siblings and were exposed to more varied adult models than they would have been in a small nuclear family. Older children often took charge of their younger siblings. Sisters, in particular, carried major responsibility for raising the youngest siblings and frequently acted as surrogate mothers if the mother worked outside the home or if she had died.

The smaller age overlap between children and their parents was also significant: the oldest child was the one most likely to overlap with the father in adulthood; the youngest child, the least likely to do so. The oldest child would have been most likely to embark on an independent career before the parents reached old-age dependency; the youngest children were most likely to carry responsibilities for parental support and to overlap in adulthood with a widowed mother. The oldest child had the greatest chance to overlap with grandparents, the youngest child the least. Late-marrying children were most likely to be responsible for the support of a widowed mother, while early-marrying children depended on their parents' household space after marriage.

The relative significance of transition into family roles has also changed. In the nineteenth century, when conception was likely to take place very shortly after marriage, the major transition in a woman's life was represented by marriage itself. But, as the interval between marriage and the first pregnancy has increased in modern society, the transition to parenthood has become more significant than the transition to marriage. Family limitation has also had an impact on the timing of marriage. Since marriage no longer inevitably leads to the birth of children, postponing marriage is no longer necessary to delay parenthood. On the other end of the life course, transitions into the empty-nest roles are much more critical today than they were in the past when parental or surrogate-parental roles encompassed practically the entire adult life span. Completion of parental roles today involves changes in residence, in work, and eventually, perhaps, removal into institutions or retirement communities.[22]

The overall historical pattern of family behavior has been marked by a shift from involuntary to voluntary control over the timing of family events. The pattern also has been characterized by increased rigidity and uniformity in the timing of the passage from one family role to another. In their comparison of such transitions in nineteenth-century Philadelphia with the present, Modell, Furstenburg, and Hershberg concluded that transitions into adult roles (departure from the family of origin, marriage, and the establishment of a household) today follow a more orderly sequence and are accomplished over a shorter time period in a young person's life than they were in the nineteenth century. Now such transitions to familial roles also coincide with transitions into occupational roles: "Transitions are today more contingent, more integrated because they are constrained by a set of formal institutions. 'Timely' action to nineteenth-century families consisted of helpful response in times of trouble; in the twentieth century, timeliness connotes adherence to a schedule."[23]

These differences in age at marriage, number of children, assigned tasks, and generational overlap, especially given the uncertainties and the economic precariousness of the period, made the present orderly progression through the family cycle impossible for the nineteenth-century family. While the major historical changes in family functions occurred in the nineteenth and early twentieth century, changes in the timing of family transitions are

[22]Tamara K. Hareven and Howard P. Chudacoff, "The Later Years of Life and the Family Cycle," in Tamara K. Hareven, ed., *Transitions: The Family and the Life Course in Historical Perspectives* (New York: Academic Press, 1978).

[23]John Modell, Frank Furstenburg, and Theodore Hershberg, "Social Change and Transitions to Adulthood in Historical Perspectives," *Journal of Family History*, 1 (Autumn 1976), 7–32.

a twentieth-century phenomenon and particularly affect the family in our times. Changes in the family cycle, such as the emergence of the empty nest, extensions of the period of widowhood, and increasing age segregation in the family and the larger society, have increased the problems in the middle and later years of life. Precisely this area needs particular concern regarding future changes in the family.

VI

A major source of anxiety about the future of the family is rooted not so much in reality as in the tension between the idealized expectation in the culture and the reality itself. Nostalgia for a lost family tradition, which, in fact, never existed, has prejudiced our understanding of the conditions of families in contemporary society. Thus, the current anxiety over the fate of the family reflects not only problems in the family but also a variety of fears about other social problems that are eventually projected onto the family.

The real problems facing American families today are not symptoms of breakdown as is often suggested; rather, they reflect the difficulties of adaptation to recent social changes, particularly to the loss of diversity in household membership, to the reduction of the variety of family functions and, to some extent, to the weakening of the family's adaptability. The idealization of the family as a refuge from the world and the myth that the work of mothers is harmful has added considerable strain. The continuous emphasis on the family as a universal private retreat and as an emotional haven is misguided in light of the historical experience. In the past, the family fulfilled a broad array of functions, not merely emotional ones. Most of its functions in the past were intertwined with the larger community. Rather than being the custodian of privacy, the family prepared its members for interaction with the larger society. Family relationships were valued not merely for their emotional contents, but for a wide array of services and contributions to the collective family unit. In contrast, a major difficulty of the nuclear family today is adapting to the emotional functions thrust upon it and to the expectations of romantic love that accompany marriage, precisely because these functions and expectations represent an artificial boundary between individuals and the larger society.

Concentration on these emotional functions has grown at the expense of another necessary role in industrial society, namely, the preparation of family members for their interaction with bureaucratic institutions. In American society, the educational and welfare systems have made dramatic inroads into areas that once were the private preserve of the family. At the same time, however, the tendency of the family to shelter its members from other social institutions has weakened its ability to influence the programs and legislation that public agencies have directed at the family.

There has been a tendency toward homogenization of American culture through the absorption of ethnic traditions on the one hand and through the acceptance by immigrants of the dominant cultural models on the other. Immigrants, primarily in the second generation, have adopted "American" family behavior, characterized by a decline in fertility, earlier marriage, growing privatization of the family, withdrawal of women and children from the labor force, and changing patterns of consumption and tastes. Nevertheless, this ongoing process did not result in total assimilation of family ways and traditional customs because the influx of new immigrants kept introducing new cultural variety. The result has been continuing diversity in family patterns. Contrary to the creed of the melting pot, many varieties of ethnic family behavior have survived in American society, and new patterns are still being introduced. It is therefore unrealistic to talk simply about *the* American family.

For over a century, until very recently, the stereotype of the private nuclear family as the American ideal has dominated. Alternative forms of family organization such as those among black families or among ethnic groups were misinterpreted as "family disorganization" simply because they did not conform to the official stereotype. Over the past decade, the strength and resilience of ethnic and black families has been recognized. Their traditional resources of family and kinship have been rediscovered as the middle-class nuclear family, besieged by its own isolation, has proven its limitations in coping with stress.[24] American families today are culturally and ethnically diverse; this diversity, which continues a historical pattern, is now being valued as a

[24]Tamara K. Hareven, Stephan Thernstrom, ed., and John Modell, "Ethnic Families," in *Harvard Encyclopedia of American Ethnic Groups* (Cambridge, Mass.: University Press, 1980), pp. 345–354.

source of strength and continuity, rather than being condemned as a manifestation of deviance.

An understanding of the historical changes over the past century illuminates family life today. There is no question that American families have been undergoing important transitions during this time. But the main question is what these changes mean—whether they represent family breakdown or threaten the disappearance of the family. Some of these transitions continue a long historical process, as do the decline in the birth rate, the earlier marriage rate, and the changes in the timing of life transitions. Similarly, the moratorium from adult responsibilities that teenagers are experiencing now and the increasing isolation of older people on the other end of the cycle result from long-term historical changes. On the other hand, the increase in divorce rates and the concomitant increase in single-parent households represent a much more dramatic transition in our time. But the rise in divorce as such, often cited as a symptom of family breakdown, should not necessarily be construed as such.

In the nineteenth century, people did not resort to divorce as frequently as they do now because divorce was considered socially unacceptable. This does not mean, however, that families were living happily and harmoniously. High rates of desertion and separation replaced legal divorce. And those couples who did not resort to divorce or separation despite incompatibility lived together as strangers or in deep conflict. Thus, the increase in divorce statistics as such is no proof of family breakdown. In some respects, it demonstrates that people care enough about the quality of family life and marriage to be willing to dissolve an unsatisfactory marriage and commonly to replace it with a more successful one.

Much anxiety has also been expressed over the higher proportion of couples living together unmarried, over homosexual partners or parents, and over a whole variety of alternative family forms and life style. What we are witnessing, in all these varieties of life style, are not necessarily new inventions. Many different forms have existed all along, but they have been less visible. More recently alternative life styles have become part of the official fiber of society because they are now being better tolerated than in the past. In short, what we are witnessing is not a fragmentation of traditional family patterns but rather the emergence of a pluralism in family ways.

Thus, from a long-range perspective, the greatest concerns

over family life in America need not be divorce, the declining birth rate, or alternative life styles. Of much greater concern for the future should be the problem of the isolation of the elderly and the inability of families in all stages to cope with inflation and with diminishing resources.

The historical lesson is valuable in demonstrating the extent to which traditional family ways and continuities with the past still survive in American society today. It is particularly powerful in pointing to the salient roles of surrogate families (taking in boarders and lodgers) and of kinship ties that have effectively coped with migration, economic insecurity, and personal family crises. The persistence of kinship ties has been a major source of resilience and strength in urban neighborhoods. This rediscovery of the strength of kin should not lead us, however, to a new myth of self-reliance. It would be a mistake to assume that the fact that family members help each other in times of crisis means that they should be left to take care of their own. This historical experience also suggests the high price that family members paid in order to support their kin and to help aging parents. The pressures on the nuclear family today, combined with economic and technological stresses, would make it difficult, if not impossible, for the family to sustain continued assistance and support for their kin, especially for aging relatives.

A creative and constructive family policy will have to take into consideration, therefore, both the survival of support networks among kin and the escalating pressures on individuals and families. Such a policy, by necessity, will have to provide public programs and assistance where informal support falls short. It will also need to strengthen kinship and neighborhood support networks without bureaucratizing them.

INDEX

Date Due